Microprocessor and Its Applications

Microprocessor and Its Applications

R. Theagarajan
S. Dhanasekaran
S. Dhanapal

PUBLISHING FOR ONE WORLD

NEW AGE INTERNATIONAL (P) LIMITED, PUBLISHERS
New Delhi • Bangalore • Chennai • Cochin • Guwahati • Hyderabad
Jalandhar • Kolkata • Lucknow • Mumbai • Ranchi
Visit us at **www.newagepublishers.com**

Published by New Age International (P) Ltd., Publishers
First Edition: 1997
Reprint: 2010

Branches:

- No. 37/10, 8th Cross (Near Hanuman Temple), Azad Nagar, Chamrajpet, **Bangalore** - 560 018.Tel.: (080) 26756823, Telefax: 26756820 E-mail: bangalore@newagepublishers.com
- 26, Damodaran Street, T. Nagar, **Chennai** - 600 017. Tel.: (044) 24353401, Telefax: 24351463, E-mail: chennai@newagepublishers.com
- CC-39/1016, Carrier Station Road, Ernakulam South, **Cochin** - 682 016. Tel.: (0484) 2377004, Telefax: 4051303, E-mail: cochin@newagepublishers.com
- Hemsen Complex, Mohd. Shah Road, Paltan Bazar, Near Starline Hotel, **Guwahati** - 781 008, Tel.: (0361) 2513881, Telefax: 2543669 E-mail: guwahati@newagepublishers.com
- No. 105, 1st Floor, Madhiray Kaveri Tower, 3-2-19, Azam Jahi Road, Nimboliadda, **Hyderabad** - 500 027. Tel.: (040) 24652456, Telefax: 24652457 E-mail:hyderabad@newagepublishers.com
- RDB Chambers (Formerly Lotus Cinema)106A, 1st Floor, S.N. Banerjee Road, **Kolkata** - 700 014, Tel.: (033) 22273773, Telefax: 22275247 E-mail:kolkata@newagepublishers.com
- 16-A, Jopling Road, **Lucknow** - 226 001. Tel.: (0522) 2209578, 4045297, Telefax: 2204098, E-mail: lucknow@newagepublishers.com
- 142C, Victor House, Ground Floor, N.M. Joshi Marg, Lower Parel, **Mumbai** - 400 013, Tel.: (022) 24927869, Telefax: 24915415 E-mail: mumbai@newagepublishers.com
- 22, Golden House, Daryaganj, **New Delhi** - 110 002. Tel.: (011) 23262370 23262368, Telefax: 43551305, E-mail: sales@newagepublishers.com

ISBN (10) : 81-224-1040-5
ISBN (13) : 978-81-224-1040-2

Rs. 200.00

C-10-08-4881

Printed in India at A.H. Print Pack, Delhi.

PUBLISHING FOR ONE WORLD
NEW AGE INTERNATIONAL (P) LIMITED, PUBLISHERS
4835/24, Ansari Road, Daryaganj, New Delhi-110002
Visit us at **www.newagepublishers.com**

PREFACE

In the recent past, the microprocessor has made enormous inpact on our day to day life. Its versatility makes it suitable for a variety of applications ranging from the personal computer to industrial control. The knowledge of microprocessor is therefore essential in understanding not only the computer hardware and but also any of the processor controlled instruments.

This book is the outcome of our experience in teaching micrprocessors at T T T I Madras. We have made an attempt to write a text, which is easy to read and understand and which covers most of the aspects of the microprocessor.

This book is intended for the students of Electronic/Electrical Engineering and also for working professionals who want to learn microprocessors. The reader is expected to have only entry level knowledge to understand the text.

The text is aimed to provide the stundents a comprehensive knowledge of programming and interfacing of Intel 8085 and its peripherals. With the knowledge of working of 8085 CPU it is easy for any one to learn any other CPU and its peripherals.

The book is divided into 14 chapters and begins with a brief overview of a microprocessor based system. It discusses the details of the building blocks of a microprocessor system.

The second chapter deals with the architecture of 8085 CPU and also its pin details. It will give an insight into the main features of the CPU.

The power of microprocessor, over discrete logical systems comes from its ability to execute instructions. Chapters 3 and 4 deal with the instruction set of 8085 CPU. The functions of different instructions are explained with the help of examples.

Chapter 5 deals with many useful programming examples. The different examples are carefully chosen so as to illustrate features of the instruction set. The reader can practice these examples on his trainer kit to familiarise himself with programming concepts.

Once the programming concepts are understood, the reader can learn interfacing techniques. Chapter 6 deals with interfacing the CPU with simple devices.

Chapter 7 deals with the concepts of interrupt, which enables the microprocessor to be used for many real life applications.

Chapter 8 deals with the details of memory as used in a microprocessor based system.

The 8085 has a number of companion peripherial devices, produced by the Intel Corporation. Chapters 9, 10 and 11 deal with programming and interfacing aspects of these peripheral devices.

Chapter 12 covers details of many real life applications of the microprocessor. The details of this chapter will help the reader in implementing microprocessor based solutions, for any new problems encountered.

An overview of other popular 8 bit microprocessors, namely Z-80, 6800 and 6502 is given in the Chapter 13.

The last chapter, introduces the 16 bit microprocessor, Intel 8086 to the reader. Details of mathematic coprocessor 8087 are also discussed.

The authors wish to thank all the persons who chose not to disturb them while they were writing this book.

Authors

Contents

CHAPTER 1

INTRODUCTION TO MICROCOMPUTER SYSTEMS

1.1 MICRO COMPUTERS

Microcomputer systems are becoming very widely used and find applications not only in the industry and laboratories, but also in homes and offices. The basic structure of a microcomputer system is the same as that of a general purpose digital computer. This chapter introduces the basic structure of a computer and its relevance to a microprocessor based system.

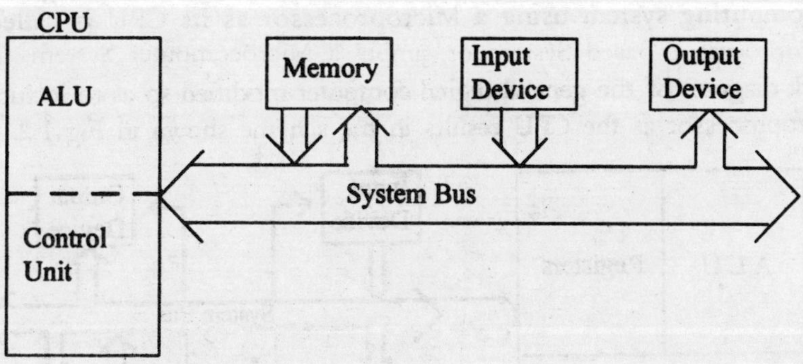

Fig 1.1 Block diagram of a computer system

Fig 1.1 gives the block diagram of a general purpose digital computer. Any problem to be solved in a computer would involve arithmetic computations and simple logical decisions. The block which handles these functions is called the Arithmetic Logic Unit (ALU). Further the computer would require mechanisms for input and output of data. Such devices are called Input and Output units. The computer remembers these data by storing them in its Memory. The Memory not only stores data but more importantly the program itself. The communication and data flow between the ALU on one hand and the Input, Output units and Memory on the other hand are controlled by the Control Unit; specifically it manages the timing needed for these operations. The ALU and Control Unit together are generally called the Central Processing Unit (CPU).

Hardware and Software

The physical components of the computer make up the Hardware. A set of instructions logically sequenced to carry out a given task is called a Program. Generally, the computer program is known as Software.

Bit and Byte

The microcomputer system recognises and operates in binary digits; 0 and 1. A *bit* is the abbrevation of Binary digit. Using binary digit, it is easier to represent electrically ON or OFF states of voltage in a cirucit. A group of 8 bits is known as a *Byte.*

1.1.1 DESCRIPTION

Advances in semiconductor technology have made available the entire CPU as a single Integrated Circuit (IC) called the Microprocessor. A computing system using a Microprocessor as its CPU is called a Microprocessor Based System or simply a Microcomputer System. The block diagram of the general digital computer modified so as to include a Microprocessor as the CPU results in the scheme shown in Fig 1.2.

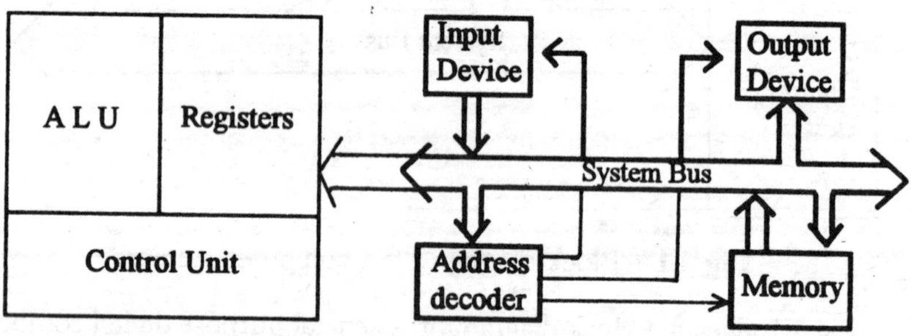

Fig. 1.2 Modified block diagram of a computer system.

The various components of such a Microprocessor Based System are explained below.

Microprocessor

The microprocessor consists of several logic circuits integrated on a single chip. It is usually built using Large Scale Integration (LSI) or Very Large Scale Integratrion (VLSI) technology. It is capable of performing arithmetic computations and making decisions. The major component blocks of a microprocessor are Arithmetic Logic Unit (ALU), Registers and Control Unit. The following explain their functions.

Arithmetic Logic Unit (ALU)

The ALU performs arithmetic operations such as addition,subtraction and logic operations such as AND, OR and Exclusive OR.

Registers

The registers are used for temporary storage of data during the execution of the program. Certain registers have special functions; for example holding the address of the next instruction to be executed

Control Unit

The control unit provides the timing and control signals to carry out different operation within as well as outside the CPU.

Input

The purpose of the input section is to accept data and programs and transfer them to the CPU and memory. The most often used input device is a keyboard. Microprocessor based systems generally use hexadecimal keyboards. These type of keyboards have 16 data keys from 0 to F, apart from some additional function keys.

Alternatively microprocessor based systems can get input from devices such as analog to digital converters (ADC) and switches as well.

Output

The results of computation/processing inside the CPU are indicated to the outside world through the output devices. The commonly used output device is a series of 7 segment display devices. Alternatively individual Light Emitting Diodes (LED) and relays can also be used as output devices.

Memory

Semiconductor memory devices are used to implement the memory. The memory device basically stores binary data ZERO or ONE. It will have provision to access an individual digit or a group of digits (4 bits/ 8 bits) together. A microprocessor based system will make use of a permanent memory device to store certain resident programs which are not changed during operation or even when power is turned off. These programs control the hardware and enable the user to enter and run his own program and data. Such programs are called Monitor programs.

This permanent memory device is called Read Only Memory (ROM) because it is not possible to overwrite the contents of such a device during the normal operations.

In addition, the microcomputer needs memory area for temporary storage of user's program, intermediate data and results of computation. This read/write type temporary memory is called Random Access Memory (RAM).

System Bus

As in Fig. 1.1, the CPU, memory and the Input/Output devices are shown interconnected by the system bus. A bus is a set of conductors carrying signals. It is called system bus since it serves the microcomputer system and is under its control. Thus the different units of the microprocessor system communicate through the system bus.

Address Decoder

To access a specific memory device or an I/O device the CPU puts its address on the address bus. However the address bus is common to all other memory devices and so the address reaches all other memory and I/O devices. To make only the specific memory device active, the address decoder circuit is used. It is designed to recognise the relevant device for a given address. It then selects that particular device through the enable signals.

1.1.2 A Working Microcomputer System

With the addition of certain other facilities and adding further details to each of the block, the schematic of a practical model of a microcomputer evolves, as shown in Fig.1.3.

Memory Organisation

The memory is organised as a sequence of identical locations. Each location can hold typically 8 bits of data. Alternatively devices with 1 or 4 bit location are also available. Each location is identified by an unique serial number which could run as 0, 1, 2,.......upto 1023 for a 1 Kilobyte memory device, (In computer terminalogy, 1 Kilobyte means 2 raised to the power 10). This serial number is known as the address of the location. Typically 4 or 5 memory IC chips, each of 2 or 4 or 8 Kilobytes of data size will make up the RAM block. ROM is also organised in a similar fashion, though total ROM size for a microcomputer will be smaller.

I/O Ports

Most applications of a microcomputer would involve controlling or reading external devices such as switches, relays, LEDs, Analog to

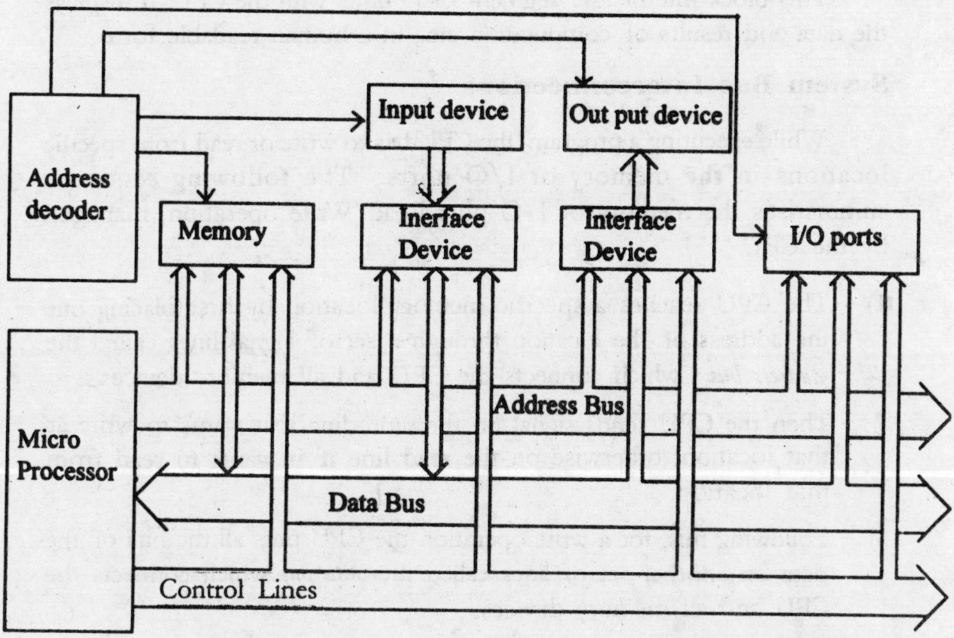

Fig. 1.3 Schematic of practical model of a Microprocessor based system

Digital (A/D) or Digital to Analog (D/A) converters, stepper motor circuits etc. For example, a microcomputer operating in a weighing machine would read a pressure sensor through an A/D converter and write data on a suitable display device. Such external devices are interfaced to the CPU through the Input/Output ports. The ports contain a number of registers through which the CPU access the different external devices. Just like a memory location, each port (register) will have an unique address.

Interface

The circuits necessary to connect the external devices with the microprocessor is called an **interface**

Keyboard Interface

This unit interfaces the keyboard with the CPU for input. It converts each keypress into a data format suitable for the CPU.

Display Interface

This block interfaces 7 segment LED units with the CPU. It displays the data and results of computation etc., in a human readable form.

System Bus Interconnections

While executing a program, the CPU has to write or read from specific locations in the memory or I/O ports. The following sequence summarises the memory or I/O port Read/Write operation, managed by the CPU.

1) The CPU reaches a specific memory location by first placing out the address of the location through a set of signal lines called the *address bus* which connects the CPU and all memory devices.

2) Then the CPU sends signal on the write line if it wants to write at that location; otherwise on the read line if it wants to read from that location.

3) Following this, for a write operation the CPU puts all the bits of the data on another set of lines called the *data bus* which connects the CPU and all memory devices.

4) Thus the data is written into the desired location of the memory.

5) For a read operation the selected location places its contents on the data bus and the CPU reads it in.

In essence the CPU manages the read/write operation by placing address and data on specific lines and every microprocessor will include such signal lines in its architecture.

Similarly, I/O read or write operations are managed by selecting the specific I/O port by sending unique I/O address.

1.2. NUMBER SYSTEM

Conventionally, we use the Decimal Number System which has numbers 0 to 9. However, Binary Number System having numbers 0 and 1 is used in digital computer systems.

1.2.1 Binary Number System

Microcomputers, as any other digital computer system use Binary Number System for all its internal representation and processing of data. Binary Number System is a base 2 number system and therefore it has only 2 digits 0 and 1. Table 1.1 shows the binary number equivalent of decimal numbers from 0 to 15. In a binary number, the place value of digits increase in powers of 2.

As an example, the binary number 1110 represents
$1 \times 2^3 + 1 \times 2^2 + 1 \times 2^1 + 0 \times 2^0 = 14$ in decimal system.

All information within a microcomputer is represented in binary form; which include the input data to be processed, the instructions themselves and the address of memory locations as well.

Table 1.1 Binary Number System

Decimal Number	*Binary Number*
0	0000
1	0001
2	0010
3	0011
4	0100
5	0101
6	0110
7	0111
8	1000
9	1001
10	1010
11	1011
12	1100
13	1101
14	1110
15	1111

1.2.2 Hexadecimal Number System

The hexadecimal system has a base of sixteen; therefore it has 16 symbols. The 10 decimal digits (0 to 9) and additionally 6 English alphabets (A to F) are made use of to represent these 16 symbols. The hexadecimal symbols and their binary and decimal equivalents are given in Table 1.2.

As the table shows hexadecimal number is a very convenient way of notation for a 4 bit long binary number. Many digital systems process binary data in groups that are multiples of 4 bits. These data can be conveniently represented in hexadecimal number system. To convert a long train of binary numbers into hexadecimal equivalent, split the binary number into groups of 4 starting from the right most digit. Assign hexadecimal equivalent to each 4 bit group.

Table 1.2 Hexadecimal Number System

Hexadecimal	*Binary*	*Decimal*
0	0000	0
1	0001	1
2	0010	2
3	0011	3
4	0100	4
5	0101	5
6	0110	6
7	0111	7
8	1000	8
9	1001	9
A	1010	10
B	1011	11
C	1100	12
D	1101	13
E	1110	14
F	1111	15

Example

Binary number 111001101011

After splitting into groups of 4 Bits 1110 0110 1011

Hexadecimal equivalent C 6 B

Usually hexadecimal numbers will have the letter H at the right end to denote that the number is a hexadecimal number.

Example

C6BH

Microcomputer systems have keyboard to enter hexadecimal numbers directly. The keyboard will have keys from 0 to F.

1.3 REVIEW OF DIGITAL CIRCUITS

In a bus oriented microcomputer system, address decoders select a specific device whenever CPU wants to read/write from/into memory, input and output devices. In order to do effectively, tri-state logic gates are needed, since the same bus lines are shared by different devices. For a total understanding of the microcomputer system, knowledge of logic circuits are essential. With this idea, a review of commonly used digital circuits is made in the following.

1.3.1 LATCH

The Latch is a digital circuit which can store a 0 or 1. Normally, latches are used in the output circuits. (Output Ports). The latch holds the data till the next data is transferred in. The simplest latch is a D type flip flop as shown in Fig. 1.4a. When the enable input E is high, the output Q changes according to the input D; when D is 1, Q is 1; when D is 0, Q is 0.

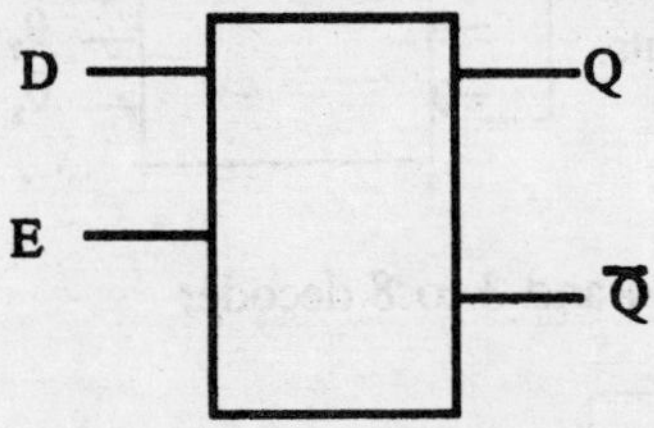

Fig. 1.4a Schmatic of a D flip-flop

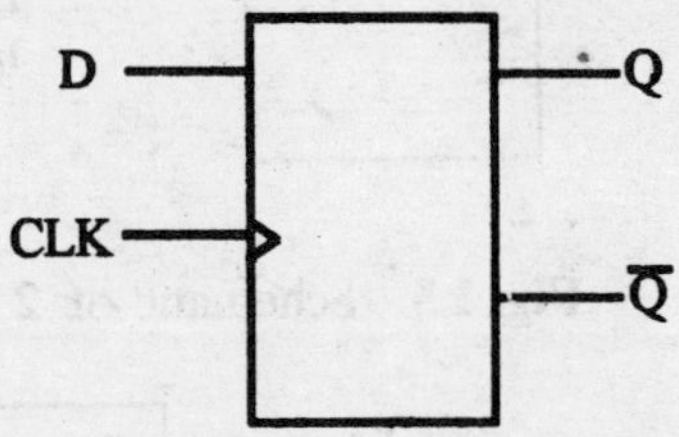

Fig.1.4b Schematic of an edge triggerred flip-flop

The moment enable input E goes low, the output Q will latch (or hold) the last value of the input D. The circuit maintains (or stores) this value until the enable goes high again.

$\overline{Q}$ always outputs the complement of Q.

A typical example of a D type latch is the TTL chip 7475 D -Flip Flop.

A positve edge triggered flip flop such as TTL chip 7474 can also be used as a latch. In this case the latching of output is done at the instant of the positive edge of a clock.

1.3.2 DECODER

A decoder detects the presence of a specified combination of bits on its input and indicate this coincidence on its output.

The decoder in Fig.1.5 has 2 input lines, and so the input combinations possible are 00, 01, 10 & 11. Therefore the decoder will have 4 output lines, one for each input combination. The input combination 10 is indicated by a high level on the output line O2, and a low on the other output lines. Such a decoder is called 2 to 4 decoder, indicating the number of inputs and outputs. It is also called 1 out of 4 decoder, since only one of the 4 outputs will be high at any time.

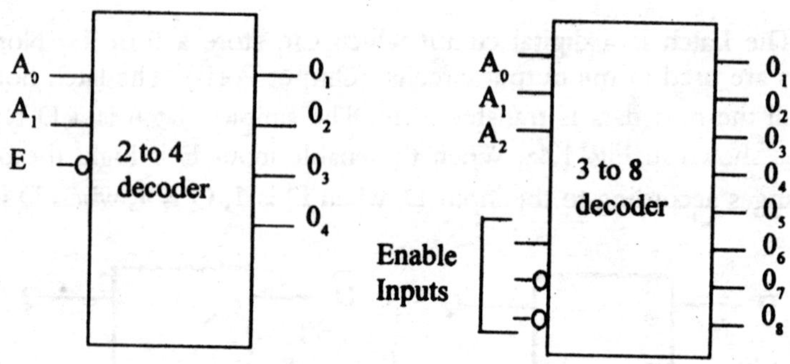

Fig. 1.5 Schematic of 2 to 4 and 3 to 8 decoder

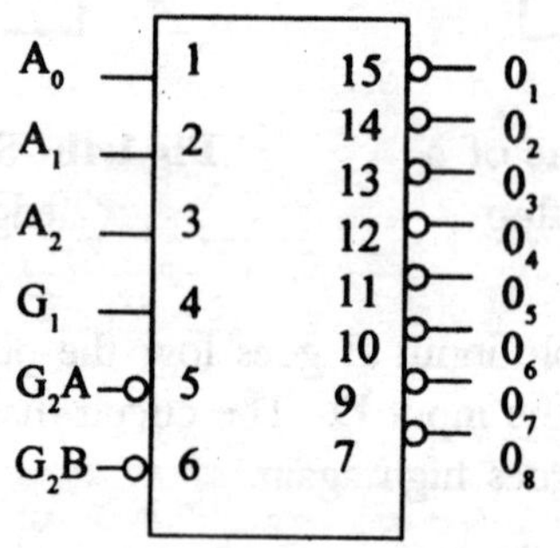

Fig. 1.6 Schematic of IC 74138

Note that a bubble at E input indicates that the decoder action will be enabled only when the Enable input is active LOW.

Note that in 3 to 8 decoder, there are two active LOW enable and one active HIGH enable inputs.

In general, for n input lines a decoder will have a maximum of 2^n output lines. Commonly used decoders are 3 to 8, 4 to 10 and 4 to 16.

The TTL chip 74138 shown in Fig. 1.6 is a 3 to 8 decoder. The three input lines (A_0, A_1, A_2) are decoded into the 8 output lines (O_1, O_2, O_3,... O_7). However the active output line (selected line) assumes a *low* level while the remaining 7 are at *high* level. Therefore the chip is called an active low output decoder. Control lines G_1 and G_2A, G_2B are provided in the chip to enable the output. G_2A and G_2B have to be *low* and G_1 has to be *high* for the decoded output line to go to *low* level. For any other combination of G_2A, G_2B and G_1, all outputs will be *high*.

Decoders are used to decode address sent out by CPU and select the relevant device as discussed earlier. It is also used in memory devices to select a particular memory IC chip for a given address.

1.3.3 TRI STATE DEVICES

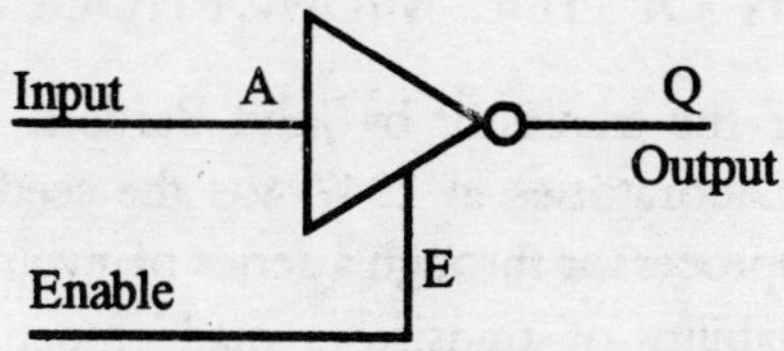

Fig. 1.7 Tri-state inverter gate

Tri-state logic devices have 3 output states; the usual *high* & *low* states and additionally a *high impedence state.* Fig. 1.7 shows the symbol of a tristate inverter gate. In addition to the data input A, the gate also has an enable input E. When E is high the gate is enabled and the output Q can be 1 or 0 (if A is 0, Q is 1, otherwise Q is 0). However, when E is low the gate is disabled and the output Q enters into a *high impedence state.*

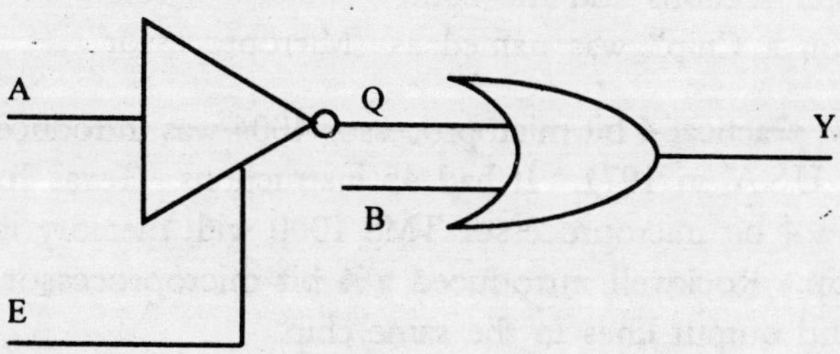

Fig. 1.8 Tri-state logic

Let us investigate what the high impedance state implies. In Fig.1.8, the output of tristate gate is connected to the input of an OR gate. When E is 1, Q can be at 0 or 1. For both these states, the output Q draws a current from the input of the OR gate. When E is low, Q enters a high impedance state; high impedance means it is electrically isolated from the OR gate's input, though it is physically connected. Therfore, it does not draw any current from the OR gate's input.

In a microcomputer, devices connected with the bus are terminated using tri-state gates. This is needed when 2 or more devices are connected to a common bus. To prevent the devices from interfering with each other, the tristate gates are used to disconnect all devices except the one that is communicating at a given instant.

1.4 EVOLUTION OF THE MICROPROCESSOR

The invention of the transistor by John Bardeen, W.H.Brattain and W.B.Shockley at Bell Laboratories in 1947 was the seed which led to the development of Microprocessor through a series of evolutionary processes. The commercial availability of transistors made most of the electronic systems "solid state". In 1959, the circuit consisting of transistors, resistors and capacitors was fabricated on a single chip of silicon. This was the basis of an integrated circuit (IC). The growth of the integrated circuit technology started with Small-Scale Integration (SSI) consisting of less than ten gates per chip. It progressed to Medium Scale Integration (MSI), with ten to hundred gates on a chip, then to Large Scale Integration (LSI) with hundred to few thousand gates per chip. With the advancement of technology, Very Large Scale Integration (VLSI) with several thousand gates on a chip could be achieved.

By 1970, it was possible to accomodate all the functional elements, of the Central Processing Unit (CPU), the Arithmetic and Logic Unit (ALU), register sections and the control units in a single IC chip. This "Computer on a Chip" was named as "Microprocessor".

The first practical 4 bit microprocessor 4004 was introduced by Intel Corporation, U.S.A. in 1971. It had 45 instructions. Texas Instruments brought out a 4 bit microprocessor TMS 1000 with memory included in the same chip. Rockwell introduced a 4 bit microprocessor PPS 4/1 with input and output lines in the same chip.

Since the capabilities of the 4 bit microprocessors were not sufficient to meet the requirements of many applications, 8 bit microprocessors were developed. Intel brought out 8008 and then the improved version 8080. It is a 40 pin I.C with 8 bit data lines and 16 bit address lines. Motorola developed MC 6800 and Zilog developed Z 80. The chip Z 80 gained popularity, since it had 158 instructions and more number of registers for easy operation. Intel modified 8080 and came up with 8085. This processor has multiplexed address/data bus and more number of hardware interrupts and serial I/O facilities. The 8 bit microprocessors are extensively used in control applications.

To meet complex computing requirements, 16 bit microprocessors were developed. Intel produced 8086, 8088 and 80286 microprocessors. Zilog produced Z8000 and Texas Instruments developed TMS 9900 and Motorola developed 68000.

Nowadays, 32 bit and 64 bit microprocessors are available. Intel 80386, 80486 and Motorola 68020, 68030 are some of the 32 bit microprocessors. The 16 bit and 32 microprocessors are capable of handling large size memory, operating at higher speed and offer higher accuracy.

1.5 ADVANTAGES OF MICROPROCESSOR SYSTEMS

For any given application, it is possible to design a circuit with discrete components and Integrated Circuits. Such a system is called a Hard Wired System.

It has a disadvantage. Once a hardwired system is fabricated and is working, making changes in the design is difficult. Even a small change in design has to be acheived by corresponding changes in the hardware.

The advantage of a microprocessor based system is that it is programmable. It has the same hardware, but carries out different functions with different software.

The following are the advantages of a Microprocessor based systems

- Simplifies system design
- Reduces development time, cost and size
- Flexible in operation.

EXERCISE 1

I. FILL IN THE BLANKS

1. The expansion of CPU is ______________________________.
2. The third state of tri-state logic is __________________.
3. Data and addresses are stored in ____________ form.
4. A group of lines is called as ____________.
5. 1 KB represents ____________ number of bytes.
6. The system bus consists of 3 sets of lines namely ____________ ____________ and ____________ .
7. The binary equivalent of the decimal number 42 is ____________.
8. The decimal equivalent of the binary number 0101 0101 is _______.
9. The binary equivalent of the hexa decimal number C5 is ________.
10. The hexa decimal number equivalent of 1010 1100 is ________ .

II. WRITE SHORT ANSWERS

1. What are the functional blocks of a microcomputer ?
2. Mention the purpose of the registers inside the CPU
3. List a few input and output devices
4. What is the purpose of the control unit of the CPU ?
5. Differentiate between ROM and RAM
6. What is interface ?
7. Why is Binary number system used in computer arithmetic ?
8. Mention the purpose of using the Hexadecimal number system ?
9. Explain the operation of a tri-state logic device
10. Explain the function of IC 74138.
11. What is the major difference between hardwired system and a microprocessor based system ?
12. What do you mean by the term VLSI ?
13. In the term 8 bit microprocessor, what does '8 bit' mean ?

CHAPTER 2

ARCHITECTURE AND PIN DETAILS OF THE 8085 MICROPROCESSORS

2.1 CONCEPT OF A PROGRAM

A Computer is a general-purpose machine or device that can be used to solve a problem or implement a particular task. A task is implemented by deciding the *sequence of operations* needed to perform it. Consider a basic electronic calculator which offers the user a variety of operations - add, subtract, multiply, etc. It is then upto the user to select the particular sequence of these operations necessary to solve a specific problem. Similarly a digital computer can perform a number of basic operations called *Instructions* which the user selects and arranges in a way, so as to solve a particular problem. This sequential list of operation is referred as a *Program.*

2.2 BASIC OPERATIONS

Once the program has been written for the task, the complete program is loaded into memory and is then executed. During program execution, each instruction is brought from the memory and then executed by the microprocessor. In executing each instruction, the microprocessor therefore operates in a two phase mode; during the first phase, the fetch cycle, the instruction is fetched from memory; then in the second phase or execution cycle, the microprocessor performs (or executes) the action specified by the instruction.

2.3 INTERNAL ARCHITECTURE

The term architecture, as used in microprocessor circuits describes the functional components that make up the CPU and the interaction between them. They include the temporary storage devices known as registers, which are used to hold data, instructions and status information. There are also devices to perform arithmetic operations such as addition and subtraction, and logic operations such as AND and OR.

The 8085 microprocessor consists of registers, an instruction decoder, a timing and control unit, an arithmetic and logic unit (ALU), an interrupt, system and serial input and output devices. The functional block diagram is shown in Fig. 2.1

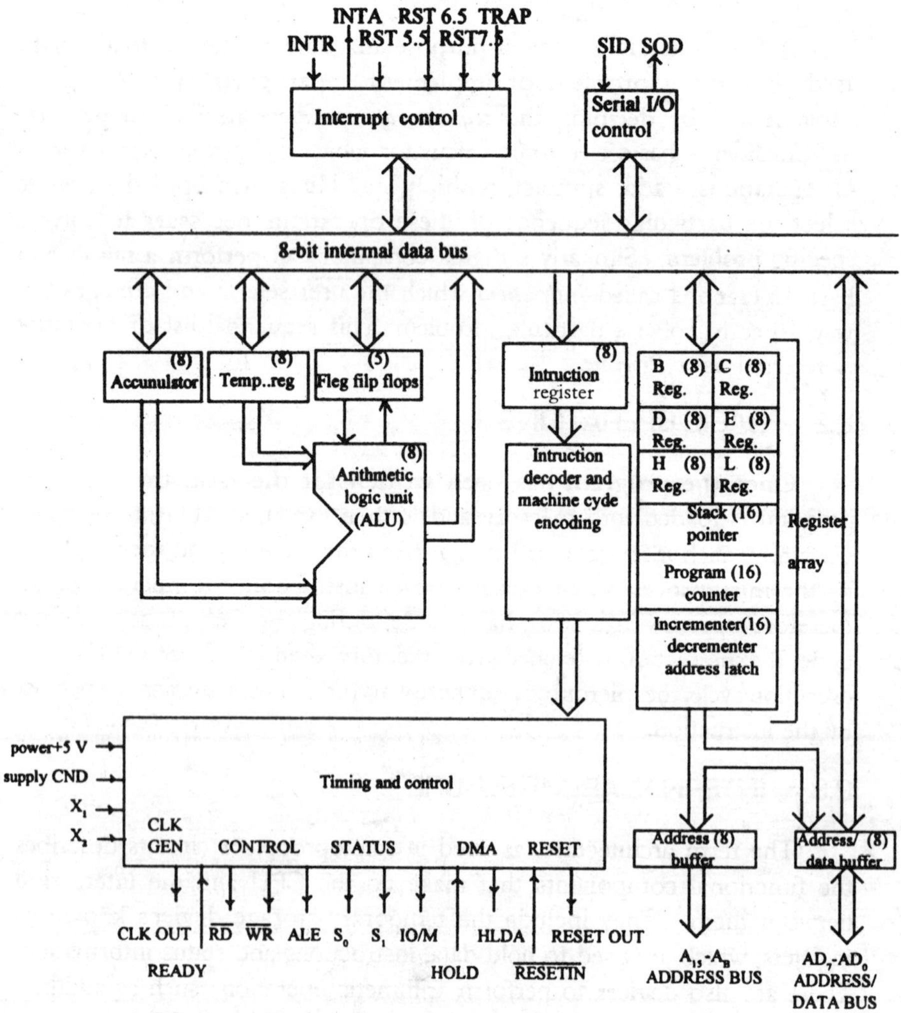

Fig. 2.1 8085 functional block diagram

2.4 EXECUTION OF AN INSTRUCTION

The functioning of the different components of a microprocessor can be best understood by learning the execution process of an instruction.

The time required to execute an instruction is called an *Instruction Cycle.* The operation durng an instruction cycle usually involves accessing memory or input/output devices. The time required ot access the memory or an input/output device *once* is called a *Machine Cycle.* These cycles are not measured in absolute time units, rather in terms of the number of periods of the system clock the microprocessor uses. The machine cycle and therefore the instruction cycle takes multiple clock periods and that portion of the operation carried out in one system clock period is called a *T state.*

The instruction cycle could consist of one or more machine cycles. The machine cycle usually consists of 3 to 6 T states. The clock period is determined by the frequency of the crystal controlled oscillator which provides the system clock. The operations of the microprocessor are therefore synchronised with the system clock.

Let us assume that the program is stored starting from the location 8C00H. Therefore the location 8C00H contains the code for the first instruction. Fig. 2.2 helps in understanding the execution sequence.

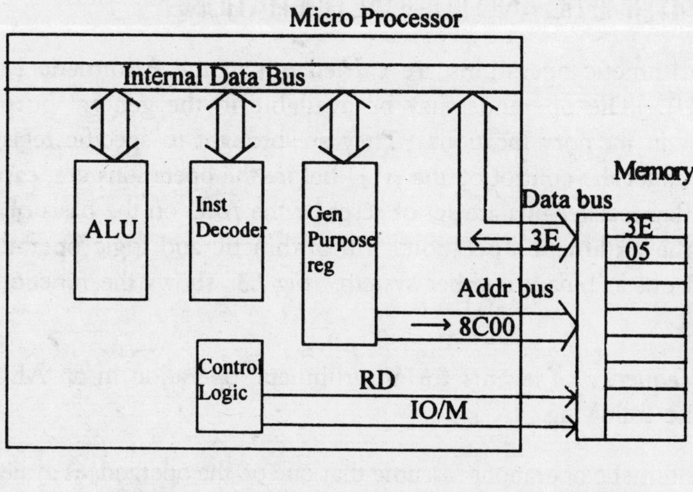

Fig.2.2 Signal flow from memory to the CPU

The following explains the purpose and interaction of different blocks as well as the stages in the execution of an instruction.

1. In order to run a program the CPU first loads the starting address of the program into one of its registers called the Program Counter (PC). The contents of the Program Counter are sent out through the address bus. In this case the address would be 8C00 H.
2. The relevant memory location is enabled and its contents are placed in the data bus. The content in this case is the operation code of the instruction MVI A.
3. The CPU reads the content of the data bus and sends it to the block called *INSTRUCTION DECODER*. It is in this block that the instruction is identified and the sequence of events that has to follow is decided. This process is called decoding the instruction and therefore the block is called so.
4. As part of the follow up sequence, the Instruction Decoder enables the *CONTROL* and *TIMING UNIT* to send the necessary signals.
5. The Instruction Decoder completes the execution by setting the ALU to add the contents of B register and A register.

Note: After sending out the content of the Program Counter as in step 1 above, its content is incremented so that it contains the address of the next instruction. Thus at any instant, the counter stores the address of the next instruction to be executed. That is why it is called the Program Counter.

2.5 ARITHMETIC AND LOGICAL OPERATIONS

All arithmetic operations are carried out in the Arithmetic Logic Unit (ALU). The operands may be available in the general purpose registers or in memory locations. They are brought to specific registers which are under the control of the ALU before the operations are carried out. The flag register bits are set or reset by the ALU on the basis of the result of the arithmetic operation. All arithmetic and logic operations are carried out in binary number system. Fig.2.3 shows the functioning of the ALU.

The sequence of events for an arithmetic operation in an ALU is listed in the following.

- All arithmetic operations assume that one of the operands is available in the A register.

- The second operand which may be at one of the CPU registers or at a memory location is taken to the Temporary register.
- The contents of these 2 registers are brought inside the ALU and the specified operation carried out in the ALU.
- Then through the internal data bus, the result is again placed in the A register. The A register is also called the *ACCUMULATOR*.
- The content of the flag register will change depending upon the result. The flag register has 5 independent bits which indicate the status of the result.
- The Carry flag bit is set (made one level) if a Carry or Borrow occurs during the arithmetic operation. The Carry flag indicates that the operation resulted in *overflow*.
- The Parity flag bit is set if the result has an *even* number of 1s, otherwise it will be reset (made Zero).
- The Sign flag bit is set if the bit D7 of the result is 1, otherwise it is reset. The sign bit indicates the sign of the number (Positive or Negative) and becomes useful in the *SIGNED* binary number system.
- The Zero flag is set if the result of the operation becomes 0. For all other values of the result the bit is reset.
- The Auxiliary Carry flag bit become one level, when a Carry is generated at digit D3 position, and passed on to digit D4. This flag is used only internally for Binary Coded Decimal (BCD) operations.

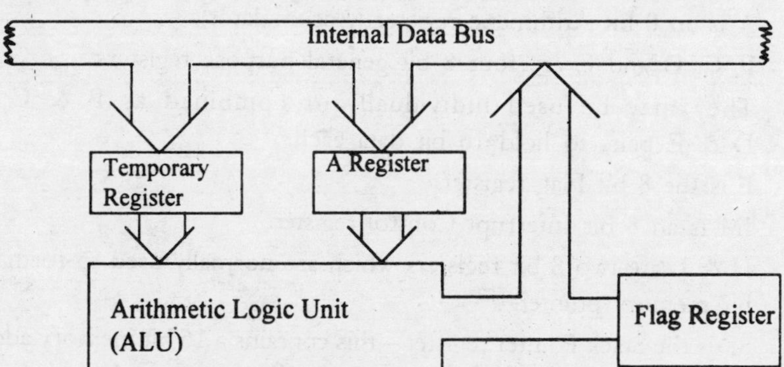

Fig. 2.3 Signal flow in ALU operation

The relative bit positions of the flag register is shown in the following Table.

D7	D6	D5	D4	D3	D2	D1	D0
S	Z	–	AC	–	P	–	CY

2.6 REGISTERS

The majority of machine instructions available with a microprocessor operate on or affect the state of various internal registers which make up the microprocessor. Therefore, it is necessary to acquire a knowledge of those processor registers which are accessible or are affected by the machine instructions. The main registers for the Intel 8085 are shown in Fig 2.4.

A	FLAG
B	C
D	E
H	L
	IM
Stack Pointer (SP)	
Program Counter (PC)	

Fig. 2.4 Main registers in the 8085 microprocessor

- A is an 8 bit Arithmetic register (Accumulator).
- B, C, D and E are four 8 bit general purpose registers.
- They may be used individually or combined as B & C and D & E pairs to hold 16 bit data each.
- F is the 8 bit Flag register.
- IM is an 8 bit Interrupt Control register.
- H & L are two 8 bit registers which are normally used to form a 16 bit memory pointer.
- SP is the Stack Pointer register – this contains a 16 bit memory address which is used as pointer to the top of a system stack.
- PC is the Program Counter register which contains a 16 bit memory address which points to the next instruction to be executed.

2.7 INTERRUPT AND SERIAL I/O

Interrupt facility is provided to enable a peripheral device to inform the microprocessor whenever it wishes to transfer data. The 8085 has 5 interrupt inputs.

The 8085 also features a serial I/O facility. This enables serial input/ output of single bit data under direct control of the CPU.

2.8 PIN DETAILS OF THE 8085 MICROPROCESSOR

Fig.2.5a shows the pin details of 8085 microprocessor. Fig.2.5b shows the logical schematic of the processor. The signals can be grouped as follows

1. Power supply and clock signals
2. Address bus
3. Data bus
4. Control and status signals
5. Interrupts and externally initiated signals
6. Serial I/O ports

1. Power supply and Clock frequency signals

V_{cc} + 5 volt power supply

V_{ss} Ground

X_1, X_2 Crystal or R/C network connections to set the frequency of internal clock generator. X_1 can also be an external clock input instead of a crystal.

Normally, a crystal is connected across X_1 and X_2 inputs. The frequency is internally divided by two. Since the basic operating timing frequency is 3 MHz, a 6 MHz crystal is connected externally.

The microprocessor performs several operations like reading instructions from memory, understanding the instructions and generate control signals accordingly to execute the instructions. It carries out the different operations synchronised with a timing signal. In 8085, the timing signal is generated internally; however only a crystal or RC network need to be connected externally.

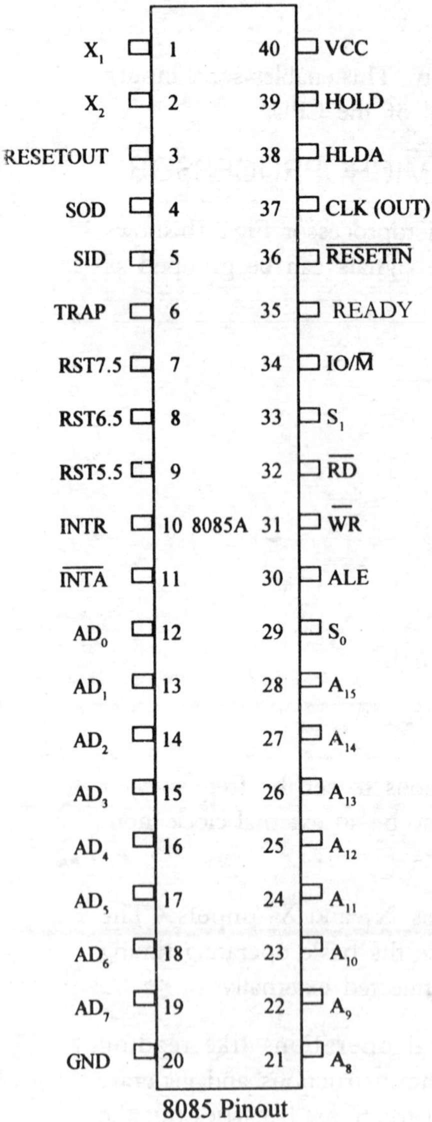

Fig.2.5a Pin details of the Microprocessor 8085

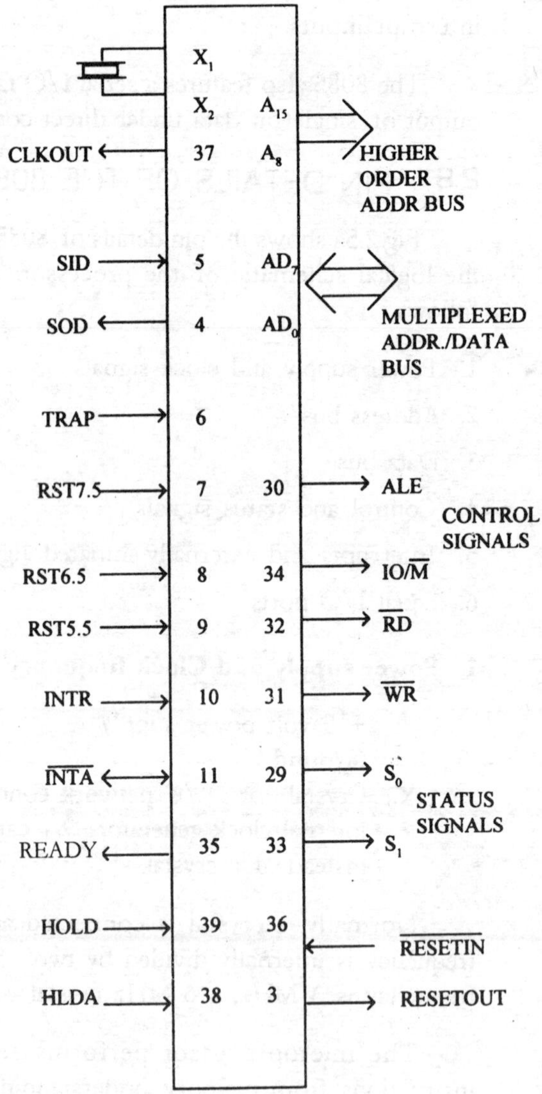

Fig.2.5b Logical Schematics of the Microprocessor 8085

CLK (output) — Clock Output

This is used as the system clock for peripheral and devices interfaced with the microprocessor.

2. Address Bus

$A_8 - A_{15}$ (output; 3-state)

The most significant 8 bits of the memory address or the 8 bits of the I/O address;

3. Multiplexed Address / Data Bus

$AD_0 - AD_7$ (input/output; 3-state)

Multiplexed Address/Data Bus.

These multiplexed set of lines serve as the lower order 8 bit address as well as data bus. During the opcode fetch operation, in the first clock cycle, the lines deliver the lower order address A0 - A7. In the subsequent I O / memory, read / write clock cycle the lines are used as data bus. The CPU may read or write out data through these lines.

4. Control and Status signals

ALE (output) - Address Latch Enable

This signal helps to capture the lower order address presented on the multiplexed address / data bus. This positive going pulse is generated whenever the CPU begins a machine cycle. It is synchronised with the appearance of **lower order address** on the address / data bus. The ALE signal enables the lower order address to be latched externally.
Basically, the microprocessors does & operations. Memory read, Memory write, I/O read and I/O write.

$\overline{RD}$(output 3-state, active low) – Read memory or IO device.

This indicates that the selected memory location or I/O device is to be read and that the data bus is ready for accepting data from the memory or I/O device.

$\overline{WR}$ (output 3-state, active low) - Write memory or IO device.

This indicates that the data on the data bus is to be written into the selected memory location or I/O device.

IO/M (output) - Select memory or an IO device.

This status signal indicates that the read / write operation relates to whether the memory or I/O device. It goes high to indicate an I/O operation and kept low for memory operations. Combined with $\overline{RD}$ and $\overline{WR}$ signals the IO/$\overline{M}$ signal directs the CPU data into I/O or memory devices.

5. S_0, S_1 status signals

S1	S0	(output) – Data bus status.
0	0	Halt
0	1	Write
1	0	Read
1	1	Fetch

These status signals may be used to know the type of current operation the CPU performs.

6. Interrupts and Externally initiated operations

Microprocessors provide a facility called an interrupt which enables a peripheral (Input/Output) device to draw the attention of the microprocessor whenever the peripheral is ready for data transfer. The 8085 architecture features 5 interrupt signals.

TRAP
RST 7.5
RST 6.5 — (inputs)
RST 5.5
INTR
INTA (active low output)

They are initiated externally by the peripheral devices. On receipt of an interrupt, the microprocessor acknowledges the interrupt by the active low INTA (Interrupt Acknowledge) signal.

Reset In (input, active low)

This signal is used to reset the microprocessor. The program counter inside the microprocessor is set to zero. The buses are tri-stated.

Reset Out (Output)

It indicates CPU is being reset. It can be used as a system RESET to reset all the connected devices when the microprocessor is reset.

7. Direct Memory Access (DMA)

Direct Memory Access operation is used for large volume data transfer between memory and an I/O device. Normally the CPU controls the data transfer operation between memory and I/O device. However for large volume data transfer, the CPU is disabled by tri-stating its buses and the transfer is effected directly by external control circuits. These two signals are used to tri-state the CPU buses.

HOLD signal is generated by the DMA controller circuit. On receipt of this signal, the microprocessor acknowledges the request by sending out HLDA signal and leaves out the control of the buses. After the HLDA signal the DMA controller starts the direct transfer of data.

READY (input)

In general memory and I/O devices will have slower response compared to microprocessors. Before completing the present job such a slow peripheral may not be able to handle further data or control signal from CPU. Therefore it resets the READY signal. It sets the READY signal after completing the present job. The microprocessor enters into WAIT state while the READY pin is disabled.

8. Single Bit Serial I/O ports

SID (input) - Serial input data line

SOD (output) - Serial output data line

One bit information can be read or sent out serially through these signal lines.

These signals can be used to read the status of a switch or light an LED. These signals can also be used for serial communication.

EXERCISE - 2

I. FILL IN THE BLANKS

1. The operations of the microprocessor are ________________with the system clock.
2. The register which holds the address of the next instruction is ________________.
3. The number of bits used in the flag register is ________________.
4. The size of the Stack pointer is ________________ bits .
5. The signal used to latch the lower order address onto the AD0- AD7 bus is ________________.
6. The control signals needed for a memory read operation are ________________ and ________________.
7. When HOLD signal is active, the address, data and control signal lines of the CPU are in ________________ condition.
8. For 0.5 micro second clock period, the crystal to be connected externally should have a frequency of ________________ MHz.
9. The register pair normally used as memory address pointer is ________.
10. The maximum addressing capacity of 8085, with 16 address lines is ________________ Kilobytes.

II. WRITE SHORT ANSWERS

1. Explain the concept of a program ?
2. What is meant by an instruction cycle ?
3. What is the purpose of the Instruction Decoder of the CPU ?
4. Mention the speciality of A register compared to any other general purpose register.
5. What do you understand by multiplexed address / data bus ?
6. What are the control signals needed for I/O write operations ?
7. What are the hardware interrupts available in 8085 ?
8. Explain the action of applying RESET to the CPU.
9. Explain the term Direct Memory Access (DMA).
10. Mention the purpose of SID and SOD lines.

CHAPTER 3

PROGRAMMING THE MICROPROCESSOR - I

3.1 INSTRUCTION SET OF 8085

A microcomputer performs a task by reading and executing a sequence of instructions stored in memory. The instructions written in a logical sequence is called a program. Each instruction in the program is a command, in binary form, to the microprocessor to perform an operation. A microprocessor will have a set of such commands which covers all required operations. This set of commands which can be executed by the microprocessor is the microprocessor's Instruction Set. The instruction set *differs* from one microprocessor to another.

Every instruction is given by the manufacturer an unique one byte code called operation code (*OP-CODE* in short). Every instruction is also given a short name called *MNEMONIC* to enable programmers to remember the different instructions.

Example	*OP-CODE*	*MNEMONIC*
	3E	MVI A
	78	MOV A, B
	0B	DCR B
	76	HLT

The instruction set of 8085 can be divided into five different groups based on the functions the instructions carry out. They are

1. Data transfer operations
2. Arithmetic operations
3. Logical operations
4. Branching operations
5. Stack, I/O and machine control operations

Instructions under each of the category is described in detail in the following units

3.2 DATA TRANSFER OPERATIONS

In a microcomputer, the memory locations, the CPU internal registers and I/O ports would be holding useful data. Programming operations would involve moving data between and among these data locations. The 8085 instruction set features a number of instructions to carry out the data movement.

3.2.1 Move from a Register to another Register

The mnemonic (short form) for this instruction is MOV followed by a pair of register names separated by a comma.

Example: MOV B,C

This instruction causes the contents of the C register to be *COPIED* to B register. The B register loses its previous content in this process. The content of the C register remains unchanged.

	Register B	Register C
Initial content	XXXX XXXX	0100 0010

After executing the instruction MOV B,C the contents of registers B and C are

Register B	Register C
0100 0010	0100 0010

In this instruction, the C register which holds the data initially is called the Source register. The B register to which the data is copied is called the Destination register. All the 7 CPU registers namely A, B, C, D, E, H and L are allowed to be source as well as destination. So the Instruction set has 49 MOV commands for the 49 combinations of registers starting from MOV A, A; MOV A,B..... to MOV L,L.

3.2.2. Move between a Memory location and a CPU Register

The mnemonic is MOV followed by a register name and M separated by a comma.

Example: MOV E,M

A memory location is considered as a register and is represented by the symbol M. This instruction causes the content of the memory location to be copied to the E register. But which memory location? For this purpose the content of the HL register pair is taken as the 16 bit address of the memory location and the *content* of that location is copied to register E. Whenever any memory location is represented as M, its address should have been already placed in *HL register pair.*

Register E	Register H	Register L
XXXX XXXX	0010 0000 (20H)	0100 0000 (40H)

Memory location	Memory content
203F	0000 0000
2040	1000 0101
2041	0000 0000
2042	0000 0000

After execution of MOV E,M instruction, the contents of the E register will be

Register E

1000 0101

Thus the H and L register pair takes the role of holding the address of the memory location (H holding the *Higher* 8 bits and L the *Lower* 8 bits of the 16-bit address), and so is known as the *Address Pointer.* This type of refering a memory location using H and L pair as address pointer is known as *Indirect Addressing.* Since each one of the CPU registers can be used as the destination register, the Instruction set has 7 MOV commands starting from MOV A, M to MOV L, M.

Additionally, the Instruction set also has 7 more commands of the type MOV M,A to MOV M,L where the memory location M is used as the destination. The address of M is held by the H and L pair. These instructions cause the content of the register to be copied to the memory location.

Each register combination of the MOV command has an unique, *one byte* operation code (op code).

Example

Mnemonic	Opcode (Hexa decimal)
MOV A,B	78
MOV E,M	5E

Since these type of instructions just contains the OP-CODE which is 1 byte long, they are called **One Byte Instructions.**

3.2.3 Move Immediate Instruction

This instruction consists of 2 parts; the mnemonic and the destination register symbol as the first part and a single byte data as the second part.

Example MVI D, A5

It causes the data A5 to be moved to the register D. Since each of the CPU registers or a memory location could be the destination register, the instruction set has 8 MVI commands starting from MVI A till MVI L and additionally MVI M. Each of this MVI command has an unique opcode.

Example

Mnemonic	Opcode (H)
MVI D	16
MVI M	36

so that complete instruction using MVI will look like

MVI D, A5	16
	A5
MVI M, 2A	36
	2A

The MVI instructions have a 2 byte code; the first one is the opcode and the 2nd one, is the operand which is the data. Hence these instructions are called Two Byte Instructions. When such instructions need to be stored in memory as part of a program, the 2 bytes are stored in adjacent memory locations as shown in the following example. When the instruction is executed the content of the immediate (next) location is treated as the data, which in this example is moved to the D register. This type of addressing the memory location *for data* is called *Immediate Addressing.*

Example

Initial content

Register D	Memory location	Memory content
XXXX XXXX	2000	0001 0110 (MVI D)
	2001	1010 0101 (data)

After execution of MVI D, A5 instruction,

Register D	Memory location	Memory content
1010 0101	2000	0001 0110 (MVI D)
	2001	1010 0101 (data)

3.2.4 Load Immediate Register Pair Instruction

This instruction consists of 2 parts; the mnemonic which is LXI and the register pair symbol in the first part and a 2 byte data in the second part. Therefore it is a *Three Byte Instruction.*

Example LXI B, 20B0

It causes the data 20B0 to be moved into the register pair B and C. The instruction set has totally 4 LXI commands LXI B, LXI D, LXI H and LXI SP to cover all allowed register pairs.

Example

Mnemonic	Opcode (Hex)
LXI B	01

so that the complete instruction would look as

LXI B, 20B0 01
B0
20

The instruction as in this example has a 3 byte code, the first one is the opcode followed by a 2 byte data needed to load the destination which is a register pair. When the instruction is stored in memory as part of a program, the 3 bytes are stored in adjacent locations as shown in the following example. The letter I in LXI indicates that the instruction uses immediate addressing mode.

Example

Initial content

Register B	Register C	Memory location	Memory content
XXXX XXXX	XXXX XXXX	2000	0000 0001 (LXI B)
		2001	1011 0000 (data)
		2002	0010 0000 (data)

After execution of LXI B, 20B0 instruction,

Register B	Register C	Memory location	Memory content
0010 0000	1011 0000	2000	0000 0001 (LXI B)
		2001	1011 0000 (data)
		2002	0010 0000 (data)

Note: As per convention the order of storage of the data in the memory is the lower order byte first followed by the higher order byte. The 2nd byte of the instruction is transferred to the C register and the 3rd byte to the B register.

When H & L registers are used as a pair to store 16 bits, by convention, the L register stores the lower byte and H the higher byte. An example would be the indirect addressing mode where the HL pair is used to store the address of a memory location.

3.2.5 Direct Load and Store Instructions

These instructions are provided to load the content of a memory location into the A register and to store the content of the A register in a memory location.

These again are 2 part instructions; the first part is the mnemonic and the second part is a 2 byte address of a memory location.

The instruction for loading the accumulator from the location 2050H is LDA 2050. It causes the accumulator to be loaded with the contents at the address 2050.

Mnemonic	HEX code
LDA 2050	3A (opcode)
	50 (address - low byte)
	20 (address – high byte)

Example

Register A	Memory location	Memory content
XXXX XXXX	2000	0011 1010 (LDA)
	2001	0101 0000 (address)
	2002	0010 0000 (address)
	—	—
	2050	0101 0111 (data)

After execution of the instruction LDA 2050, the content of A register is

Register A
0101 0111

The instruction for storing the accumulator content in the memory location 2060 is STA 2060

It causes the accumulator content to be stored at the memory location 2060

Mnemonic	HEX code
STA 2060	32 (opcode) 60 (address - low byte) 20 (address - high byte)

Example

Register A	Memory location	Memory content
0110 0101	2000	0011 0010 (STA)
	2001	0110 0000 (address)
	2002	0010 0000 (address)
	—	—
	2060	XXXX XXXX

After executing the instruction STA 2060,

Register A	Memory location	Memory content
0110 0101	2060	0110 0101 (data)

The mode of addressing uses in these instruction is known as *Direct Addressing,* since the memory address is directly available in the instruction itself.

3.3 ARITHMETIC OPERATIONS

Any microcomputer program would involve adding or subtracting numbers and incrementing or decrementing a counter as in repeat operations. The instruction set of 8085 offers a number of instructions for such arithmetic operations.

3.3.1 ADD THE CONTENT OF A REGISTER

The mnemonic is ADD followed by register name

Example: ADD E

In this operation, one of the operands is assumed to be in the A register. The content of E register is added to the content of the accumulator (A register). The result is placed in the A register itself. The flag register contents are changed to reflect the addition operation results.

The instruction set has 7 ADD register instructions for each of the CPU registers.

Example

	Register A	Register E
Initial content	0010 0000	0110 0101

After executing ADD E

A = 0010 0000 +
E = 0110 0101

A = 1000 0101

The sign flag bit is made as 1, since D7 bit of the result is 1, other flag bits will be at zero.

In the above instruction register A is assumed as one of the operands. Hence this type of addressing is called *Implied addressing.*

3.3.2 ADD THE CONTENT OF A MEMORY LOCATION

The mnemonic is ADD M

The content of the memory location whose address is stored in HL register pair is added to the content of the Accumulator (A register). The result is placed in the A register. Flag register content is accordingly changed.

Example

Assume the content of HL register pair is 2050H.

Register A	Register H	Register L
0100 0100	0010 0000	0101 0000

Memory location	Memory content
204F	xxxx xxxx
2050	0001 0010
2051	yyyy yyyy

After executing ADD M

M = 0001 0010 +
A = 0100 0100

A = 0101 0110

The parity flag bit is made as 1 since the number of 1s in the result is *even*.

The Add instruction adds the content of a CPU register or a memory location with the content of accumulator. The result is left in the accumulator. The flags are affected.

3.3.3 ADD IMMEDIATE

The first part of this 2 part instruction is the mnemonic which is ADI, and the 2nd part is a *single* byte data.

Example

ADI 75 (where 75 is the data)

It causes the data 75 to be added with the content of the accumulator. The result is stored in the accumulator. Flags are affected.

Example

Initial content of A = 1100 0000

After executing ADI 75

A = 1100 0000 +
Data = 0111 0101

A = 0011 0101

The carry flag is set to 1, since the addition results in overflow. (exceeds 8 bits)

3.3.4 SUBTRACT THE CONTENT OF A REGISTER

The mnemonic is SUB register

Example SUB C

The content of the register C is subtracted from the accumulator content. The result is placed in the accumulator. Flags are affected. The subtraction is carried out by using 2's complement method.

Example

	Register A	Register C
Initial content	0110 0010 (62H)	0010 0100 (24H)

The content of C is 2's complemented

Content of C is	0010 0100
1's complement of C is	1101 1011
2's complement of C is obtained by adding 1 to the 1's complement, which is	1101 1100

ADD 2's complement to the accumulator.

A = 0110 0010 +
C = 1101 1100

A = 0011 1110

Carry flag is set to 1.

When there is a carry, the result is assumed as positive, and the result is available in normal form. If there is no carry the result is a negative number and it is available in 2's complement form.

The instruction set has 7 SUB instructions to cover all the CPU general purpose registers.

3.3.5 SUBTRACT THE CONTENT OF A MEMORY LOCATION

The mnemonic is SUB M

The content of the memory location pointed by HL register pair is subtracted from the accumulator content. The result is left in the accumulator. Flags are affected.

3.3.6 SUBTRACT IMMEDIATE

The first part is the mnemonic which is SUI, and the 2nd part is a single byte data.

Example: SUI 2B (where 2B is Data)

It causes the data 2B to be subtracted from the content of accumulator. The result is left in accumulator. Flags are affected.

Note: The addition and subtraction instructions carry out the operations on BINARY numbers, not on decimal numbers. Since the 8 bit binary numbers are represented as two digit HEX numbers the binary addition is called as hex addition and the binary subtraction is called as hex subtraction.

3.3.7 INCREMENT / DECREMENT THE CONTENT OF A REGISTER

The mnemonic is

INR Register (for incrementing)
DCR Register (for decrementing)

Example: INR B

Increments the content of B register by one

DCR H

Decrements the content of H register by one. All the Flags except the *CARRY* flag are affected in both cases.

The instruction set has 8 INR and 8 DCR instructions for each of the CPU registers and memory M.

Example :-

Initial content	B = 0000 0100
After executing INR B	B = 0000 0101
Initial content	H = 0000 0011
After executing DCR H	H = 0000 0010

3.3.8 INCREMENT / DECREMENT THE CONTENT OF A REGISTER PAIR

The mnemonic is

INX Register pair (for incrementing)
DCX Register pair (for decrementing)

Example

INX H Increments the content of HL register pair by 1
DCX B Decrements the content of BC register pair by 1

No Flags are affected in both cases.

The instruction set has 4 INX and 4 DCX instructions to cover each of the 3 available pairs of CPU registers and the stack pointer.

Example

Initial content H = 0100 0000 L = 1111 1111
After executing INX H, H = 0100 0001 L = 0000 0000

Initial content B = 0010 0000 C = 1111 1111
After executing DCX B, B = 0010 0000 C = 1111 1110

3.4 PROGRAM EXAMPLES

The following are simple programs, which show the usage of data movement and arithmetic instructions discussed so far.

3.4.1 EXAMPLE

Problem statement

To add 2 numbers 25H and 43H and store the result in the memory location 2050H.

Steps:

1. Move the number 25H to the accumulator.
2. Add the number 52H to the accumulator content.
3. Store the accumulator content at memory location 2050H.

To carry out the tasks 1 to 3 the relevant instructions are written in the same sequence. While writing the program the following points are observed:

- With each instruction (opcode) the memory location where it has to be stored is also written.
- The mnemonic is also written with each instruction
- A short explanation is also given with each instruction. This is known as comment. The comment is written following the semicolon (;).

Memory location	Hex code	Mnemonic	Comments
2000	3E	MVI A, 25	; Move the number 25 to the
2001	25		accumulator (acc.)
2002	C6	ADI A, 52	; Add the number 52 with acc.
2003	52		
2004	32	STA 2050	; Store the acc content at 2050
2005	50		
2006	20		
2007	76	HLT	; End of the program

The last instruction HLT is the Halt instruction. This instruction stops the execution of the program and makes the processor to enter a wait state.

A microprocessor training kit is ideally suited to test this program. The program may be entered into the user memory area of the microprocessor training kit and executed. After running the program, if the content of the memory location 2050H is read, the result 77 may be found stored.

Note: The starting address 2000H to load the program mentioned in the example is only a typical value. For exact user area address, the training kit manual may be referred.

For each instruction, only the hex code has to be entered into the kit's memory. The information following the (;) is just a comment on the instruction. It explains the programming step.

3.4.2 Example 2

Problem statement

Subtract the number 43 H from 78 H and store the result in location 2050.

Steps:

1. Move the number 78 H to the accumulator
2. Subtract 43 H from the accumulator content
3. Store the accumulator content at memory location 2050H

Memory location	Hex code	Mnemonic	Comments
2000	3E	MVI A, 78	; Move 78 into acc.
2001	78		
2002	D6	SUI 43	; Subtract 43 from acc.
2003	43		
2004	32	STA 2050	; Store the result at the
2005	50		; location 2050H
2006	20		
2007	76	HLT	; end of the program

Note: If the second number (minuend) which is being subtracted is more than the first number (subtrahend), then the result will be a negative number and so it is available in the 2's complement form.

In the case of subtraction the carry flag acts as the borrow flag. If the subtraction results in a negative number, the carry flag is set to 1.

3.5 LOGICAL OPERATIONS

Many applications of a microprocessor, particularly those involving control of a piece of hardware would involve operations like logical ANDing and ORing of data.

The 8085 instruction set includes logical functions such as AND, OR, EX-OR and NOT (complement).

These logic instructions have some common features which are given below :-

- They assume that the accumulator has one of the operands.
- The result is always placed in the accumulator.
- The Zero, Parity and Sign flags are affected according to the result.

In general carry and auxiliary carry flags are reset. ANA, ANI and CMA instructions are exceptions to this.

3.5.1 LOGICAL AND THE CONTENT OF A REGISTER

The mnemonic is ANA followed by the register name.

Example ANA B

The content of B register is logically ANDed *bitwise* with the content of the accumulator, *Bitwise* ANDing means every bit of the B register data is ANDed with the corresponding bit of the accumulator data. The result is placed in the accumulator.

The instruction set has 8 ANA instructions for each of the CPU registers and memory.

Example

Initial content	Register A	Register B
	0101 0101	0010 0111

After executing ANA B instruction, A = 0101 0101
B = 0010 0111 AND
A = 0000 0101

Register A	Register B
0000 0101	0010 0111

The operation sets AC and resets CY flag.

Table 3.1 Truth table for AND logical function

Bit 1	Bit 2	Output
0	0	0
0	1	0
1	0	0
1	1	1

The instruction set also has an AND immediate instructions. The syntax is ANI 8 bit data. The 8 bit data given in the instruction is logically ANDed with accumulator content. Result is left in the accumulator.

Note: Just to clear the Carry flag and to retain the accumulator content, *ANA A* instruction may be used in a program.

3.5.2 LOGICAL OR THE CONTENT OF A REGISTER

The mnemonic is ORA followed by a register name.

Example: ORA D

It carries out *bitwise* ORing the D register and accumulator contents. Result is placed in the accumulator.

The instruction set has 8 ORA instruction for each of the CPU registers and memory.

Example

Initial content

Register A	Register D
0101 0101	0010 0111

After execution of ORA D instruction,

A = 0101 0101
D = 0010 0111 OR
A = 0111 0111

Register A	Register D
0111 0111	0010 0111

S, Z and P flags are changed to reflect the results of the operation, CY and AC flags are reset.

Table 3.2 Truth table for OR logical function

Bit 1	Bit 2	Output
0	0	0
0	1	1
1	0	1
1	1	1

The instruction set also has an OR immediate instruction. The syntax is ORI 8 bit data. The 8 bit data given in the instruction is logically ORed with the accumulator content. The result is left in the accumulator.

3.5.3 EXCLUSIVE-OR (EX-OR) THE CONTENTS OF A REGISTER

The mnemonic is XRA followed by a register name

Example: XRA C

It carries out the *bitwise* exclusive ORing of the C register and accumulator contents. The result is stored in the accumulator.

The instruction set has 8 XRA instructions for each of the CPU registers and memory.

Example:

Initial content

Register A	Register C
0101 0101	0010 0111

After executing XRA C instruction,

A = 0101 0101
C = 0010 0111 EX - OR
A = 0111 0010

Register A	Register C
0111 0010	0010 0111

Flags Z, P are altered to reflect the results of the operation, CY and AC flags are reset.

Table 3.3 Truth table for EX–OR logic function

Bit 1	Bit 2	Output
0	0	0
0	1	1
1	0	1
1	1	0

The instruction set also has an Exclusive OR immediate instruction. The syntax is XRI 8 bit data. The 8 bit data given in the instruction is logically exclusive ORed with the accumulator content. Result is left in the accumulator.

Note: To clear the accumulator content and Carry flag, *XRA A* instruction may be used in a program.

3.5.4 Complement the Accumulator

The mnemonic is CMA. The content of the accumulator is complemented. Every bit is inverted so that 0 becomes 1 and 1 becomes 0.

Example:

Intial content Register A
0110 1001

After executing CMA instruction,

Register A
1001 0110

No flags are affected.

3.6 PROGRAM EXAMPLE

3.6.1 Example - 3

Problem statement :

To check the status (level) of the D3 bit in a given 8 bit data (D0 - D7) stored at the location 2050H.

Steps :

1. Load the accumulator with the data from the location 2050H
2. Logically AND accumulator content with 08H (0000 1000), $D_3 = 1$.

Programming:

Memory location	Hex code	Mnemonic		Comments
2000	3A	LDA 2050	;	Contents of location 2050
	50		;	is loaded into accumulator
	20			
2003	E6	ANI 08	;	Logically AND accumulator
	08		;	content with 0000 1000 (08H)

By ANDing with 08 all bits except D3 are made zero. This process is called *masking* the unwanted bits.

The result will be 0 if the D3 bit of data at location 2050 is 0; otherwise it would be 08. The content of accumulator can be verified by checking the content of the *zero flag.*

3.7 BRANCHING OPERATIONS

In section 3.2 to 3.6, instructions related to data transfer and data manipulation groups have been discussed. The flexibility and versatility of the stored program concept on which computers are based, however results primarily from the computer's ability to transfer control, or branch, to an instruction that is not in sequential order. This is achieved with instructions from the Branching group. All these instructions act on the program counter and, as will be shown, it is possible to execute a block of instructions many times.

3.7.1 UNCONDITIONAL JUMP

A JUMP instruction is used to break the normal sequential execution and branch to a different part of the program. This is accomplished by loading the address of the next out-of-sequence instruction into the program counter, thus forcing the processor to fetch the contents of this new location as its next instruction. The new address is usually specified in the jump instruction.

For example,

Memory	Mnemonic
2005	JMP 2040

Execution of this instruction, causes an unconditional, jump to memory location 2040 for the next instruction.

Memory location	Hex code	Mnemonic	Comments
2005	C3	JMP 2040	; continue execution from
2006	40		; 2040H onwards
2007	20		

Note: When the mnemonic is coded into Hex code, the lower byte of the address is given first followed by the higher byte.

When jump instruction is executed, no flag is affected.

3.7.2 Use of Labels

When writing a program, the programmer may not know the exact address of instructions which appear in later part of the program. If the program needs jump to such an instruction, instead of giving the address, a label (name) is given in the jump instruction. Later when that part of the program is written the same label is referred at the statement to which execution has to jump.

Memory location	Hex code	Label	Mnemonic
2005	C3		JMP LOOP1
2006	40		
2007	20		
....			..
....			..
....			..
....			..
2040	3E	LOOP1	MVI A, 01
2041	01		
2042			..

Initially the program is written using mnemonics. Then for each instruction the Hex code is written. While Hex code, in the place of the label, the actual address is as shown.

3.7.3 Conditional Jumps

Conditional jump instructions allow the processor to make decisions on certain conditions indicated by the flags. After every logical and arithmetic operation, flags are set or reset to reflect the status of result. The conditional jump instructions check the flag status and make decisions about changing the sequence of the program.

FLAGS

The 8085 status register has 5 flags, one of which (Auxiliary Carry) is used internally. The other four flags used by the jump instructions are

1. Carry flag
2. Zero flag
3. Sign flag
4. Parity flag

All conditional jump instructions in the 8085 are *3 byte instructions* just like the unconditional jump instructions.

Mnemonic		Description
JC	16 bit address	Jump on Carry (if the operation generates carry)
JNC	16 bit address	Jump on No Carry (CY = 0)
JZ	16 bit address	Jump on Zero (When the result is 0000 0000 (Z=1)
JNZ	16 bit address	Jump on No Zero (Z = 0)
JP	16 bit address	Jump on Plus (S = 0)
JM	16 bit address	Jump on Minus (S = 1)
JPE	16 bit address	Jump on Even Parity (P = 1)
JPO	16 bit address	Jump on Odd Parity (P = 0)

3.8 PROGRAM EXAMPLES

3.8.1 EXAMPLE 4

Problem statement

Load a hexadecimal number in D register and another hexadecimal number in E register and add them. If the sum is greater than FFH, store 01 at the location 2050H; otherwise 00 at 2050H.

Steps:

1. Load the numbers in the respective registers
2. Add them
3. Check the sum
4. If the sum > FFH, branch to a program segment which stores 01 at 2050H and halt.
5. Otherwise store 00 at 2050 and halt.

To find out whetner sum > FFH, the carry flag status is checked. This is because when the sum of 2 unsigned 8 bit numbers exceed FFH, the carry flag is set.

Programming

Memory location	Hex code	Label	Mnemonic	Comments
2000	16	START:	MVI D, A0	; A0 is loaded
2001	A0			;in reg. D
2002	1E		MVI E, B7	; B7 is loaded
2003	B7			; in reg. E
2004	7A		MOV A,D	
2005	83		ADD E	
2006	DA		JC STORE	; If CY = 1, then
2007	10			;jump to 2010H
2008	20			
2009	97		SUB A	; Make accumulator ;content 0
200A	32		STA 2050	;Store 0 in the
200B	50			;location 2050H
200C	20			

Memory location	Hex code	Label	Mnemonic	Comments
200D	C3		JMP HALT	; Jump to location
200E	15			; 2015H (to HLT
200F	20			; instruction)
2010	3E	STORE	MVI A, 01	; Move 01 into
2011	01			; Accumulator
2012	32		STA 2050	; Store 01 in the
2013	50			; location 2050H
2014	20			
2015	76	HALT	HLT	

EXERCISE - 3

1. What are the major categories under which the instructions can be grouped?
2. Explain the operation carried out by each of the following instructions.

   MOV A,M

   LXI H,3002

   STA 2003

   ADI 14
3. Compare the following instructions.

   SUI 23 and ANI 23

   LDA 2012 and STA 3011
4. What is the instruction to be used to retain the accumulator content and to clear the carry flag simultaneously ?
5. Write a program to find out number of data less than 40 in a given set of ten values.
6. Write a program to add 14, 21, 45 and 20 and store the result in the memory.
7. What are the components of flag register ? Mention the purpose of the flag register ?
8. What is the advantage of using labels in writing a program?
9. Explain the 2s complement method of subtractionfor different numbers.

CHAPTER 4

PROGRAMMING THE MICROPROCESSOR - II

4.1 INTRODUCTION

The basic data movement and arithmetic instructions are discussed in Chapter 3. The indirect addressing discussed in Chapter 3 uses HL register pair to hold the address. However for data movement into and out of the accumulator, it is possible to make other register pairs to hold the address. The 8085 has also provisions to add or subtract 16 bit numbers and to handle BCD addition. Details of these advanced instructions are discussed in this chapter. The concept of stack and the related data movement instructions are also discussed.

4.2 DATA TRANSFER INSTRUCTIONS

4.1.2 Load Accumulator Indirect

Syntax : LDAX B
LDAX D

Action: The register pair specified in the instruction holds a 16 bit address. The contents of the memory location of that address is copied into the accumulator. The contents of the register pair or the memory location *are not changed.*

This is an *indirect addressing instruction* since the address of the memory location is stored in a register pair.

Example: LDAX B

Initial Register content	Reg. A	Reg. B	Reg. C
	42	20	50
Memory Content	Location	Content	
	2050	75	

After executing the instruction LDAX B

Register content	Reg. A	Reg. B	Reg. C
	75	20	50

4.2.2 Store Accumulator Indirect

Syntax: STAX B
STAX D

Action: The register pair specified in the instruction holds a 16 bit address. The contents of the accumulator is stored at the memory location of that address. The contents of the register pair or the accumulator *are not changed.*

As the address is stored in a register pair, this is an *indirect addressing instruction.*

Example: STAX B

Register content	Reg. A	Reg. B	Reg. C
	42	20	50
Memory Content	Location	Content	
	2050	B8	

After executing STAX B,

Register Content	Reg. A	Reg. B	Reg. C
	42	20	50
Memory Content	Location	Content	
	2050	42	

4.2.3 Load H and L Register Direct

Syntax: LHLD address

Example: LHLD 2050

Action: A valid 16 bit address of a memory location is specified as part of the instruction. The *content of the location* of that address is stored in the *L register.* The *content of the next memory location* is stored in the *H register.* The content of the 2 memory locations are not changed.

As the address of the memory location is supplied as part of the instruction, it is a *direct addressing instruction.*

Initial Content	Register H	Register L
	34	85
Memory Content	Location	Content
	2050	A4
	2051	7B

After executing LHLD 2050,

Register Content	Regisater H	Register L
	7B	A4
Memory content	Location	Content
	2050	A4
	2051	7B

4.2.4 STORE H AND L REGISTER DIRECT

Syntax: SHLD address

Example: SHLD 2050

Action: A valid 16 bit address of a memory location is specified as part of the instruction. The content of the L register is stored at the location specified by the address. The content of H register is stored in the next location. The content of the HL register pair is *not changed.*

As the address of the memory location is specified as part of the instruction, it is a *direct addressing instruction.*

Initial Content	Register H	Register L
	34	B5
Memory Content	Location	Content
	2050	F9
	2051	7B

After executing SHLD 2050,

Register Content	Register H	Register L
	34	B5
Memory Content	Location	Content
	2050	B5
	2051	34

4.2.5 EXCHANGE H AND L REGISTER CONTENT WITH D AND E REGISTER CONTENT

Syntax: XCHG

Action: The *contents* of registers *H* and *D* are *exchanged* and the *contents* of the registers *L* and *E* are *exchanged.*

Initial content	Register H	Register L
	05	02
	Register D	Register E
	FF	A4

After executing XCHG instructions,

The register contents are	Register H	Register L
	FF	A4
	Register D	Register E
	05	02

4.3 ARITHMETIC INSTRUCTIONS

The arithmetic instructions discussed in Chapter 3 perform arithmetic operations basically on 8 bit (1 byte) numbers. The 8085 instruction set also features the following instructions for the sake of performing arithmetic operations on 16 bit (2 bytes) and larger numbers.

4.3.1 ADD Register Pair to H and L Register Pair

Syntax: DAD B
DAD D
DAD H
DAD SP

Action: The 16 bit content of the specified register pair are added to the *content of H and L pair. The result is placed in the H L register pair.* The content of the source register pair is not changed. *The Carry flag is set if the result is larger than 16 bit.*

Example Register HL pair = 1234

Register BC pair = 4567

After executing DAD B instruction

the register pair contents are

Register HL pair = 579 B

Register BC pair = 4567

The carry flag is reset, since the result is only 16 bit.

4.3.2 ADD Register Content to Accumulator with Carry

Syntax: ADC register

Example ADC B
ADC M

Action: The contents of the registers specified and the Carry flag are added to the content of the accumulator and the result is placed in the accmulator. The content of the register is not changed. The Carry flag is set/reset based on the result.

The 8085 instruction set has 7 ADC instructions for each of the 7 CPU registers and ADC M for memory location. For ADC M instruction, the address of the memory location is stored in HL register pair.

The instruction set also has an ADD immediate with carry instruction. The syntex is ACI 8 bit data. The 8 bit data given in the instruction is addeed with carry with the content of the accumulator and the result is stored in the accumulator.

Program Examples

Addition of 3 Byte numbers

If numbers longer than 16 bits are required to be added/subtracted, then such operations can not be carried out using single instructions. Instead a number of instructions must be used. Consider the addition of two 24 bit (3 byte) numbers. A and B.

The addition operation requires 3 separate 8 bit additions. Further it is also necessary to add the Carry bit while adding the second and third pair of bytes.

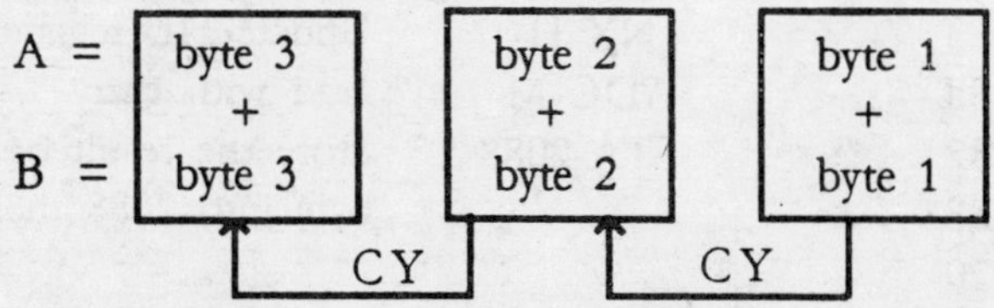

For this purpose the ADC instruction is used while adding the second bytes and third bytes of the 2 numbers.

Problem Statement

To add two 24 bit (3 byte) numbers.

One of the numbers is stored in three consecutive memory locations starting at address 2080 and the next number is stored in the three memory locations starting at address 2083. The 24 bit result is stored in 2086 onwards.

Location	Hex op-code	Label	Mnemoric	Comments
3000	21	START	LX1 H, 2083	; Initialise HL reg.
3001	83			; with start address of
3002	20			; one number
3003	3A		LDA 2080	; Load accumulator first ; byte
3004	80			; from the second ; number.
3005	20			
3006	86		ADD M	
3007	32		STA 2086	; Store the result of first ; byte into 2086 memory.
3008	86			
3009	20			
300A	23		INX H	; Update HL register
300B	3A		LDA 2081	; Load accumulator ; second byte from ; second number
300C	81			
300D	20			
300E	8E		ADC M	; Add with carry
300F	32		STA 2087	; Store result of second
3010	87			; byte into 2087 memory.
3011	20			
3012	23		INX H	; Update HL register
3013	8E		ADC M	; Add with carry
3014	32		STA 2088	; Store the result of third
3015	88			; byte into 2088 memory.
3016	20			
3017	76	STOP	HLT	; Stop execution.

Note that the first byte addition is done using ADD instruction and the other addition operations are done using ADC instructions.

Remember that these additions and subtractions are carried out on binary numbers, not on decimal numbers. *For convenience we represent binary numbers as Hex numbers.* Hence the binary addition or subtraction is called Hex addition or Hex subtraction.

4.3.3 Subtract Register Content from Accumulator with Borrow

Syntax: SBB register

Example: SBB C
SBB M

Note: In 8085 micro processor, the carry flag also acts as Borrow flag.

Action: The contents of the register specified and the carry flag is substracted from the content of the accumulator and the result is placed in the accumulator. The content of the register is not changed. However the BORROW flag is reset.

The 8085 instruction set has 7 SBB instructions and further SBB M for memory location. For SBB M instruction, the address of the memory location is stored in HL register pair.

The instruction set also has an SUBTRACT Immediate with BORROW instruction. The syntex is SBI 8 bit data. The 8 bit data given in the instruction is subtracted with carry from the accumulator content and the result is placed in the accumulator.

4.3.4 Binary Coded Decimal (BCD) Arithmetic

Since we readily understand and recognise the decimal numbers, any man-machine interface such as thumbwheel switches, seven segment display devices would ideally require data presentation in decimal form. However all digital devices operate with only binary numbers. To bridge these two requirements Binary Coded Decimal number system, in which each decimal digit is represented independently as its 4 bit binary equivalent is used.

However when microprocessors carry out arithmetic operations on BCD numbers, certain extra steps are required as shown in the following example. Consider the addition of the following 2 BCD numbers.

79	Decimal	0111 1001	BCD
+16	Decimal	0001 0110	BCD
95	Decimal	1000 1111	BCD

The microprocessor applies binary addition rules to the two **8** bit binary numbers. Therefore the result is 1000 1111 where as the required BCD number is 95 of binary equivalent 1001 0101 which is different from the result.

However this can be corrected using 2 rules as explained in the following.

Rule 1:

In BCD arithmetic, any 4 bit number larger than 9 (A to F of hexa decimal system) is invalid, and needs a correction by adding 6 to bring to valid BCD number system.

For example, to get the BCD equivalent of 12 for the hexadecimal number C :

```
C =    0000 1100  +
       0000 0110
       ---------
       0001 0010     which is the BCD equivalent of 12.
       ---------
```

Likewise any BCD sum can be adjusted to proper BCD sum by adding 6 when the sum exceeds 9.

Example

```
 6      0000 0110   BCD
 8+     0000 1000   BCD
        ---------
        0000 1110   Lower 4 bits have value more than 9
             0110   So ADD 6
        ---------
14      0001 0100
        ---------
```

Example

```
 52      0101 0010   BCD
 74+     0111 0100   BCD
         ---------
         1100 0110   Upper 4 bits have value more than 9
126      0110        So ADD 6 to upper 4 bits
      ------------
      01 0010 0110
      ------------
```

Rule 2:

If there is a Carry during the addition add number 6 to the upper 4 bits to get the correct BCD number. When there is an auxiliary carry add 6 to the lower A bits.

Example

91	1001 0001	BCD
84 +	1000 0100	BCD
175	01 0001 0101	Carry is set. So ADD 6 to the
	0110	Upper 4 bits.
	01 0111 0101	

If there is a Carry from the 4th bit during the addition, it is termed as *Auxilary Carry.* When there is an auxiliary Carry, the binary equivalent will not be the same as the BCD number. We have to add 0110 to the lower 4 bits.

Example

38	0011 1000	BCD
49+	0100 1001	BCD
	1000 0001	Auxiliary carry is set. So ADD 6
	0110	to the lower 4 bits.
87	1000 0111	

Example

57	0101 0111	BCD
58 +	0101 1000	BCD
	1010 1111	Lower 4 bits have value more than
	0000 0110	9, so ADD 6 to lower 4 bits
	1011 0101	Upper 4 bits have value more than
	0110	9, so ADD 6 to upper 4 bits
115	0001 0001 0101	

The 8085 instruction set has a specific instruction to carry out these corrections as per rules explained above.

Syntax : DAA Decimal Adjust Accumulator

Action : The content of the accumulator is adjusted to change 8 bit binary number into two 4 bit Binary Coded Decimal (BCD) digits.

The following process is followed.

- If the value of the least significant 4 bits of the A register is greater than 9 or if the AC flag is set, 6 is added to the A register.

- If the value of the most significant 4 bits of the A register is greater than 9 **or** if the Carry flag is set, 6 is added to the most significant 4 bits of the A register.

Since both halves of the A register are corrected and also the Carry (CY) and auxiliary Carry (AC) flags are affected, it is clearly possible to perform multiprecision BCD arithmetic using the same instruction.

Program Example
Problem statement

The program example adds together two 4 digit (16 bit) BCD numbers, and forms the corrected 4 digit BCD sum. The first number is stored in the two consecutive memory locations starting at address 2080 and the second is stored in the two locations starting at address 2082 and the result is stored in the address 2084 onwards.

Memory Location	Opcode	Label	Mnemonics	Comments
3000	21	START	LXIH, 2082	; Initialise HL reg. ; with start address
3001	82			
3002	20			
3003	3A		LDA 2080	; Load accumulator from ; memory location 2080
3004	80			
3005	20			
3006	86		ADD M	; Add first byte.
3007	27		DAA	; Decimal adjust
3008	32		STA 2084	; Store the result in ; memory
3009	84			
300 A	20			; Location 2084.
300 B	23		INX H	; update HL
300 C	3 A		LDA 2081	; Load accumulator
300 D	81			; from memory
300 E	20			; location 2081
300 F	8E		ADC M	; Add with carry
3010	27		DAA	; Decimal adjust
3011	32		STA 2085	; Store the result in
3012	85			; memory location 2085
3013	20			
3014	76	STOP	HLT	; Stop execution.

4.4 LOGICAL INSTRUCTIONS

The logical instructions discussed in the Chapter 3 performed bit by bit logical operations between two 8 bit words. Additionally, the 8085 instruction set features instructions for rotating/shifting the bits of a 8 bit word. These instructions are useful for implementing binary multiplication and division, since

- a left shift of the bits of word by one bit position is equivalent to multiplying it by 2.
- while a right shift is equivalent to dividing it by 2.

These additional logical instructions are discussed in the following.

4.4.1 Rotate Accumulator Content Left

Syntax : RLC

Action: The content of the accumulator is rotated to the left by one bit. The MSB is shifted out to the LSB position as well as to the Carry flag.

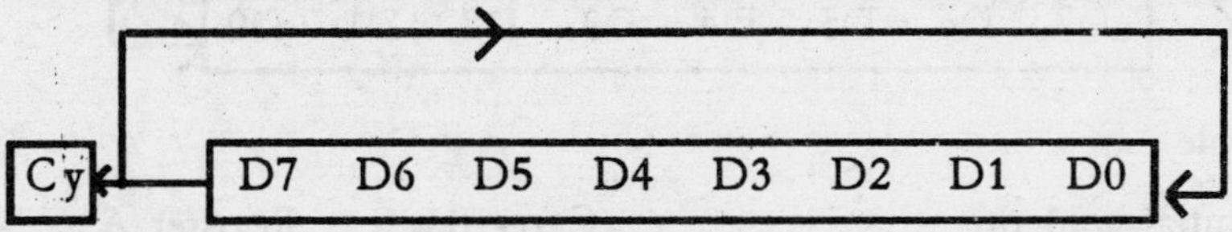

Example

Initial Content	Carry flag	Register A
	0	1001 0110

After executing RLC,

	Carry flag	Register A
	1	0010 1101

4.4.2 Rotate Accumulator Right

Syntax: RRC

Action: The content of the Accumulator is rotated to the right by one bit. The LSB is shifted out to the MSB as well as to the Carry flag.

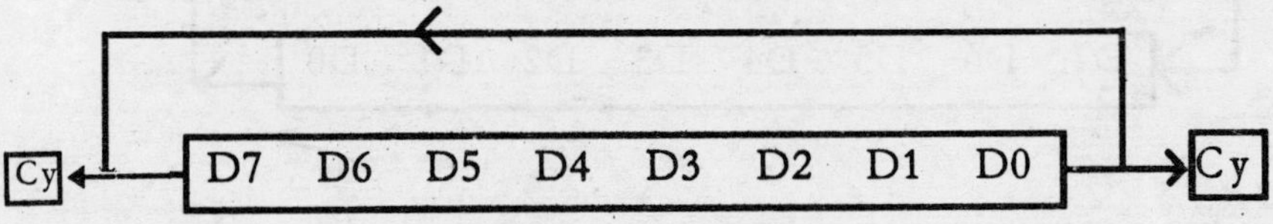

Example

Initial Content	Carry flag	Register A
	0	0110 1001
After executing RRC,		
	Carry flag	Register A
	1	1011 0100

4.4.3 Rotate Accumulator Left through carry

Syntax: RAL

Action:The content of the accumulator is rotated to the left by one bit through the Carry flag. This means that the MSB is shifted to the Carry flag, the Carry flag content shifted to the LSB.

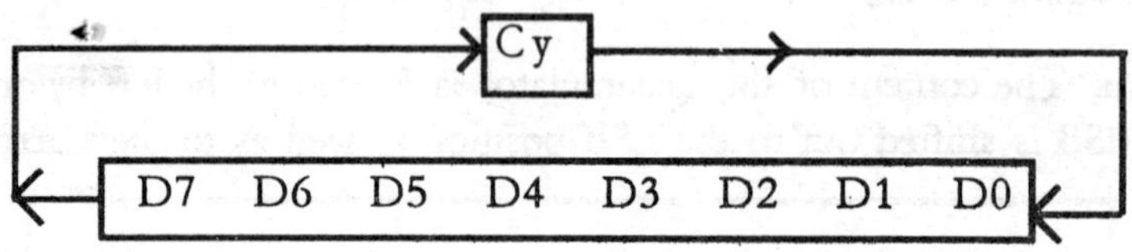

Example

Initial content	Carry flag	Register A
	0	1010 0011
After executing RAL		
	Carry flag	Register A
	1	0100 0110

4.4.4 Rotate Accumulator Right through carry

Syntax: RAR

Action: The content of the accumulator is rotated right by one bit through the Carry flag. The LSB is shifted to the Carry flag and the Carry flag content is shifted to the MSB.

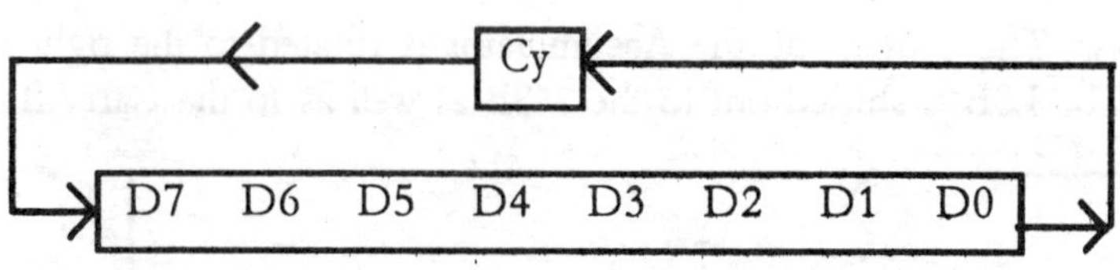

Example

Initial content	Carry flag	Register A
	0	1001 1011

After executing RAR,

	Carry flag	Register A
	1	0100 1101

4.4.5 Compare Instruction

The instruction set also has an instruction to compare the accumulator content and the content of any of the CPU registers or a memory location, to determine which is bigger. The result of the comparison may be used to decide the next operation to be performed.

Syntax: CMP register

Example: CMP H

Action: The content of the register specified is compared with the content of the accumulator The Zero flag is set if the values are equal. The Carry flag is set if the Accumulator content is smaller.

Note that the accumulator content and the specified register content does not change, only the flag register is affected.

The instruction set has 7 CMP instructions for each of the 7 CPU registers and CMP M for memory location. For CMP M, the HL register pair points to the address of memory location. Further it also features a Compare Immediate instruction of syntax CPI data, which compares the data specified with the accumulator content.

4.5 SUBROUTINE AND STACK

Very often a program logic would require a specific sub-task performed at one point in the program need to be performed at many other places in the program as well.

One approach would be to repeat the machine code instructions of the sub-task at each point in the program as shown in Fig.4.1 However this makes the program code very large.

Program: __________________

____

____

____

Sub-task instructions

____

____

Sub-task instructions

____

____

____

Sub-task instructions

Fig.4.1 Sub-task instruction used many times in the main program

Instead, it is desirable to have just one set of machine instructions for the sub-task within the program, and the same set is used whenever the sub-task is wanted in the program. This is acheived by transferring the execution to the sub-task instructions so that they are performed once and then transferring the control back to the main sequence, as shown in Fig.4.2.

Main program: __________________

____

____

Subroutine called

____

____

____

Subroutine called

____

____

____

Subroutine called

____

____

Subroutine xxxxxxxxxxxxxxxxx

xxxxxxxxxxxxxxxxx

xxxxxxxxxxxxxxxxx

Return to main program.

Fig.4.2 Sub-task instructions made into subroutine

Thus the set of sub-task instructions become a *Subroutine* and the *Main Program* uses the subroutine at all desired points.

The instruction set has separate instruction to invoke (to call) subroutine and to return from a subroutine.

Syntax: CALL addr

Example: CALL 2320H

Action : The address specified is the starting address of the *Subroutine.* The CALL instruction causes the control to be transferred to the address specified, and thus to the subroutine. Therefore, the next instruction executed is the first instruction of the subroutine. However there is a major difference between a simple Jump (JMP) instruction and the subroutine CALL instruction. The CALL instruction before transfering the control to the subroutine, stores the content of the Program Counter (address of the next instruction in the main program) in an area of RAM called *Stack*. This enables the control to return to proper address of the main program after executing the subroutine.

The stack is a set of memory locations in the *RAM* area *specifically* used to store certain temporary data. The starting address of the stack area is stored in the 16 bit CPU register called *Stack Pointer.* Data is stored in subsequent *lower addresses*.

For example, assume the Stack Pointer (SP) is initialised to 2FF0H. If 2 bytes needed to be stored on the Stack, then the SP is *decremented* by one so that it is pointing to 2FEFH. The first byte is stored at 2FEFH. The SP is again decremented by 1 and the 2nd byte stored at 2FEEH. Notice that in this process the SP is pointing to the latest byte stored.

For retreiving data from the Stack (reading the stack) the procedure is reversed. The data is first read from the location pointed by SP. Then SP is *incremented* by 1. The data is read from the new location. Then SP is incremented again. Thus the Stack Pointer tracks the storage and retreival of data from the stack.

Further the Stack always grows to lower addresses of RAM.

Therefore it is usual prctice to initialise the starting of the Stack to the *highest RAM address* of a microprocessor based system.

The location of the latest byte stored on a stack is known as the top of the stack as shown in Fig.4.3.

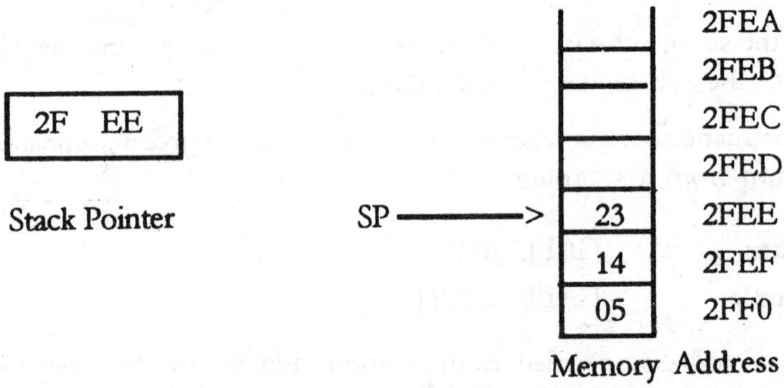

Fig.4.3 Stack storage details

Like conditional JUMP instructions, there are 8 conditional call instructions to go to the subroutine from main program. No flags are affected.

4.5.1 RETURN FROM SUBROUTINE

Syntax: RET

Action: Causes the control to return from the subroutine to the calling program. The top of the stack holds the 2 byte return address. The instruction causes the address to be copied to the Program Counter, thereby return to proper address of the calling program. is made. *The last statement of every subroutine is the RET statement.*

Program Example

The time delay program is made as a subroutine. Assume that the stack pointer content is 27E2H

	Memory Location	Op-codes	Mnemonics
Main program	1FFD	..	
	1FFE	..	
	1FFF	..	

	Memory Location	Op-codes	Mnemonics
PC =>	2000	CD	CALL TIMEDLY
	2001	90	(Subroutine)
	2002	20	
	2003	y y	
	....	..	
Subroutine	2090	XX	
	2091	XX	
	2092	..	
	....	..	
	....	C9	RET
Stack	27E0	..	
	27E1	..	
SP =>	27E2	14	

When the CALL instruction is executed, the Program Counter content will be 2003H. This value is stored on the stack as the return address. Following this, the address of the subroutine which is 2090H is placed in the Program Counter. Thereafter the instructions in the subroutine are executed. The last instruction of the subroutine is the RET instruction. This instruction causes the return address to be retrieved from the stack and put into the Program Counter. Thus the execution of the main program resumes from the address 2003H.

The process of loading the return address on the stack following a subroutine call is illustrated below.

At the time of executing CALL instruction, the following action takes place.

	Memory Location	Op-codes	Mnemonics
Main program	1FFD	..	
	1FFE	..	
	1FFF	..	
	2000	CD	CALL TIMEDLY
	2001	90	(subroutine)
	2002	20	
PC =>	2003	y y	
	....	..	

	Memory Location	Op-codes	Mnemonics
Subroutine	2090	XX	
	2091	XX	
	2092	..	
	....	..	
	....	C9	RET
Stack	27E0	..	
	27E1	..	
SP =>	27E2	14	

STATUS before execution of CALL instruction

PC => 2003
SP => 27E2

STATUS after execution of CALL instruction

PC => 2090
SP => 27E0

PC contents are saved and contents of SP are decremented twice.

The process of loading the stack content into the program counter while returning from a subroutine is illustrated below

	Memory Location	Op-codes	Mnemonics
Main program	1FFD	..	
	1FFE	..	
	1FFF	..	
	2000	CD	CALL TIMEDLY
	2001	90	(subroutine)
	2002	20	
	2003	y y	
	....	..	
Subroutine	2090	XX	
	2091	XX	
	2092	..	
	....	..	
PC =>	2111	C9	RET
	2112	..	

	Memory Location	Op-codes	Mnemonics
Stack SP =>	27E0	20	
	27E1	03	
	27E2	14	

STATUS before execution of RET instruction

PC => 2112
SP => 27E0

STATUS after execution of RET instruction

PC => 2003
SP => 27E2

When the RET statement is executed, the stack pointer is incremented and PC is loaded with 2003 from the stack. The stack pointer value becomes 27E2.

Normally, in the microprocessor kit, the stack pointer is initialised by the monitor program itself at the time of switching on the kit. However, the stack pointer can also be initialised in the beginning of the main program.

```
Main Program     LXI SP, 27E2     ; initialise stack pointer
                 MVI C, 41        ; load TIMEDLY parameter
                 CALL TIMEDLY     ; call subroutine
                 ....
```

Like conditional CALL instructions there are 8 conditional RET instructions to return from the subroutine to the main program on condition. In executing this instruction no flags are affected.

4.6 PUSH AND POP INSTRUCTIONS

The stack may also be used as a temporary storage for the contents of processor registers.

Example:

PUSH PSW (Push processor status word)

This instruction pushes (saves) the combined 16 bit contents of A register and Flag register on the top of the stack. There are also instructions to push contents of register pairs BC, DE and HL on the stack.

To transfer the content of the stack back to the register pair, the POP instruction is used.

Example POP H

Transfers the contents of stack memory to the register L and H, where the address is given by stack pointer (SP). The PUSH and POP instructions are particularly useful when writing subroutines. If a subroutine requires B and C register pair to perform a subtask, then user has to save the current contents of these registers into the stack memory using PUSH B instruction. After performing the subtask, the saved contents has to be restored back to the B and C registers using POP C instructions, before transfering the control back to the main program.

4.7 OTHER INSTRUCTIONS

STC and CMC instructions

The carry flag can be set using the STC instruction. The CMC instruction will complement the content of CY flag. By executing any one of logical instructions the carry flag can be cleared.

NOP instruction

When this instruction is executed, NO-oPeration is performed. It is mainly used to fill in time delays and to accommodate one machine cycle time. This instruction may be used in the main program to eliminate some of the unwanted instructions for checking purpose.

PCHL instruction

The contents of register H and L are copied into the Program Counter (PC). The contents of H are placed as a high order byte and L as a low order byte. No flags are affected. *This instruction is equivalent to a one byte unconditional jump instruction.* A program execution sequence can be changed to any location by loading the H and L registers with the appropriate address and by executing this instruction.

SPHL instruction

The contents of register H and L are loaded into stack pointer. The contents of the H and L registers are not altered. No flags are affected.

XTHL instruction

The content of the L register is exchanged with the stack location pointed by stack pointer. The contents of the H register is exchanged with the next stack memory location (SP+1). The content of the stack pointer remains same. No flags are affected.

The content of the registers are given below

HL	SP
2003	5000

Stack Memory Content

5000 — 14
5001 — 41

After executing this XTHL instruction, the content of register are shown below

HL	SP
4114	5000

Stack Memory Content

5000 — 03
5001 — 20

4.8 TIMING DIAGRAM

The basics of the timing aspects of the instruction execution was discussed in chapter 2. The instructions of a program are stored in the memory of a microcomputer. In general to execute an instruction, the CPU has to do the following operations.

- Fetch the opcode from the memory through the data bus.
- If required read a memory location for data.
- Perform the relevant operation on the data.

Each of these operations is synchronised with the system clock. The timing diagram of an instruction shows the operation sequence in terms of the system clock period.

The following terms are used in explaining the sequence of instruction execution.

Instruction Cycle

Time required to complete the execution of an instruction.

Machine Cycle

The time required to access the memory or the input or output device once. (either for read or write operation)

T State

The portion of the operation performed in one clock period.

4.8.1 Timing Diagram for Execution of MOV reg, reg Instruction

The timing for execution of MOV reg, reg is illustrated with the help of the instruction MOV A,B.

It is assumed that the instruction MOV A,B is stored at the location 2040H.

Memory Location	Opcode	Mnemonics
2040	78	MOV A,B

It is also assumed that all the previous instructions are executed and the program counter has presently the address of MOV A,B

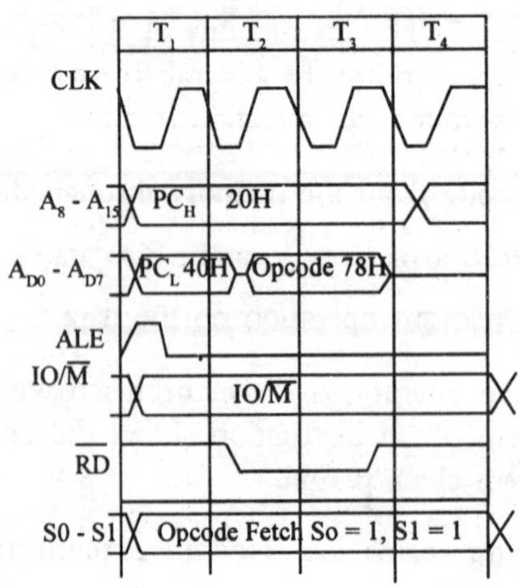

Fig.4.4 Timing diagram for execution of MOV A,B instruction.

Fig.4.4 shows the timing diagram for the execution of the MOV A,B instruction.

The following is the sequence of events in executing the MOV A,B instruction.

1. First Clock Cycle (T1) (First T state)

a. The CPU places the content of the program counter on the address bus; 20H on the higher order bus and 40H on the lower order bus.

b. It raises the ALE signal, so that external circuit can latch the lower order address.

c. IO/$\overline{\text{M}}$ becomes low in order to select the memory device.

2. Second Clock Cycle (T2) (Second T state)

a. $\overline{\text{RD}}$ signal is made low to read the memory device.

b. Following $\overline{\text{RD}}$ going low, the memory device puts the content of the selected memory location, which is the opcode of MOV A,B on to the data bus.

3. Third Clock Cycle(T3) (Third T state)

a. The CPU reads the data bus content, and puts it in its instruction decoder.

b. After reading the data, the $\overline{\text{RD}}$ signal is made high.

4. Fourth Clock Cycle (T4) (Fourth T state)

a. The instruction is decoded and relevant operation is carried out. In this case the B register content is copied to A register.

The 4 T states (T1 to T4) together make a machine cycle. This machine cycle is called opcode fetch cycle, as that was the main activity in that cycle. The opcode fetching, decoding and execution of MOV A,B is enterely carried out in the opcode fetch cycle. Therefore the instruction cycle of MOV A,B just has one machine cycle.

4.8.2 Timing Diagram for Execution of MVI Reg, data Instruction

The timing for MVI reg,data instruction is illustrated with the help of the instruction MVI C, 75.

It is assumed that the instruction MVI C, 75 is stored at locations 2050H and 2051H.

Memory Location	Opcode	Mnemonics
2050	0E	MVI C, 75
2051	75	

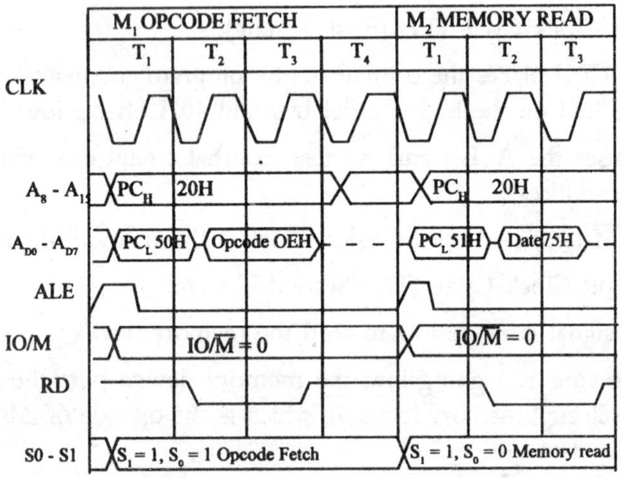

Fig. 4.5 Timing diagram for executing MVI C,75 instruction

This instruction needs two machine cycles

- The Opcode fetch cycle to read the opcode from memory and to decode it.
- An additional memory read cycle to read the operand (data) from the next memory location.

The following is the sequence of events in executing MVI C,data instruction.

I Machine Cycle: Opcode fetch cycle

The sequence of operations for the opcode fetch cycle is exactly similar to the opcode fetch cycle of MOV A,B instruction discussed in the previous section. During T1 cycle the address is placed on the address bus and ALE is enabled. During T2, RD is enabled and data is placed on the data bus. The data is read in during T3 and the instruction decoded in T4. However after decoding the instruction, the CPU realises, it has to read memory once more, to get the operand (data). Therefore it executes the 2nd machine cycle (memory read cycle).

Note: When the content of the program counter is sent out for the above opcode fetch cyle it is incremented automatically, so as to point to the next location.

II Machine Cycle: Memory read cycle

1. First clock cycle (T1) (First T state) the content of program counter is sent out through the address and data bus and ALE is enabled.
2. Second clock cycle (T2) (Second T state): $\overline{RD}$ is made low.
3. Third clock cycle (T3) (Third T state): The content of data bus is read in and transferred to the C register:

Thus the memory read cycle requires only 3 clock cycles.

4.8.3 TIMING DIAGRAM FOR EXECUTION OF STA ADDR INSTRUCTION

The STA address instruction is explained with an example STA 2450.

It is assumed that the instruction STA 2450H is stored at 2100H location onwards.

Memory Location	Opcode	Mnemonics
2100	32	STA 2450H
2101	50	
2102	24	

The instruction needs four machine cycles.

- The opcode fetch cycle to read the opcode from 2100H
- A memory read cycle to read the lower order address from 2101H
- Another memory read cycle to read the higher order address from 2102H.
- The fourth machine cycle to store the contents of A register at the specified location (2450H).

Fig.4.6 shows the Timing diagram for the execution of STA instruction.

The opcode fetch cycle and the first memory read cycle are exactly similar to the MVI C instruction, discussed in the previous section. In addition, the STA instruction has the second read cycle to read the higher order address. In the *fourth machine cyle* the CPU executes a memory write cycle of following sequence.

1. First Clock Cycle (T1) (First T state)

- The CPU places the content of the program counter on the address bus; 24H on higher order bus and 50H on lower order bus.
- The ALE signal is made high.
- IO/$\overline{M}$ is made low so as to indicate that it is a memory operation.

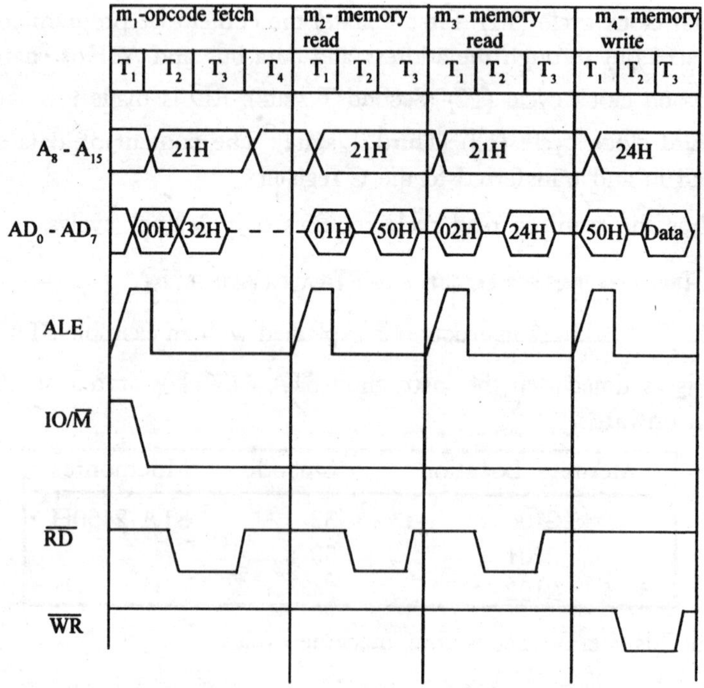

Fig.4.6 Timing diagram for the execution of STA instruction

2. **Second Clock Cycle (T2) (Second T state)**

- The CPU places the A register content on the data bus.
- The WR signal is enabled.

3. **Third Clock Cycle (T3) (Third T state)**

- The data bus content are written into the memory device at the selected location.
- The WR signal is disabled by making it high.

4.8.4 Timing diagram for Execution of RST Instruction

As an illustration, the instruction RST 3 is explained in the following. It is assumed that the instruction RST 3 is stored at location 2050H.

Memory Location	Opcode	Mnemonics
2050	DF	RST3

The instruction needs three machine cycles.

- The opcode fetch cycle to read opcode of RST 3 instruction
- A memory write cycle to store the higher order byte of the program counter
- Another memory write cycle to store the lower order byte of the program counter.

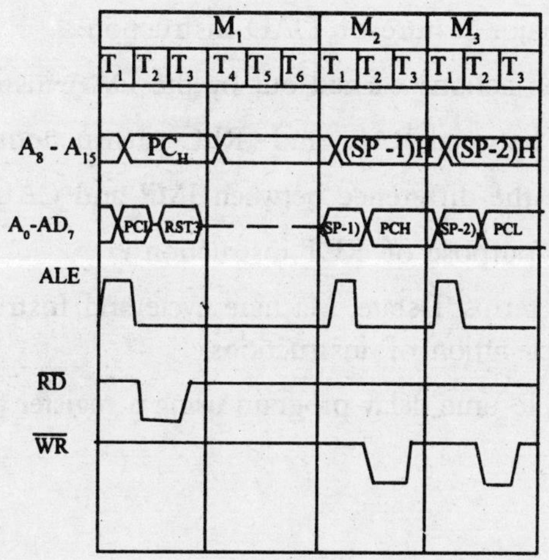

Fig.4.7 Timing diagram for RST 3 instruction.

The opcode fetch cycle reads the opcode and decodes it. However the RST 3 is an interrupt instruction. It requires the execution of its service routine and after execution, the control has to return to the instruction following RST 3 (location 2051 H), This return address has to be stored on the stack memory.

The second machine cycle is a memory write cycle. The content of stack pointer is decremented by one and its 16 bit content is placed on the address bus. The higher order byte of program counter (the return address) is stored at this location.

The third machine cycle is again a memory write cycle. The content of stack pointer is further decremented by 1 and its content placed on the address bus. The lower order byte of the program counter is stored at this location.

EXERCISE - 4

1. Distinguish between the following instructions.

   a) MOV A,M and LDAX D

   b) CMP B and SUB B

2. Discuss the addressing modes of the instructions :

   LDAX B and LHLD addr.

3. Write down the register pairs used with the XCHG instruction.
4. Write the major feature of DAD instruction.
5. What are the actions carried out by the DAA instruction ?
6. Distinguish between RAL and RLC instructions.
7. Write down the difference between JMP and CALL instructions.
8. What is the purpose of RET instruction ?
9. Explain the terms T-state, Machine cycle and Instruction cycle with respect to execution of instructions.
10. Write a simple time delay program using a register pair as a counter.

CHAPTER 5

PROGRAMMING EXERCISES

INTRODUCTION

The exercises discussed in this chapter can be entered into a microprocessor trainer kit and executed. The kit on which the authors developed and tested these programs has the user RAM area as given in the programs. The readers have to refer the operation manual of their trainer kits for the user RAM area and load the programs at suitable locations.

5.1 EIGHT BIT ADDITION

Problem Statement

Add the two hexadecimal numbers stored at the consecutive memory locations 2000H and 2001H and leave the result at the next location 2002H.

Memory Initialisation

Through the kit's memory access commands load the desired numbers at 2000H and 2001H.

Program Listing

Memory Location	Opcode	Label	Mnemonics	Comments
3000	21		LXI H,2000	Load HL register with
3001	00			the address of the first
3002	20			number
3003	7E		MOV A, M	Bring data into A reg.
3004	23		INX H	Point to next location
3005	86		ADD M	Add the two numbers
3006	23		INX H	Point to next location
3007	77		MOV M,A	Transfer the result into memory location.
3008	76		HLT	Stop execution.

Result after executing the program

Check the content of the location 2002H for the result.

5.2 EIGHT BIT SUBTRACTION

Problem Statement

Subtract the hexadecimal number stored at 2001H from the content of 2000H and leave the result at 2002H.

Memory Initialisation

Load the two desired numbers at 2000H and 2001H through the memory access commands.

Program Listing

Memory Location	Opcode	Label	Mnemonics	Comments
3000	21		LXI H,2000	Load the HL register with
3001	00			the starting address of
3002	20			data
3003	7E		MOV A, M	Bring data into A reg.
3004	23		INX H	Point to next location
3005	96		SUB M	Subtract the 2nd number
3006	23		INX H	Point to next location
3007	77		MOV M, A	Transfer the result into memory location
3008	76		HLT	Stop execution.

Result

After executing the program, check the content of the location 2002H for the result.

5.3 MULTI - BYTE ADDITION

Problem Statement

Add 2 multibyte numbers. The location 2000H stores the size (number of bytes) of the number. The first data is stored starting from 2001H and the second data is stored starting from 2010H. Store the result starting from the location 2001H (Replace the first number with the result)

Memory Initialisation

Let us assume that the two hex numbers to be added are

746A5F and 4D23C5

So the size in bytes of the number is 3 which is stored in location 2000H. The data 5F is stored in 2001H, 6A in 2002H and 74 in 2003H.

The data C5 is stored in location 2010H, 23 in 2011H and 4D in 2012H.

Flow Chart

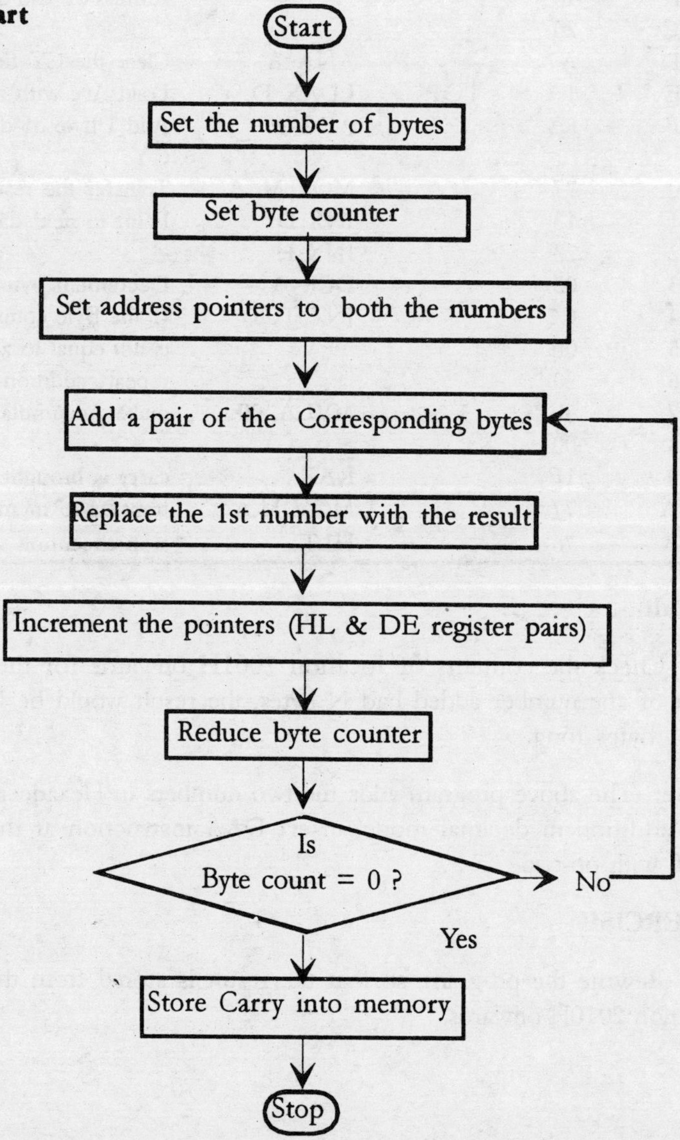

Program Listing

Memory Location	Opcode	Label	Mnemonics	Comments
3005	21		LXI H,2000	Load HL register with
3006	00			address 2000
3007	20			
3008	46		MOV B,M	Set byte counter
3009	23		INX H	Point first byte of data1
300A	11		LXI D,2010	Load DE register with
300B	10			address of 2nd data
300C	20			
300D	A7		ANA A	Clear the CY flag.
300E	1A	TOP	LDAX D	Load Acc with a byte data
300F	8E		ADC M	Add 1 byte of data2 with CY
3010	77		MOV M, A	Transfer the result
3011	13		INX D	Point to next data byte
3012	23		INX H	
3013	05		DCR B	Decrement byte counter
3014	C2		JNZ TOP	If the Byte count
3015	0E			is not equal to zero
3016	30			repeat addition
3017	3E		MVI A, 00	make Accumulator = 0
3018	00			
3019	1F		RAR	carry is brought to bit 1
301A	77		MOV M,A	transfer to memory
301B	76		HLT	stop execution

Result

Check the contents of location 2001H onwards for the result. If each of the number added had N bytes, the result would be N bytes or N+1 bytes long.

Note: The above program adds the two numbers in Hexadecimal mode. For addition in decimal mode, insert DAA instruction at the location 3010 with op-code as 27.

EXERCISE

Rewrite the program, so that the result is stored from the memory location 2010H onwards.

5.4 BLOCK TRANSFER OF DATA

Problem Statement

A block of data is available starting from 2003H (Source block). Transfer the block so that it is stored starting from 2050H (Destination block). The number of bytes in the block (Size of data) is stored in 2002H.

Flow Chart

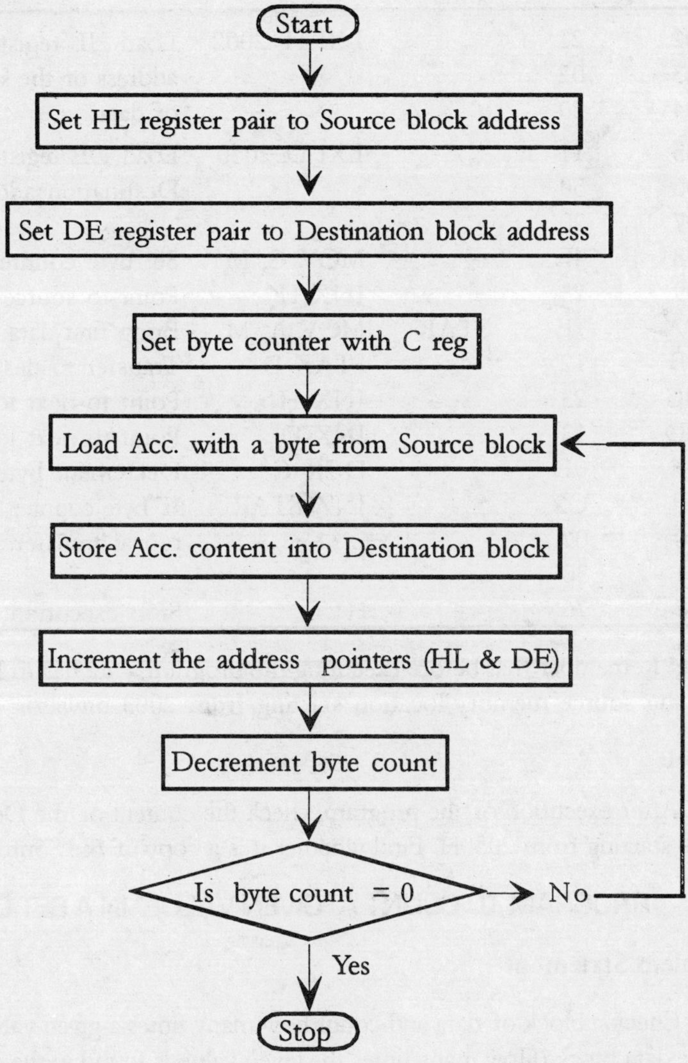

Memory Initialisation

Load the data of specified bytes starting from 2003H onwards.
Load the number of bytes in location 2002.

Program Listing

Memory Location	Opcode	Label	Mnemonics	Comments
3002	21		LXI H, 2002	Load HL register with
3003	02			address of the size
3004	20			of data
3005	11		LXI D, 2050	Load DE register with
3006	50			Destination address
3007	20			
3008	4E		MOV C, M	Set byte counter
3009	23		INX H	Point to source block
300A	7E	STAR	MOV A, M	Bring first data to Acc.
300B	12		STAX D	Transfer to destination
300C	23		INX H	Point to next location
300D	13		INX D	Point to next location
300E	0D		DCR C	Decrement byte counter
300F	C2		JNZ STAR	If byte counter not 0
3010	0A			repeat transfer.
3011	30			
3012	76		HLT	Stop execution.

Note: Remember that before executing the program, data has to be loaded into the source memory location starting from 2003 onwards.

Result

After execution of the program, check the content of the Destination block starting from 2050H. Find whether it is a copy of the Source block.

5.5 PROGRAM TO COUNT A "GIVEN VALUE" IN A SET OF DATA

Problem Statement

Check a block of data and count how many times a given value occurs in the data block (How many times the given value is found in the data) The size of data to be checked is stored in 204FH. The data is stored starting from 2050H. The result (number of occurances) is to be placed in 2075H.

Flow Chart

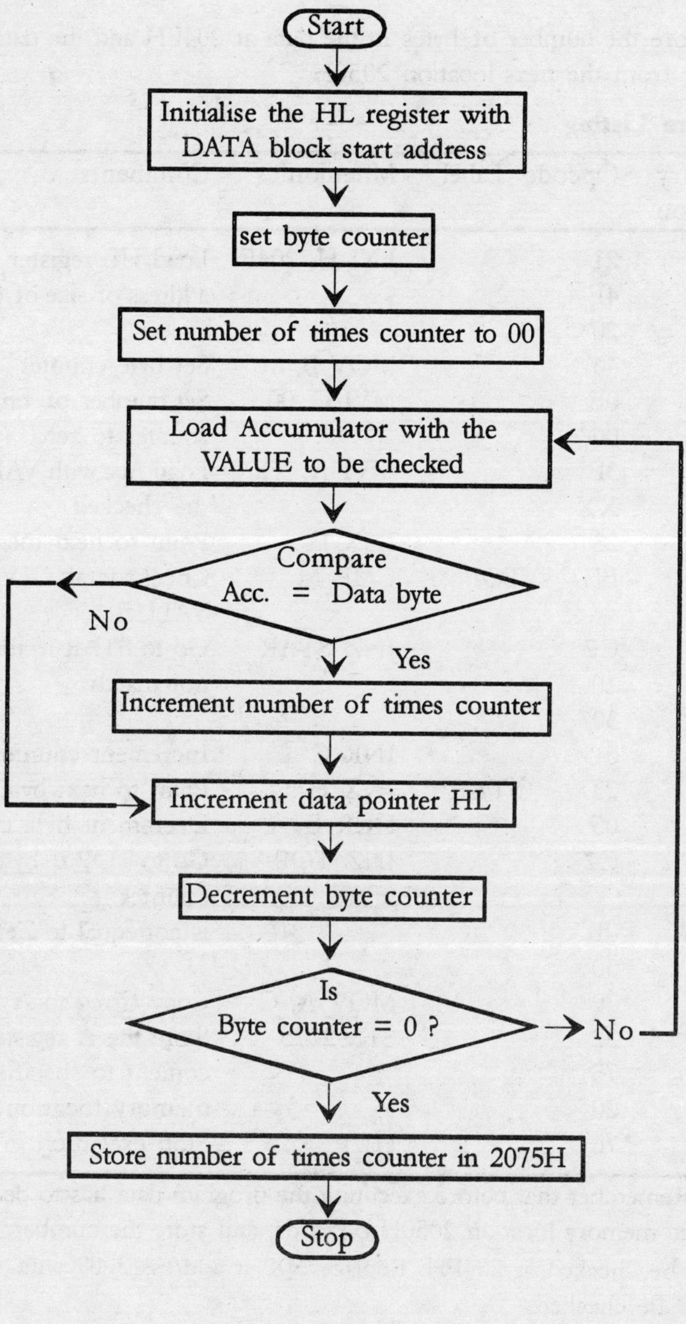
Start
Initialise the HL register with DATA block start address
set byte counter
Set number of times counter to 00
Load Accumulator with the VALUE to be checked
Compare
Acc. = Data byte
No
Yes
Increment number of times counter
Increment data pointer HL
Decrement byte counter
Is
Byte counter = 0 ?
No
Yes
Store number of times counter in 2075H
Stop

Memory Initialisation

Store the number of bytes in the data at 204FH and the data block starting from the next location 2050H.

Program Listing

Memory Location	Opcode	Label	Mnemonics	Comments
3002	21		LXI H, 204F	Load HL register with address of size of data
3003	4F			
3004	20			
3005	46		MOV B, M	Set byte counter
3006	0E		MVI C, 00	Set number of times counter to zero
3007	00			
3008	3E		MVI A, XX	Load Acc with VALUE to be checked
3009	XX			
300A	23		INX H	Point to next memory
300B	BE	TOP	CMP M	Check data=GIVEN VALUE
300C	C2		JNZ STAR	Go to STAR if they do not match
300D	10			
300E	30			
300F	0C		INR C	Increment counter
3010	23	STAR	INX H	Point to next byte data
3011	05		DCR B	Decrement byte counter
3012	C2		JNZ TOP	Go to TOP if byte counter is not equal to Zero
3013	0B			
3014	30			
3015	79		MOV A, C	Copy C reg to A reg.
3016	32		STA 2075	Store the A register content to specified memory location.
3017	75			
3018	20			
3019	76		HLT	Stop execution.

Note: Remember that before executing the program data has to be loaded from the memory location 2050H onwards, and store the number of data to be checked at 204FH. Replace XX at address 3009 with desired value to be checked.

Result

After execution of the program, check the location 2075H for the number of occurances of the given value in the set of given data.

Exercise

The content of 2075H may be displayed at the data field of the microprocessor trainer kit. Refer the operation manual for using the relevant utility routine for this purpose.

5.6 FINDING THE BIGGEST VALUE IN A BLOCK OF DATA

Problem Statement

Check a block of data and find the biggest value stored in that block. The size of the block is stored at 2000H. The data is stored from 2001H onwards. The result has to be displayed at the data field of the kit.

Flow Chart

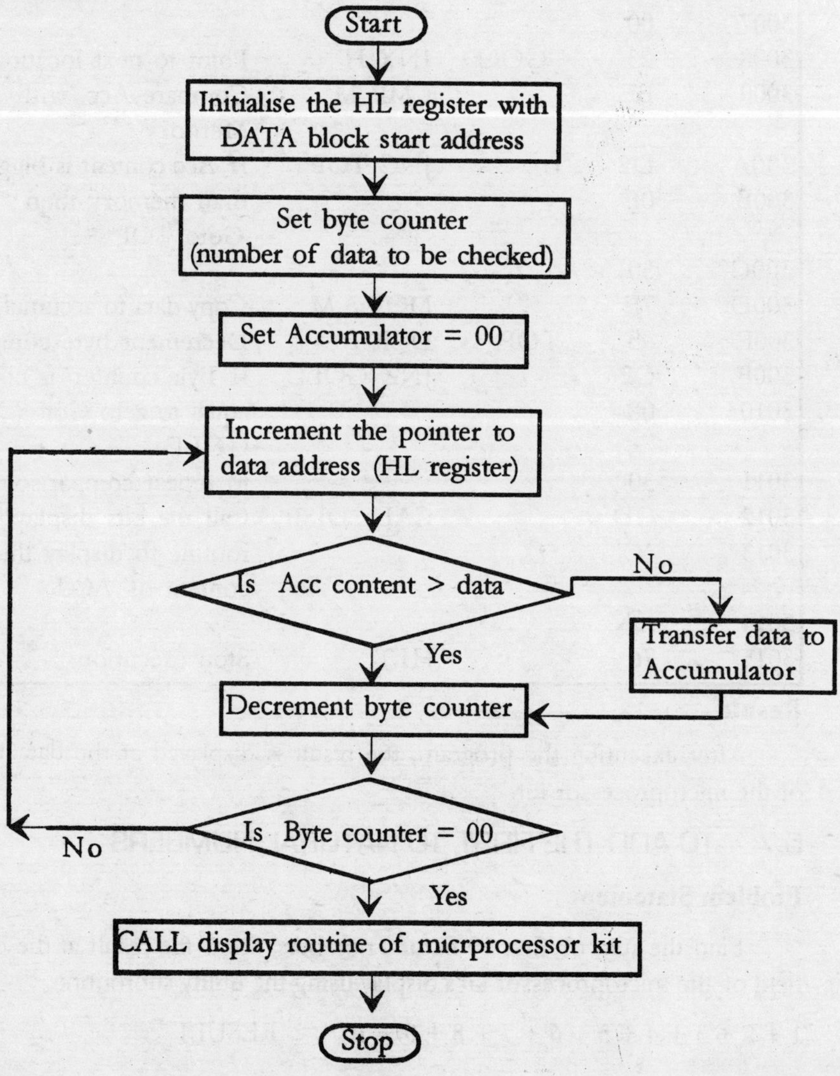

Memory Initialisation

Store the number of bytes in the data at 2000H and the data starting from 2001.

Program Listing

Memory Location	Opcode	Label	Mnemonics	Comments
3002	21		LXI H, 2000	Load HL register with address
3003	00			
3004	20			
3005	46		MOV B, M	Set byte counter
3006	3E		MVI A,00	Load Acc. with Zero
3007	00			
3008	23	GOLD	INX H	Point to next location
3009	BE		CMP M	Compare Acc. with Memory
300A	D2		JNC TOP	If Acc content is bigger than memory then Goto TOP
300B	0E			
300C	30			
300D	7E		MOV A,M	Copy data to accumulator
300E	05	TOP	DCR B	Decrement byte counter
300F	C2		JNZ GOLD	If Byte counter is not equal to zero Goto GOLD
3010	08			
3011	30			to repeat comparison
3012	CD		CALL DISP	Call the kits display routine to display the content of ACC.
3013	XX			
3014	XX			
3015	76		HLT	Stop execution

Result

After executing the program, the result is displayed at the data field of the microprocessor kit.

5.7 TO ADD THE FIRST 10 NATURAL NUMBERS

Problem Statement

Find the sum of first 10 natural numbers. Show the result at the data field of the microprocessor kit's display using the utility subroutine.

1 + 2 + 3 + 4 + 5 + 6 + 7 + 8 + 9 + 10 = RESULT

Flow Chart

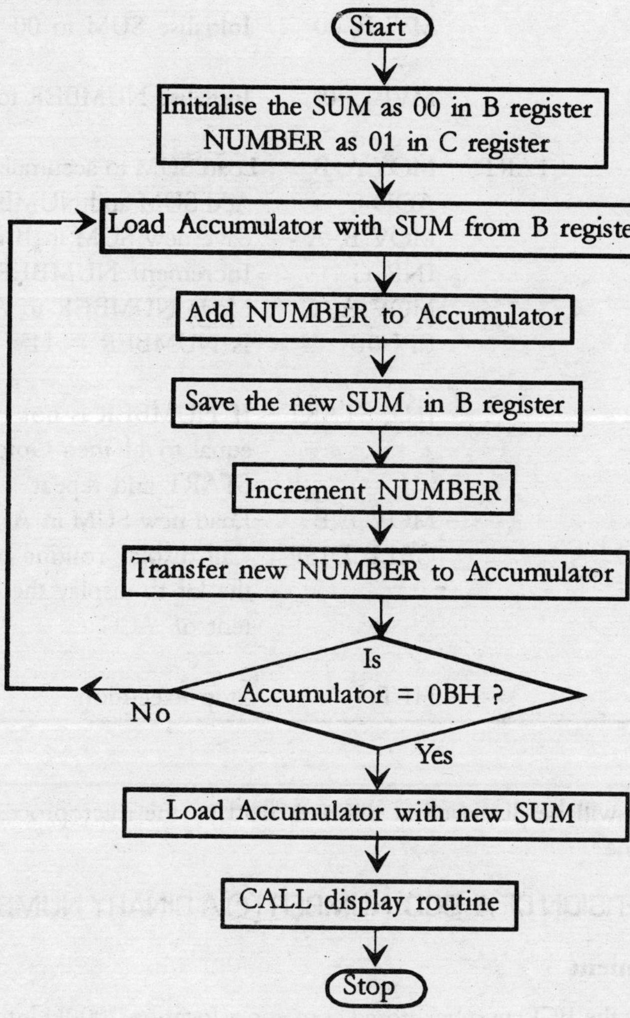
Start
Initialise the SUM as 00 in B register
NUMBER as 01 in C register
Load Accumulator with SUM from B register
Add NUMBER to Accumulator
Save the new SUM in B register
Increment NUMBER
Transfer new NUMBER to Accumulator
Is
Accumulator = 0BH ?
No
Yes
Load Accumulator with new SUM
CALL display routine
Stop

Program Listing

Memory Location	Opcode	Label	Mnemonics	Comments
3002	06		MVI B, 00	Initialise SUM to 00
3003	00			
3004	0E		MVI C, 01	Initialise NUMBER to 01
3005	01			
3006	78	START	MOV A, B	Load SUM to accumulator
3007	81		ADD C	Add SUM and NUMBER
3008	47		MOV B, A	Save new SUM in B reg.
3009	0C		INR C	Increment NUMBER
300A	79		MOV A, C	Move NUMBER to Acc.
300B	FE		CPI 0B	Is NUMBER = 11
300C	0B			
300D	C2		JNZ START	If NUMBER is not
300E	06			equal to 11 then Goto
300F	30			START and repeat
3010	78		MOV A,B	Load new SUM in A reg
3011	CD		CALL DISP	Call display routine of
3012	xx			the kit to display the con tent of ACC.
3013	xx			
3014	76		HLT	Stop execution

Result

The result will be displayed at the data field by the microprocessor kit display routine.

5.8 CONVERSION OF A BCD NUMBER TO A BINARY NUMBER

Problem Statement

To convert the BCD number stored at memory location 2000H into its binary equivalent and store the result at 2001H.

Background Information

An example of a two digit decimal number is 96

The BCD equivalent of 96 is 1001 0110

However the true binary equivalent of 96 is 0110 0000

Flow Chart

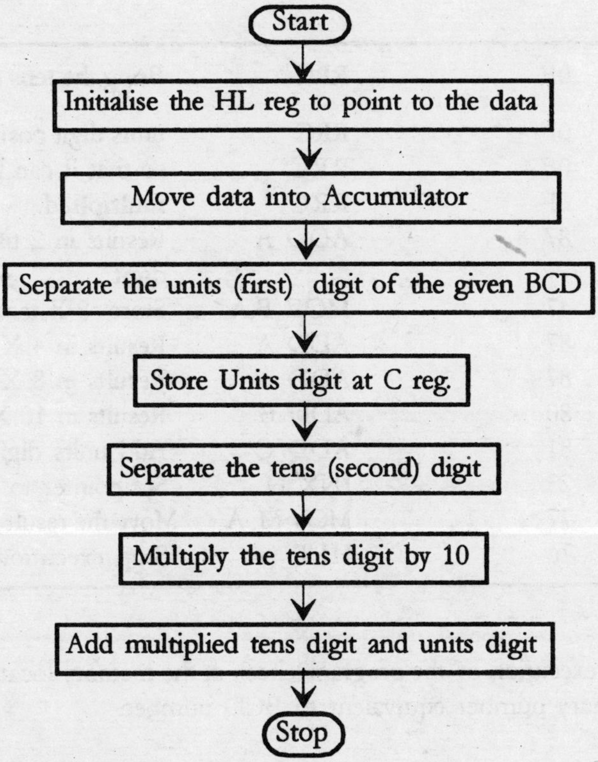

Memory Initialisation

Load a BCD number at memory location 2000H.

Program Listing

Memory Location	Opcode	Label	Mnemonics	Comments
3005	21		LXI H, 2000	Load HL pair with the
3006	00			address of the data
3007	20			
3008	7E		MOV A, M	Bring data to A register
3009	E6		ANI 0F	Mask units digit
300A	0F			
300B	4F		MOV C, A	Store units digit to C reg
300C	7E		MOV A, M	Bring data to A register
300D	E6		ANI F0	Mask tens digit
300E	F0			

Memory Location	Opcode	Label	Mnemonics	Comments
300F	0F		RRC	Bring the tens digit into
3010	0F		RRC	units digit position
3011	0F		RRC	so that it can be
3012	0F		RRC	multiplied.
3013	87		ADD A	Results in 2 times tens digit
3014	47		MOV B,A	Store 2 X tens digit
3015	87		ADD A	Results in 4 X tens digit
3016	87		ADD A	Results in 8 X tens digit
3017	80		ADD B	Results in 10 X tens digit
3018	81		ADD C	Add units digit
3019	23		INX H	Set pointer to 2001H
301A	77		MOV M, A	Move the result to memory
301B	76		HLT	Stop execution.

Result

After execution of the program, check at the memory location 2001H for the binary number equivalent to BCD number.

Exercise

Extend the program to include the display routine for displaying the result. The binary result will be displayed in HEX form.

5.9 FIND SQUARE-ROOT OF A GIVEN NUMBER

Problem Statement

Calculate the square root of a given number and display it if it is a perfect square, if not display an error message.

Background Information

The square root can be calculated by subtracting from the given number natural old numbers starting from 1. That is first subtract 1, then 3, 5, 7, 9 ... etc. For a perfect square the remainder becomes zero after certain subtractions. The square root is given by the number of times subtraction is carried out. For non-perfect squares the remainder does not become 0, but becomes negative.

Examples

Find square root of 36.		Find square root of 39.	
Given number	Number of subtraction.	Given number	Number of Subtraction.
36		39	
−1	1	−1	1
35		38	
−3	2	−3	2
32		35	
−5	3	−5	3
27		30	
−7	4	−7	4
20		23	
−9	5	−9	5
11		14	
-11	6	-11	6
0		3	
		-13	7
Remainder becomes ZERO for a perfect square.		–10	
Therefore the Square root of 36 is equal to the number of subtractions carried out, that is 6.		Remainder becomes –ve, which indicates that the given number is a non-perfect square.	

Flow Chart

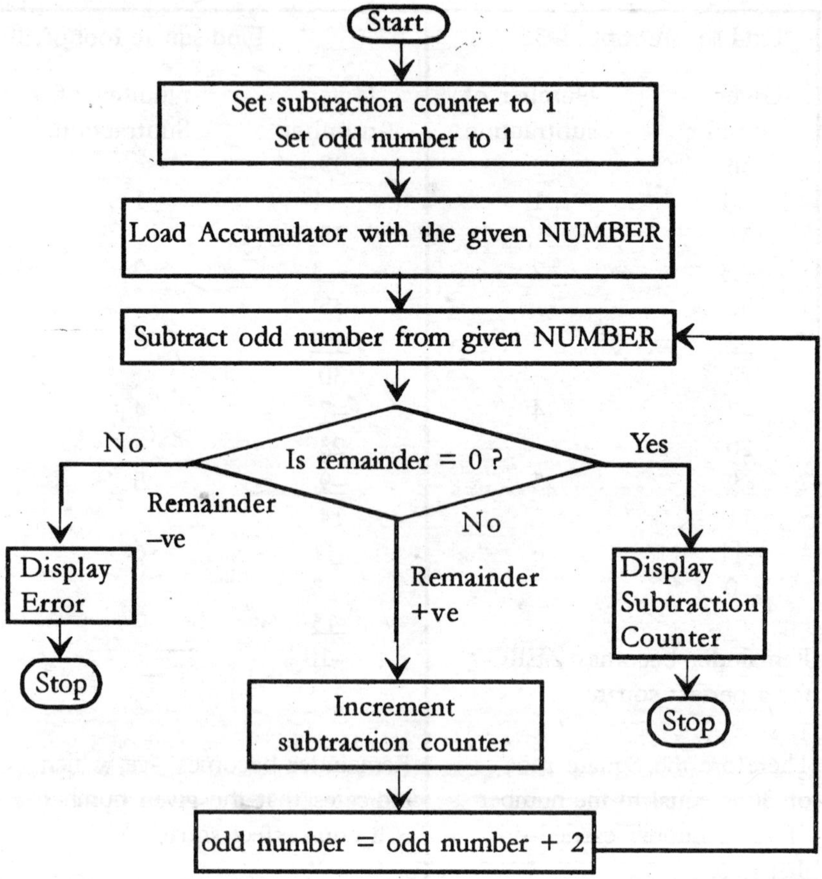

Program Listing

Memory Location	Opcode	Label	Mnemonics	Comments
4001	0E		MVI C, 01	Set subtraction counter
4002	01			to 1
4003	06		MVI B, 01	Set odd number to 1
4004	01			
4005	3E		MVIA, NUM	Load Acc with NUMBER
4006	NUM			
4007	90	LOOP	SUB B	Subtract odd number
4008	CA		JZ KING	If Acc content equal to
4009	14			zero, then Goto DISP

Memory Location	Opcode	Label	Mnemonics	Comments
400A	40			
400B	DA		JC BAD	If Acc content less than
400C	19			B reg, then Goto ERR
400D	40			Otherwise
400E	0C		INR C	Increment C register
400F	04		INR B	Increment odd number
4010	04		INR B	Increment odd number
4011	C3		JMP LOOP	Repeat subtraction
4012	07			
4013	40			
4014	0C	KING	MOV A,C	Move C reg to Accumulator
4015	CD		CALL DISP	Call display routine
4016	XX			
4017	XX			
4018	76		HLT	Stop execution.
4019	CD	BAD	CALL ERROR	If given NUMBER is not a perfect square then call ERROR routine
401A	YY			
401B	YY			
401C	76		HLT	Stop execution.

Note: For the MVI A instruction the user has to insert at the memory location 4006, the actual number whose square root has to be calculated. In the program the symbolic name NUM is given.

Result

The result will be displayed on the data field of the microprocessor kit.

5.10 CALCULATION OF FACTORIAL OF A GIVEN NUMBER

Problem Statement

Calculate the factorial of a given number. Use the HL register pair as an extended 16 bit accumulator. Use repeated addition to implement multiplication.

Background Information

Factorial of a number n is given by

n(n-1)(n-2)(n-3)..................4 x 3 x 2 x 1

In other words, the given number n is multiplied by (n-1) that is the next lowest number, then by (n-2) and so on by all lower numbers upto 1. Since there is no instruction for multiplication, it is implemented by repeated addition in this problem. To multiply n and n-1, n is added to itself n-1 times.

Flow Chart

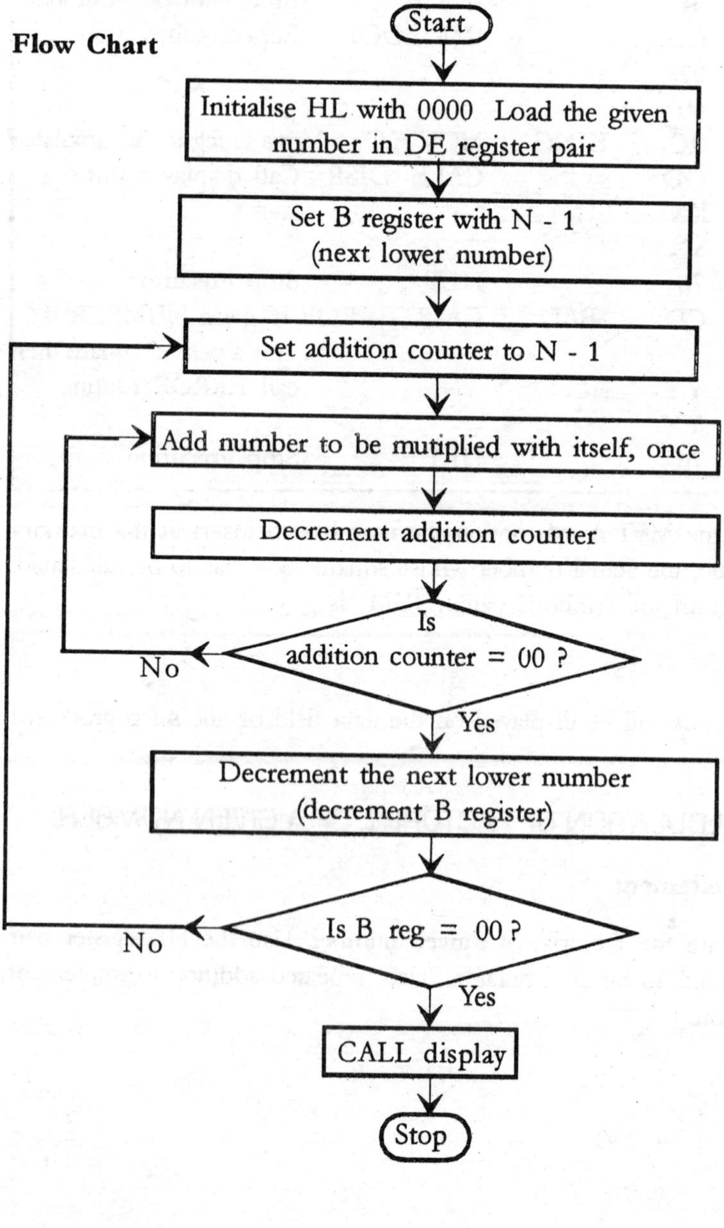

PROGRAM TO FIND THE FACTORIAL VALUE OF A GIVEN NUMBER

The program finds the fatorial value of N. The HL register pair is used as a 16 bit accumulator to find the multiplied value for

N(N-1)(N-2)......

which is then stored in DE register pair, the HL register pair is initialised to 0000 to repeat the operation to complete the entire process.

Memory Location	Opcode	Label	Mnemonics	Comments
4001	21		LXI H, 0000	Load HL register with
4002	00			0000.
4003	00			
4004	1E		MVI E, Num	Load DE register pair
4005	Num			with given number
4006	16		MVI D, 00	
4007	00			
4008	43		MOV B,E	Set next lower number
4009	05		DCR B	to N-1
400A	48	KING	MOV C, B	Set addition counterN-1
400B	19	TOP	DAD D	Add the number to itself
400C	05		DCR B	Decrement addtion counter
400D	C2		JNZ TOP	If addition counter not
400E	0B			zero, repeat addition
400F	40			
4010	EB		XCHG	Store the result in DE
4011	21		LXI H, 0000	Load HL with zero
4012	00			
4013	00			
4014	41		MOV B, C	Decrement the next lower number
4015	05		DCR B	
4016	C2		JNZ KING	If next lower number is
4017	0A			not zero, repeat
4018	40			multiplication goto KING
4019	CD		CALL DISP	Call display after moving
401A	ZZ			the result into specific
401B	ZZ			register pairs ormemory
401C	76		HLT	Stop execution.

Result

The result will be shown on the address field of the microprocessor kit.

Note: At memory location 4005 the reader/user has to enter the given number whose factorial has to be calculated. In the program the symbolic name NUM is given.

5.11 CONVERSION OF A BINARY NUMBER TO A DECIMAL NUMBER – [Method-1]

Problem Statement

Convert the binary number stored at the location 2003H into decimal form and display the decimal number on the address field of the microprocessor trainer kit.

Background Information

The maximum number that can be formed with an 8 bit binary number is 255. To represent and display 255 as decimal number, 3 digits are required. Hence address field of the kit may be used to display the result.

Example

Binary number = 1111 0111

Equivalent decimal number = 247

To seperate the Hundreds, Tens and Ones digit the following method may be used.

Hundreds digit

Subtract repeatedly 100 from the given number, until the remainder becomes less than 100. The number of 100s subtracted gives the Hundreds digit.

Tens digit

After seperating the hundreds digit, the remainder would be less than 100. Subtract repeatedly 10 from the remainder until it becomes less than 10. The number of 10s subtracted gives the Tens digit.

Units digit

The remainder gives the units digit straight away.

The flow chart represents the exact sequence of the process for conversion of a given Binary number into decimal number.

Note: Depending on the microprocessor kit, transfer the result into the required registers or memory locations. Then call the routine meant for displaying the result in the address field.

Flow Chart

CONVERSION OF A BINARY NUMBER INTO DECIMAL NUMBER (Method-1)

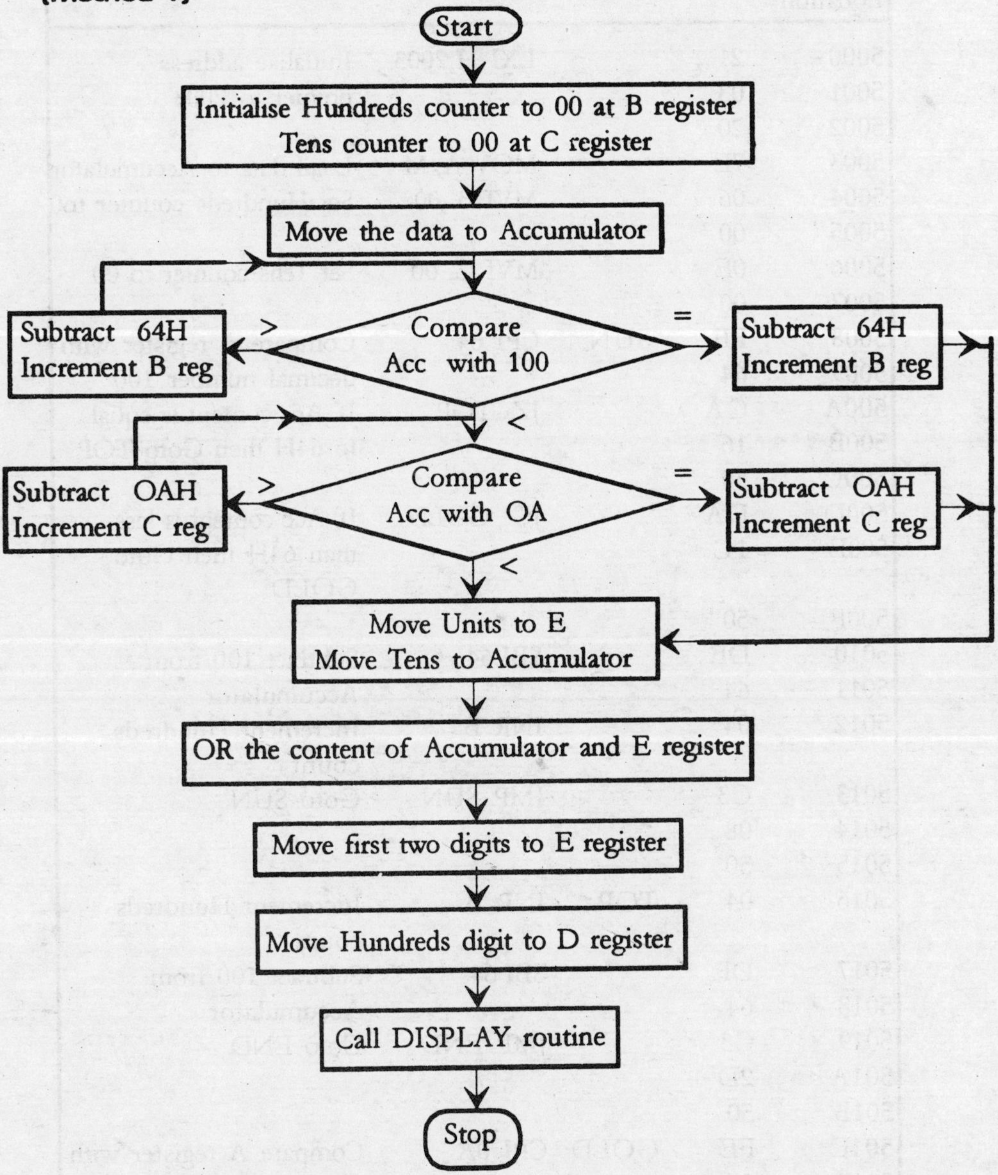

PROGRAM FOR BINARY TO DECIMAL CONVERSION: (Method-1)

This program converts the binary numbers in memory location 2003H into its equivalent decimal number and displays the result in address field of the kit.

Memory Location	Opcode	Label	Mnemonics	Comments
5000	21		LXI H,2003	Initialise address pointer to 2003
5001	03			
5002	20			
5003	7E		MOV A, M	Load data to Accumulator
5004	06		MVI B ,00	Set Hundreds counter to0
5005	00			
5006	0E		MVI C, 00	Set Tens counter to 00
5007	00			
5008	FE	SUN	CPI 64	Compare A register with decimal number 100
5009	64			
500A	CA		JZ TOP	If Acc content is equal to 64H then Goto TOP
500B	16			
500C	50			
500D	DA		JC GOLD	If Acc content is less than 64H then Goto GOLD
500E	1C			
500F	50			
5010	DE		SBI 64	Subtract 100 from Accumulator
5011	64			
5012	04		INR B	Increment Hundreds count
5013	C3		JMP SUN	Goto SUN
5014	08			
5015	50			
5016	04	TOP	INR B	Increment Hundreds count
5017	DE		SBI 64	Subtract 100 from Accumulator
5018	64			
5019	C3		JMP END	Goto END
501A	2D			
501B	50			
501C	FE	GOLD	CPI 0A	Compare A register with decimal number 10
501D	0A			

Memory Location	Opcode	Label	Mnemonics	Comments
501E	CA		JZ LUX	If Accumulator content
501F	2A			equal to 10 Goto LUX
5020	50			
5021	DA		JC END	If Accumulator content
5022	2D			less than 10, Goto END
5023	50			
5024	DE		SBI 0A	Subtract immediately 10
5025	0A			from the Accumulator
5026	0C		INR C	Increment Tens counter
5027	C3		JMP GOLD	Goto GOLD
5028	1C			
5029	50			
502A	0C	LUX	INR C	Increment Tens counter
502B	DE		SBI 0A	Subtract 10
502C	0A			from the Accumulator
502D	57	END	MOV D, A	Copy Units to D register
502E	79		MOV A,C	Bring Tens to Accumulator
502F	07		RAL	Change the first digit
5030	07		RAL	position to second
5031	07		RAL	digit position.
5032	07		RAL	
5033	B2		ORA D	OR the Tens and Unit digit
5034	5F		MOV E,A	Copy Accumulator to E reg.
5035	50		MOV D, B	Copy D reg. from B reg.
5036	CD		CALL DISP	Call Display routine
5037	ZZ			after storing the
5038	ZZ			result into reg or memory
5039	76		HLT	Stop execution.

Result

The equivalent decimal number will be displayed on the address field of the microprocessor kit.

The content of memory location 2003H = FE (Hex)

The content displayed in the address field of microprocessor kit = 0254 (Decimal)

Note: Consult your microprocessor kit to use the routine for displaying the result at the address field. The routine may require the result to be stored at a specific register or memory location.

5.12 A 16 BIT BINARY NUMBER TO A DECIMAL NUMBER (Method 2)

Problem Statement

Convert the 16 bit binary number stored at 2003H (lower byte) and at 2004H (higher byte) into decimal equlent number and display it on the address field of the kit.

Background Information

A simple method is used to convert the binary number into decimal number. The binary number is moved into the BC register pair. The DE register pair is initialised to zero.

The BC register pair is decremented and the DE register pair is incremented. For every decrement of BC, the DE pair gets one increment. This is repeated until the BC content becomes zero. The DE register pair at this stage will contain the required number. However the DE pair has to be made to increment in decimal mode, so that finally it gets the decimal equivalent of the binary number. This is achieved in the following way.

For every decrement of BC register pair, the E register is incremented. Its content is brought to A register and DAA instruction is applied. Then the A register content is transferred to E register. Thereby the register is incremented in decimal format. When the E register content reaches 99 it will becomes 00 in the next increment instead of 100. Therefore when E register content becomes 00, the D register is incremented once. The decimal adjustment is also applied to the D register. Thus the DE pair counts in BCD mode.

Finally the DE register pair contains the equivalent decimal number for the binary number stored at memory locations 2003 and 2004H.

Note : Consult your microprocessor kit to use the routine for displaying the result at the address field. The routine may require the result to be stored at a specific register or memory location.

Flow chart

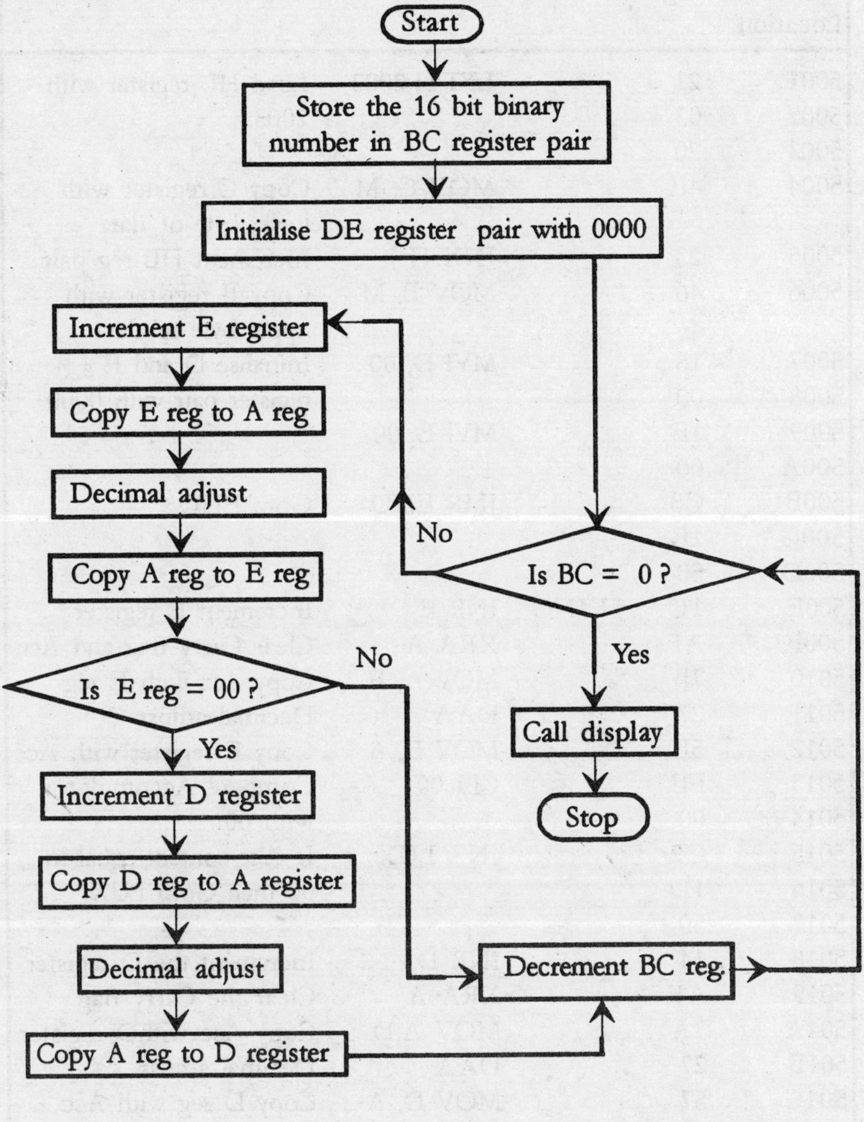

PROGRAM FOR BINARY TO DECIMAL CONVERSION

This program converts the 16 bit binary number at memory location 2003H and 2004H into its equivalent number in decimal form which will be displayed at the address field of the microprocessor kit.

Memory Location	Opcode	Label	Mnemonics	Comments
5001	21		LXI H,2003	Load HL register with 2003
5002	03			
5003	20			
5004	4E		MOV C, M	Copy C register with lower byte of data
5005	23		INX H	Increment HL reg pair
5006	46		MOV B, M	Copy B register with upper byte of data
5007	16		MVI D, 00	Initialise D and E register pair with 0000
5008	00			
5009	1E		MVI E, 00	
500A	00			
500B	C3		JMP END	Goto END
500C	1E			
500D	50			
500E	1C	KING	INR E	Increment E register
500F	AF		XRA A	Clear Carry flag and Acc
5010	7B		MOV A, E	Copy Acc with E reg
5011	27		DAA	Decimal adjust
5012	5F		MOV E, A	Copy E register with Acc
5013	FE		CPI 00	Compare Accumulator with 00
5014	00			
5015	C2		JNZ LUX	If Acc content equal to 00 then Goto LUX
5016	1D			
5017	50			
5018	14		INR D	Increment the D register
5019	AF		XRA A	Clear the Carry flag
501A	7A		MOV A,D	Copy Acc withD register
501B	27		DAA	Decimal adjust
501C	57		MOV D, A	Copy D reg with Acc
501D	0B	LUX	DCX B	Decrement BC reg pair
501E	78	END	MOV A, B	Copy Acc with B reg
501F	B1		ORA C	OR Acc with C register
5020	C2		JNZ KING	If B reg and C reg is equal to 00 then Goto KING
5021	0E			
5022	50			
5023	CD		CALL DISP	Call display routine after storing the result
5024	xx			

Memory Location	Opcode	Label	Mnemonics	Comments
5025	ZZ			into specific register or memory location
5026	76		HLT	Stop execution.

Note: zzzz is the starting address of the display routine to display the content of register or memory location in the address field.

5.13 ARRANGING DATA IN ASCENDING ORDER

Problem Statement

Arrange the ten numbers stored starting from memory location 3002H, in ascending (increasing) order.

Background Information

The method of arranging numbers in ascending order can be expiained with an example. Consider the following 5 numbers which have to be arranged in ascending order

18, 13, 41, 35, 12

The following four cycles of comparison are needed.

First Cycle

The first two numbers are compared. If the first number is larger than the second number, the location of the numbers are interchanged. If the first number is smaller, then they are not interchanged. Thus this comparison ensures that the second number is the larger of the two. After this, every one of the other remaining pairs namely 2&3, 3&4 and 4&5 are compared.

18	13	13	13	13	
13	18	18	18	18	I Cycle
41	41	41	35	35	4 pairs compared
35	35	35	41	12	
12	12	12	12	41	← Largest of 5 numbers.

Second cycle

The last number is already the largest of 5 numbers. Therefore in the II cycle only 3 pairs namely 1&2, 2&3 and 3&4 are compared.

13	13	13	13	
18	18	18	18	II Cycle
35	35	35	12	3 pairs compared
12	12	12	35 ← Second Largest of 5 numbers.	
41	41	41	41	

Third Cycle

The two pairs 1&2 and 2&3 are compared.

13	13	13	III Cycle
18	18	12	2 pairs compared
12	12	18 ← Third Largest of 5 numbers.	
35	35	35	
41	41	41	

Fourth Cycle

The only pair compared is 1&2.

13	12	IV Cycle
12	13 ← Fourth Largest of 5 numbers.	1 pair compared
18	18	
35	35	
41	41	

After four cycles of comparison the five numbers are arranged in ascending order.

In general to arrange n numbers, (n-1) cycles of comparisons are needed. In I cycle (n–1) comparisons are made. In II cycle (n–2) comparisons and so on and in the last cycle only one comparison is made.

Flow Chart for arranging 10 numbers in ascending order

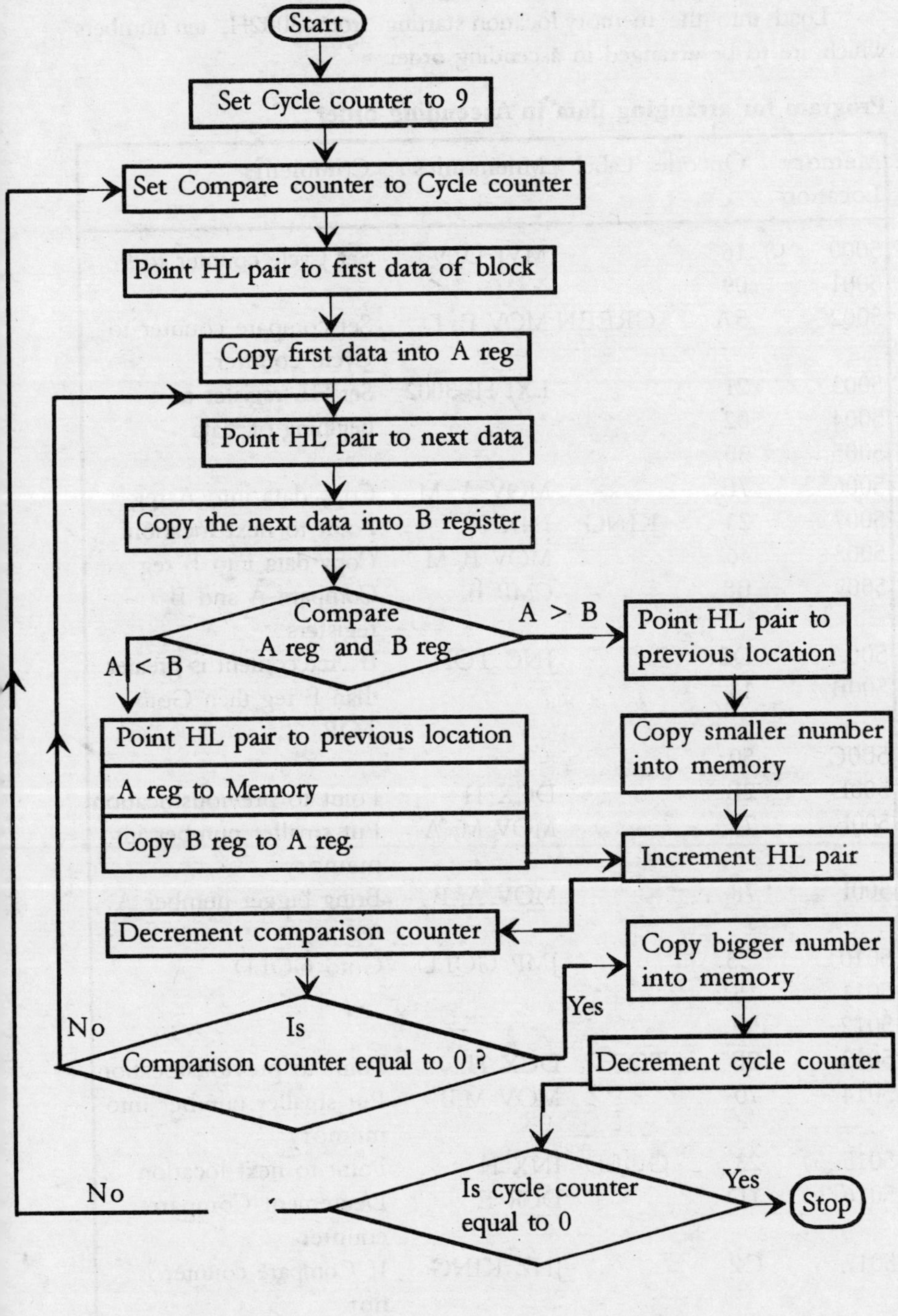

Memory Initialisation

Load into the memory location starting from 3002H, ten numbers which are to be arranged in ascending order.

Program for arranging data in Ascending order

Memory Location	Opcode	Label	Mnemonics	Comments
5000	16		MVI D,09	Set Cycle counter to 9
5001	09			
5002	5A	GREEN	MOV E, D	Set compare counter to Cycle counter
5003	21		LXI H, 3002	Set HL register to begining of data
5004	02			
5005	30			
5006	7E		MOV A, M	Copy data into A reg.
5007	23	KING	INX H	Point to next location
5008	46		MOV B, M	Copy data into B reg
5009	B8		CMP B	Compare A and B registers
500A	D2		JNC TOP	If Acc content is greater than B reg then Goto TOP
500B	13			
500C	50			
500D	2B		DCX H	Point to previouslocation
500E	77		MOV M, A	Put smaller number into memory
500F	78		MOV A, B	Bring bigger number A reg
5010	C3		JMP GOLD	Goto GOLD
5011	15			
5012	50			
5013	2B	TOP	DCX H	Point to previouslocation
5014	70		MOV M,B	Put smaller number into memory
5015	23	GOLD	INX H	Point to next location
5016	1D		DCR E	Decrement Compare counter
5017	C2		JNZ KING	If Compare counter is not

Memory Location	Opcode	Label	Mnemonics	Comments
5018	07			equal to zero then Goto
5019	50			KING
501A	77		MOV M,A	Copy Big number to memory
501B	15		DCR D	Decrement Cycle counter
501C	C2		JNZ GREEN	If Cycle counter is not
501D	02			equal to zero then Goto
501E	50			GREEN
501F	76		HLT	Stop execution.

Result

Check the memory content from the location 3002H onwards for arranged data in ascending order.

Note: Think what is the suitable modification to be made in the above program so as to arrange the given data in descending order

5.14 EIGHT BIT MULTIPLICATION (Method-1)

Problem Statement

Multiply the two eight bit numbers stored at memory location 2000H and 2001H and display the result in the address field of the microprocessor kit.

Background Information

The common method of multiplication of two decimal numbers is as follows.

```
To multiply   125 X 32
                 125     (multiplicand)
                 x 32    (multiplier)
                 250 ← Partial result of multiplying 125 with 2
          ←     375   ← Partial result of multiplying 125 with 3
                4000
```

The process is started from the units digit end of the multiplier. The units digit multiplies the multiplicand and partial result written. Then the tens digit multiplies and the partial result written shifted left by 1 digit. The two numbers are added to give the result.

The same procedure can be applied for multiplying two binary numbers.

Example

To multiply 1010 (decimal 10) by 0110 (decimal 6)

```
          1 0 1 0   (multiplicand)
          0 1 1 0   (multiplier)
          -------
          0 0 0 0
        1 0 1 0
      1 0 1 0
    0 0 0 0
    -------------
Result= 0 1 1 1 1 0 0
```

3C Hex (60 in decimal)

The LSB of the multiplier is 0. Therefore the partial result is 0000. The next bit is 1, therefore the multiplicand is shifted left by 1 bit and added to 0000. The next bit is also 1, therefore the multiplicand is shifted by 1 more bit and added. The MSB is 0 and so only 0000 is added. The total is 0111100 which is the decimal number 60.

Flow Chart

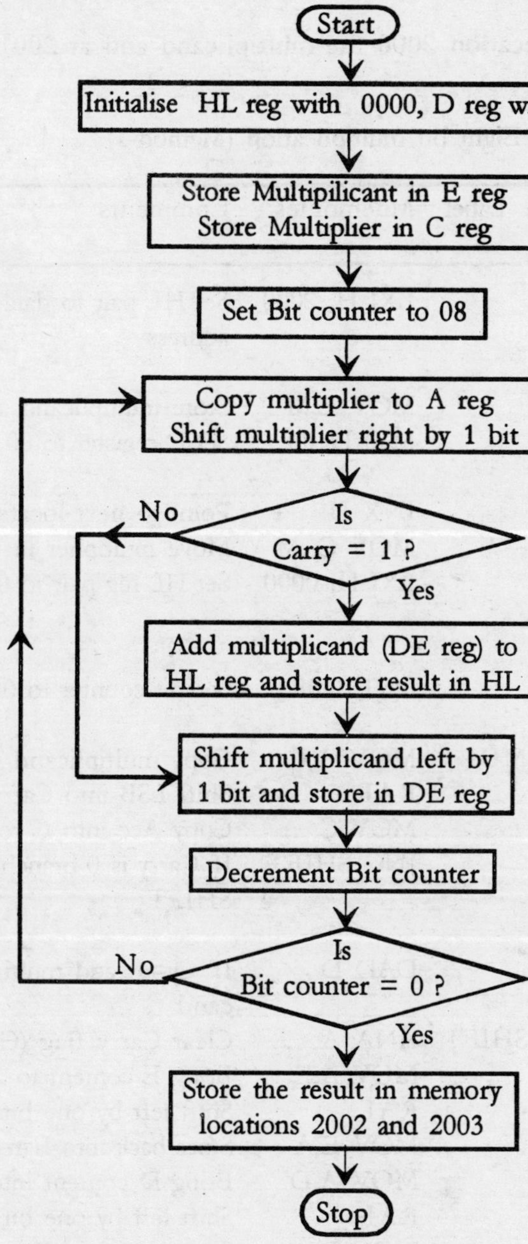
Start
Initialise HL reg with 0000, D reg with 00
Store Multipilicant in E reg
Store Multiplier in C reg
Set Bit counter to 08
Copy multiplier to A reg
Shift multiplier right by 1 bit
Is Carry = 1 ?
No
Yes
Add multiplicand (DE reg) to HL reg and store result in HL
Shift multiplicand left by 1 bit and store in DE reg
Decrement Bit counter
Is Bit counter = 0 ?
No
Yes
Store the result in memory locations 2002 and 2003
Stop

Memory Initialisation

Store at the location 2000 the multiplicand and at 2001H the multiplier.

Program Listing for Eight bit multiplication (Method-1)

Memory Location	Opcode	Label	Mnemonics	Comments
6001	21		LXI H, 2000	Set HL pair to data address
6002	00			
6003	20			
6004	5E		MOV E,M	Store multiplicand at E
6005	16		MVI D, 00	Set D register to 00
6006	00			
6007	23		INX H	Point to next location
6008	4E		MOV C, M	Move multiplier in C reg
6009	21		LXI H, 0000	Set HL reg pair to 0000
600A	00			
600B	00			
600C	06		MVI B, 08	Set Bit counter to 08
600D	08			
600E	79	MUL	MOV A,C	Copy multiplicand in A
600F	1F		RAR	Shift LSB into Carry flag
6010	4F		MOV C, A	Copy Acc into C reg
6011	D2		JNC SHIFT	If Carry is 0 branch to SHIFT
6012	15			
6013	60			
6014	19		DAD D	If Cy=1, add multipli cand
6015	A7	SHIFT	ANA A	Clear Carry flag (Cy)
6016	7B		MOV A,E	Bring E content to Acc
6017	17		RAL	Shift left by one bit
6018	5F		MOV E,A	Store back into E reg
6019	7A		MOV A,D	Bring D content into Acc
601A	17		RAL	Shift left by one bit
601B	57		MOV D,A	Store back into D reg
601C	05		DCR B	Decrement bit counter
601D	C2		JNZ MUL	Repeat the process, If B register is not zero
601E	0E			
601F	60			

Memory Location	Opcode	Label	Mnemonics	Comments
6020	76		XCHG	Exchange DE and HL reg
6021	CD		CAL DISP	Call the display to
6022	10			show the result in
6023	05			address field
6024	76		HLT	Stop execution

Result

The result will be displayed in the address field of the microprocessor kit.

5.15 EIGHT BIT MULTIPLICATION (Method-2)

Problem Statement

Multiply the two 8 bit numbers stored at 2000H and 2001H and display the result in the address field of the microprocessor kit.

Background Information

In this second method, the multiplication starts from the most significant digit as shown in the example.

Multiply 125 by 32.

	1 2 5 x	125 x 32
	3 2	= 125 (3 x 10 + 2 x 1)
Partial result of	———	= 3750 + 250
Multiplying by tens	3 7 5	= 4000
by units digit	2 5 0	
	———	
	4 0 0 0	

The tens digit multiplies first and partial result written. The units digit multiplies next and the partial result is shifted right by one digit. The two partial results are added to get the final result. Similar procceducre can be used for multiplying binary numbers.

To multiply 1011 (decimal 11) by 0101 (decimal 5)

```
                                        1 0 1 1   x
                                        0 1 0 1
Partial result of multiplying 1 0 1 1   -------
            by 0                        0 0 0 0
            by 1                          1 0 1 1
            by 0                            0 0 0 0
            by 1                              1 0 1 1
                                        -------------
       Total    = >                     0 1 1 0 1 1 1
                = >   37H
                = >   55 (decimal)
```

The most significant digit multiplies first. The partial results of other digits are shifted one digit right to account for their place value. The total gives the final result.

The same procedure slightly modified so as to add the partial results to produce partial sum inbetween is shown in the following.

Note that the procedure shown below assumes a 0 (zero) at the square positions. This implies that the intermediate sum is shifted left before the next partial result is added.

```
                                  1 0 1 1  x
                                  0 1 0 1
Partial result of multiplying    ---------
        1011  with 0              0 0 0 0[0]    partial sum
              with 1                1 0 1 1
                                 ---------
                                0 1 0 1 1[0]    partial sum
              with 0                0 0 0 0
                                 ----------
                              0 1 0 1 1 0[0]    partial sum
              with 1                1 0 1 1
                               ------------
              Result =        0 1 1 0 1 1 1

                     =        3 7 H
                     =        5 5  (decimal)
```

Flow Chart

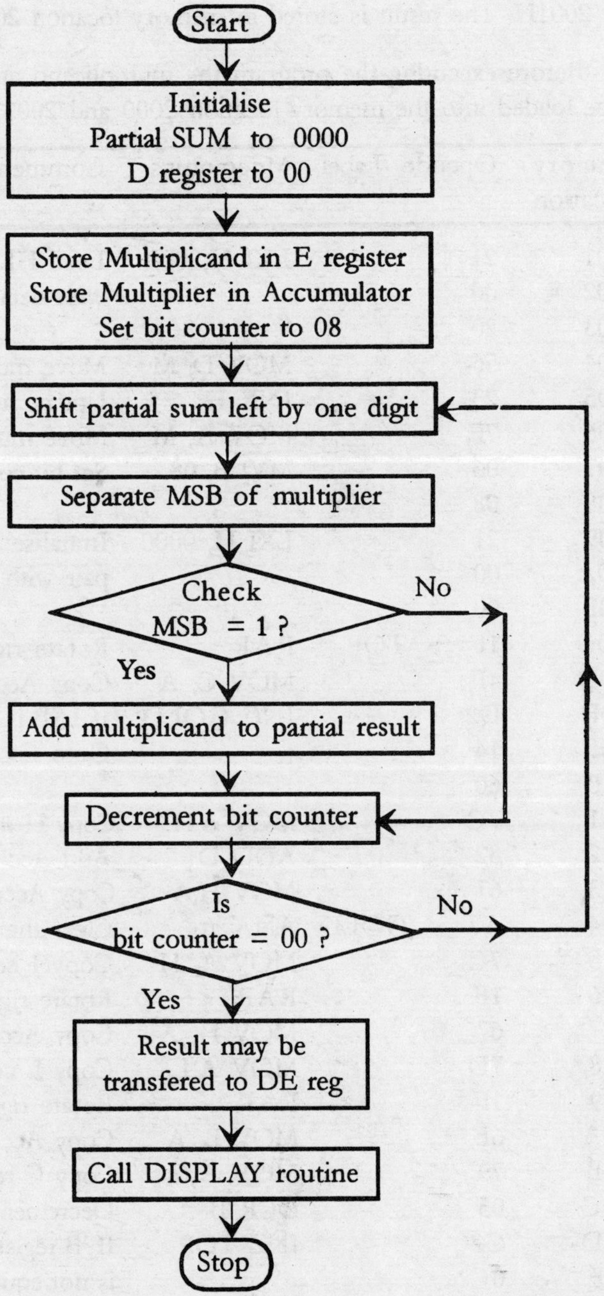
Start
Initialise
Partial SUM to 0000
D register to 00
Store Multiplicand in E register
Store Multiplier in Accumulator
Set bit counter to 08
Shift partial sum left by one digit
Separate MSB of multiplier
Check
MSB = 1 ?
No
Yes
Add multiplicand to partial result
Decrement bit counter
Is
bit counter = 00 ?
No
Yes
Result may be
transfered to DE reg
Call DISPLAY routine
Stop

Program for eight bit multiplication (Method – 2)

This program multiplies the content of memory location 2000H and 2001H. The result is stored in memory location 2002 and 2003H.

Before executing the program the multiplicand and multiplier are to be loaded into the memory location 2000 and 2001 respectively.

Memory Location	Opcode	Label	Mnemonics	Comments
6001	21		LXI H,2000	Load HL register pair
6002	00			with data address
6003	20			
6004	56		MOV D, M	Move multiplicand intoD
6005	23		INX H	Update address pointer
6006	7E		MOV A, M	Move multiplier into Acc
6007	06		MVI B, 08	Set bit counter to 08
6008	08			
6009	21		LXI H, 0000	Initialise HL register
600A	00			pair with 0000
600B	00			
600C	1F	TOP	RAR	Rotate right multiplier
600D	4F		MOV C, A	Copy Acc content into C
600E	D2		JNC GOLD	If LSB is ONE then
600F	14			Goto GOLD
6010	60			
6011	7C		MOV A,H	Copy H into Accumulator
6012	82		ADD D	Add Acc content with D
6013	67		MOV H,A	Copy Accumulator into H
6014	A7	GOLD	ANA A	Clear the carry flag
6015	7C		MOV A, H	CopyH content into Acc
6016	1F		RAR	Rotate right Acc content
6017	67		MOV H, A	Copy Acc into H register
6018	7D		MOV A,L	Copy L content into Acc
6019	1F		RAR	Rotate right Acc content
601A	6F		MOV L, A	Copy Acc into L register
601B	79		MOV A,C	Copy C reg into Acc.
601C	05		DCR B	Decrement B register
601D	C2		JNZ TOP	If B register content
601E	0C			is not equal to zero
601F	60			Goto TOP

Memory Location	Opcode	Label	Mnemonics	Comments
6020	EB		XCHG	Exchange DE with HL
6021	CD		CALL DISP	Call display routine
6022	XX			
6023	XX			
6024	76		HLT	Stop execution.

Note: XXXX is the starting address of the display routine to display the content of DE register pair in the address field.

To store the result in memory locations 2002 and 2003, enter the instructions given below from memory locations 6021 in the above program.

Memory Location	Opcode	Label	Mnemonics	Comments
6021	23		INX H	Update the address pointer
6022	73		MOV M, E	Transfer lower byte to memory
6023	23		INX H	Update the address pointer
6024	72		MOV M, D	Transfer higher byte to memory
6025	76		HLT	Stop execution

5.16 16 BIT BY 8 BIT BINARY DIVISION

Problem Statement

Divide the 16 bit unsigned number by the 8 bit unsigned number. Store the quotient in memory location 8150H and the remainder in memory location 8151H.

Background Information

You can perform division on the microprocessor kit just like you do division with pen and pencil, ie subtraction method. Since the numbers are binary, the question is whether to store the quotient bit as 1 or 0, ie whether the divisor can be subtracted from the dividend.

If the divisor can be subtracted from the eight most significant bit of the dividend without a borrow, the corresponding bit in the quotient is 1, otherwise store the quotient bit as 0.

The above process has to be repeated for eight times by arranging the dividend and quotient properly. This can be done by shifting the dividend and quotient left by one bit before each time you do the subtraction.

In this problem we can take care of sharing the 16 bit register for dividend and quotient, since the procedure clears one bit of the dividend at the same time as it determines one bit of the quotient.

To do the division follow the procedure given below -

FIRST CYCLE: Initialization
Counter register C = 08
Store B register = Divisor
Store HL registers = Dividend

SECOND CYCLE: Shift left the dividend and quotient. This is to keep bit position vacant to accept the appropriate quotient bit.
Dividend = 2 * Dividend
Quotient = 2 * Quotient

THIRD CYCLE: Perform the subtraction, ie subtract the divisor from the dividend. If no borrow, add one to quotient, then
New partial dividend = MSB of dividend – Divisor

FOURTH CYCLE:	Decrement the counter and check for zero. New counter = Counter - 1 If new counter is not equal to zero, then goto second cycle. If new counter is zero, then the remainder is 8 MSB of partial dividend.

Example:

Dividend = 0040H (64 in decimal)
Divisor = 08

Initialization

HL register pair= 0040 (Dividend)
B register = 08 (Divisor)
C register = 08 (Counter)
Quotient = 00

After the First iteration of steps 2 to 4 :

Divident = 0080
Divisor = 08
Counter = 07
Quotient = 00

After the Second iteration of steps 2 to 4 :

Divident = 0100
Divisor = 08
Counter = 06
Quotient = 00

After the Third iteration of steps 2 to 4 :

Divident = 0200
Divisor = 08
Counter = 05
Quotient = 00

After the Fourth iteration of steps 2 to 4 :

Divident = 0400
Divisor = 08
Counter = 04
Quotient = 00

After the Fifth iteration of steps 2 to 4 :

Divident = 0801
Divisor = 08
Counter = 03
Quotient = 01

After the Sixth iteration of steps 2 to 4 :

Divident = 0002
Divisor = 08
Counter = 02
Quotient = 02

After the Seventh iteration of steps 2 to 4 :

Divident = 0004
Divisor = 08
Counter = 01
Quotient = 04

After the Eigth iteration of steps 2 to 4 :

Divident = 0008
Divisor = 08
Counter = 00
Quotient = 08

When the counter value becomes zero, the content available in H register will be remainder and the content available in L register will be quotient.

Hence in the above example, the remainder is zero and the quotient is 08.

Flow Chart for the 16 bit by 8 bit DIVISION:

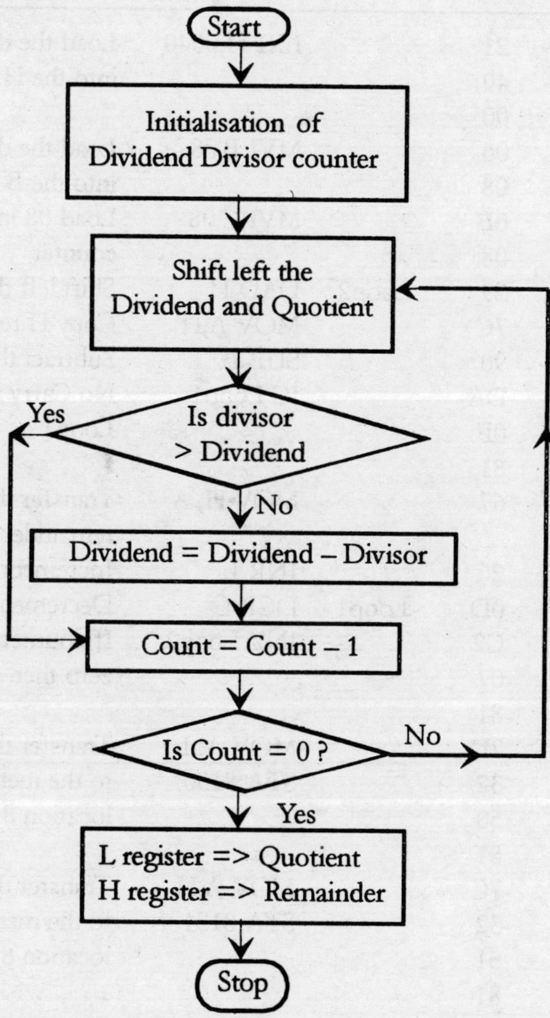

Program for the 16 bit by 8 bit division:

Memory Location	Opcode	Label	Mnemonics	Comments
8100	21		LXI H,0040	Load the dividend into the HL register
8101	40			
8102	00			
8103	06		MVI B,08	Load the divisor into the B register
8104	08			
8105	0E		MVI C,08	Load 08 into the counter
8106	08			
8107	29	Loop2	DAD H	Shift left the dividend.
8108	7C		MOV A,H	Copy H reg to Acc.
8109	90		SUB B	Subtract the Divisor
810A	DA		JC Loop1	No Carry means goto Loop1
810B	0F			
810C	81			
810D	67		MOV H, A	Transfer the partial remainder back to H.
810E	2C		INR L	Increment the L reg.
810F	0D	Loop1	DCR C	Decrement the counter
8110	C2		JNZ Loop2	If counter is not zero then goto Loop2
8111	07			
8112	81			
8113	7D		MOV A, L	Transfer the quotient to the memory location 8150
8114	32		STA 8150	
8115	50			
8117	81			
8118	7C		MOV A,H	Transfer the remainder to the memory location 8151
8119	32		STA 8151	
811A	51			
811B	81			
811C	76		HLT	Stop execution.

CHAPTER 6

INTERFACING INPUT AND OUTPUT DEVICES

6.1 INTRODUCTION

The primary function of a microprocessor is to process data according to the instructions stored in its memory. However the data meant for processing by the microprocessor, originate from outside, from different devices such as keyboard, switches, analog to digital converters etc. Therefore the microprocessor has to read data from these input devices. Further the results of the processing may be used to control devices such as digital to analog converters, relays or may be communicated to human users through LEDs, seven segment displays etc. These devices form the output devices for the data from the microprocessor. The different approaches in connecting such devices to the microprocessor are discussed in the following.

6.2 INTERFACING AND ADDRESS DECODING CIRCUITS

A single pole switch can produce a 1 bit signal input to a microprocessor as shown in figure 6.1 a. The switch position sets the input level which could be 0 or 1. Likewise, a simple logical output from a microprocessor can be displayed using an LED as shown in figure 6.1 b. When the output is 1 level, the LED glows.

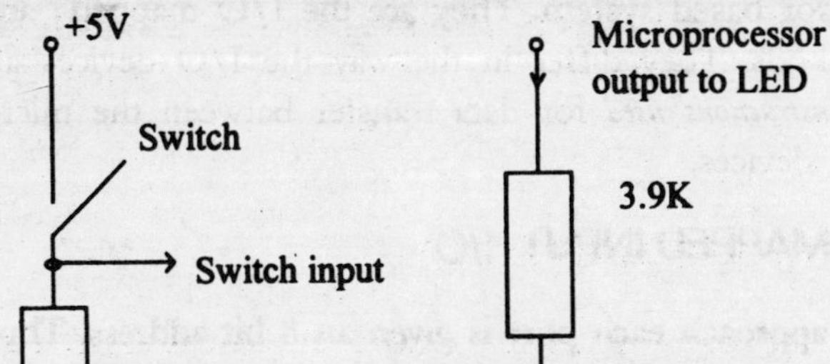

Fig. 6.1 Logical input and Logical output

However simple I/O devices such as the switch or the LED can not be directly connected to the data bus of the microprocessor. Because, the bus is used by the microprocessor to communicate with all the devices in the system. The information on the bus is therefore continuously changing as instructions are fetched from memory and executed. Information intended for an output indicator must therefore be latched by a suitable circuit. The processor can then send data to the output latching device which captures the data at the appropriate time determined by the bus control signals and then provides a continuous output until new data is sent out to it. Similarly, an input from a switch must be isolated from the data bus until the microprocessor is ready to read its status (0 or 1).

Thus additional circuits are required to connect the microprocessor to specific external input and output signals. Such circuits are called *INTERFACE CIRCUITS*. A group of inputs/outputs is called as an I/O port. The interface circuits are usually organised into I/O ports of 8 bits.

The microprocessor reads or writes different I/O devices at different instants. But how does it inform an I/O device whenever it wants to select that device? Each device is given a number which is its address. The microprocessor puts this address on the address bus for selecting a device. Thus each I/O device needs a circuit to recognise its own address on the address bus. Such a circuit is called *ADDRESS DECODER*. Address decoder is a part of the interface circuit.

There are two approaches in organising the I/O devices in a microprocessor based system. They are the I/O mapped and memory mapped methods. They differ in the way the I/O devices are *addressed* and in tne *instructions used* for data transfer between the microprocessor and the I/O devices.

6.3 I/O MAPPED INPUT I/O

In this approach each port is given an 8 bit address. Thus an input port can have any address ranging from 00H to FFH. The output ports is also allowed to have any address in the same range of 00H to FFH. Thus a microcomputer can have 256 input and 256 output ports. Further 2 exclusive instructions are used for moving data between the port and the microprocessor. *They are the IN and OUT instructions.*

Instruction to output data into a port

Syntex: OUT address
Example: OUT 23H

It causes the accumulator content to be latched to the output port whose address is specified in the instruction.

Instruction to input data from a port

Syntex: IN address
Example: IN 41H

It transfers data from the addressed port to the accumulator.

A special feature is while the microprocessor executes the IN or OUT instruction *the specified address is put in the higher order address bus A15..A8 as well as in the lower order address bus A7..A0.*

An Output Port Implementation

The circuit in Fig. 6.2 shows an array of 8 LEDs connected to an interface circuit. The interface circuit forms an output port. The LED array can be used to display an 8 bit word. The address of the port may be assumed to be 80H.

In order to switch on the LED, L4, the D4 bit of the data, has to be made 1 and the rest of the bits 0. Initiallly, the data byte 00010000 which has to be latched at the output port is to be placed in the accumulator and then an OUT instruction is to be executed. The following sequence of instructions implement the data transfer to the port 80H.

Memory Location	Opcode	Mnemonics	Comments
2000	3E	MVI A,10	; data with a 1 in D4 bit and 0
2001	10		; in rest of the bits is placed
			; in the accumulator
2002	D3	OUT 80	; data is latched to the output
2003	80		; port 80H

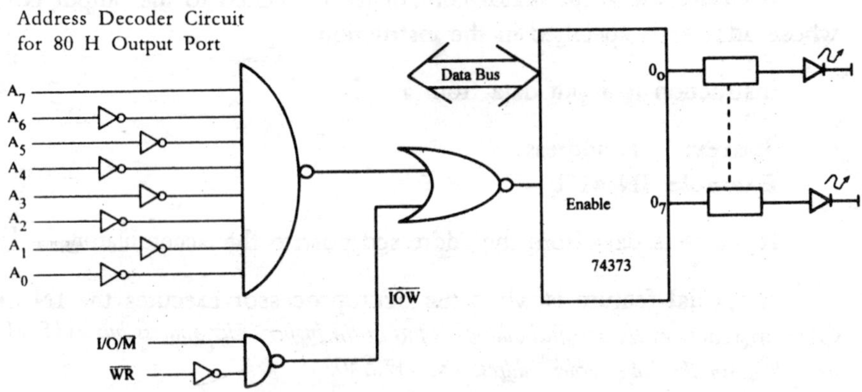

Fig. 6.2 Interfacing circuit for 8 bit output port.

CIRCUIT DESCRIPTION

Fig. 6.3 shows the timing diagram of the OUT instruction.

- **When the OUT instruction is executed, the CPU places the 8 bit address 1000 0000 (80H) on the higher order address bus A15-A8 and the lower order address lines A7-A0**
- **The address lines A6 to A0 are connected to the inputs of the 8 input NAND gate after inversion through the NOT gates. The A7 bit is directly connected to one of the inputs of the NAND gate. Thus when the address is 80H all the inputs to the NAND gate are 1 and so it gives an output of 0. For all other address inputs the NAND gate output is 1. Therefore the NAND-NOT gate combination decodes the address 80H.**
- The IO/$\overline{M}$ signal and $\overline{WR}$ signals from the CPU are gated to produce $\overline{IOW}$ (write on the I/O port) signal.
- The address decoder output and $\overline{IOW}$ signal are gated further to produce the positive going enable pulse.
- The CPU after placing the address on the address bus, puts the accumulator content on the data bus.
- The address decoder output enables the latch to capture the data bus content. The output of the latch drives the LEDs.

- Thus a simple output port at address 80H can be realised using this circuit.

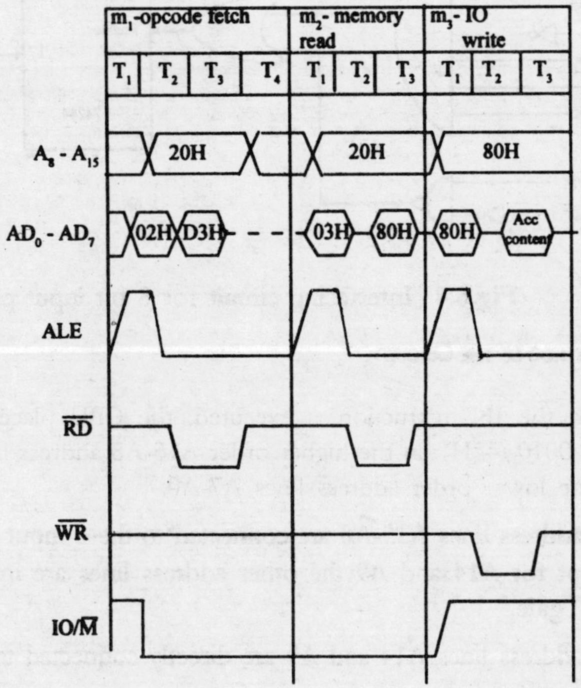

Fig. 6.3 Timing diagram of the OUT instruction.

An Input Port Implementation

The circuit in Fig.6.4 shows an array of 8 switches connected to an interface circuit. The interface circuit shown forms an input port. The array of switches can be used to input an 8 bit word to the CPU. The address of the port may be assumed to be 42H. The following sequence of instructions implement the data reading from the port

Memory Location	Opcode	Mnemonics	Comments
2050	DB	IN 42	; reads the data from the port
2051	42		; at address 42H and sends the
			; data to the accumulator.

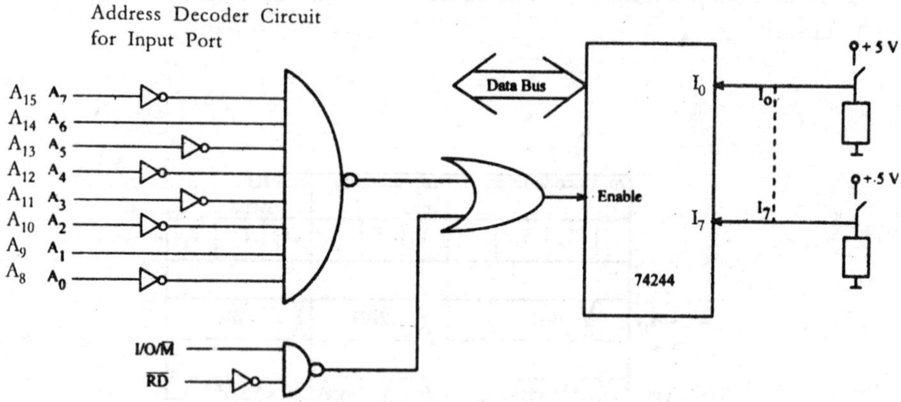

Fig.6.4 Interfacing circuit for 8 bit input port

WORKING METHOD OF THE CIRCUIT

- When the IN instruction is executed, the CPU places the address 0100 0010 (42H) on the higher order A15-A8 address lines as well as on the lower order address lines A7-A0.
- **The address lines A15-A8 are connected to the 8 input NAND gate. Except for A14 and A9 the other address lines are inverted at the NOT gate.**
- **The address lines A14 and A9 are directly connected to the NAND gate inputs.**
- **When the address is 42H all the inputs to the NAND gate are 1 and so it gives an output of 0. For all other address values the output is 1. Thus the NAND-NOT gate combination decodes the address 42H.**
- The IO/$\overline{M}$ signal and $\overline{RD}$ signals from the CPU are gated to produce $\overline{IOR}$ (read the I/O port) signal.
- The $\overline{IOR}$ and NAND gate output are combined to produce the positive going enable pulse.
- **This signal enables the tristate buffer, which connects the switch status at that instant to the data bus.**
- **The data bus content is read and placed in the accumulator.**
- **Thus a simple input port at address 42H can be realised using this circuit.**

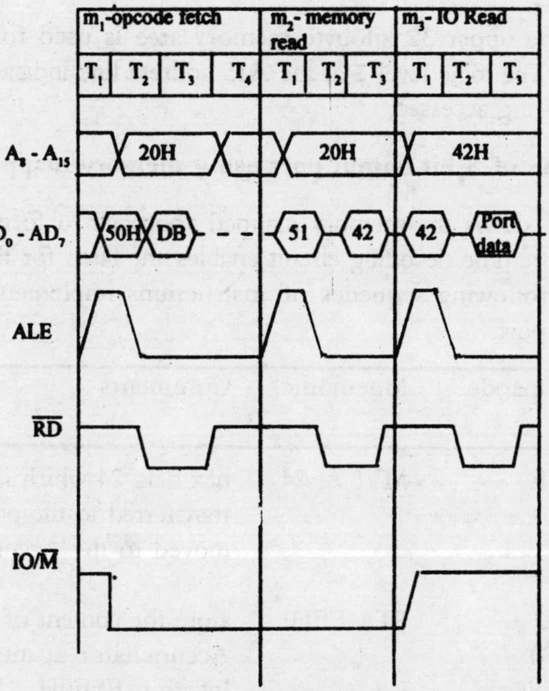

Fig. 6.5 Timing diagram for IN instruction

6.4 MEMORY MAPPED I/O METHOD

In memory mapped I/O, the microprocessor treats an I/O device *as if it is a memory location,* and therefore it is identified with a 16 bit address. Data trasnfer is implemented by using *memory related instructions such as MOV, STA and LDA.*

With memory mapped I/O the available memory of the microprocessor based system is partitioned into two areas. One area is allocated for the system memory (RAM and ROM). Other area is reserved for I/O devices. A *typical* memory map showing this approach is shown in fig. 6.6.

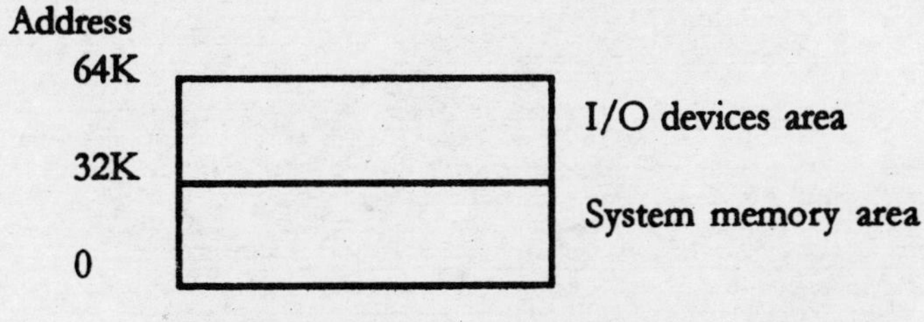

Fig.6.6 Memory mapped input / output.

Usually, the upper 32 kilobyte memory area is used for the I/O device address. The logic level 1 at the A15 address line indicates that an I/O device is being accessed.

Implementation of 8 bit output port using memory mapped I/O

Figure 6.7 shows the memory mapped approach to form an 8 bit LED output port. The decoding circuit enables the latch for the address FFF0H. The following sequence of instructions implement the data transfer to the port.

Memory Location	Opcode	Mnemonics	Comments
2000	3E	MVI A, 24	hex data 24 which is to be
2001	24		transferred to the port is moved to the Accumulator
2002	32	STA FFF0	store the content of the
2003	F0		Accumulator at memory
2004	FF		location FFF0H

WORKING OF THE CIRCUIT

- The address decoding circuit for the address FFF0H and the IO/$\overline{M}$ and $\overline{WR}$ signals are used to enable the latch of the output port. The rest of the operation is similar to storing the content of the accumulator in the memory location FFF0H.

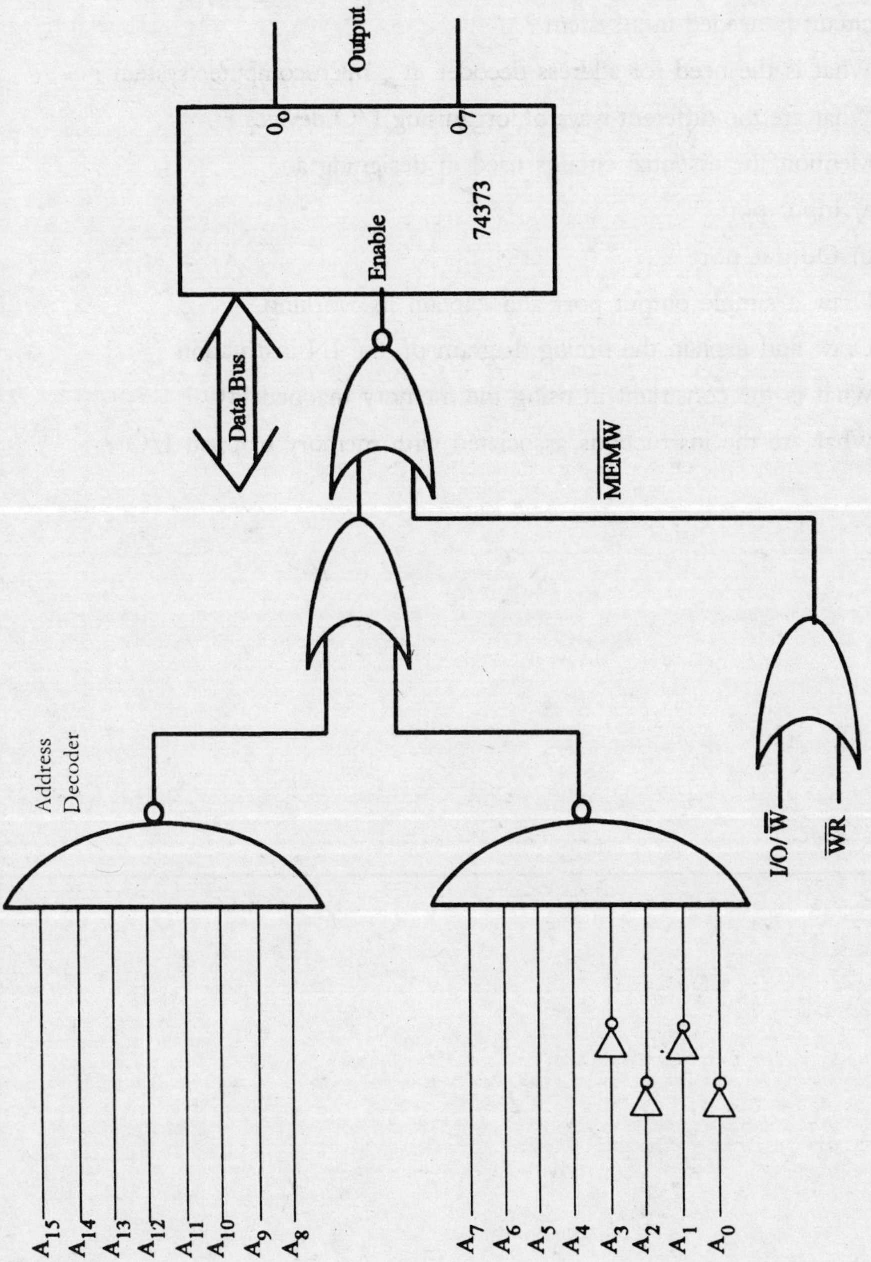

Fig. 6.7 Interfacing circuit for output port using memory mapped I/O technique.

EXERCISE - 6

1. What do you understand by the term interface ? Why interface circuit is needed in a system ?
2. What is the need for address decoder in a microcomputer system ?
3. What are the different ways of organising I/O devices ?
4. Mention the essential circuits used in designing an

   a) Input port

   b) Output port
5. Draw a simple output port and explain its working.
6. Draw and explain the timing diagram of the IN instruction
7. What is the constraint in using the memory mapped I/O ?
8. What are the instructions associated with memory mapped I/O ?

CHAPTER 7

INTERRUPTS

7.1 THE INTERRUPT CONCEPT

The CPU in a microcomputer system may be in the process of executing a program. Meanwhile there could be many requirements in the microcomputer to stop the execution of current program and execute another brief program and resume the current program afterwards. For example a peripheral may be ready with data and wants the CPU to read its data. The CPU meets such requirements through a process called *Interrupt.*

Imagine that a teacher is delivering a lecture in a class room. In the middle, one of the students may want to raise a question. That is the interrupt to the delivering of the lecture. The teacher stops the lecture and answers the student's question. Afterwords he resumes his lecture. Answering the question is analogous to executing an Interrupt program.

For the purpose of Interrupt, the 8085 CPU offers 5 hardware interrupt inputs on the CPU chip itself. Besides it also offers 8 interrupt instructions in the instruction set. Thus the CPU can respond to events occuring at the hardware as well as at the software level. The CPU on receipt of any one of these interrupts, leaves its current instruction sequence and enters a new sequence relevant for the interrupt. After completing the new sequence it resumes the earlier sequence. In otherwords the CPU upon receipt of the interrupt, services the interrupt by executing the relevant set of instructions stored at a *predetermined* memory *block area.* Therefore that set of instructions is known as the Interrupt Service Routine (ISR). Each interrupt can be made to do a specific task by writing a suitable service routine.

The Fig.7.1 shows the way in which the interrupt is executed.

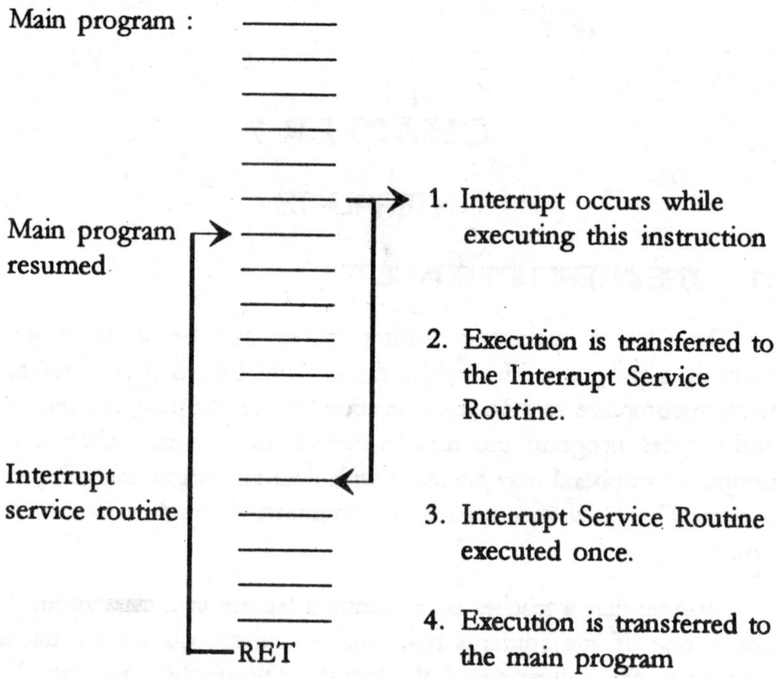

Fig. 7.1 Interrupt execution

7.2 ACCESSING AN INTERRUPT SERVICE ROUTINE

7.2.1 Interrupt Vector Table

It is not possible to give each Interrupt Service Routine (ISR) a fixed slot in the memory, since the different routines may be of different size. The user has the freedom to store within memory the different ISRs at suitable locations. In such a case the access to the right routine is managed in the following way.

When an interrupt occurs the control does not go to the ISR directly. Instead a CALL instruction to a predetermined location on the 00 page of the memory is executed. 256 bytes of memory is called a page. At that particular location a JMP instruction to the relevant ISR is stored and so the control then goes to that ISR. This predetermined location is a part of table called the Interrupt Vector Table, which contains the JMP instructions for every ISR of the system.

7.2.2 Software Interrupt

The syntax for the interrupt instruction is

RST n

where n ranges from 0 to 7.

Example RST 1
RST 5

These are single byte instructions and the hex code with the address in the Vector Interrupt Table for these instructions are listed below in the table. Table 7.1 List of vector address for RSTn interrupts :

Table 7.1

Instruction Op-code	*Hex code in Hex*	*Vector address*
RST0	C7	0000
RST1	CF	0008
RST2	D7	0010
RST3	DF	0018
RST4	E7	0020
RST5	EF	0028
RST6	F7	0030
RST7	FF	0038

Action

When any of these instructions are executed a CALL to the specified address is executed. That is the contents of the program counter (address of the instruction next to the RST instruction) is saved in the stack memory. Then the control goes to the address specified in the table. Note that the vector addresses of the instructions are spaced 8 bytes apart. Thefore 8 bytes of instructions can be stored begining at any vector address. Usually a 3 byte JMP instruction to the corresponding ISR is stored here so that the control is transferred to the desired ISR.

7.2.3 Hardware Interrupt

The 8085 CPU has 5 hardware interrupts as given below

Interrupt	Vector address in Hex
TRAP (RST4.5)	0024
RST 5.5	002C
RST 6.5	0034
RST 7.5	003C
INTR	—

The space between RST 5 (software interrupt) and RST 5.5 (hardware interrupt) is only 4 bytes which is adequate to wite 3 byte JHP instruction.

The predetermined addresses of the hardware interrupts are in the first page of the memory area. The initial portion of the memory is occupied by the monitor program in EPROM (say 0000 to 0FFFH, which is 4K). Note that the vector addresses of the hardware interrupts are spaced only 8 bytes apart (for example the space between RST5.5 & RST 6.5). Normally a three byte jump instruction is written in this space. The jump address may point to either another portion of EPROM or RAM from which the corresponding interrupt service routine starts or another jump address table to make the system flexible since the first page is in EPROM, which content cannot be changed.

The first 4 hardware interrupt signals are directly vectored to the address specified in the Interrupt vector table. They are also called *vector interrupts.* However the Interrupt request, INTR is handled in a slightly different way. When INTR interrupt is activated, the CPU produces an Interrupt Acknowledgement INTA (active LOW) signal.

INTR INTERRRUPT

When INTR signal is made high, the CPU produces $\overline{\text{INTA}}$ signal. The CPU expects the opcode of the next instruction in the *data bus.* The INTA signal is used to enable a buffer which is set to input to the databus, the opcode of any one of the software RST interrupts, which is a single byte instruction. The CPU reads it and executes the ISR of that RST interrupt.

Another way of using INTR interrupt :

When INTR is actuated,the CPU produces $\overline{\text{INTA}}$ signal. It is used to enable a complex circuit to place the code for CALL instruction (CD) in the data bus. The CPU reads it and understands. It sends another $\overline{\text{INTA}}$ signal. This signal is used to place the lower order eight bit address of the CALL instruction in the data bus. After reading the lower order address,the CPU sends another $\overline{\text{INTA}}$ signal. It is used to place the higher order eight bit address in the data bus. The CPU reads and executes the interrrupt service routine available in that call address. In this way, by sending CALL address instruction through the data bus INTR interrupt can be handled.

The RST hardware interrupts can be classified as maskable and nonmaskable interrupts. Except TRAP, the others are maskable interrupts. The maskable interrupts may be enabled and disabled by software instructions. When they are disabled the CPU ignores them when they occur.

When a hardware interrupt is actuated, *it is sensed only after completing the present instruction cycle.* If more than one interrupt are actuated at the same time, they are serviced on *priority* basis. TRAP has the highest priority. It is always serviced first then RST 7.5, then RST 6.5 and finally RST 5.5. At the end of every instruction cycle, internally, the interrupt lines are scanned in priority.

7.2.4 Summary of Interrupt service sequence

1. A hardware interrupt occurs or a RST n instruction is encountered in the program.
2. CPU completes the execution of the current instruction and scans the interrupt lines. If there is any interrupt,
3. The contents of program counter is stored in the stack memory
4. The CPU sends out an $\overline{\text{INTA}}$ signal (for hardware interrupt only) CPU branches to the vector table location.
6. Executes a JMP to the specified ISR
7. Carries out the ISR
8. When RET instruction is encountered, the CPU loads the return address from the stack into the program counter and returns to the main program.

7.3 WORKING OF THE INTERRUPT CONTROL CIRCUIT

7.3.1 Trap

Trap being non-maskable, it is used to handle very important functions. In general it is used to take care of sudden power failures. It may execute a routine to transfer the contents of the main memory to the back up memory (if any). It is *edge and level sensitive* which means the input has to go HIGH and stay HIGH to be recognised. Refering Fig. 7.2 the rising edge triggers the D flip-flop. The D flip-flop and the AND output together triggers the TRAP interrupt.

Once TRAP is recognised, further inputs at TRAP will not be considered unless the interrupt is cleared. The TRAP is cleared by either

- The RESET (active low) signal or
- Internal TRAP acknowledge signal

As soon as it is recognised the internal trap acknowledge signal will reset the D flipflop.

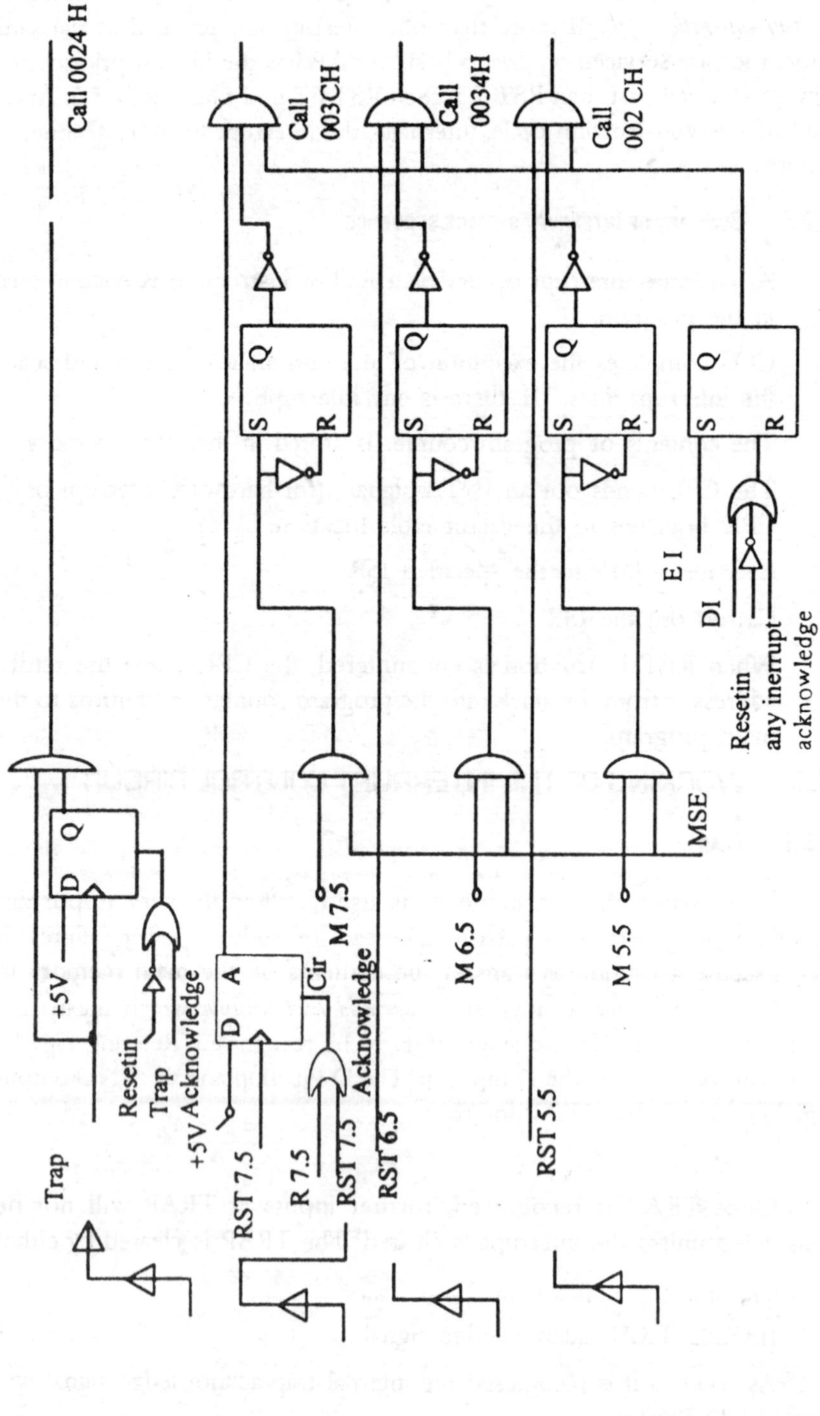

Fig. 7.2 Circuit of Interrupt control block of 8085

7.3.2 RST 7.5 AND OTHER VECTOR INTERRUPTS

The RST 7.5 is *edge sensitive.* In the fig. 7.1 the D flip-flop is actuated by the rising edge and its output becomes ONE level and triggers the RST7.5 interrupt. The RST7.5 interrupt is cleared by internal RST7.5 interrupt acknowledge signal or R7.5 bit in mask register.

The RST6.5 and RST5.5 are level sensitive interrupt inputs.

7.3.3 ADDITIONAL INSTRUCTIONS RELATED TO INTERRUPT

The 8085 has the following additional instructions related to the interrupt.

Enable Interrupt (EI) and Disable Interrupt (DI) instructions:

These instructions enable or disable all the interrupts execept the TRAP. The EI and DI instructions produce internally the EI and DI signals. Refer fig. 7.2. The EI signal sets the SR flip-flop and produces an Interrupt Enable (IE) signal which enables the AND gates at the RST7.5, RST6.5 & RST5.5 inputs. The DI signal resets the SR flip-flop and makes the IE output LOW and all the maskable interrupts are disabled.

Further Resetin (active low) or any Interrupt Acknowledge signal also disables all the maskable interrupts.

The mask bits M7.5, M6.5 and M5.5 for the interrupts are set using the SIM instruction.

Need for EI & DI Instructions

Once the CPU recognises any of the interrupts, it immediately *disables all interrupts* (except, of course TRAP). This is done just to ensure that the CPU is not further interrupted while it is executing the current ISR. Once the current ISR is completed the program is required to enable the interrupts back. The EI (Enable Interrupt) instruction is therefore introduced just before the last instruction (RET instruction) of the ISR. However if the EI instruction is placed at the begining itself, the interrupts are enabled all through the ISR execution. This is done if it is desired to allow further interrupts during the current ISR execution.

The programmer may want certain portions of the main program to be executed without being stopped by interrupt signals. He can disable the interrupts by placing the DI instruction and later enable them by placing EI as shown in Fig.7.3 .

```
Program:    ________
            ________
            ________
            DI          Disable the interrupts
            ________  |
            ________  | Instructions are
            ________  | executed independent of any
            ________  | Interrupt
            ________  |
            EI          Enable the interrupts
            ________  |
            ________  | Program continues.
            ________  |
```

Fig.7.3 Use of EI and DI.

7.4 SET INTERRUPT MASK (SIM) INSTRUCTION

Often it is required to selectively enable a few interrupts and disbale others. This selective enabling is done through, the Set Interrupt Mask instruction.

The accumulator (A register) is first loaded with the required mask bits. The SIM instruction reads the accumulator content and enables or disables the interrupts.

The meaning of different mask bits are as shown in table 7.3.

Table 7.3

D7	D6	D5	D4	D3	D2	D1	D0
SOD	SDE	XXX	R7.5	MSE	M7.5	M6.5	M5.5

D3 bit (Mask Set Enable)

- When LOW, the bits D2 to D0 are ignored
- When HIGH, the bits D2 to D0 are valid.

This MSE signal enables the masked interrupts (see fig. 7.2)

D2 to D0 bits

- A LOW level *enables* the corresponding interrupt.
- A HIGH level *masks* the corresponding interrupt.

D4 bit

- When HIGH, RST7.5 flip-flop in Fig.7.2 is reset, in order to override RST 7.5, without servicing it.

D6 and D7 bits

- Used for serial transfer of data through the SOD pin.

The correct sequence of using these instructions is, the SIM instruction is executed first to set the masking scheme. The EI is introduced at desired points later, to further enable those unmasked interrupts set by the SIM instruction.

Example

```
MVI A,08     ; Load bit pattern to enable 7.5, 6.5 & 5.5
SIM          ; Set the mask scheme.
EI           ; Enable the interrupts.
```

7.5 READ INTERRUPT MASK INSTRUCTION -

This instruction loads the accumulator with the 8 bits shown in table 7.4, giving the *status* of the interrupt mask, the interrupt enable, the pending interrupts and one bit of serial input data. The meaning of different bits are as follows

Table 7.4 Bits representing the status in RIM instruction

D7	D6	D5	D4	D3	D2	D1	D0
SID	I7.5	I6.5	I5.5	IE	M7.5	M6.5	M5.5

D2, D1 & D0 bit

- Represents masking of 7.5, 6.5 & 5.5 interrupts
- A HIGH level shows that interrupt is masked
- A LOW level shows that interrupt is not masked.

D3 bit

- Interrupt Enable flag
- A HIGH level shows interupt is enabled
- A LOW level shows that interrupt is disabled.

D6, D5 & D4 bits

- Represents pending interrupts
- A HIGH level shows that interrupt is pending
- A LOW level shows that interrupt is not pending.

SID bit

- Serial input through SID pin.

USE OF RST INSTRUCTIONS: PROGRAM BREAK POINTS

When a complex program is being developed, often it would have *logical errors*. Locating the errors is called *debugging*. A popular debugging method uses many *breakpoints* within a program at different places. A breakpoint in a program is an instruction where the execution is temporarily stopped. Then the programmer examines the contents of different registers. After that, he allows the execution to proceed. The contents of the registers may give him certain idea about the errors. An RST n instruction can be used to implement the breakpoint. Upon execution of RST n instruction the program executes an ISR which shows the contents of different registers.

POLLED I/O METHOD FOR DATA TRANSFER

Polled input / output is another method of accessing the I/O devices. In this method the CPU polls or samples the I/O devices at regular interval for their readiness for data transfer. If they are ready the required operations are carried out. Since the CPU has to probe each I/O device often, most of its time is wasted in this operation. However the programming becomes simpler in this method.

7.6 EXAMPLE OF INTERRUPT HANDLING

Problem Statement

To use accumulator as a counter when the main program is executes and display its content at the Data display field of a trainer, whenever KBINT key is pressed.

Interrupt handling

Normally one of the RST interrupts is connected to the KBINT key of the keyboard in the microprocessor kit. Let us assume that the RST7.5 interrupt is connected to the KBINT key of the kit. Whenever this key is pressed, 7.5 interrupt pin is made active. The Program Counter value is saved in stack area and it is loaded with predetermined address 003CH (vector table address of RST7.5). Normally in the kit the JMP instruction is stored in that location. The jump address will be in user RAM area.

Assuming the monitor program of the trainer has a JMP 8000 stored at 003CH, the RST7.5 interrupt routine can be directly written at 8000.

The main program acts as a serial number generator. The main program implements a loop which increments the accumulator content. The accumulator counts in BCD mode from 00 to 99.

When the KBINT interrupt key is pressed, the RST7.5 interrupt service routine stored at 8000 is executed. The ISR reads the accumulator content and displays it at the data field of the microprocessor kits display. Thereafter the control returns again to the main program.

The microprocessor trainer kit has a built in subroutine which displays a number at the data field of the display. In a particular kit it is assumed that the subroutine is UPDAT and it requires the number for display to be stored at memory location yyyy H.

The above problem explains the concept of triggering by an interrupt and branching to an ISR.

Memory Location	Opcode	Label	Mnemonics	Comments
3002	3E		MVI A,0B	; Mask 5.5 & 6.5 and
3003	0B			; Unmask 7.5 interrupt
3004	30		SIM	
3005	FB		EI	; Enable interrupt
3006	AF		XRA A	; Make Acc content 00
3007	7D	TOP	MOV A,L	
3008	3C		INR A	; Increment accumulator
3009	27		DAA	; Implement BCD addition
300A	6F		MOV L,A	
300B	CD		CALL DELAY	
300C	YY			
300D	YY			
300E	C3		JMP TOP	; Loop back to TOP
300F	07			
3010	30			

The above program is executed continuously till the interrupt key is pressed. When interrupt key is pressed the program given below is executed.

Second part:

Memory Location	Opcode	Label	Mnemonics	Comments
8000	F5		PUSH PSW	; Save PSW in stack
8001	32		STA yyyy	; Store accumulator content
8002	yy			; at yyyy for use by UPDAT
8003	yy			
8004	CD		CALL UPDAT	; Call subroutine meant
8005	xx			; for display in DATA
8006	xx			; FIELD
8007	F1		POP PSW	; Load PSW
8008	FB		EI	;
8009	C9		RET	; Go back to main program

After execution of the program from location 8000, it will display the content in the data field, then it goes back to the main program to increment the counter value continuously.

This process continues till the next keyboard interrupt occurs.

EXERCISE - 7

1. Explain the concept of interrrupt and the interrupt vector table.
2. What are the interrupt facilities available in 8085 ?
3. What do you understand by priority interrupt ?
4. How is the INTR interrupt used in 8085 ?
5. Explain the RST interrupt control circuit of 8085.
6. Explain the need and the use of EI and DI instructions.
7. Explain SIM and RIM instructions.
8. Write down the procedure to mask the RST 6.5 insterrupt.
9. Using a software interrupt, write a main program to call a time delay program as an interrupt service routine.
10. Assume that an interrupt routine is called from a main program and within this interrupt routine another interrupt routine is also called. Write down the content of stack memory while the second interrupt routine is being executed.

CHAPTER 8

MEMORY IN A MICROPROCESSOR BASED SYSTEM

8.1 INTRODUCTION

Memory in a microcomputer stores the program and data. The input/output of data is routed through the memory. At present semiconductor memory devices are widely used in microcomputer and other systems.

The memory can be thought of as a collection of thousands of registers similar to the CPU registers. Microcomputer systems use two types of memory, namely the Read Only Memory (ROM) and Read Write Memory (RWM or RAM). The microcomputer has to store certain fixed program and data which should not be altered. The monitor program of a microprocessor trainer kit, the BIOS program of a personal computer are examples of this type of program. Such programs are stored in Read Only Memory. As the name of the memory suggests such memory devices allow only reading of the content, but not writing in the normal course of operation.

The microcomputer also uses the other type of memory the Read Write Memory whose content can be changed any number of times. As the name suggests this type of memory allows reading as well as writing. User program and data are stored in such a type of memory. Fig.8.1 shows different memory devices available under each category.

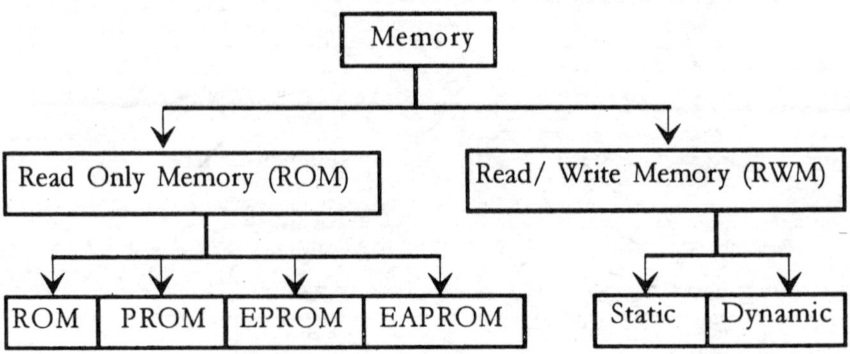

Fig. 8.1 Types of memory

8.2 READ WRITE MEMORY

Read Write Memory is also popularly known as Random Access Memory (RAM), because it takes the same amount of time to access any storage location.

STATIC RANDOM ACCESS MEMORY (SRAM)

The static RAM makes use of flip-flops to store bits of data The flip-flops may be constructed with bipolar transistors or MOS switches. The bipolar devices will have a fast switching speed of 40 nano second. But they occupy a large physical area and therefore offer a low packaging density - around 1024 memory cells per IC chip. A bipolar memory retains its data as long as power is ON.

The Fig.8.2 shows one of the flip-flops used in a static MOS RAM. Q1 and Q2 act like switches. Q3 and Q4 are active loads (acting like resistors). The circuit action is similar to the transistor latch. Either Q1 conducts and Q2 is cut off or vice versa. A static RAM will contain thousands of flip-flops, one for each stored bit. As long as the power is ON, the flipflop remains latched and can store the bit indefinitely.

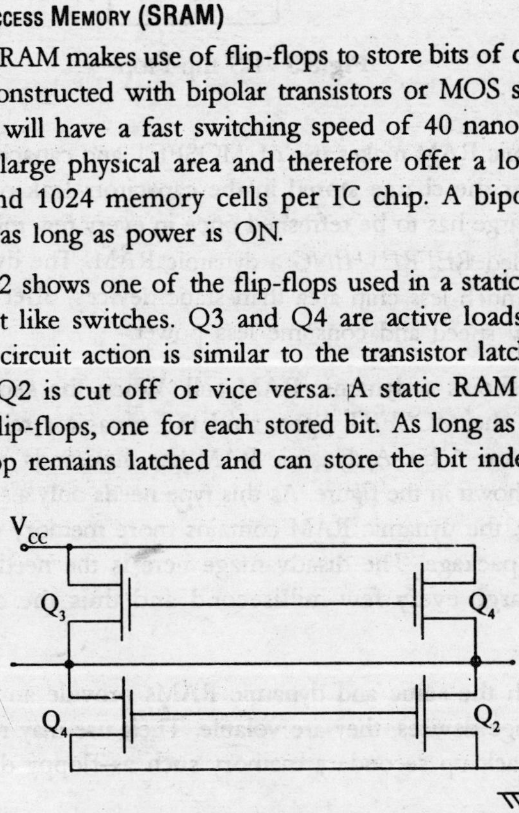

Fig.8.2 Flip-Flop circuit diagram

In Fig.8.3 the NAND gates are coupled back to back. So two stable states are available. When Q is HIGH, it is logic '1' state, and when Q is LOW, it is logic '0'. A momemtary low applied to set input guarantees that Q will be set to 1 and a low on RESET that it will be reset to 0. If no external input is given, the flip-flop will remain in its current state as long as power is applied.

DYNAMIC RANDOM ACCESS MEMORY (DRAM)

Though the static RAM retains its data indefenitely, due to the power consumption and area occupied by the transistors the packaging density is low. Therefore large capacity memory devices can not be made out of static RAM.

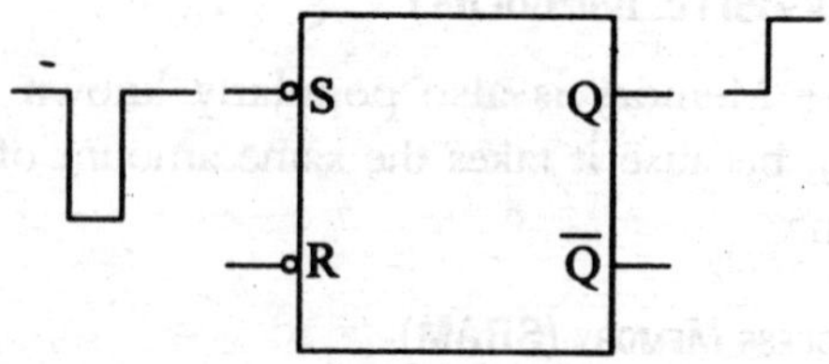

Fig.8.3 RS flip-Flop

A dynamic RAM makes use of MOSFET and capacitors to store the data. However the charge stored in the capacitors leak off gradually, so the stored charge has to be refreshed once in every few milliseconds. This process is called *REFRESHING* a dynamic RAM. The dynamic memory cells occupy much less chip area than static devices, offer high packaging densities, slow speed and consume less power.

Fig.8.4 shows a dynamic RAM cell. When the sense and control lines go low, the MOSFET opens and the capacitor retains its charge. Thus it can store 1 bit. A dynamic RAM has thousands of memory cells like the one shown in the figure. As this type needs only a single MOSFET and capacitor, the dynamic RAM contains more memory cells than static RAM in the package. The disadvantage here is the need to refresh the capacitor charge every few millisecond and thus the design is more complex.

Although the static and dynamic RAMs provide an attractive form of main storage devices, they are volatile. Their use may require auxiliary power or a back up secondary memory such as floppy disk.

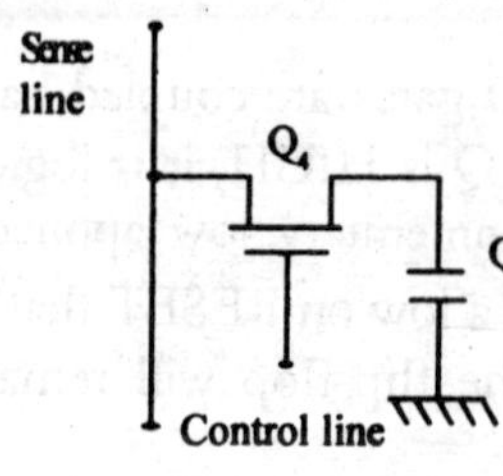

Fig.8.4 Dynamic RAM cell

Table 8.1 compares the parameters of RAM made with different device technologies.

Table 8.1

Technology	Maximum size in bits	Access time in Nanosec	Dynamic or Static
PMOS	4 K	1000	Both
NMOS	16 K	300 to 500	Both
CMOS	1 K	100 to 500	Static
STTL	1 K	50 to 100	Static
ECL	1 K	10 to 50	Static
IIL	4 K	100	Static

ROM Memory

The data is entered into a ROM at the device manufacturing stage itself. Entering data into ROM is called *PROGRAMMING* the device The manufacturer makes a special mask while fabrication and the device is programmed using this mask. Since the mask making is an expensive process, ROM is used only in systems which are mass produced, for example printers, photo copying machines etc. In these systems the ROM usually stores the *FIRMWARE* program. The FIRMWARE is a fixed program which looks after the operation of the system. The storage content of ROM is fixed so that only the read operations are permitted. Once the ROM is produced, its contents can not be changed.

The ROM design is a custom technology, and it is expensive. ROMs are available in both BI-POLAR and MOS technologies. Bi-polar ROMs are extremely fast, some having access time of less than 50 nano sec.

A PROM is a Programmable Read Only Memory that is programmed in the field by the user. The PROM is constructed with tiny silicon oxide or nichrome fuses that are burnt open in a device called a PROM programmer. When a fuse is burnt open, the bit position being programmed is usually set to a logic 0 level. The PROM is a TTL device that contains a small number of high speed memory locations. For this reason, its use has fallen off in recent times except when high speed is an important consideration. Access time for PROM are normally 25 nano sec. Once a PROM is programmed its content *can not be changed.*

The EPROM is an Erasable Programmable Read Only Memory that can be programmed as well as erased at the site. As with the PROM, the EPROM is programmed in a device called an EPROM programmer. The EPROM programmer applies a 25 or 12 Volt pulse to the memory location being programmed and traps charges in a special MOSFET transistor. All memory cells must be programmed sequentially. This trapped charge remains there until it is erased by ultra violet light (UV light) or until it bleeds off through the insulator. By exposing UV light source for a period of approximately 30 minutes the entire content is erased. There is no possibility of erasing a single cell or a part of the EPROM. The manufacturers of this device claim that it will retain a charge for over 20 years.

The EEPROM is an Electrically Erasable Programmable Read Only Memory. It is a device that is programmed and erased in the system. No special programmer kit is needed for this type of ROM. Cost and reliability seem to be at the present very high. It lasts for 10,000 programmings and costs considerably more than an EPROM.

The EAPROM is an Erasable Alterable Programmable ROM. Here it is possible to alter some of the cell contents in the memory. However this needs a special circuitry and care. So this type is costlier than the other types.

Table 8.2 compares read only memory devices made with different device technologies.

Technology	Maximum size in bits	Typical access time.
PMOS	64 K	800 ns to 1.5 microsec
NMOS	64 K	100 ns to 1 microsec
CMOS	12 K	100 to 500 nanosec
STTL	16 K	50 to 100 nanosec

Memory Device Internal Configurations

One of the parameters of a memory device would be the total number of bits that can be stored in it. This capacity will be equal to 2 raised to some integer value. The capacity would be say 1024, 2048, 4096 etc. However, usually the memory devices are described not by this exact value of bits, but by the nearest multiple of 1024. Thus 1024 and 4096 bit devices are known as 1K and 4K devices respectively.

Another important parameter of the memory device would be the number of bits per location. The usual values are 1, 4 and 8. Thus a 1K memory device could be internally organised as 1K locations of 1 bit each or 256 locations of 4 bit each. The 1K memory device was popular with the 8 bit microprocessor systems. Presently with availability of higher density systems 4K and 16K units are widely used. Memory devices can be connected in parallel to realise larger bits per location. For example to realise a device with 8 bits per location 2 devices of 4 bits per location can be connected in parallel. A typical scheme to realise *256 by 8 bit* memory system is shown in Fig.8.5. The 8 address lines needed are connected to both devices in parallel. The chip enable signal enables both the chips.

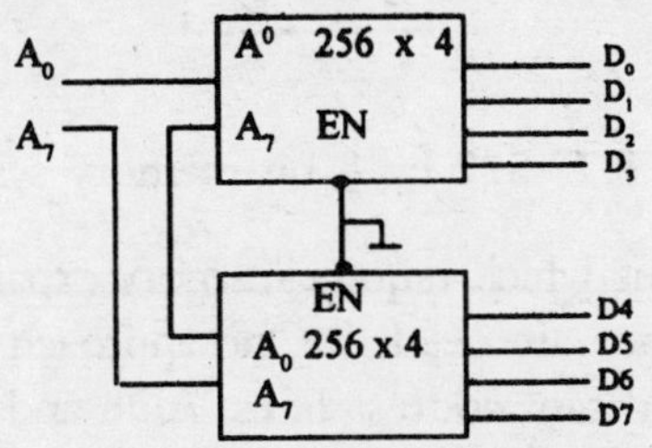

Fig. 8.5 256 by 8 bit memory system.

The same scheme with a minor change can be converted into a *512 by 4 bit* memory system as shown in Fig.8.6. To access 512 locations 9 address lines are required. However since a 256 location memory device has provision for only 8 address lines, the nineth address line is used as the chip enable (CE) signal of the memory device. As shown in the Fig.8.7 the zero level in the nineth address line A8, enables one memory device and whereas one lvel enables the other memory device.

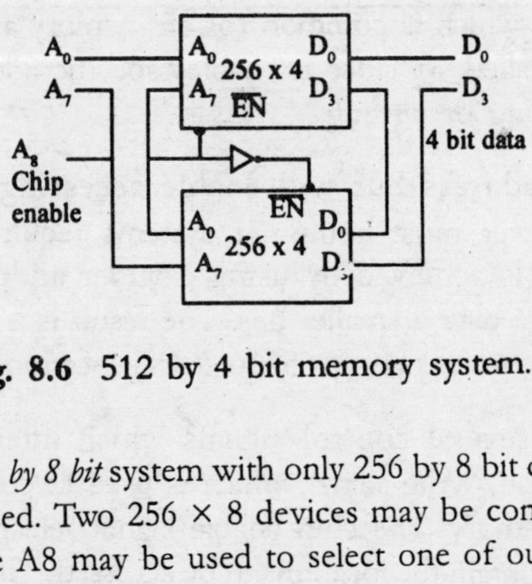

Fig. 8.6 512 by 4 bit memory system.

To realise a *512 by 8 bit* system with only 256 by 8 bit devices, the above approach may be used. Two 256 × 8 devices may be connected in parallel and the address line A8 may be used to select one of out of 2, as shown in Fig. 8.7.

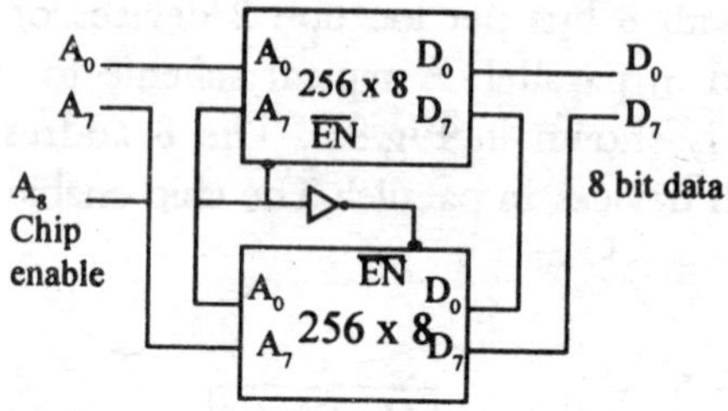

Fig. 8.7 512 by 8 bit memory system.

For larger systems which require memory expansion, such as 1K x 8 system, 10 address lines are needed. One approach is to utilize decoders on the two most significant address lines, AD8 and AD9. Since there are four possible states (with two inputs) each output of the decoder will be used with a 256 x 8 memory configuration.

Memory Addressing

Every location in memory is uniquely specified by a serial number called *address*. To select a location the CPU has to send the location address in binary form to the memory device. This action is commonly known as addressing the memory. The first location usually has the address 0000 and the following locations are sequentially numbered. The 66th location will have the address 65 which has the binary code of 0100 0001 (41H). The CPU sends these binary digits through a set of lines called the address bus, which is common for all memory and I/O devices. The address bus is called so, since it enables specific address locations to be chosen for reading or writing.

An 8 bit address bus will enable accessing only 256 memory locations. However most computer systems require a large addressing capability. This is achieved by using a wider address bus rather than transmitting twice over a smaller bus. The result is a standard 16 bit wide address bus which will permit 65536 (64K) locations to be accessed.

There are several control signals which interface with memory, including the Read/Write signal, which is used to control the operational mode of the memory. The chip enable signal selects those chips in the memory which contain the locations to be accessed. The schematic in Fig.8.8 illustrates the memory interface.

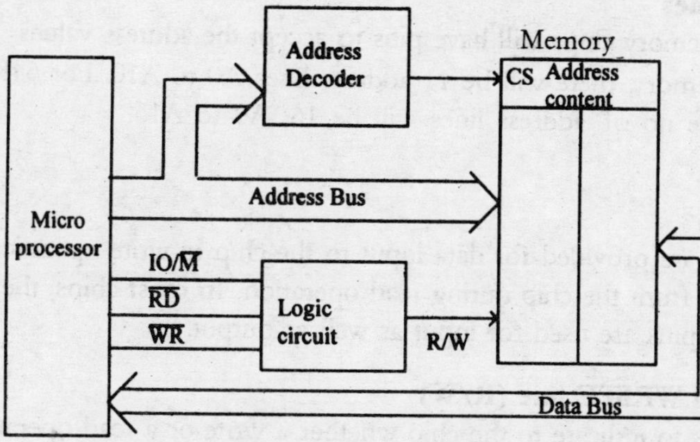

Fig. 8.8 Memory interface with Microprocessor.

To communicate with memory, the microprocessor should be able to

- Select the chip
- Identify the location
- Read from or Write into that location

Presently a variety of memory chips are available to meet any design requirements of a microprocessor based system. In general, the memory chip will have the signal lines shown in Fig.8.9.

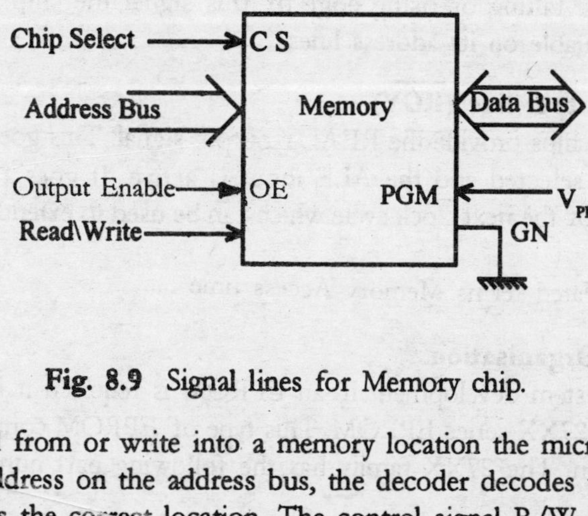

Fig. 8.9 Signal lines for Memory chip.

To read from or write into a memory location the microprocessor places the address on the address bus, the decoder decodes the address and identifies the correct location. The control signal R/W enables the I/O lines and the data byte is either read from or stored into the memory location.

Address Lines

The memory chips will have pins to accept the address values For a 2K byte memory, there will be 11 address lines A0 to A10. For 64K byte memory, the no of address lines will be 16, A0 to A15.

Data Lines

These are provided for data input to the chip in write operation and data output from the chip during read operation. In most chips, the same set of data pins are used for input as well as output.

READ and WRITE line (R/W)

This is to indicate to the chip whether a write or a read operation is performed. In some chips, there is only one input to indicate the operation. It will be HIGH for read operation and LOW for write operation.

Chip Enable / Select line (CS)

Before any operation can be performed on the chip, the chip must be enabled (selected) by activating this input line.

Output Enable line (OE)

The data bus is common for all memory devices. Therefore the data output of a device normally remains tristated. The output enable signal is used to connect the output with the data bus.

Address Latch Line (ALE)

On the falling or rising edge of this signal the chip reads in the address available on its address lines.

READY output line ($\overline{\text{RDY}}$)

Some chips provide the READY output signal. This goes LOW after the chip is selected and the ALE input is active. It goes HIGH at the rising edge of the next clock cycle which can be used to extend the machine cycle.

Memory related terms Memory Access time .....

EPROM Organisation

For system development if an EPROM is required it is most often one of the 27XX series EPROM. This type of EPROM contains 8 bits in one location. The 27XX family has the following part numbers :

2716	2048 locations, 8 bits	24 pin
2732	4096 locations, 8 bits	24 pin
2764	8192 locations, 8 bits	28 pin

27128	16 K locations, 8 bits	28 pin
27256	32 K locations, 8 bits	28 pin
27512	64 K locations, 8 bits	32 pin

In the 27XX family, the 2716 and 2732 ICs are almost obsolete, hence details of 2764 is discussed here.

In the 27xxx series, the capacity of the memory IC can be calculated by dividing the number xxx by 8.

For example, in memory IC 2764, the capacity is calculated as

64 / 8 = 8K

Suffix to the IC number denotes the requirement of different programming voltages. For example

2764 requires 21 volts and
2764A requires only 12 volt.

2764 EPROM details

- HMOS technology, TTL compatible
- 200 nanosecond access time
- Two line control
- Pin compatible with 27128 EPROM
- Low active current; 100 milliamps
- Compatible with high speed microprocessor IAPX186
- Compatible with microcontroller 8051 family

Important feature of this IC is the separate Output Enable (OE) and Chip Enable control (CE). It has a standby mode which reduces power consumption without increasing access time. The maximum active current is 100 mA while the maximum standby current is only 40 mA. The standby mode is selected by applying a TTL high signal to the CE input. This EPROM allows the microprocessor to operate wihtout the addition of WAIT states. It can work with temperature between -10 to + 80 deg. Centrigrade

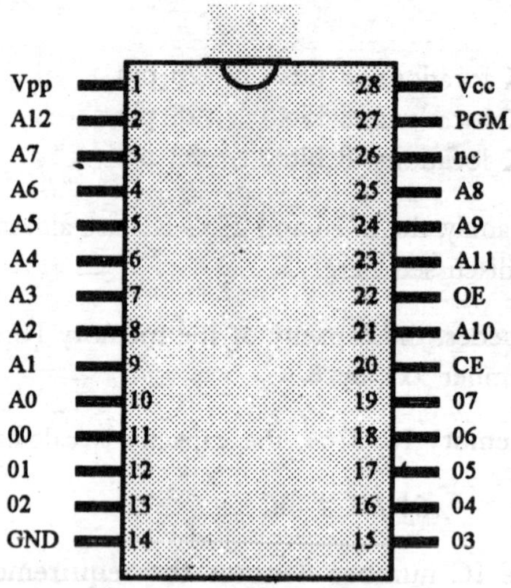

Fig. 8.10 Pin Details of 2764

PIN names

- A0 to A12 address lines
- O0 to O7 output lines
- $\overline{OE}$ Output Enable (active LOW)
- $\overline{CE}$ Chip Enable (active LOW)
- $\overline{PGM}$ program
- nc Not Connected
- Vcc = + 5 volt
- Vpp = +21 volts during programming
- Vpp = +5 volt during read mode
- PGM, CE and OE must be active LOW

Read Mode

The 2764 has two control functions, both of which must be logically active in order to obtain data at the outputs. Chip Enable (CE,active LOW) is the power control and should be used for device selection. Output Enable (OE,active LOW) is the output control and should be used to gate data from the output pins.

Programming Mode

Data is written by selectively programming 0s into the desired location. Even though only 0s will be programmed, both 1s and 0s can be present in the data word. The only way to change 0 to 1 is by keeping the device under ultra violet light.

This IC can be programmed only when Vpp input is at 21 volt or 12 V depending upon the IC and CE & PGM are both at TTL low. The data to be programmed is applied 8 bits in parallel to the data output pins. The levels required for the address and data inputs are TTL. Exceeding 22 volts on Vpp will permanently damage the 2764 IC.

Details of Static RAM 6264

The 6264, CMOS static RAM is a memory device with an internal organisation of 8192 × 8 bits. It has 13 address lines and 4 control inputs the 8 data lines are used for both input and output. These four control inputs include a pair of complementary chip enable inputs, an active low write enable input and an active low output enable input. It is an 28 pin Dual in Line package.

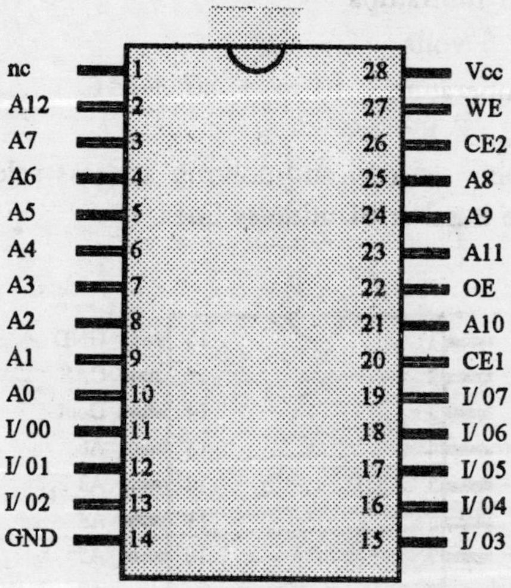

Fig. 8.11 PIN details of 6264

PIN names

- A0 to A12 address lines
- I/00 to I/07 input/output lines
- $\overline{OE}$ Output Enable (active LOW)
- $\overline{CE1}$ Chip Enable (active LOW)
- CE2 Chip Enable (active HIGH)
- nc Not Connected
- Vcc = + 5 volt
- $\overline{WE}$ Write Enable (active LOW)
- GND Ground

Data Retention	2.0 to 5.5 volts
Read time	Read cycle 120 to 150 nanosecond Address Access 120 to 150 nanosecond
Write time	Write cycle 120 to 150 nanosecond Write enable width 80 to 100 nanosecond

Details of Dynamic RAM 2164

- 64 K, 1 bit RAM
- HMOS technology
- TTL compatible
- Industry standard
- Access time < 200 nanosec
- Current < 50 milliamps
- Power supply 5 volts
- Operating temperature – 10 to + 80 deg. C

RAS and CAS pins are row and column address select lines. They are used to reduce the number of address lines.

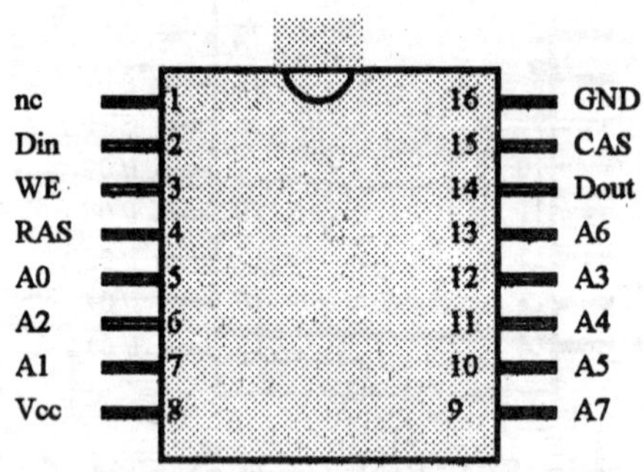

Fig. 8.12 Pin details of 2164

Details of EEPROM 2816

- 2 K, 8 bit PROM
- HMOS technology
- JEDEC standard
- Access time < 450 nanosecond
- Erase time < 10 millisecond
- Power supply +5 volt
- Operating temperature 0 to + 70 deg. C

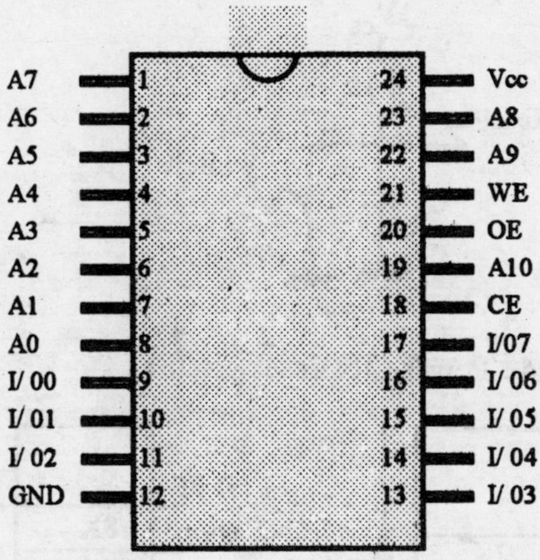

Fig. 8.13 Pin details of 2816

MEMORY MAP AND MEMORY USAGE IN A 8085 MICROPROCESSOR SYSTEM

The addressing capability of 8085 CPU is 64K. A portion of this 64K memory space will be used by EPROM, and the rest by RAM. A figure showing the utilisation of the memory area by different memory ICs is called the memory map of the system.

Fig:8.15a shows a memory map inwhich 2K EPROM and 2K static RAM are used. The address of EPROM is between 0000H and 07FFH. The 2K RAM address is from 8800H to 8FFFH. The remaining area is vacant and it can be used.

Fig.8.15b shows a memory map consisting of 8K EPROM and 8K RAM. In this example 8K EPROM occupies the addresses 0000H-1FFFH and the 8K RAM occupies the addresses 8000H-9FFFH.

A typical example of 8085 based microcomputer system would be the microprocessor trainer kit. As soon as the kit is switched ON, or reset, certain house keeping activities like displaying the *SIGN ON MESSAGE* and recognising keypress have to be done. The routines doing these house keeping job have to be invoked. These routines are available in EPROM. A set of such routines is called *Monitor program.* When the processor is reset, the program counter is initialised to 0000H. Hence, the EPROM is placed at 0000H address. It is to be noted that, without monitor program the microprocessor based *system will not work.*

Power on Reset Circuit

When the power is switched on, through this circuit, (active low). Reset in signal is given to microprocessor. Initially, the capacitor is at 0V level. Through R, it charges. It takes a little time. Till, then, the Reset in signal will be low. Thus, at the time of switching on, Reset of the microprocessor is ensured.

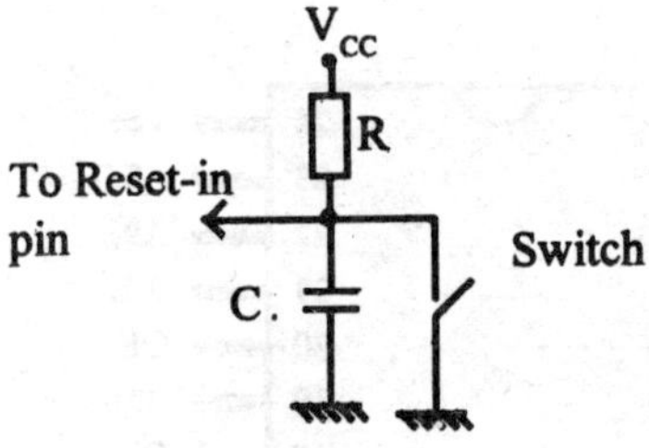

Fig.8.14 Power-ON reset circuit

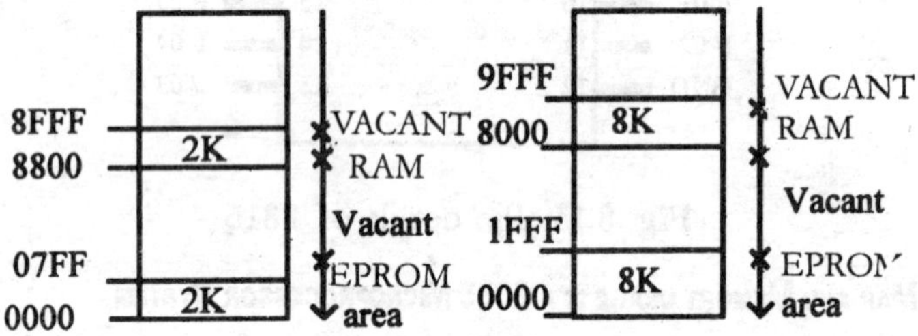

Fig. 8.15 (a) and **8.15** (b)

SEPARATING ADDRESS AND DATA BUS IN 8085 SYSTEM

The 8085 is having multiplexed lower order address and data bus (AD0-AD7). During each machine cycle at the first clock state, the program counter releases the address in AD0-AD7 (lower order address) and in A8-A15 (higher order address). Simultaneously it rises the ALE signal to indicate that the information available in AD0-AD7 is lower order address, and not data. So it is the responsibility of the external circuit to latch the address at this instance from AD0-AD7. This idea is shown in Fig.8.16. Thus the address bus A0-A7 and the data bus D0-D7 are separated.

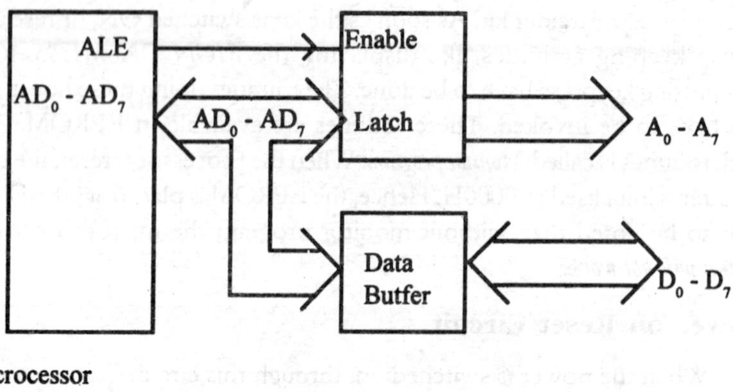

Fig. 8.16 Circuit for separation of lower address lines

Memory Address Decoding

Assume that the microprocessor based system use one number of 8K EPROM and one number of 8K RAM. Each of the devices require the address lines A0 to A12. These address lines are connected to both the memory ICs. But at any time only one device is to be selected for reading or writing. This is achieved by properly enabling chip select pin (CS, normally active LOW) of the particular IC. The circuit involved in enabling the *chip select* is called *memory address decoder.*

In Fig.8.15b, the EPROM occupies the address 0000H-1FFFH and RAM occupies the address 8000H-9FFFH. For accessing these memory locations the address lines are needed are A0-A12. The remaining address lines of the processor namely A13, A14 and A15 are to be used in the memory address decoder circuit. In this case a simple 3 to 8 decoder circuit (IC74138) can be used as shown in the Fig.8.17.

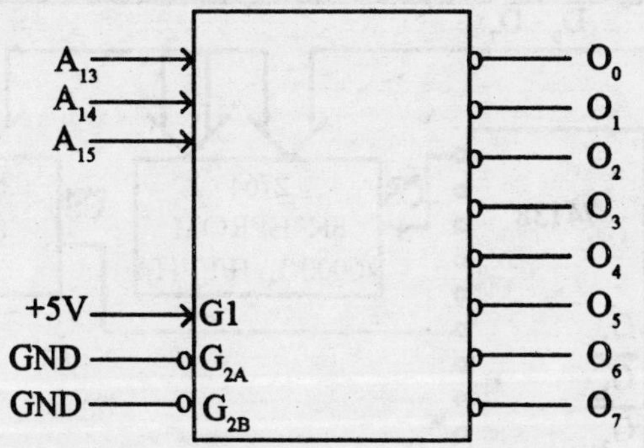

Fig.8.17 Memory address Decoder — 3 to 8 Decoder circuit (IC 74138)

Based on combination of A13, A14 and A15, any one of the outputs (O0-O7) will become *active low,* other output lines remain in high state. These output lines are connected to the chip select of the memory ICs. For example O0 output line is connected to the chip select of the 8K EPROM IC

The following table shows the output lines and corresponding memory address capability.

Table.8.3 Address selected by the decoder

O0	0000H to 1FFFH
O1	2000H to 3FFFH
O2	4000H to 5FFFH
O3	6000H to 7FFFH
O4	8000H to 9FFFH
O5	A000H to BFFFH
O6	C000H to DFFFH
O7	E000H to FFFFH

Thus using a simple decoder, CE signals for 8 nos of 8K devices are selected.

The Fig.8.18 shows the complete memory and address decoder circuit of the example of Fig.8.15b.

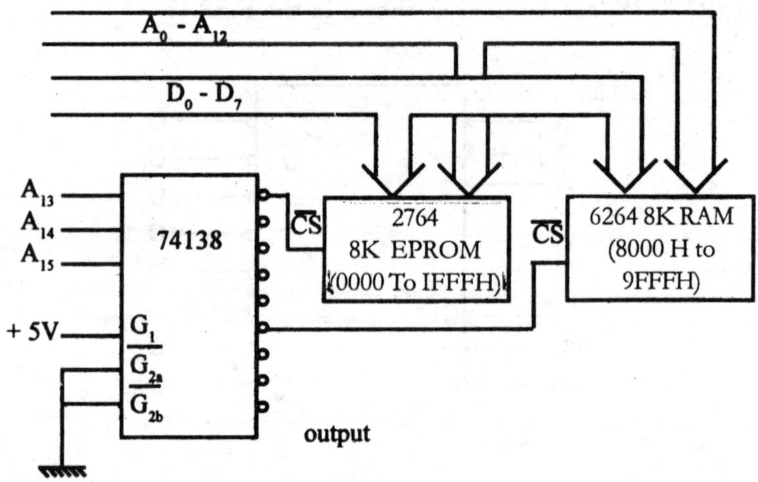

Fig. 8.18 Complete memory and address decoder circuit

Basic Hardware of a Microprocessor based system

The basic hardware of a 8085 microprocessor based system consists of

- The CPU and system bus
- Memory and decoder circuits
- I/O and decoder circuits
- Circuit for handling external signals (which include RESET, Interrupts etc).

The system bus is buffered so that it can be used by many devices. Several I/O devices are interfaced with the system as required by the application.

The I/O devices interfaced are display devices, keyboard, analog to digital converters, digital to analog converters, thumb wheel switches and relays. A number of programmable ICs peripheral are available to work with the 8085 CPU.

- 8255 to interface I/O ports
- 8253 for timer/counter aplication
- 8279 to interface keyboard and display
- 8251 for serial communication implementation
- 8259 for handling multiple interrupts.

MONITOR PROGRAM

The monitor program of a trainer kit starts working as soon as the power is switched ON. It is responsible for the house keeping activities of the kit. It allows the user to enter and execute a program. It detects and reports certain errors. The monitor program also contains several utility routines like

- Time delay program
- Read key board
- Update address field
- Update data field.

The monitor program is stored in EPROM located at the lowest region of the memory map, so that it is activated as soon as power is switched ON.

The keyboard of the kit consists of HEX keys and number of function keys. For example EXAM MEMory key, GO key, NEXT key. As soon as the kit is switched ON the following sequence of operation is carried out.

- Sign ON message is displayed
- Wait for a key press
- If any key is pressed, the key code is checked and according to the key code, specific subroutine is executed.

Normally, when the kit is switched ON, it expects the function key to be pressed first, otherwise the *ERROR* message is displayed. If any function key is pressed the specific subroutine is executed.

The sequence for entering a program in the microprocessor kit is

- Initially EXAM MEMory key is pressed
- The routine meant for this function key expects the starting address of the program from the user.
- Through HEX keys the starting address is entered
- Once the correct address is entered, the NEXT key is pressed
- Following this the memory location address and its content are displayed
- Using HEX keys, the content of that location is modified
- The NEXT key is pressed
- The displayed content is stored in the memory location
- The memory address is incremented
- The incremented address and its contents are displayed

This procedure is continued to enter the complete program. To come out of this EXAM MEMory function routine, RESET key is pressed. The subroutine meant for EXAM MEMory key should take care of all the above steps.

The subroutines corresponding to different function keys are available in the monitor program. The monitor program cannot be written in isolation. It is to be written based on the hardware design.

System RAM area

Certain fixed locations of the RAM area are used by some of the routines of the monitor program. For example the Update the data field routine displays the content of a given memory location. It requires the user to place the data at a specified location of the RAM. The set of such RAM memory locations used by the monitor program is called system RAM area. Normally the system RAM memory lies in the last portion of the user memory area. Since this system memory is fixed one, the stack memory starts just above the system RAM area.

Development and Trouble shooting tools

The development of an application program for a 8085 system involves writing the program and testing it on a system. The program is written with mnemonics (assembly language). However when it is entered nto the system for testing, opcodes corresponding to the mnemonics have to be used. It is a tedious process for the user to relate every mnemonics with the equivalent opcode. Further the user also has to take care of JUMP, CALL addresses at the time of coding the program.

A development tool called *ASSEMBLER* helps in such sitution. Using a personal computer the user can enter a 8085 program written in assembly language. The assembler converts each instruction into its opcode. It also converts the labels used in JMP and CALL statements into actual address values.

The user can get the printout of HEX code for manual entry of the program into the user memory of the system. Otherwise these HEX codes can be transferred to the user memory of the system through the serial port of the system from the personal computer. In this way the Assembler can be used as a simple development tool.

In-circuit Emulator

The in-circuit emulator consists of two subsystems

- Controller module.
- Personality module.

and a 40 pin Dual-Inline-Package (DIP) plug with the ribbon cable.

This emulator is interfaced with personal computer through serial port. In the target board (prototype of microprocessor based system), the 8085 processor is removed and the 40 pin DIP plug of the personality subsystem is fixed in the 8085 socket. The user can operate or control the target board from the computer through the emulator. The emulator consists of assembler and disassembler software in EPROM. It understands the single line command from the computer and executes.

The User can write a program using mnemonics and labels. He can also transfer the program to the target board memory and execute the same. Single step facility, exam register facility and break point facility are also available in the emulator system to test the prototype. It helps the developer to detect the logical errors in the program and the hardware faults in the prototype. The emulator performs all the functions of the replaced microprocessor in the prototype.

The user can store the program as a file in the computer and download the program whenever it is needed. The clock and the memory of emulator can also be shared by the prototype system. This helps the user to develop the microprocessor based system from the minimum hardware to a complex one in stages.

EXERCISE - 8

1. What do you mean by the term memory ? What is Volatile and Non-volatile memory ?
2. Distinguish between static and dynamic memory.
3. What do you mean by memory access time ? ice heirarchy
4. Compare ROM and EPROM. Distinguish between RAM and ROM.
5. What is a memory map ? The starting address of a 4K RAM is 4000H. What is the end address ?
6. Draw a memory address decoder circuit using two numbers of 74138 decoder devices, for a 2K RAM starting from B000H.
7. Why is the monitor program stored in an EPROM and placed at 0000H location in 8085 based system ?
8. What do you understand by the system RAM area ?
9. What are the advantages of using Assembler software ?
10. Write the pin details of 27128 EPROM IC.

CHAPTER 9

PROGRAMMABLE PERIPHERAL INTERFACE — 8255

9.1 INTRODUCTION

Most of the microprocessor applications will have two things in common

- Reading data from an external device
- Writing data into another external device

Special interface circuits are available for this purpose. Such interface circuits are called peripheral interface circuits. They are also called I/O ports. They can be programmed to do a specific interfacing function. Therefore they are called programmable peripheral interface. They are available in IC form.

The Intel 8255 is one such peripheral interface chip. It can be used with the Intel 8085 CPU. The 8255 is one of the most widely used interface devices.

9.2 INTERNAL DETAILS OF 8255

The device comes in a 40 pin dual-in-line package format. Fig.9.1a shows the pin detail and Fig.9.1b shows the schematic of 8255.

The major features are

The device features three numbers of ports namely A, B and C. Each one of them is an 8 bit port. However port C can be divided into two 4 bit ports and used separately. The device also has an 8 bit internal register to store the control word. The control word is used to configure the three ports of device either as input or as output.

Port A and Port C upper are grouped together as Group A and Port B and Port C lower are grouped together as Group B as shown in the Fig.9.2.

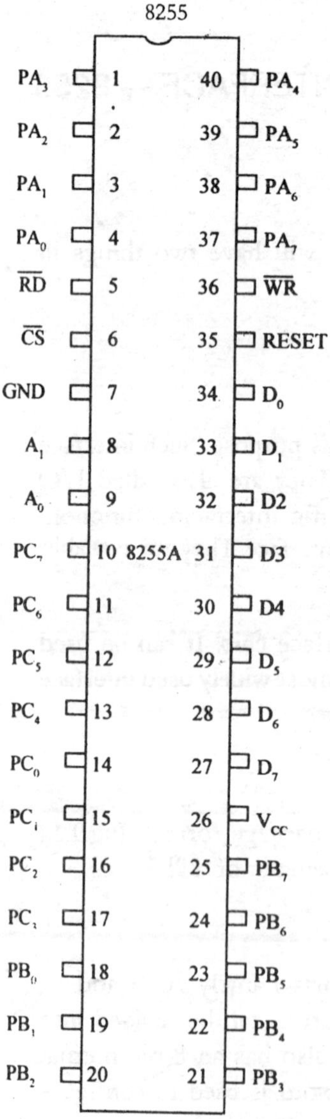

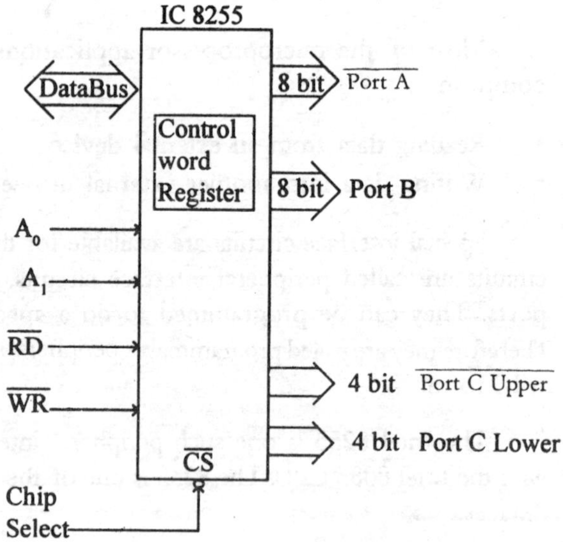

D_7 - D_0	Data Bus (Bidirectional)
RESET	Reset Input
CS	Chip Select
RD	Read Input
WR	Write Input
A_0, A_1	Port Address
PA_7- PA_0	Port A (8 Bit)
PB_7- PB_0	Port B (8 Bit)
PC_7-PC_0	Port C (8 Bit)
V_{CC}	+5 Volts
GND	0 Volts

Fig.9.1 (a) and **9.1** (b)

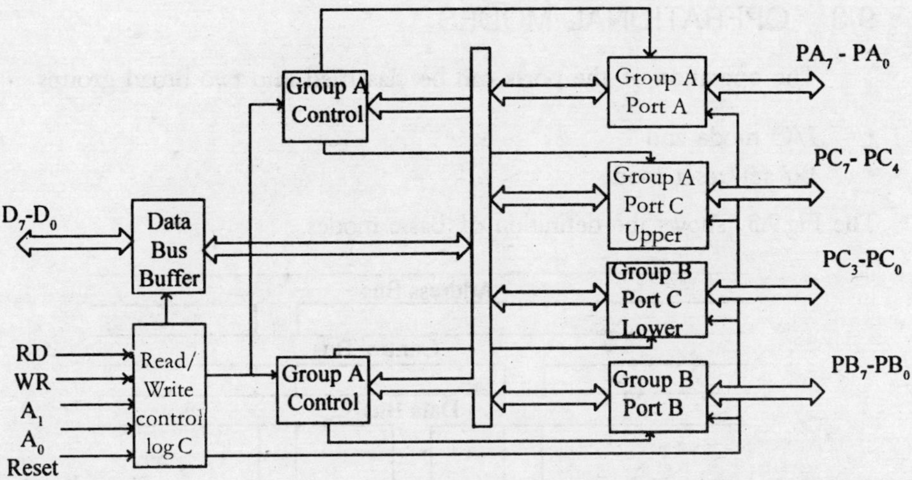

Fig.9.2 Block diagram of IC 8255

Signals necessary to interface with the Microprocessor

The lines A0 and A1 are used to address the three ports and the Control Word Registers (CWR).

A1	A0	
0	0	Port A
0	1	Port B
1	0	Port C
1	1	Control Word Register

The device is enabled when the CS (active LOW) pin is made LOW. The output of the address decoder is connected to this pin. For the CPU each port appears as a logical register. The CPU can read or write into these registers. The $\overline{RD}$ and $\overline{WR}$ signals are used for this purpose. The data lines D0 to D7 are connected to the data bus of the CPU.

The RESET input is normally connected to the RESET OUT signal of the microprocessor., so that whenever the CPU is reset the 8255 is also reset. The internal control word register is cleared and all ports are set to the *input mode.*

9.3 OPERATIONAL MODES

The operation of the ports can be classified into two broad groups

- I/O mode and
- Bit set/reset mode.

The Fig.9.3 shows the definition of basic modes.

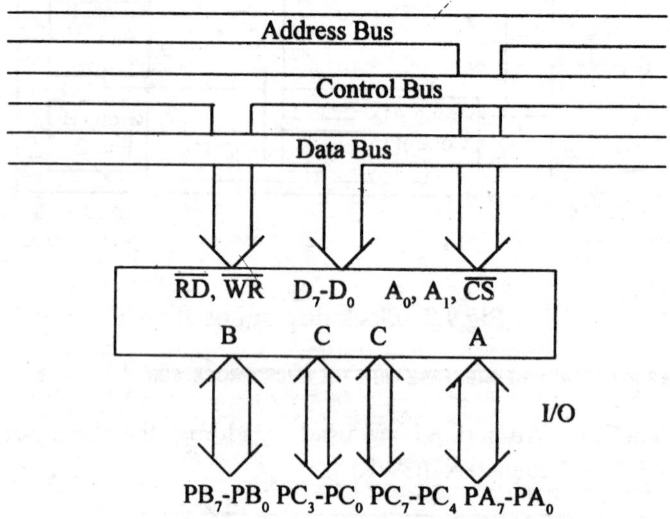

Fig.9.3 (a) Mode 0

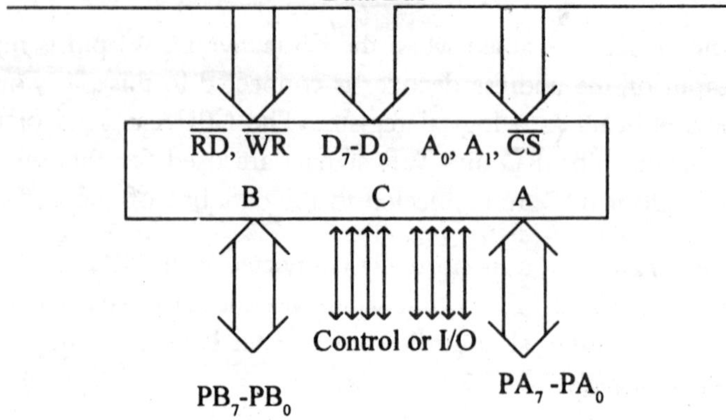

Fig.9.3 (b) Mode 1

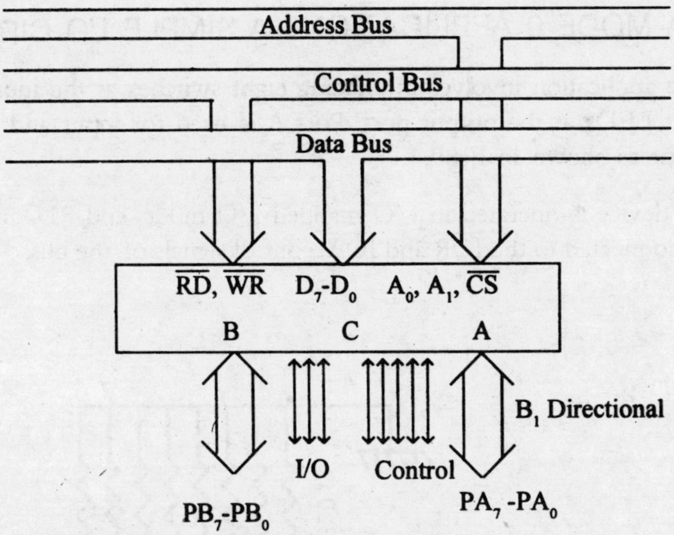

Fig.9.3 (c) Mode 2

I/O Mode

Under the I/O mode, the device offers three specific modes of operation as mode 0, mode 1 and mode 2 as shown in Fig. 9.3.

Mode 0 - Simple I/O mode

Under mode 0, the port A can be set as either input or output port. In the same way the port B can also be set for input or output operation. However there is a flexibility in port C. It can be divided into two 4 bit ports, the C lower and C upper. Each of them can be set independently for input or output operation.

Mode 1 - Handshake mode :

Under mode 1, the port A or B can be set for input or output operation. The bits from port C are used as control signals. These control signals are used for handshaking.

Mode 2 - Bi-directional mode :

In mode 2 the port A is used as a bi-directional port with simultaneous input and output capability. Port C is used as control signals.

Bit Set/Reset Mode

The Bit Set/Reset mode makes use of only port C. Any bit of this port can be set or reset.

9.4 A MODE 0 APPLICATION—A SIMPLE I/O CIRCUIT

The application involves interfacing eight switches at the input port and eight LEDs at the output port. Port A is used for input and port B for output as shown in Fig.9.4.

The device is operated in I/O mapped I/O mode, and $\overline{RD}$, and $\overline{WR}$ lines are connected to the $\overline{IOR}$ and $\overline{IOW}$ control signals of the bus.

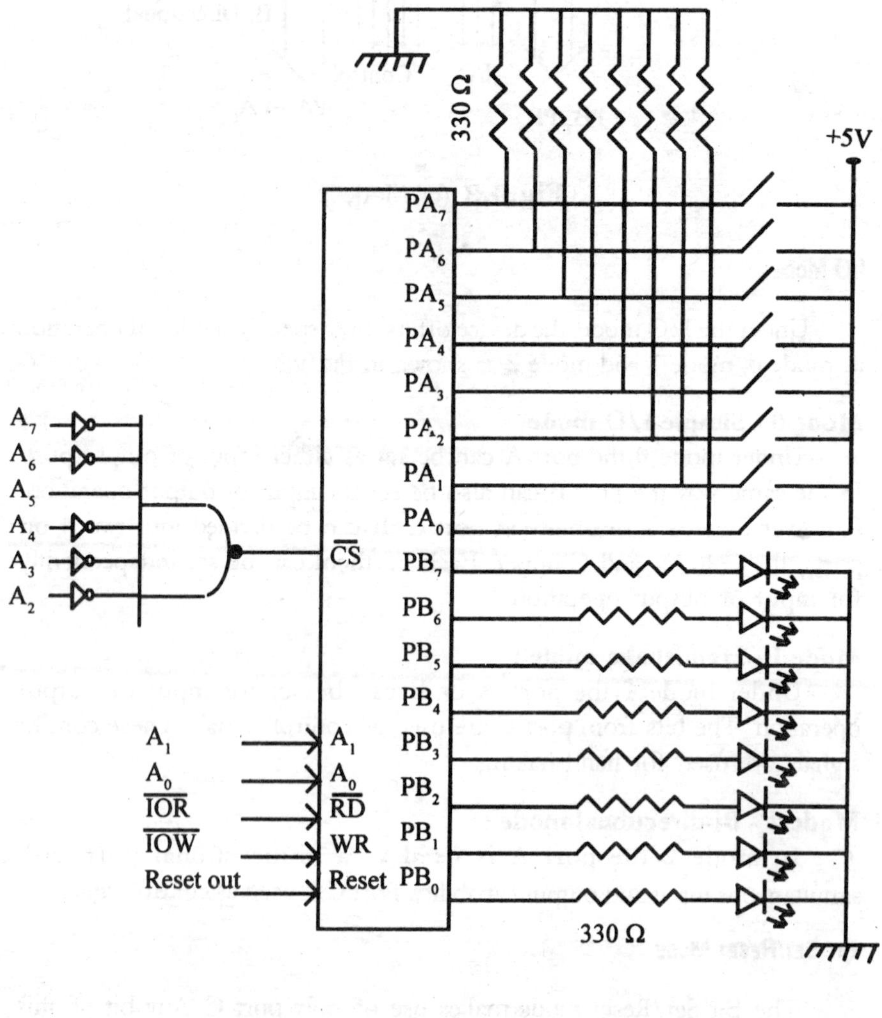

Fig. 9.4 IC 8255 Mode 0 operation

The A0 and A1 inputs of the device selects the 3 ports and the control word register (CWR). The A0 and A1 inputs are connected to the A0 and A1 lines of the address bus.

The address decoder uses the rest of the 6 address lines A2 - A7. The address decoder is designed for address 20H, 21H, 22H and 23H and the output is connected to the $\overline{CS}$ pin of 8255. The addresses of the ports and CWR become

Port A	20H	Port B	21H
Port C	22H	Contol Word Register	23H

9.5 PROGRAMMING THE 8255

As 8255 is a programmable I/O device and, it has to be programmed for desired operation before using the ports. Programming is also called *initialisation* or *configuring* the device. Programming assigns an input or output mode for each port. Writing the control word into the control word register completely configures the device. Each bit encodes certain detail about the operational mode.

CONTROL WORD FORMAT

The details of control word is shown in Fig.9.5.

The bit D7 chooses between I/O mode or Bit set reset mode. When it is 1, I/O mode is selected. When it is 0, bit set reset mode is selected.

The bit D6 and D5 determine the I/O mode of group A. Since group A can be operated in mode 0, mode 1 and mode 2 , two bits are needed to select the mode of operation.

The bit D4 sets the port A for input or output function. When it is 1, the port A becomes input port. When it is 0, the port A becomes output port.

The bit D3 sets the port C (upper) input or output.

The bit D2 determines the I/O mode of Group B. Since Group B can be used in mode 0 or mode 1, one bit is enough to decide.

The bit D1 sets the port B for input or output.

The bit D0 sets the port C (lower) for input or output.

Since this application needs I/O mode, D7 is set to one.

The group A has to be operated in simple I/O. So the bits D6 and D5 are made zero.

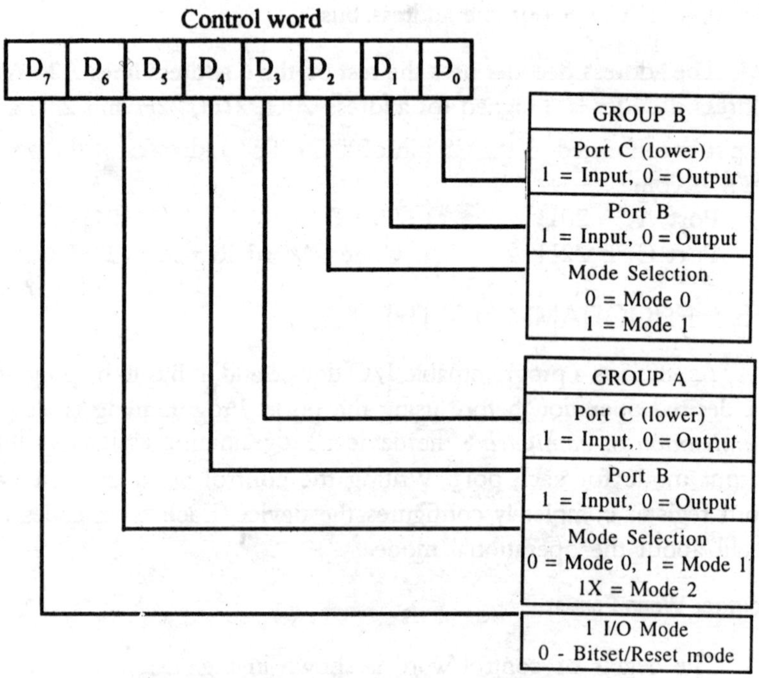

Fig. 9.5 IC 8255 Command word format

Since port A has to be input port, D4 is made one.

Port C is not used, therefore D3 can be zero or one.

Group B has to work in simple I/O mode, therefore bit D2 is zero.

Port B has to be output port, so bit D1 is made zero.

Port C is not used, therefore bit D0 is made zero or one.

For our application, the control word works out to

D7	D6	D5	D4	D3	D2	D1	D0
1	0	0	1	0	0	0	0
			9	0	H		

For the configuration of mode 0 operation with port A as input and port B as output, the control word works out to 90H, which has to be written into the control word register through an OUT instruction.

Memonic	Comment
MVI A, 90H	; The control word 90H is placed ; in the accumulator.
OUT 23 H	; Output to the I/O port 23, ; the control word register.

After these instructions are executed, the port A will act as input port and port B will act as output port.

For example, to light the last LED of the output port the, D7 bit is to be made 1 level. The data bit pattern which is to be output is

1 0 0 0 0 0 0 0
8 0 H

The instructions

```
MVI A, 80H    ; To make the D7th bit to 1 level.
OUT 21 H      ; Output to the LED port to glow
              ; the LED connected to the D7th bit.
```

will output 80H into port B.

To read the status of the 8 switches, the switch port is to be read as follows.

```
IN 20H        8 bit input from the switch port is
              available in accumulator.
```

9.6 A PROGRAMMING EXAMPLE

Problem
Switch ON and OFF the LEDs in Fig.9.6 in sequence.

The following program switches ON the LEDs in sequence.

Label	Mnemonic	Comments
	MVI A, 90H	; Control word is written in the CWR
	OUT 23H	
	MVI A, 01H	; make the first LED on
	OUT 21H	

Label	Mnemonic	Comments
repeat	PUSH PSW	; A register is stored in stack
	CALL DELAY	; time delay routine is called
	POP PSW	; A register content is retrieved
	RRC	; rotate the content right by one bit.
	OUT 21H	; output to the port B
	JMP repeat	; it is repeated

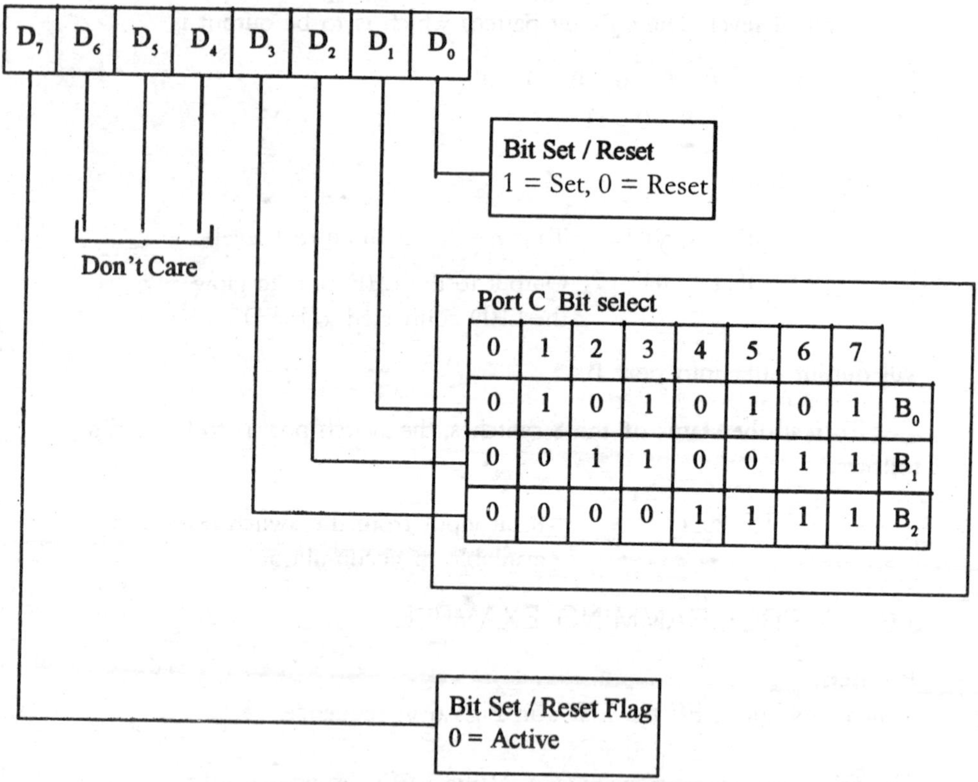

Fig. 9.6 IC 8255 Bit set / Reset format

9.7 COMMON APPLICATIONS OF MODE 0

Mode 0 is the most widely used modes of IC 8255. It finds many common applications. An example would be the traffic control lights. The ports of 8255 can be made to switch ON and OFF, an array of lights with certain time delay.

Another common example would be the washing machine. CPU would read water level through one port and switch on the relay for a pump through another port. In short one port is made to read the *status* of various devices and another port is used to *control* certain other devices.

Any such interface application can be best implemented with Mode 0

9.8 BIT SET/RESET OPERATION

Before learning mode 1, let us learn the Bit Set Reset mode. This mode makes use of port C. Any bit of port C can be set or reset. Consider a group of bits that are used as control signals applied to a device. If any of the bits need to be selectively changed, this mode is the best suited mode.

In order to operate 8255 in this mode, the control word is to be structured as shown in Fig.9.6

D7	D6	D5	D4	D3	D2	D1	D0
0	X	X	X	Bit select		Set/Reset	
BSR mode		Not used		Position of the bit in Binary		Set = 1 Reset = 0	

For example, in order to set the bit 4 of the Port C (PC4), the control word would be

D7	D6	D5	D4	D3	D2	D1	D0
0	0	0	0	1	0	0	1
			0	9	H		

The following program segment will set the bit PC4.

```
MVI A,09H
OUT 23H
```

This operation is mainly used where manipulation of bits at the output is needed.

9.9 MODE 1 OPERATION

The details of mode 1 is illustrated with an example of interfacing a peripheral. A good example of a peripheral that is going to have a mode 1 interface is the printer used with computers.

The printer is an electro mechanical device. Its printing speed is much slower than the CPU's operating speed. Though printer can receive data from CPU at any rate, it can print the data only at slower rate. Therefore the data transfer between the CPU and the printer proceeds as follows.

The printer has a memory buffer within it.

The CPU sends out *a byte* of data to printer.

The printer receives it, stores it in the buffer, then sends out an acknowledgment to the CPU.

The CPU sends out one more byte. The process repeats until the memory buffer is full.

Then the printer stops sending the acknowledgment.

The CPU stops sending further data.

The printer prints part of the buffer content.

Then it starts sending acknowledgment and then the CPU sends data.

This process of data transfer is known as *Handshake* method.

The advantage of handshake method is that the CPU can do another task when the printer is printing. In this way the CPU time is effectively used. Now let us see how to implement handshake method usding mode 1.

In mode 1 operation, Port A and Port B are independently used either for input or output. Port C is used for control signals. Mode 1 operation is also called as Strobed Input/Output operation or Handshake mode operation.

Fig.9.7 shows mode 1 operation in which the Port A is used as input port and Port B as output port.

INPUT PORT OPERATION

When Port A is used for input, PC3, PC4 and PC5 of port C are used as the associated control lines.

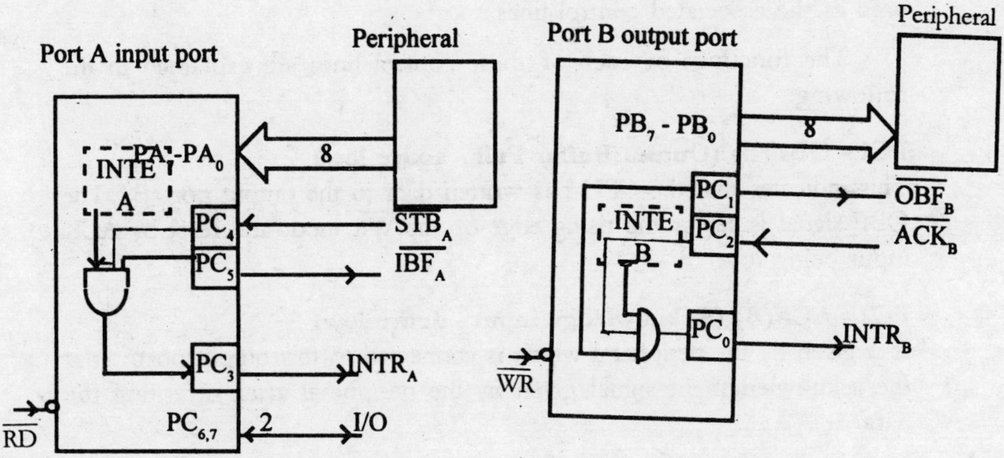

Fig. 9.7 IC 8255 Mode 1 operation

The functions of each of these control lines are explained in the following :

PC4 - $\overline{STB}$(A) (Strobe - active low)

When a peripheral wants to input an 8 bit data to the microprocessor it places the 8 bit data in the input lines of the Port A and make STB control line low.

PC5 - IBF(A) (Input Buffer Full - active high)

Following the strobe signal the input data is latched into port A and acknowledgement signal is given to the peripheral device through the IBF line. IBF is set by $\overline{STB}$ input being low and is reset by the rising edge of the $\overline{RD}$ input.

PC3 - INTR(A) (Interrupt request - active high)

After latching the data into port A the device raises the INTR line to indicate that there is a valid data to be read by the CPU. This line can be used as the interrupt to the CPU, which in turn can read the data from the input port. It is reset by the falling edge of $\overline{RD}$ signal.

To enable INTR (A) line active, the internal flip flop is to be set earlier. This is done by making the PC4 bit 1 level. It is to be done before using the IC in mode 1 I/O operation.

Output Port Operation

When port B is used for Output, PC2, PC1 and PC0 of port C are used as the associated control lines.

The functions of each of these control lines are explained in the following:

PC1 - OBF(B) (Output Buffer Full - active low)
This indicates that the CPU has written data to the output port B. The OBF signal is set by the rising edge of the $\overline{WR}$ input and reset by ACK input being low.

PC2 - ACK(B) (Acknowledge input - active low)
It is given by the peripheral which is connected to this output port. It is the acknowledgment signal given by the peripheral after accepting the data.

PC0 - INTR(B) (Interrupt Request - active high)
After receiving the ACK (active low) signal, INTR signal goes high. It can be used as interrupt request to the CPU to send another byte of data to the output port which is connected to the peripheral. It is reset by the falling edge of the $\overline{WR}$ signal.

To enable the INTR line, the internal flip flop is to be set. It is done by making the bit PC2 to 1 level initially before using the IC 8255 in mode 1.

We have seen that data transfer between the I/O ports and the CPU in mode 1 can be done using INTR line both in the case of input port and output port. However, without using the INTR line, it can be effected after reading the Status Word from 8255 through the Port C.

Status word

The status word is read from 8255 by reading the Port C. If both Group A and Group B are used as INPUT ports in mode 1, and if the address of the port C is 22H, the instruction

```
IN 22H          read Port C
```

will bring the following status word into the accumulator

D7	D6	D5	D4	D3	D2	D1	D0
I/O	I/O	IBF A	INTE A	INTR A	INTE B	IBF B	INTR B

If both groups A and B are used as OUTPUT ports, then the Status word will be

D7	D6	D5	D4	D3	D2	D1	D0
OBF A	INTE A	I/O	I/O	INTR A	INTE B	OBF B	INTR B

For input operation, the status word is checked for IBF bit (active 1 level). After that, the input port is read by the CPU.

Similarly, for output operation, the status word is checked for OBF bit (inactive level). It indicates that the output port does not contain any 8 bit data to be transferred to the peripheral device. The CPU can transfer the next byte data to the output port.

Thus the data transfer between I/O ports and the CPU can be done by checking the status word.

9.10 A MODE 1 APPLICATION

The Mode 1 operation can be better understood with an A/D converter application as shown in the fig.9.8.

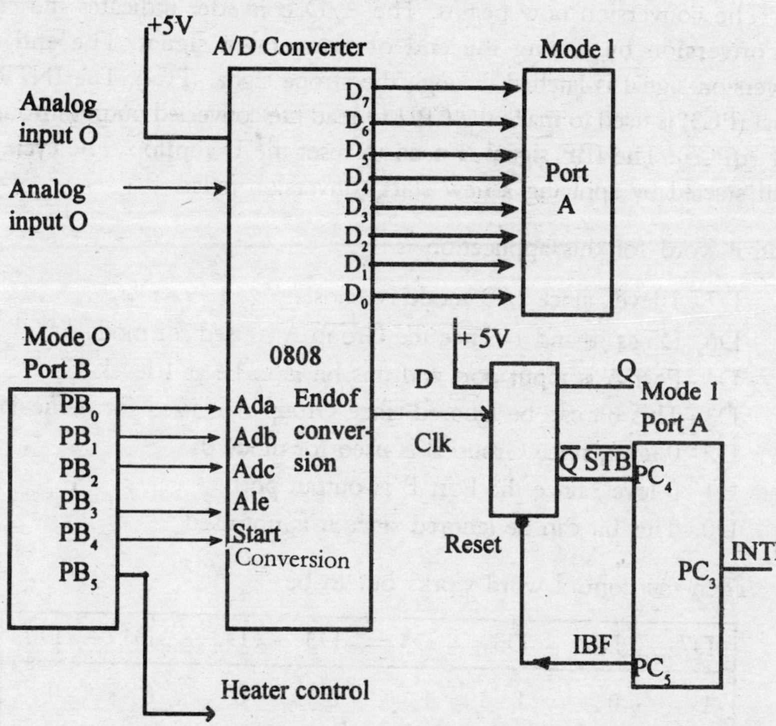

Fig. 9.8 IC 8255 Interfacing with A/D converter

The A/D converter is triggered by a signal called start conversion. After a small time delay, the conversion gets over and the valid data is available at the output. The device indicates this by a signal called end of conversion. Now the CPU can read the data. These control signals call for application in mode 1. In addition,certain A/D converters also require an address input to select an analog signal. This calls for operation in mode 0.

Therefore port A is operated in mode 1 and port B is operated in mode 0. Port A is used to read data from the A/D converter. Port B is used to address the channels in the A/D converter to start conversion.

The A/D converter 0808 can take-in 8 analog channels. To select any one of them, it needs a 3 bit address input. To select channel 0, the address is 000.

First the address is put out through the bits PB2, PB1 and PB0. This address is latched into the A/D converter by sending out a 1 on PB3. After this the conversion is triggered by putting a 1 on PB4 and then 0 in that control line.

The conversion now begins. The A/D converter indicates the end of conversion by raising the end of conversion signal. The end of conversion signal is latched through the strobe signal (PC4). The INTRA signal (PC3) is used to make the CPU to read the converted output through port A(PC5). The IBF signal is used to reset the D flipflop. The cycle is again started by applying a new start conversion pulse.

Control word for this application is

D7 - 1 level, since I/O mode is chosen

D6, D5 as 0 and 1 since the Group A is used for mode 1

D4 –Port A is input port and this bit is to be at 1 level

D3 –This bit can be ignored since Group A is used for mode 1

D2 - 0 level, since Group B is used for mode 0

D1 - 0 level, since the Port B is output port

D0 –This bit can be ignored since it is not used

Then the control word works out to be

D7	D6	D5	D4	D3	D2	D1	D0
1	0	1	1	0	0	0	0
			B	0	H		

9.11 A PROGRAM TO READ THE DATA FROM AN A/D CONVERTER

Label	Mnemonics	Comments
	MVI A, B0H OUT 23H	control word is written in CWR
start	MVI A, 00H OUT 21H	channel address is written in Port B
	MVI A, 08H OUT 21H	ALE signal is made to 1
	CALL DELAY	Delay routine is called
	MVI A, 18H OUT 21H	start conversion signal is made 1 level
	CALL DELAY	again delay routine is called
	MVI A, 00H OUT 21H	both ALE signal and start conversion signal becomes 0 Conversion starts
status	IN 22H	port C, status word is read
	ANI 20H	IBF signal PC5 is checked for 1 level. If it is so, then Port A is to be read.
	JZ status	Otherwise, status word is read till PC5 becomes 1 level.
	IN 20H	A to D converter data is read by reading the port A.
	JMP START	sampling the channel 0 is repeated.

9.12 OTHER EXAMPLES

To illustrate the mode 1 operation, let us take another example of handling a keyboard and a printer.

Printer Operation

The data transfer operation between a printer and CPU can be carried out as explained below.

1. The CPU places an 8 bit data in the output port.

2. The interface circuit sends out $\overline{OBF}$ (Output Buffer Full), active low level signal to the printer to indicate that the data is available for taking inside the printer memory buffer.
3. If the printer buffer is empty enough to receive the data, it will read the data into the printer buffer and if it is ready to receive next byte of data, then it will acknowledges the output port through the $\overline{ACK}$ active low signal.
4. The active $\overline{ACK}$ level is sensed by the interface circuit and an interrupt is raised to inform the CPU to place the next data from the computer memory to the output port.
5. Steps 1, 2, 3 and 4 are repeated.
   This operation is continued till the active $\overline{ACK}$ signal is received from the printer.

Keyboard Operation

When a key is pressed in the keyboard, an 8 bit code is formed.

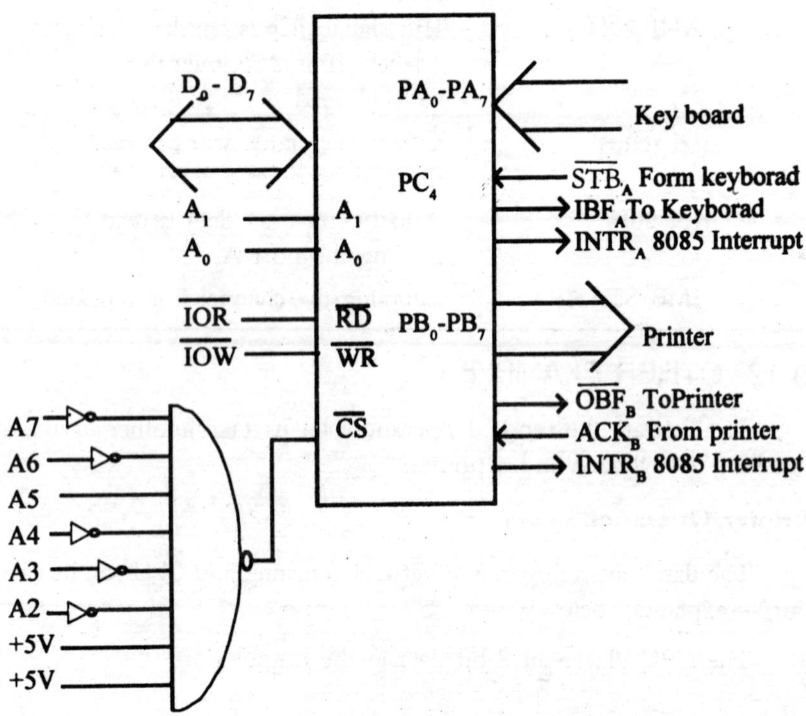

Fig. 9.9 Keyboard input and printer output operation 8255 Mode 1

1. The 8 bit code is placed as data to the input port.
2. The keyboard circuit sends the STB (Strobe Input) LOW signal to the interface circuit to indicate that the keyboard circuit has placed the data to the input port.
3. The interface circuit acknowledges the receipt of the data by raising the output signal IBF (input buffer full).
4. Then an interrupt signal INTR is actuated to enable the CPU to read the data available in the input port.

Thus the keyboard data is read. Here, STB and IBF are handshaking control signals.

In the example shown in Fig.9.9, the Keyboard and the Printer are connected to the CPU using 8255 operating in mode 1.

The Port A is used to handle Keyboard and Group B is used to handle Printer. Group A is configured for input operation and Group B is configured for output operation.

Port C is used as control lines for both the ports.

Input Control Lines

In our example, Group A is used as input port.

PC3 - INTR (A)
PC4 - STB (A)
PC5 - IBF (A)
PC6 and PC7 are used as I/O lines

To enable INTR (A) line active, the internal flip flop is to be set. It is achieved by making the PC4 bit 1 level initially. This PC4 bit is made 1 level by Bit Set/Reset mode.

Port B is used as the output port. The following lines are used as follows.

PC0 - INTR (B)
PC1 - ACK (B)
PC2 - OBF (B)

To enable INTR (B) line active, the internal flip flop is to be set. It is achieved by making the PC2 bit 1 level initially. This PC2 bit is made 1 level by Bit Set/Reset mode.

WORKING OF THE INTERFACE

For Mode 1 operation, the control word is formed as follows

D7	D6	D5	D4	D3	D2	D1	D0
1	0	1	1	X	1	0	X

Port C (upper) and Port C (lower) are treated as control lines. Therefore in the control word, bits representing the port C, namely D0 and D3 are assumed as don't care conditions. Thus the control word can be written as

D7	D6	D5	D4	D3	D2	D1	D0
1	0	1	1	0	1	0	0
			B	4	H		

1. The control word which is formed is entered into the control word register by the instructions.

   MVI A, B4H
   OUT 23H

2. The bits PC4 and PC2 are to be made 1 level using Bit Set Reset mode in order to enable INTR (A) and INTR (B).

D7	D6	D5	D4	D3	D2	D1	D0
0	0	0	0	1	0	0	1
			0	9	H		

MVI A, 09H
OUT 23H

will enable the INTR (A)

Similarly, in order to enable INTR (B), the following instructions are executed.

MVI A, 05H
OUT 23H

Thus the IC 8255 is initialised to be operated in mode 1 for both the groups.

If the ports are to be operated in Interrupt driven I/O mode, then the INTR(A) and INTR(B) are to be connected to hardware interrupt lines and suitable routines are to be executed.

If the ports are to be operated in Polled method, status word is checked for IBF bit and OBF bit and then accordingly, I/O operations are carried out.

9.13 TIMER / COUNTER 8253 – AN INTRODUCTION

Many industrial applications would need precise time delays. An example would be the sequence timer in a process control application. The sequence timer has to switch on and off a heater or a motor or close or open valves with specified time delay. A simple application such as traffic control also involves switching on and off the lamps with specified time delay.

Time delays are generated using mechanical timers or electronic timers using logic gates and circuits. In a microprocessor based system the time delay can be generated using software.

Similarly many industrial application will also involve counting certain events. For example the number of bottles coming out of a bottle filling plant or the number of medicine tablets filled into a bottle need to be counted. Counting of such events can also be done under software control in a microprocessor based system, using suitable sensors.

The time delay or counting can be done under the direct control of the CPU. This approach places heavy demand on the CPU's time. A better approach would be to use a dedicated device for time delay and counting applications.

The device Intel 8253 is a timer/counter to be used with Inlel 8085 system. It can be used to generate accurate time delays and square waves and many more. This device 8253 comes in a 24 pin dual-in-line package. It consists of 3 numbers of independent 16 bit counters. Each counter has a separate clock input, count enable (gate) input lines and an output line. The 16 bit divisor value is loaded into the counter. The gate enables counting. The output pulse is obtained at the end of the counting. The device offers 6 different counting modes which include square were generation and monostable operation. The counters can be operated at count rates upto 2 MHz.

9.14 BLOCK DIAGRAM OF 8253

The device can be divided into two functional blocks, namely

- the counter/timer section and
- the CPU interface section.

Timer Section

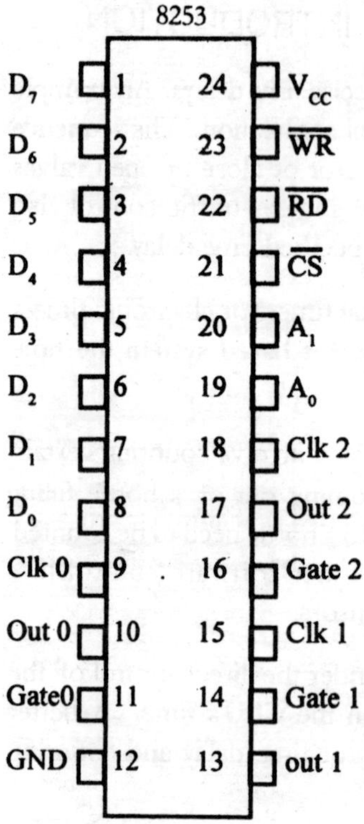

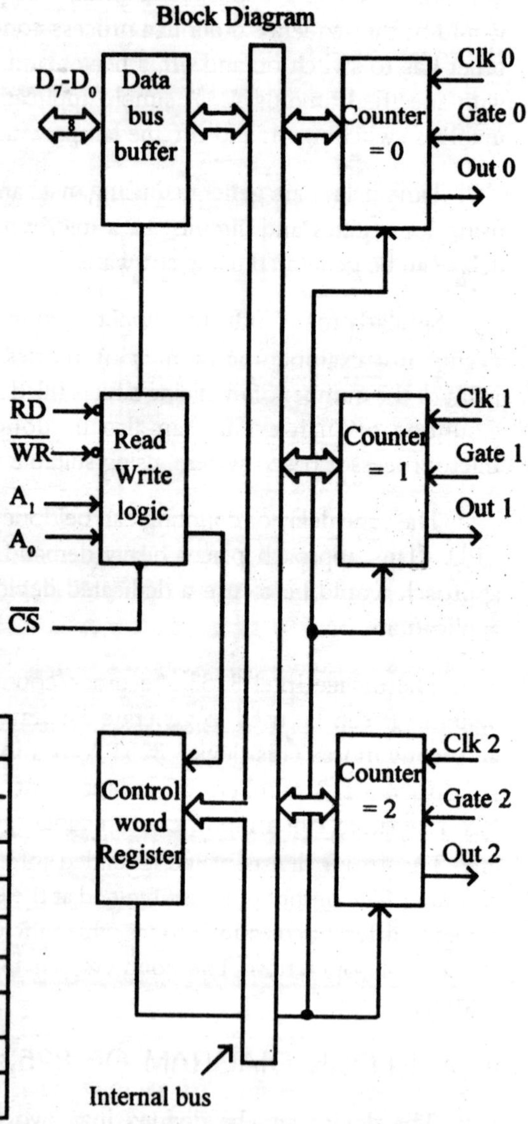

D_7-D_0	Data bus (8 bit)
Clk N	Counter clock inputs
Gate N	Counter gate inputs
Out N	Counter outputs
RD	Read counter
WR	Write Command or date
CS	Chip select
A_0-A_1	Counter Select
V_{CC}	+5 Volts
GND	Ground

Fig. 9.10 Block diagram of 8253

The device has 3 independent counter/timers

- counter 0.
- counter 1 and.
- counter. 2.

Each is a 16 bit down counter. Each of them can be operated independent of the others. Each counter has a clock input, gate input and one output. The gate input enables the counting process. The counting may be started using this gate signal.

Thus the starting of counting may be synchronised with an external event. The counter indicates the completion of the counting process through the OUT signal.

Each counter can be operated in any one of 6 modes.

CPU Interface Section

The 8 data lines D0 to D7 are connected to the data bus of the microcomputer. Each counter appears as a logical register to the CPU. The device appears as a total of 4 logical registers to the CPU; one for each counter and one more for the control. The A0 and A1 lines are connected to the A0 and A1 lines of the address bus.

A1	A0		Meaning
0	0	-	Counter 0
0	1	-	Counter 1
1	0	-	Counter 2
1	1	-	Control word register

The $\overline{CS}$ pin enables the device. The $\overline{RD}$ and $\overline{WR}$, signals allow the CPU to read and write into the 4 logical registers.

Fig. 9.11 shows the method of interfacing the device with the CPU. The device can be operated in I/O mapped I/O mode or memory mapped I/O mode. In the example shown, it is connected for I/O mapped I/O mode and hence $\overline{RD}$ and $\overline{WR}$ signals are connected to the $\overline{IOR}$ and $\overline{IOW}$ controls signals of the bus.

In the example the device is enabled for the I/O addresses of 80H, 81H, 82H and 83H

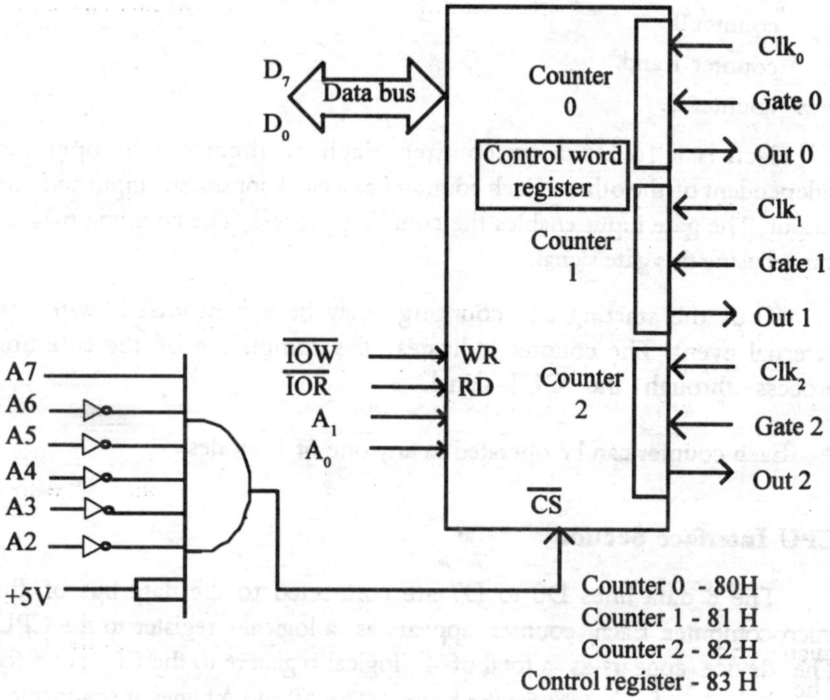

Fig. 9.11 Interfacing the IC 8253

Programming the 8253

8253 is a fully programmable device.

It is programmed

- to select the counter mode
- to initialise the counter
- and to read the count value

The first step in programming the device is to load the control word into control word register. It is followed by loading a 16 bit count value into the selected counter.

The control word specifies the counter to be used, loading and reading modes and the format of the count value.

Following table shows the control word format :

D7	D6	D5	D4	D3	D2	D1	D0

D7	D6	Select counter
0	0	0
0	1	1
1	0	2
1	1	illegal

D5	D4	Read/Load
0	0	Latch counter
0	1	LSB only
1	0	MSB only
1	1	LSB first MSB next

D3	D2	D1	Mode
0	0	0	Mode 0
0	0	1	Mode 1
0	1	0	Mode 2
0	1	1	Mode 3
1	0	0	Mode 4
1	0	1	Mode 5

D0	Code
0	Binary
1	BCD

The programming of 8253 is explained with the following example.

9.16 A TIMER/COUNTER EXAMPLE

Assume that the clock pulse input has a frequency of 1 KHz. It is required to generate square pulse of frequency 1 Hz, using Counter 0.

Address of the counter 0 is 80H

Address of the control word register is 83H

For the requirement specified, the control word is framed as follows

D7	D6	D5	D4	D3	D2	D1	D0	
0	0							counter 0
		1	1					Loading 16 bit value
			0	1	1			Mode 3 is used
							1	BCD Code
0	0	1	1	0	1	1	1	
			3	7	H			

The control word works out to 37H

The following program will load the control word and the 16 bit divisor value to the counter 0.

Program

Label	Mnemonics	Comments
	MVI A, 37H	framed control word is written into the control word register
	OUT 83H	
	MVI A, 00H	lower order byte 00 is loaded first into the counter
	OUT 80H	
	MVI A, 10H	higher order byte 10 is loaded into the counter (the divisor is 1000 decimal)
	OUT 80H	

After executing the program, when the gate signal becomes ONE, a 1 Hz wave is obtained at the output pin.

Note: The counters in this device are down counters. Thus the value loaded into the count register will actually be decremented. Loading all zeroes into a count register will result in the maximum count (2 raised to the power 16 for binary or 10 raised to the power 4 for BCD).

In most counter applications, it becomes necessary to read the value of the count in progress and make a decision based on this quantity. Event counters are probably the most common applications that use this function. There are two methods to read the value of the counters.

The first method requires that the actual counting be stopped by disabling the gate input or stopping the clock signal. The counting process is stopped to ensure a stable reading of the count value.

Format for reading the coutent is:

The first I/O read gets the least significant byte (LSB) of the count.

The second I/O read gets the most significant byte (MSB) of the count.

For example,

IN 80H instruction will read the least significant byte of the counter 0. Next IN 80H instruction will read the most significant byte of the counter 0.

9.18 READING WHILE COUNTING

The device 8253 offers another method of reading the count value without stopping the counting. The device has special internal logic to acheive this. The counter value is read after giving suitable control word.

For example, in order to read the content of the counter 0, the control word works out to be

D7	D6	D5	D4	D3	D2	D1	D0
0	0	0	0	X	X	X	X

bits D7 and D6 represents the counter number.

bits D5 and D4 values 0 and 0 represents latching operation.

Other bits are not checked when D5 and D4 are 0 and 0.

For example, the following instructions will read the counter0 value, while counting.

```
MVI A, 00    to load the control word into the control word register
OUT 83H

IN 80        to read the least significant byte of the count value

MOV C, A
IN 80        to read the most significant byte of the count value
```

MOV B,A the register pair BC contains the present value of the counter0

9.19 OPERATIONAL MODES OF 8253

The 8253 features 6 modes of operation. Each mode basically implements down counting. When the counting is completed an output is provided. Six different output formats are provided to meet diverse application requirements.

In addition, the counter may be initialised by software or hardware This improves the flexibility further.

For certain modes loading of the count value itself starts the counting. For certain other modes the starting is synchronised with a hardware input called gate. Thus the software or hardware triggering and the output format define a mode.

MODE 0 : Interupt on terminal count

As soon as the control word is written into the control word register, the output is made low. After the count is loaded into the count register, the counter starts counting. When the terminal count is reached, the

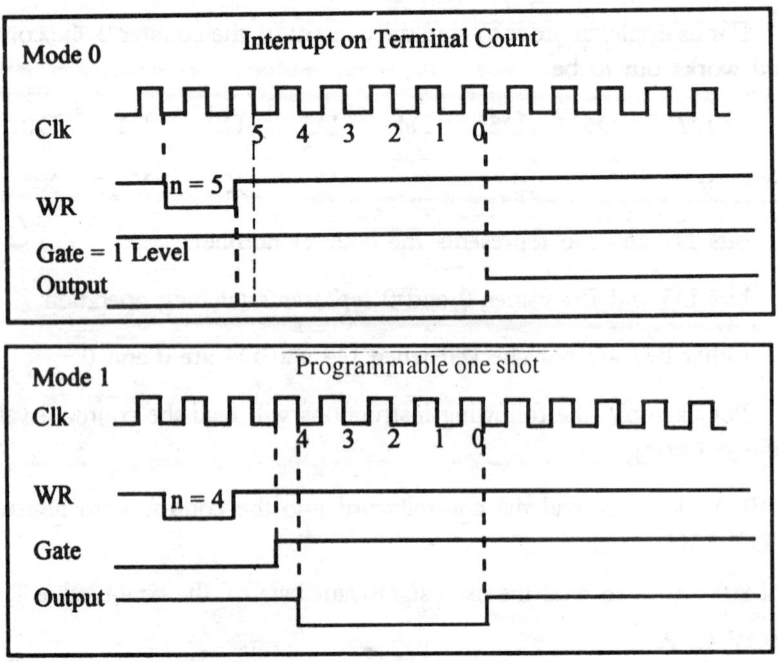

Fig.9.12 shows the Mode 0 and Mode 1

output will go high and remain high until the selected count register is reloaded with the mode.

The gate input will enable the counting when high and inhibit counting when low. Mode 0 can be used to generate specified time delays.

MODE 1 : Programmable one shot (hardware triggered monostable)

The control word and the count value are loaded into the device registers. This mode needs a *rising edge* trigger signal given at the gate input. At the *next falling edge of clock,* the output goes low. And the counter starts counting. When the number of pulses counted reaches the count value, the output goes high. The counter can be used as a triggered mono shot of desired width. The mono shot is retriggerable. That is a trigger at the gate starts the counting process. Before termination of the count if another trigger appears at the gate the counting starts again. Change in count value is allowed when the count is in progress. However the change becomes effective only after the next trigger.

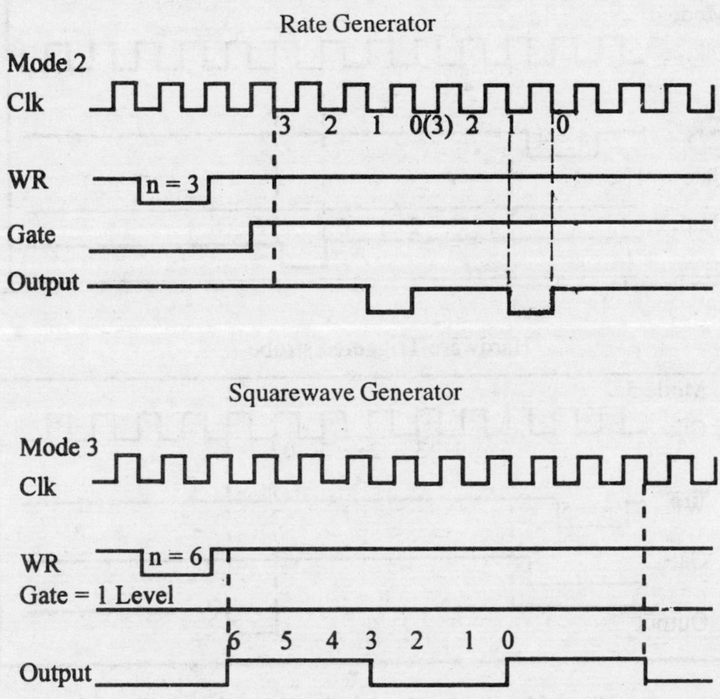

Fig.9.13 shows the Mode 2 and Mode 3

MODE 2 : RATE GENERATOR

Count by N counter:

The mode value and the count value are loaded into the register. A high level at the gate starts the counting. The output will be low for one period of the last clock pulse. The period from one output pulse to the next equals the number of input counts in the count register. If the count register is reloaded between output pulses, the present period will not be affected, but the subsequent period will reflect the new value.

The gate input when low, will force the output high. When the gate input goes high, the counter will start from the initial count. Thus the gate can be used to synchronise the counter.

MODE 3: Square Wave Rate Generator

The control word and the count value are loaded. A high level at the gate starts the counting. The output remains high for exactly half of the count value. It remains low for the rest of the count value.

Thus this mode generates a square wave of period specified by the count value. Any change in count value becomes effective, after the present count is over.

Software Triggered strobe

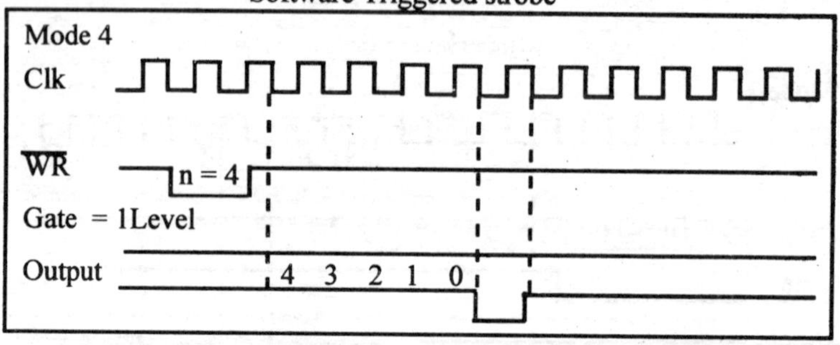

Hardware Triggered strobe

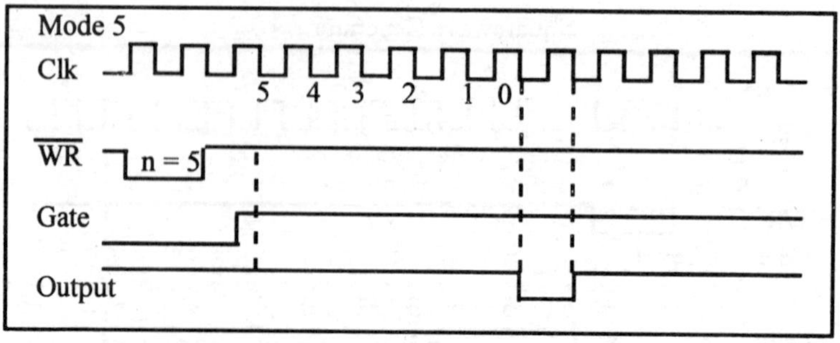

Fig.9.14 shows the Mode 4 and Mode 5.

MODE 4: Software Triggered Strobe

After the mode is set, the output will be high. When the count is loaded, the counter will begin counting. On terminal count, the output will go low for one input clock period then will go high again.

If the count register is reloaded between output pulses, the present period will not be affected, but the subsequent period will reflect the new value. The count will be inhibited while the gate input is low. Reloading the counter register will restart counter beginning with the new number.

MODE 5: Hardware Triggered Strobe

The control world and count value are loaded. The counting is started by the *rising edge,* that is by hardware. A low level pulse of 1 clock duration is generated when the count reaches the count value.

The counter is retriggerable. That is when the counting is on, if gate is retriggered. the counting is made to start from the beginning.

The counting and timing applications implemented in a microprocessor based system may be efficiently handled by 8253 device.

If the count value is odd, the output will be high for (N+1)/2 counts and low for (N–1)/2 counts.

CHAPTER 10

KEYBOARD AND DISPLAY INTERFACE - 8279

10.1 INTRODUCTION

Most of the microprocessor based systems will have an input and output device for the use of the human operator. The most common input device used is the keyboard and the output device is seven segment display.

The keyboard has to be constantly scanned to detect a key press. The display has to be constantly supplied with data to hold it steady. However if the CPU is required to do these operation itself, it will be heavily loaded and it will have lesser time left for other processing. On the other hand if these routines are managed by another device the CPU time can be efficiently utilised.

The Intel 8279 is one such device which interfaces a matrix type keyboard and multiplexed display.

10.2 DETAILS OF 8279

Fig.10.1 shows the pin details and the logic schematic of 8279.

The 8279 has the necessary facilities to connect a matrix type of keyboard and a multidigit seven segment display unit with the CPU.

The display section uses the scan lines A3-A0 and B3-B0. The scan lines SL_0–SL_3 are used as digit driver lines, the A3-A0 and B3-B0 lines put together will be used as segment lines. BD line is also available to blank the display.

In the keyboard section, the return lines RL0 to RL7 are the column lines of a keyboard. The shift and control lines read the status of the shift and control keys of the keyboard. The scan lines SL_2 to SL_0 play the additional role of selecting one row out of the many rows of the keyboard. The Interrupt Request (IRQ) line becomes active for every keypress.

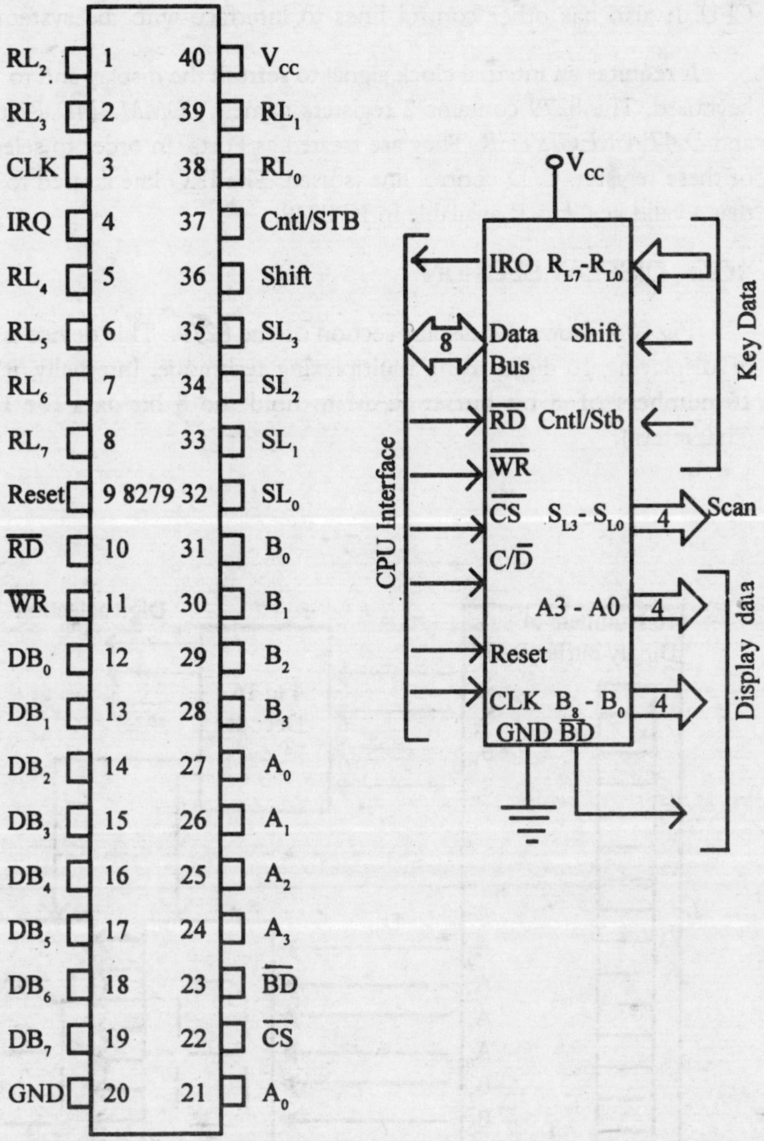

Fig.10.1 Pin details and the logic schematic of 8279.

The CPU interface section has 8 data lines for data transfer with the CPU. It also has other control lines to interface with the system bus.

It requires an internal clock signal to refresh the display and to scan the keyboard. The 8279 contains 2 registers namely *COMMAND REGISTER* and *DATA REGISTER*. They are treated as Ports. In order to select either of these register, $C/\overline{D}$ control line is used. The IRQ line is used to indicate that a valid key data is available in IC 8279.

10.3 DISPLAY SECTION

Fig.10.2 shows the display section of the 8279. This device is capable of displaying 16 digits using multiplexing technique. Internally, it contain 16 numbers of 8 bit buffer RAM to hold the 8 bit data for 16 digits (characters).

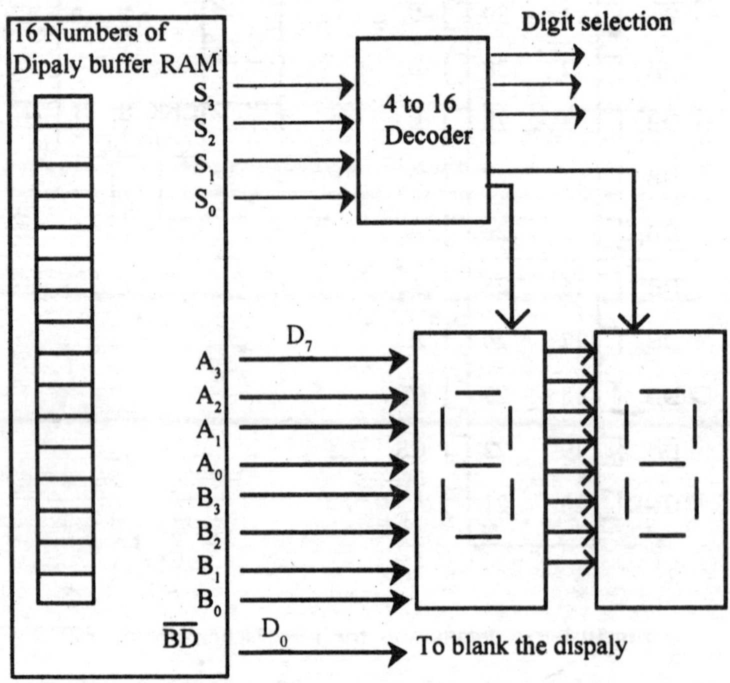

Fig.10.2 Display section of the 8279

The different display digits are multiplexed. This means all the digits are not turned ON together, but one after the other. The 4 scan lines output 0 (0000) to 15 (1111) in a periodic fashion, which can be decoded externally into 16 lines, to select any one of the 16 display digits.

The lines A3 to A0 together with B3 to B0 provide the 8 bit segment information for the display digits. The $\overline{BD}$ line can be used to blank all display digits. When the first digit is switched on, the first display buffer content is placed in A3 - A0 and B3 - B0 lines.

10.4 KEYBOARD SECTION

Fig.10.3 shows the keyboard section of the 8279. To capture the keyboard data the device features a keyboard buffer RAM.

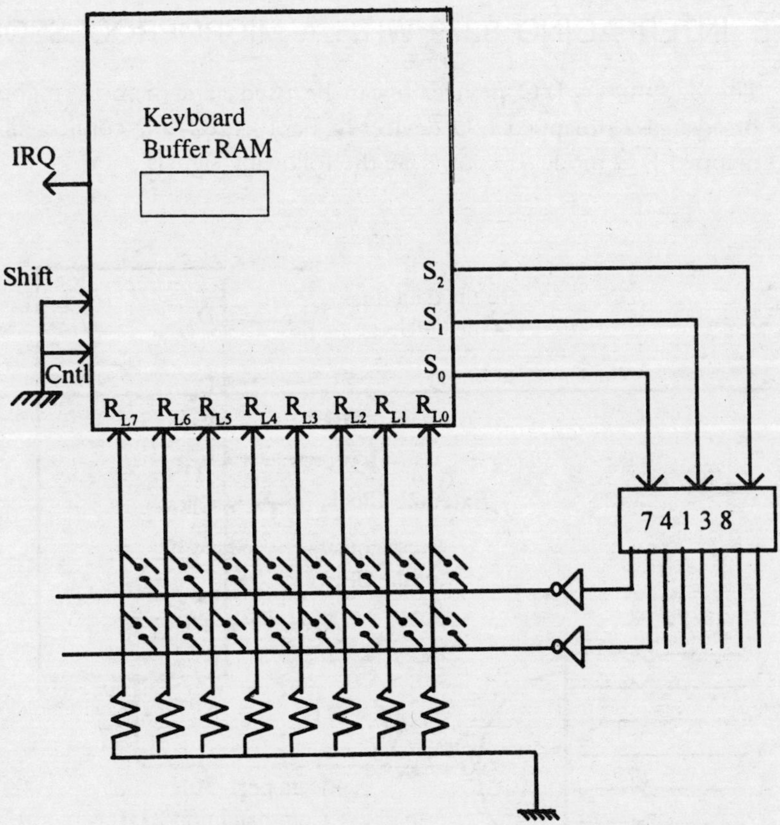

Fig.10.3 Keyboard section of the 8279.

The scan lines S_2, S_1 & S_0 are decoded to 8 lines to drive upto 8 rows of keys. The return lines RL7 to RL0 are used as column lines for the keyboard. The 8 row and 8 column signals enable the device to handle a 64 key keyboard.

However each key can have more than one function. This is made possible through the use of shift and control keys. Pressing together any key and either shift or control or both can give three more functions for each key. Thus 64 keys effectively could become 256 single function keys. Therefore, 2 exclusive lines *control* and *shift* take care of the control and shift keys.

When a key is pressed, its 8 bit code is loaded into the buffer RAM. The Interrupt Request is raised to indicate that the buffer RAM is not empty.

10.5 INTERFACING 8279 WITH A MICROPROCESSOR

The 8279 is an I/O device. It can be used as a memory mapped I/O or as an I/O mapped I/O device. In Fig.10.4, 8279 is connected in I/O mapped I/O mode. It consits of the following signals.

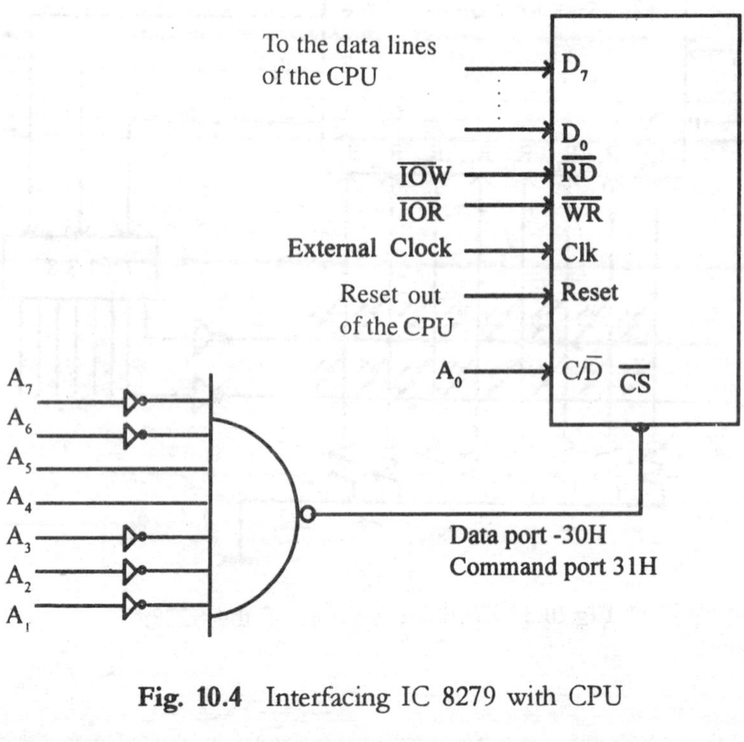

Fig. 10.4 Interfacing IC 8279 with CPU

- 8 data lines are connected to the data bus of the CPU.
- RESET signal is connected to the RESET OUT of the CPU.
- $\overline{RD}$ and $\overline{WR}$ signals are connected to $\overline{IOR}$ and $\overline{IOW}$ control signals.
- The output of the address decoder circuit is connected to $\overline{CS}$ pin in order to access the I.C as an I/O mapped device. The $\overline{CS}$ signal is active in this example for addresses 30H and 31H.
- C/$\overline{D}$ (Command/Data) signal is connected to A0 address line of the CPU in order to address Data register and Command register sequentially. It is connected to A0 address line so that the I/O address of the Data register is 30H and the Command register is 31H.
- The clock signal CLK, is connected to system clock.

10.6 CONCEPTS RELATED TO KEYBOARD AND DISPLAY

Encoded Scan and Decoded Scan

It was discussed earlier that the 4 scan lines S_3, S_2, S_1 and S_0 periodically output 0 to 15. This mode is called encoded scan mode. There is another type of scan called Decoded Scan. In this, the least 2 bits are decoded and decoded outputs are available in the scan lines S3, S2, S1 and S0. Note that when the keyboard is in decoded scan so is the display. This means that only the first 4 rows can be used and 4 characters in the display RAM are displayed.

S3	S2	S1	S0
0	0	0	1
0	0	1	0
0	1	0	0
1	0	0	0

The above table shows decoded scan output and the sequence is repeated again and again.
The disadvantage of the decoded scan is that the number of combinations is only 4. Hence only 4 rows can be used in the case of the keyboard or only 4 digits can be switched on in the case of the display.

Display – Left entry mode

In the left entry mode, the first location of the display RAM data is treated as the segment data for the Left most digit and and second location of the display is treated as the segment data for the second digit from the left and so on. This is also called typewriter display mode.

Display – Right entry mode

The right entry mode is also known as calculator mode. The first location of the display RAM indicate the display data for the right most digit. Therefore on the display, the data appears to start from right and shift towards left.

Keyboard Operation

Most of the keyboard use mechanical switches as keys.

The mechanical keys used in the keyboard have a problem. When a key is pressed the contacts bounce back and forth and settle down only after a small time delay. This is called bouncing. Bouncing may cause multiple entries made for the same key. To avoid this, after a key press is sensed the device is made to wait for few milliseconds. Then the key is checked again to ensure it is still pressed. If it is still pressed it is taken as a valid key press. This process is called debouncing. Debouncing is a builtin feature of IC 8279.

Two key lockout

If two keys are depressed within the debounce cycle, it is a simultaneous depression. Neither key will be recognised until one of the keys is released. The final key released will be recognised and entered.

N Key Roll Over

In this mode, each key depression is treated independently. If simultaneous depressions occurs, then keys are recognised and entered according to the order the keyboard scan found them.

10.7 PROGRAMMING 8279

The 8279 is a programmable interface device. Before using the 8279, it has to be programmed for desired operation. There are 8 commands that can be used in 8279. However, in this chapter, let us learn about four frequently used commands.

The different commands are entered in only one command register. The most significant 3 bits of the command tells the function of the command. The remaining 5 bits of the command tells about the parameters of the command.

The commands which are discussed are

1. Keyboard / Display Mode set
2. Program Clock
3. Write display buffer
4. Read Keyboard data from Buffer RAM.

1. Keyboard/Display Mode set command

The command bit pattern is as follows

D7	D6	D5	D4	D3	D2	D1	D0
0	0	0	D	D	K	K	K
		000		DD		KKK	

DD is the display mode and KKK is the keyboard mode.

This command sets up the operation of keyboard and display. D4 and D3 are meant for display while D2, D1 and D0 are used for keyboard.

D4 and D3 could be 0 0. This indicates that 8 digits are displayed and each digit has 8 bits. It also means that the data storage in RAM starts from the left most digit. This is known as the left entry mode or typewriter mode.

The other options available for display are :

D4	D3	Display option
0	1	16 digits, 8 bit Left entry
1	0	8 digits, 8 bit right entry
1	1	16 digits, 8 bit right entry

The D2, D1 and D0 bits could be 0 0 0. This sets up the device for 2 key lockout and also means the keyboard uses encoded scan. If two keys are pressed at the same time the last key released will be entered.

D2	D1	D0	Keyboard option
0	0	1	Decoded scan, 2 key roll over
0	1	0	Encoded scan, N key roll over
0	1	1	Decoded scan, N key roll over

The other 4 options are related with Sensor matrix mode which is not discussed in this lesson.

In order to set encoded scan and 2 key lock out and 8 bit 8 digit, left entry display mode, the command word works out to

D7	D6	D5	D4	D3	D2	D1	D0
0	0	0	0	0	0	0	0
			0	0	H		

When the following instructions are executed,

```
MVI A, 00H
OUT 31H
```

the keyboard and display will (command port) function as described above.

2. Program Clock Command

The device scans the different keys one by one to detect a keypress. It turns on the display devices one after another in sequence. It also implements key debouncing. All these operations require a timing signal. Therefore the device needs an internal clock. The design is such that the frequency of this clock has to be around 100 KHz.

The device receives clock signal through one of its pins. It can be the system clock or an external clock signal. This clock signal is divided by a suitable number to get the 100 KHz clock. Therefore the system provides a command word to set the division factor for the clock. The division factor is so chosen that after dividing the clock by this amount, it results in 100 KHz. For instance if the clock is 2 MHz, a scale factor of 20 will provide a internal clock of 100 KHz.

D7	D6	D5	D4	D3	D2	D1	D0
0	0	1	P	P	P	P	P

The 5 bits PPPPP (in binary) define the scale factor. To have a scale factor of 20 the command word works out to

D7	D6	D5	D4	D3	D2	D1	D0
0	0	1	1	0	1	0	0
			3	4 H.			

The instructions

```
MVI  A, 34H
OUT  31H
```

will set program clock to 100 KHz, if the external clock is 2 MHz.

Normally, the system clock-out signal will be in the order of 3 MHz. It can be connected to the CLK pin of the 8279. In this case, this Program clock command need not be executed because the default value is 32 and hence approximately an internal frequency 100 K Hz is obtained *even if this command is not executed.*

3. Write Display RAM Command

In the example shown in Fig.10.5, A3 A2 A1 A0 lines from 8279 are connected to the segments d c b a. B3 line is connected to decimal point and B2 B1 B0 lines are connected to the segments g f and e of the common cathode display.

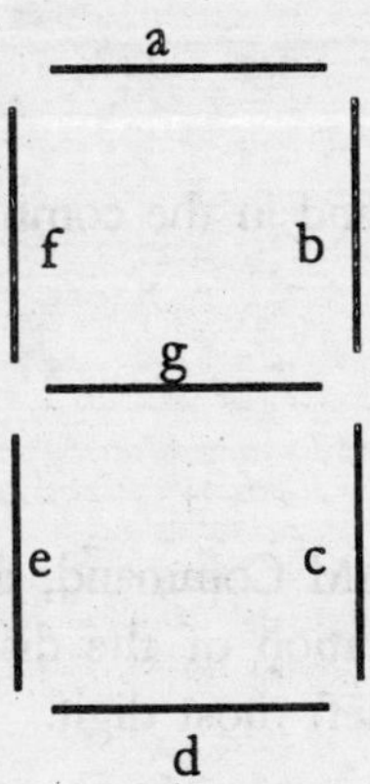

D_7	D_6	D_5	D_4	D_3	D_2	D_1	D_0
A_3	A_2	A_1	A_0	B_3	B_2	B_1	B_0
d	c	d	a	dp	g	f	e

Fig. 10.5 Display segment details

A3	A2	A1	A0	B3	B2	B1	B0
D7	D6	D5	D4	D3	D2	D1	D0
d	c	b	a	dp	g	f	e

When a bit is one level, the corresponding segment is switched ON. For instance, to display "C" the segment code becomes 93H; and to display "2" the segment code is B5H.

To display information, the segment data has to be written in the internal display buffer. To enable writing into the display buffer, *the write display RAM*

Write Display RAM Command format:

D7	D6	D5	D4	D3	D2	D1	D0
1	0	0	AI	A	A	A	A

The AI is the auto increment flag. AAAA is the address of the digit that the CPU is going to write into the buffer. Four bit address is provided to select any one of the digits.

For example to write the segment code 93H into the first location of the display RAM, the command would be

1	0	0	1	0	0	0	0
			9	0	H.		

```
MVI A, 90H
OUT    31H (command register)
```

These instructions will write the display command in the command register.

```
MVI A, 93H
OUT    30H (data register)
```

Following the loading of the Write Display RAM Command, these instructions will write the data 93H in the first location of the display RAM. Now the letter "C" will be displayed in the left most digit.

The Auto Increment flag of the command has been set to 1. This causes the next OUT data register operation to write the data in the next location; that is the 2nd location of the display RAM.

MVI A, B5H
OUT 30H. (data register)

Execution of these instructions will cause the segment code B5 to be written in the second location. The numeral "2" is displayed in the second digit from left.

4. Read FIFO Command

When a key is pressed the key code is formed and placed in the Keyboard Buffer RAM. Simultaneously the Interrupt Request line is raised. This interrupt request line may be used to interrupt the CPU, which then reads the data from the Buffer RAM. This method is called the INTERRUPT mode.

Alternatively, the status word of the device can also be read. The status word indicates the valid key press. When a valid key press is detected, the D0 bit of the status word goes high. Therefore the CPU has to look for a one at D0 bit of the status word. If one is found, the buffer RAM content may be read for the keycode. This approach is known as *POLLED* mode.

The keycode format is as follows :

D7	D6	D5	D4	D3	D2	D1	D0
CTRL	SHIFT	S2	S1	S0	R2	R1	R0

The D7 bit represents the control key status. The D6 bit represents the shift key status. The D_4, D_3 and D_2 bits represent status of the scan lines. D_2, D_1, D_0 bits represent the status of the return lines RL0 to RL7 in encoded form. Thus the status of the scan and return lines essentially form the keyboard data.

10.8 STATUS WORD

The status word can be read by reading the *COMMAND REGISTER*.

IN 31H

In order to check whether a key has been pressed or not, the status word is to be checked for 1 in D0 bit. Thereafter, the keydata is to be read.

Before reading the FIFO RAM, a *READ FIFO RAM command* has to be written into the command register.

D7	D6	D5	D4	D3	D2	D1	D0
0	1	0	AI	X	A	A	A

The AI flag and the address lines AAA are relevant only in sensor matrix mode. They are not applicable to the keyboard mode. Therefore the command word to read the keyboard would be

0	1	0	0	0	0	0	0
			4	0	H		

```
MVI A, 40H
OUT    31H
```

After executing these commands the FIFO RAM may be read for keyboard data.

```
IN 30H
```

This instruction will read data from the FIFO RAM. 30H is the address of the data register.

If the next key data is to be read, then again IN 30H instruction is to be executed because the buffer RAM works in First In First Out mode.

There are 4 more commands associated with I.C. 8279 to clear the buffer and to read the write display RAM, to inhibit writing into the display buffer RAM and to blank the display.

10.9 PROGRAM TO CHECK THE STATUS WORD

Label	Mnemonic	Comments
	MVI A, 00 OUT 31 H	; encoded scan, 2 key lockout and ; left entry mode is written in command ; register.

Label	Mnemonic	Comments
LOOP	IN 31H	; read the status word
	ANI 01	; check whether D0 becomes 1. If so, ; one character is available in keyboard ; buffer RAM. It indicates ; that one key has been pressed.
	JZ LOOP	; the loop is repeated till a key is ; pressed. The processor waits in this ; loop. If D0 becomes 1 level, it ; comes out of the loop.
	MVI A, 40H	; enter the Read FIFO RAM command
	OUT 31H	; into the command register
	IN 30H	; read the data register to take the key data

Now, the keydata is available in the accumulator.

Thus the I.C. 8279 can be used for keyboard and display interface purpose in microprocessor based systems.

SERIAL COMMUNICATION INTERFACE—8251

10.10 SERIAL COMMUNICATION FORMATS

Serial transmission is always preferred for transmission where the distance is longer than about 5 meters. The reason is it requires fewer data lines than parallel transmission. Serial communication requires *timing signals* added along with the data bits. According to the type of timing signals added serial transmission is divided into

- synchronous and
- asynchronous types

Asynchronous transmission adds timing signals to each character of data. A START bit is added at the begining. A STOP bit is added at the end. A LOW level signal is used for start bit. A HIGH level signal is used for stop bit. This process of adding start and stop bits to a character is known as *FRAMING*. Fig.10.6 explain the framing process of character.

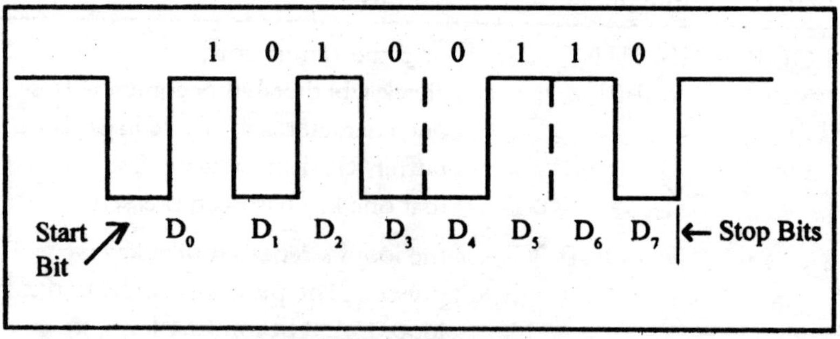

(a) Framing a character

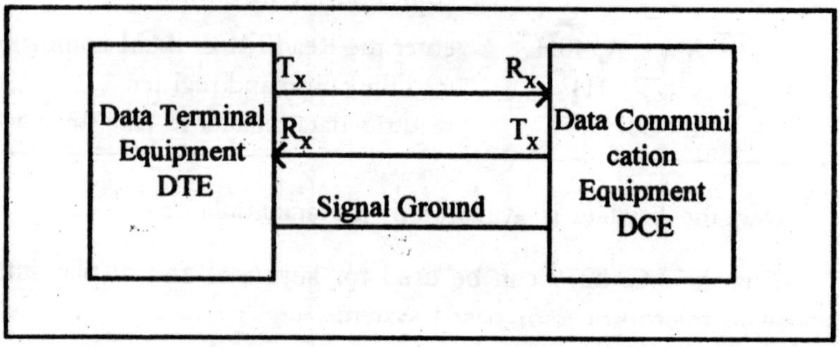

Fig. 10.6 (b) RS 232C Connection

The *falling edge* of the start bit is the timing reference. Therefore the start bit causes synchronisation of the receiver with the transmitter. A *PARITY* bit is also added to the data bits before the stop bit.

Synchronous format does not add timing signals to each character. Instead, the data is divided into fairly large blocks, typically 1000s of bytes. *Synchronising signals* are added once before each block. The synchronisation characters mark the begining of transmission. Since the receiver has to remain synchronised through out the transmission period, a clock signal is extracted from the received data. Otherwise the clock is supplied from an external source. Timing from this clock is used to detect the individual bits of the received data.

Framing overhead for synchronous transmission is much smaller and therefore it is much efficient. It is used for high speed data transfer. However it requires complex circuitry at the receiver for clock and data recovery.

The asynchronous transmission uses simple circuitry. It is used for low speed data transmission up to a speed of 20 kbit/second.

The number of bits transmitted per second is called *Bit Rate.* The bit rate is also known as *BAUD Rate.*

10.11 SIMPLEX AND DUPLEX TRANSMISSION

In SIMPLEX TRANSMISSION, data is transmitted in only one direction. A typical example is the transmission of data from a computer to a printer.

In DUPLEX TRANSMISSION, data flows in both directions. However, if the transmission goes one way at a time, it is called HALF DUPLEX; if it goes both ways simultaneously, it is called FULL DUPLEX. The old version of walkie talkie is an example of half duplex. The telephone conversion and the communication between the computers are examples of full duplex.

10.12 SERIAL COMMUNICATION STANDARDS

The current pulse method is known as current loop. For a logical 1 level current flows through the line and for a logical 0 level no current flows.

The two standards for the current loop are

- 20 milliamps loop
- 60 milliamps loop.

A current loop reduces noise pickup. And so is suitable for long distance transmission.

When data is transmitted as voltage, the standard used is RS232C.

A 1 level signal is transmitted as -12 V.
A 0 level signal is transmitted as +12 V.

A device called line driver does this voltage level shifting at the transmitter end. A line receiver does the reverse shifting at the receiver. This level shifting is done to overcome losses and for better noise performance.

Fig. 10.6 (b) shows the minimum connection required for RS 232C connection.

10.13 MODEM

One of the most common applications of serial transmission would be data trnasmission between large computers. The physical connection between the computers can be readily set up using *telephone lines.* However the telephone lines are designed to carry analog voice frequency signals. They will not readily support digital signals. Therefore the digital data is to be translated into audio frequency analog format (Modulator and Demodulator).

A device called MODEM does this signal translation. A sending modem converts digital data into audio frequency analog format. A receiving modem converts audio signal back to digital data.

Modems often use a technique called frequency shift keying for this conversion. This technique converts a 1 level signal into an audio signal at 1200 Hz and 0 level into audio signal at 2200 Hz. The calling computer simply dials the receiving one and a link is thus established whenever there is need to send data.

10.14 SERIAL I/O USING 8085 CPU

The 8085 CPU has a serial output data pin SOD and a serial input data pin SID. They can be used for software controlled serial data transfer. The SIM and RIM instructions are used for this purpose.

Serial data output through SOD pins

A 0 or 1 can be transferred out through SOD pin by executing the SIM instructions. The first step is to load the data bit into the accumulator.

The data byte format is

D7	D6	D5	D4	D3	D2	D1	D0
serial data	SOE 1 - Enable SOD 0 - Disable SOD			Not used			

The single bit data to be transmitted is placed at the *D7 th bit.* A one level at D6 bit enables the SIM instruction.

To send a 1 through the SOD pin, the data byte pattern would be

D7	D6	D5	D4	D3	D2	D1	D0
1	1	0	0	0	0	0	0
			C	0 H			

The following program segment will send out one bit through the SOD pin

```
MVI A,C0H
SIM
```

Serial Data input through SID

The SID pin can be used to receive serial data. The RIM instruction is used for this purpose. When the RIM instruction is executed once, the single bit data available at the SID pin is brought into the accumulator as the D7 th bit. All other bits are made 0.

Thus the SID and SOD bins may be used to transmit and receive serial data through the microcomputer The framing of the data for synchronous or asynchronous format can be done using software.

10.15 SOFTWARE APPROACH TO IMPLEMENT SERIAL TRANSMISSION

Transmit Operation

The SOD pin is used for serial transmit operation. The parallel data must be converted into a sequence of serial bits through the rotate instruction. The following sequence is used for serial transmission through the SOD pin.

- At the begining of every character the 0 level of the start bit is sent out
- This is followed by the data bits, parity bit and the stop bit
- The bit which is to be transmitted is placed in the most significant bit of the accumulator.
- It is sent out using SIM instruction
- A time delay suitable for the Baud rate has to be added in between the transmission of the bits.
- For 110 Baud the time delay works out to around 9 millisecond.

Receive Operation

The SID pin is used for reception. The received serial data is internally converted into parallel data. The sequence for receiving a byte of data is given in the following

- The SID pin has to be read every 9 millisecond to find out its level, for 110 baud.
- When no character is transmitted it would be getting repeated 1s.
- The first 0 received indicate the start bit.
- With reference to the start bit the other data bits, parity bit and stop bit are identified.
- The reading of the SID pin is done using RIM instruction.

10.16 PROGRAMMABLE HARDWARE APPROACH

There are powerful programmable communication interface ICs through which the serial data transfer can be effectively carried out. Thereby CPU time can be effectively used for job processing. 8251 is one such programmable communication device.

Programmable Communication Interface 8251

The 8251 is a programmable I/O device designed for serial communication. It can be used either in synchronous mode or asynchronous mode. It is also called as Universal Synchronous Asynchronous Receiver and Transmitter (USART). It comes in a 28 pin dual in line package. It has got facilities to

- generate the baud rate clock using external clock
- convert outgoing parallel data into serial data
- convert incoming serial data into parallel data
- control a modem.

This device is mainly used as the asynchronous serial interface between the processor and the external equipment.

10.17 BLOCK DIAGRAM

Fig.10.7 shows the block diagram of 8251. It consists of mainly four major sections which communicate with each other on an internal data bus. The four sections are

- Receiver
- Transmitter
- Modem control
- Microprocessor Interface section

10.18 THE RECEIVER

Fig.10.8 shows the detailed diagram of the receiver and transmitter sections. The receiver section consists of Receiver buffer register, Receiver control logic and input register. The receiver accepts serial data on the RxD pin and converts it to parallel data according to the appropriate format. When the 8251 is in the asynchronous mode and it is ready to accept a character, it looks for a low level on the R x D line. When it gets a low level, it assumes that it is a START bit and enables an internal counter. At a count equivalent to one-half of a bit time, the R x D line is sampled

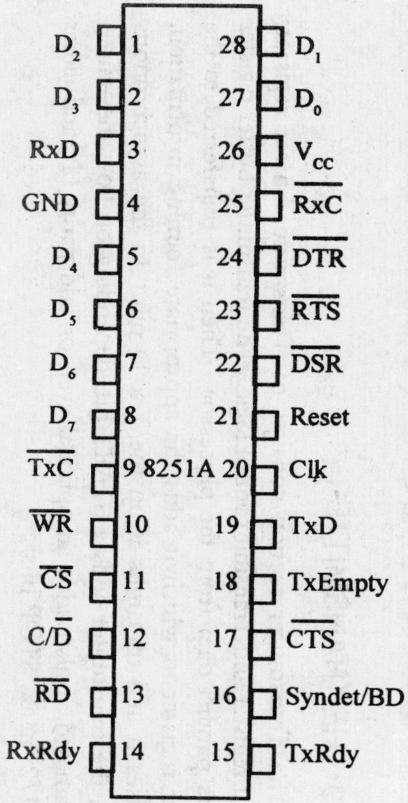

D_7-D_0	Data Bus (8Bits)
$C/\overline{D}$	Control or data is to be Written or Read
$\overline{RD}$	Read Data Command
$\overline{WR}$	Write Data or Control Command
$\overline{CS}$	Chip Enable
RESET	Reset
$\overline{TxC}$	Teansmit Clock
TxD	Transmit Data
$\overline{RxC}$	Receiver Clock
RxD	Receiver Data
RxRDY	Receiver Ready
TxRDY	Teansmit Ready
DSR	Data Set Ready
DTR	Data Terminal Ready
SYNDET /BD	Sync Detect/ Break Detect
RTS	Request to Send Data
CTS	Clear to Send Data
TxE	Transmitter Empty
Vcc	+5 Volt supl;y
GND	Ground

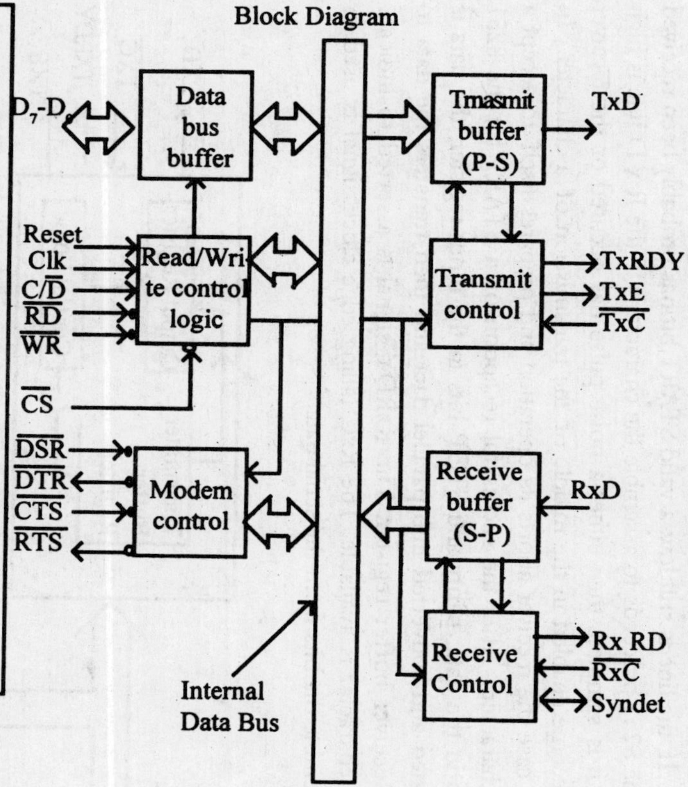

Fig. 10.7 8251 Block diagram and pin details

again. If the line is still low, a valid START bit has probably been received and the 8251 proceeds to assemble the character. If the R x D line is high when it is sampled, then either a noise pulse has occured or the receiver has become enabled in the middle of the transmission of a character. In either case the receiver aborts its operation and prepares itself to accept a new character. After the successful reception of a START bit the 8251 clocks in the data, parity and STOP bits in the input register, the data is separated and converted into parallel data and then transfers the data to The Receiver buffer register. The RxRDY signal is asserted to indicate that a character is available. The RxC falling edge clock signal is used to disassemble the bits from the serial data.

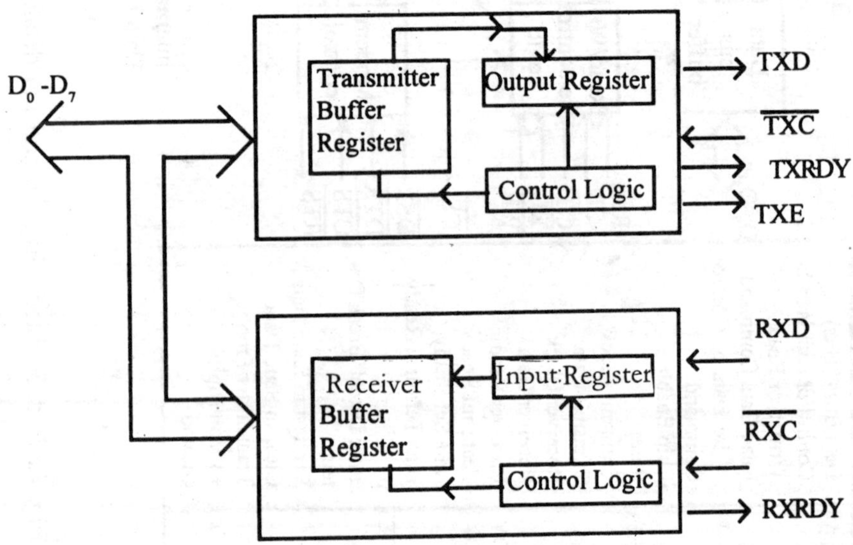

Fig. 10.8 Block diagram of transmitter and receiver

10.19 THE TRANSMITTER

The Transmitter section consists of Transmitter buffer register, Output register and Transmit control logic. The transmitter buffer register accepts parallel data from the processor. Then it is transferred to the output register in which it adds the appropriate framing information, serialises it and transmits it on the T x D pin. In the asynchronous mode, the transmitter adds a START bit, depending on how the unit is programmed, it also adds an optional even or odd parity bit, and either 1, 1 1/2 or 2 STOP bits.

When the transmitter buffer register is empty, then it outputs a signal Tx RDY. It indicates to the CPU that the 8251 is ready to accept a data character. This signal can be used as interrupt line. This signal is reset when a byte of data is loaded by the CPU into the transmitter buffer register.

When there is no data in the transmitter output register, then it raises Tx E signal to indicate that the transmission is stopped. It is reset when the data is transferred from the buffer register.

10.20 MODEM CONTROL

Fig. 10.9 shows the modem connection to the IC 8251. The modem control section provides for the generation of $\overline{RTS}$ and the reception of $\overline{CTS}$. In addition, a general purpose output and a general purpose input are provided. The output is labeled $\overline{DTR}$ and the input is labeled $\overline{DSR}$. $\overline{DTR}$ (Data Terminal Ready) is normally assigned to modem, indicating that the terminal is ready to communicate and $\overline{DSR}$ (Data Set Ready) is a signal from the modem indicating that it is ready for communication.

10.21 MICROPROCESSOR INTERFACE SECTION

Fig.10.10 shows the connection of 8251 with the microprocessor.

1. It consists of 8 data lines connected to the data bus of the CPU.
2. Since the IC is serial I/O interface, it can be used either in I/O mapped I/O or memory mapped I/O mode. In the following example, since it is used as I/O mapped I/O, the $\overline{RD}$ and $\overline{WR}$ lines are connected to $\overline{IOR}$ and $\overline{IOW}$ control lines.
3. CLK pin is connected to the CLK OUT of the CPU to provide synchronisation for the CPU interface section.
4. RESET pin is connected to the RESET OUT of the CPU. When it is in high level, the I.C 8251 is forced into the idle mode.
5. $\overline{CS}$ pin is connected to the address decoder output.
6. C/$\overline{D}$ line is used to select internal registers; either CONTROL REGISTER or DATA REGISTER. Normally it is connected to the A0 address line.

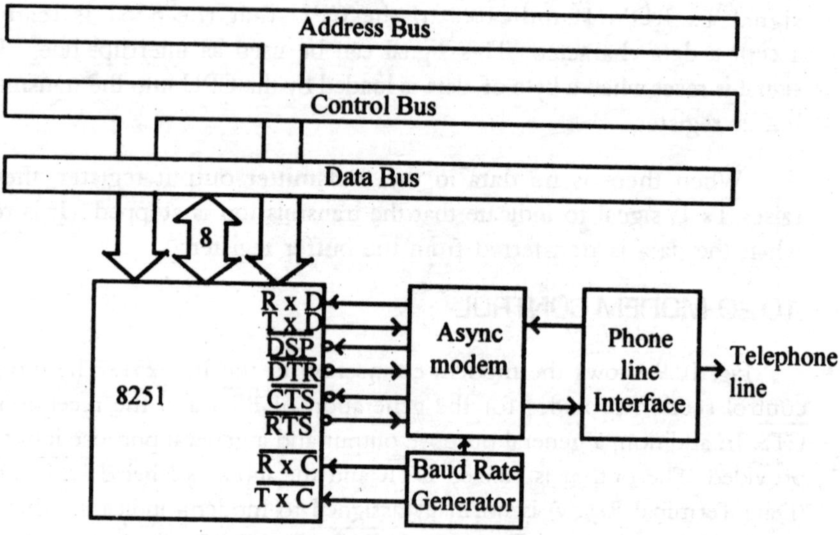

Fig. 10.9 Asynchronous interface to telephone lines

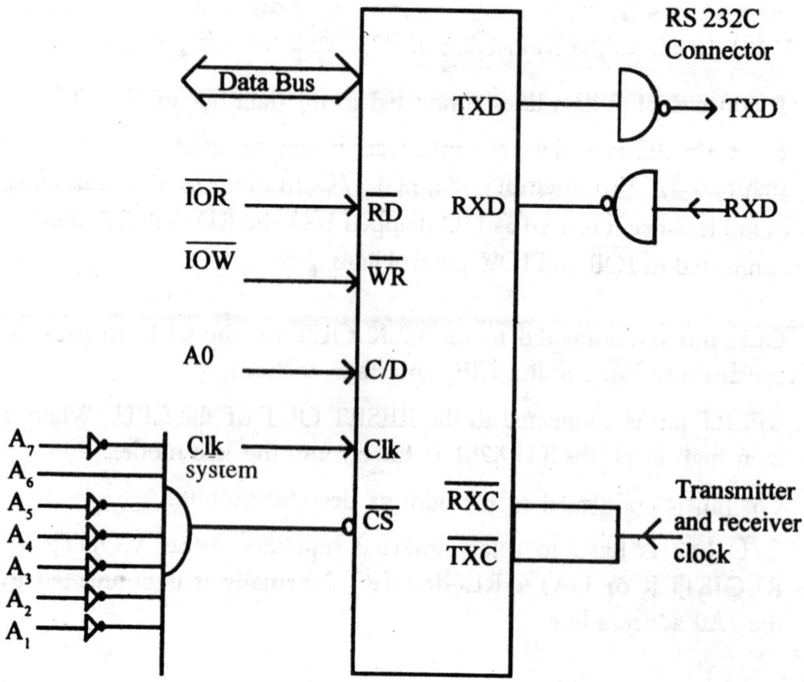

Fig. 10.10 Interfacing of RS 232C with 8251

10.22 PROGRAMMING 8251

Inside the 8251, there is a pair of 8 bit control registers (totally 16 bit) to load mode word and to load command word. Fig.10.11 shows the control logic and registers inside the IC. Mode word tells about the initialisation parameters like Mode, Baud, Stop bits and Parity. Command word tells about enabling the transmitter and receiver section. Like other programmable peripheral devices, the readiness of the peripherals can also be checked by reading the status word.

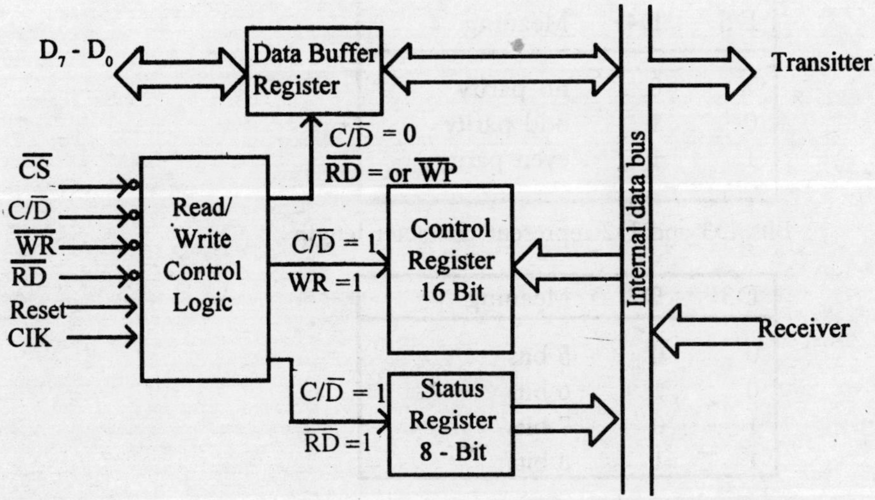

Fig. 10.11 Control logic and registers inside the IC

To initialise the device for asynchronous mode, a certain sequence of control words must be followed.

After a Reset operation, a mode word must be written in the control register followed by a command word. Any control word written into the control register immediately after a mode word will be interpreted as a command word, that means a command word can be changed anytime during the operation. However, the 8251 should be reset prior to writing a new mode word, and it can be reset by using Internal Reset bit (D6) in the command word.

Mode Word

The mode word format is described below.

D7	D6	D5	D4	D3	D2	D1	D0

Bits D7 and D6 represent number of stop bits

D7	D6	Meaning
0	0	not valid
0	1	1 stop bit
1	0	1 1/2 stop bits
1	1	2 stop bits

Bits D5 and D4 represent parity control

D5	D4	Meaning
X	0	no parity
0	1	odd parity
1	1	even parity

Bits D3 and D2 represent character length

D3	D2	Meaning
0	0	5 bits
0	1	6 bits
1	0	7 bits
1	1	8 bits

Bits D1 and D0 represent Baud rate factor

D1	D0	Meaning
0	0	Sync mode
0	1	Asyn x 1
1	0	Asyn x 16
1	1	Asyn x 64

10.23 EXAMPLE

The mode word is coined for the following requirements

1. 8251 is operated in asynchronous mode for transmit
2. Baud rate is 1200
3. Character length is 8 bits and number of stop bits is 2
4. Odd parity

5. Clock rate is 76.8 KHz. Since the baud rate is 1200, Asyn x 64 is to be selected 64 × 1200 = 76.8 KHz.
6. Addresses of the control register is 41H and data register is 40H

The mode word becomes

D7	D6	D5	D4	D3	D2	D1	D0
1	1	0	1	1	1	1	1
			D	F	H		

The statements

```
MVI A, DFH
OUT 41H
```

will load the mode word for the above environment into the control register.

Command Word

Once the functional definition of the 8251 has been programmed by the mode instruction, the device is ready for data communication. The command instruction controls the actual operation of the selected format. Functions such as Enable Transmit / Receive, Error Reset and Modem Controls are provided by the Command Instruction. The Command Instruction format is discussed below.

D7	D6	D5	D4	D3	D2	D1	D0
EN	IR	RTS	ER	SBRK	RXE	DTR	TXEN

The D7 bit is used in synchronous mode. It enables the receiver to look for the synchronizing data.

The D6 bit is used as the internal reset. A high level resets the device, so that a new mode word can be entered.

The D5 bit controls the request to send pin of the device. A 1 level at this bit makes the RTS pin to become active.

The D4 bit resets the error flags. It resets the parity, overrun and framing error flags.

The D3 bit makes the transmitter to send continuous break characters.

The D2 bit enables the receiver.

The D1 bit controls the Data Terminal Ready pin.

The D0 bit enables the transmitter.

In order to set the device for transmission the command word would be

D7	D6	D5	D4	D3	D2	D1	D0
0	0	0	1	0	0	0	1
			1	1	H		

The statements

MVI A, 11H
OUT 41H

will load the command word into the control register.

Before actually sending the 8 bit data to the transmitter section, the STATUS WORD can be checked. The status word tells about the current activity of the device. It can be read by the CPU by reading the control register. Some of the bits in the Status word format have identical meanings to external output pins so that the 8251 can be used in completely polled environment or in an interrupt driven environment.

10.23 STATUS WORD REGISTER FORMAT

D7	D6	D5	D4	D3	D2	D1	D0
DSR	SYNDET	FE	OE	PE	TXE	RXRDY	TXRDY

- D7 reflects the logic level of the DSR (Modem Control) pin.
- D6 is used for synchronous mode (SYNDET)
- D5 represents Framing error. It is set when a valid stop bit is not detected.
- D4 represents Overrun error. It is set when the CPU does not read a character before the next one becomes available.
- D3 represents Parity error. It is set when there is a parity error.

All these error bits are reset by the ER bit of the command instruction.

- D2 represents the status of the pin T x E.
- D1 represents the status of the pin R x RDY.
- D0 represents the status of the pin T x RDY.

In serial transmission, the 8 bit data can be sent to the 8251 through the data register (40H) after checking the T x RDY bit. It is done by checking the D0 bit of the status word.

```
STATUS    IN 41H
          ANI 01H
          JZ  STATUS
          MVI A, 8 bit data
          OUT 40H
```

These instructions will send the 8 bit data. There should be repeated before sending the next byte data from the CPU.

With the serial interface, the microprocessor based system can be connected to the PC for uploading and downloading programs. It can also be connected to the other serial devices.

CHAPTER 11

PRIORITY INTERRUPT CONTROLLER - 8259

11.1 INTRODUCTION

Interrupts are used in a microcomputer system for a variety of applications. The interrupt facility allows many devices to access the CPU. For example, reading a keyboard on an interrupt basis. It can also be used to detect an emergency. When more number of interrupts are used from different sources, an external device is required to control the interrupt servicing. This device is called the Priority Interrupt Controller (PIC). In this section, let us learn how the Priority Interrupt Controller 8259A is connected in a system, how it is initialised and how it is used to handle interrupts from multiple sources.

The device 8259A is a programmable controller designed to be used with 8085, 8086 and 8088 processors. The features of the device are

- it can handle 8 external interrupts
- the starting address of the interrupt service routine can be vectored (pointed) to any location in the memory map, unlike the predetermined starting addresses for RST instructions as well as RST hardware interrupts of 8085.
- it can be set to accept level triggered or edge triggered inputs
- at any instant, the status of pending interrupts, under service interrupt and masked interrupts can be read
- the interrupt system can be expanded to 64 interrupt inputs by cascading many 8259 devices. The first device will be the Master and other 8259 will be Slaves.

It is to be noted that using 8259A in 8086/8088 processor based system is different from using it in 8085 based system. In this chapter, we are going to learn the interfacing the device with the 8085 based system.

11.2 OVERVIEW OF THE 8259A

Fig.11.1 shows the internal block diagram of 8259A. The data bus allows the processor to send the control words to the device and read status word from it and to read the CALL instruction and starting address of the Interrupt Service Routine. The $\overline{RD}$ and $\overline{WR}$ input signals are used to control these transfer, provided that the Chip Select ($\overline{CS}$) input is low.

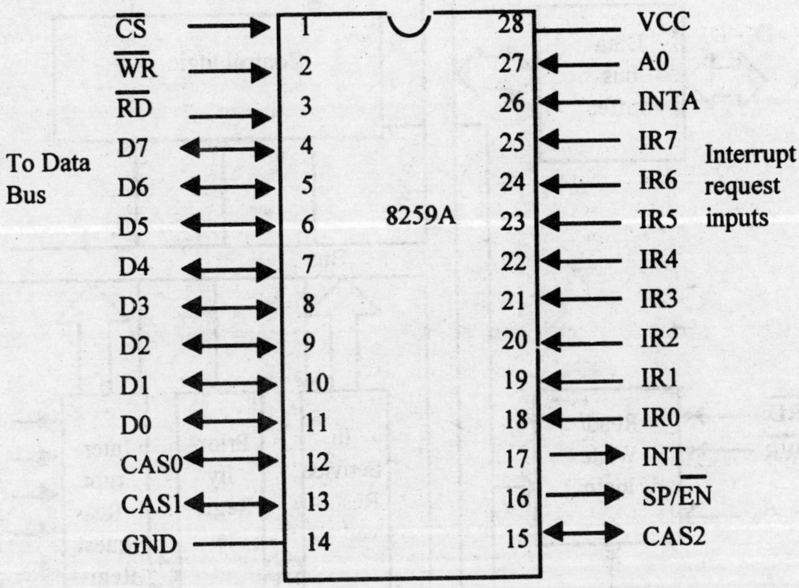

Fig. 11.1 Pin configuration of programmable interrupt control IC 8059A (Top view)

The 8 interrupt inputs are labelled as IR0, IR1,....IR7. If the IC is enabled, an interrupt signal applied to any one of these interrupts will cause the 8259A to generate an INT output signal. Normally it is connected to the INTR pin of the processor. The $\overline{INTA}$ signal of the processor is connected to the $\overline{INTA}$ signal of the 8259A. When the CPU acknowledges the interrupt by through $\overline{INTA}$, the 8259A places the opcode for the CALL instruction on the data bus.

The CPU understands the CALL instruction opcode and places two more $\overline{INTA}$ signals. When the 8259A receives the second $\overline{INTA}$, it places the low-order byte of the CALL address on the data bus. At the third $\overline{INTA}$, it places the high-order byte of the address on the data bus. Then the corresponding interrupt service routine is executed. This starting address for the particular interrupt request should have been placed in the control registers of the 8259A during the initialisation.

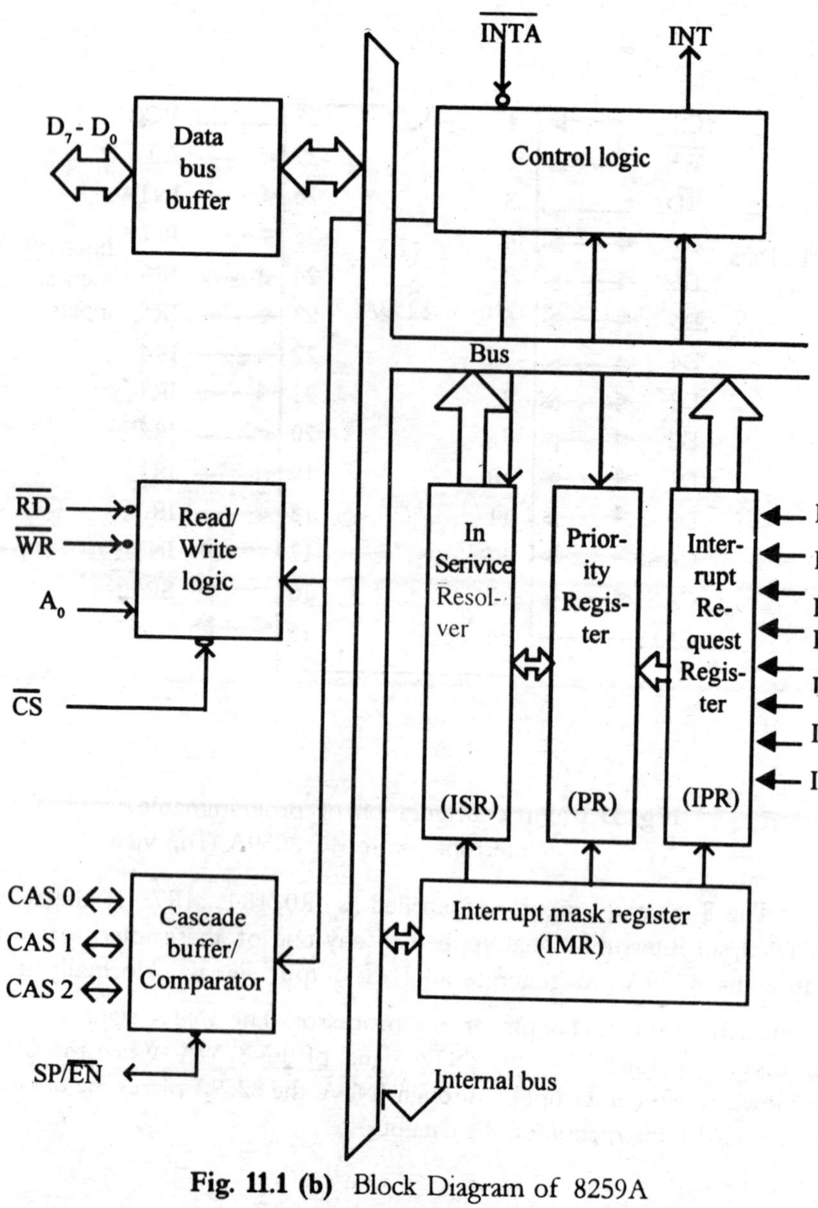

Fig. 11.1 (b) Block Diagram of 8259A

The 8259A is a Priority Interrupt Controller. There are different priority modes. In the *FIXED PRIORITY* mode, the IR0 input has the highest priority and IR7 has the lowest priority.

In the block diagram, there are 4 boxes labelled as

- Interrupt Request Register (IRR)
- Interrupt Mask Register (IMR)
- In Service Register (ISR)
- Priority Resolver

The 8 bits of the interrupt mask register are used to disable or enable individual interrupt inputs; writing 0 in the corresponding bit location enables the interrupt.

The interrupt request register keeps track of which interrupt inputs are asking for service. When the interrupt input arrives, the corresponding mask bit is checked and if it is enabled, then the corresponding bit in the interrupt request register is set.

The in-service register keeps track of which interrupt inputs are currently being serviced. More than one bit may be in the set level. It is a priority interrupt controller, this means, even while executing an interrupt, it will accept and service a higher priority interrupt; but it will reject a lower priority interrupt. The priority resolver does the job of judging whether to allow another interrupt to be executed in the middle of executing one interrupt service routine. It is detailed in the Fig.11.2

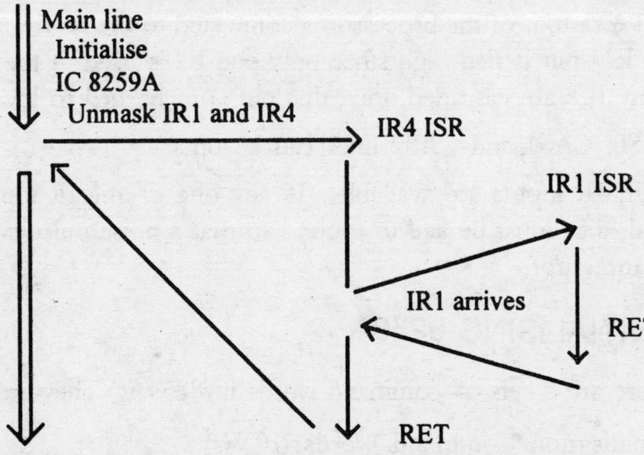

Fig.11.2 Execution of Interrupt Service Routines

1. Assume that the bits for IR1 and IR4 are unmasked in the interrupt mask register
2. Assume that initially IR4 input arrives.
3. The bit 4 in the in service register is set. The INT pin is made high and in response to the processor, the calling address of the IR4 is sent and the processor executes the interrupt service routine for IR4
4. It is assumed that the chip works in the fixed priority basis
5. Now, assume that the interrupt IR1 arrives.
6. Since IR1 has higher priority than the interrupt which is being currently serviced, it will set the bit 1 in the in service register and makes the CPU to execute the interrupt service routine for IR1.
7. At the end of the ISR of IR1, a command word is sent to 8259A to reset the bit (belonging to IR1) in the in service register. The last instruction RET will make the remaining portion of the ISR of the IR4 executed.

11.3 CONNECTION DIAGRAM OF 8259A

1. The address decoder asserts the $\overline{CS}$ input of the IC
2. A0 line is used to select one of the 2 internal addresses in the device. It is connected directly to A0 of the address lines of the system
3. Since the device is used in I/O mapped I/O mode, the $\overline{RD}$ and $\overline{WR}$ signals are connected to $\overline{IOR}$ and $\overline{IOW}$ signals respectively.
4. INT output of the device is connected to the INTR input of the processor 8085
5. $\overline{INTA}$ output of the processor is connected to the $\overline{INTA}$ input.
6. SP/EN pin is tied high since only one IC is used in the system. If many ICs are cascaded, then this pin is to be tied to low
7. CAS0, CAS1 and CAS2 lines can be open
8. Eight IR inputs are available. If any one of the IR inputs are not used, they must be tied to ground so that a noise pulse cannot cause an interrupt.

11.4 INITIALISING 8259A

There are 2 sets of command words in 8259A. They are

1. Initialisation Command Words (ICWs)
2. Operation Command Words (OCWs)

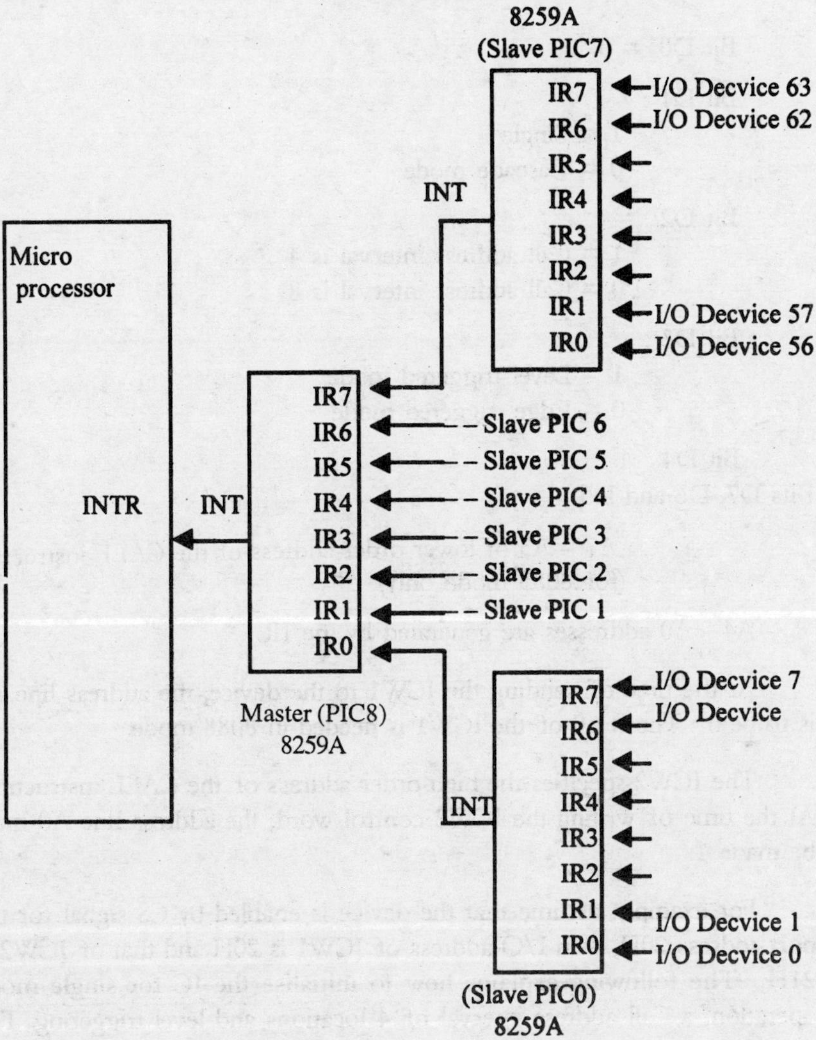

Fig.11.3 shows the connection diagram of 8259A with the system.

Initialisation command words

There are 4 Initialisation Command Words. ICW1 and ICW2 must be sent to every 8259 system. If the system has any slave 8259s (cascade mode) then an ICW3 must be used. For special operations like special fully nested mode, ICW4 is to be used.

Format of ICW1 :

D7	D6	D5	D4	D3	D2	D1	D0
A7	A6	A5	1	LTIM	ADI	SNGL	0

Bit D0 = 0

Bit D1 :

1 = Single
0 = Cascade mode

Bit D2 :

1 = Call address interval is 4
0 = Call address interval is 8

Bit D3 :

1 = Level triggered mode
0 = Edge triggered mode

Bit D4 : 1

Bits D7, D6 and D5 :

A7 – A5 of lower order address of the CALL instruction.
(for 8085 mode only)

A4 - A0 addresses are generated by the IR.

At the time of sending the ICW1 to the device, the address line A0 is to be 0. The Bit 0 of the ICW1 is needed in 8088 mode.

The ICW2 specifies the high order address of the CALL instruction. At the time of writing the ICW2 control word, the address line A0 must be made 1.

For example, assume that the device is enabled by $\overline{CS}$ signal for the port address 20H, then I/O address of ICW1 is 20H and that of ICW2 is 21H. The following explains how to initialise the IC for single mode operation, a Call address interval of 4 locations and level triggering. The Call address table starts from 8EA0H onwards.

```
DI              to avoid interrupts at the time of initialisation
MVI A, BEH      Hex code for ICW1
OUT 20 H
MVI A, 8EH      Hex code for ICW2
OUT 21H
```

Coding of ICW1

D7	D6	D5	D4	D3	D2	D1	D0
1	0	1	1	1	1	1	0
			B	E			

For IR_0 interrupt, the lower order address is obtained from D7, D6 and D5 bits

D7	D6	D5	D4	D3	D2	D1	D0
1	0	1	0	0	0	0	0

and placing zeros in the position D4, D3, D2, D1 and D0 for IR_1 interrupt, the lower order address is 10100100 since the call address interval is chosen as 4 in the example and so on as higher order address is written as ICW_2.

After writing ICWs, the OCWs are to be written. OCW1 is written to *unmask any IR inputs.* OCW2 is mainly used to *reset a bit in the in-service register.* OCW2 is called as the *End-of-Interrupt (EOI)* command. It is usually written at the end of the interrupt service routine.

Format of OCW1

D7	D6	D5	D4	D3	D2	D1	D0
M7	M6	M5	M4	M3	M2	M1	M0

1 = mask set
0 = mask reset

For example, in order to enable the interrupts IR5,IR3 and IR1 then the bit pattern of the OCW1 is to be

1 1 0 1 0 1 0 1

While writing the OCW1, the A0 D5H address line must be in one level. The simple program segment will be MVIA, D5H out 21H.

Format of OCW2

D7	D6	D5	D4	D3	D2	D1	D0
R	SEOI	EOI	0	0	L2	L1	L0

In our example, we have seen how to service higher priority interrupts. When the IR1 is serviced, the bit4 and bit 1 of the in-service register are set. At the end of the IR1 service routine, the bit1 of the in-service register is to be reset. Otherwise, other priority interrupts cannot interrupt while the remaining part of the IR4 service routine is executed. The effect of resetting the in-service register (ISR) for an interrupt level is that once the bit is reset, the 8259A can respond to interrupt signals of lower priority. At the time of issuing the OCW2, the address line A0 is to be 0 .

The End-of-Interrupt command can be issued in three formats :

Nonspecific EOI Command: This command resets the highest priority ISR bit in the in-service register. For this, the bit pattern in the format of OCW2 is

D7	D6	D5	D4	D3	D2	D1	D0
0	0	1	0	0	0	0	0 => 20H

EOI bit is to be 1 level.

The program segment is MVIA, 20H OUT 20H

Specific EOI command: This command resets the specific ISR bit in the in-service register. The bit pattern for this command is

D7	D6	D5	D4	D3	D2	D1	D0
0	1	1	0	0	L2	L1	L0

SEOI and EOI bits must be in 1 level and the encoded 3 bit value of the specific bit is written in L2,L1 and L0. For example, in order to reset the bit 2 of the in-service register corresponding to the IR2, then the bit pattern of the OCW2 must be

D7	D6	D5	D4	D3	D2	D1	D0
0	1	1	0	0	0	1	0 => 62H

Automatic EOI: If this mode is set, no command is necessary to reset the highest priority ISR bit in the in-service register. During the **third** INTA (active low) sent by the processor, the in-service register bit is set. Hence the in-service register does not have information on which IR is being serviced. Thus any IR can interrupt irrespective of its priority. Automatic EOI is actuated by writing initialisation command ICW4 and making the D1 bit to 1 level. At the time of writing the ICW4, the A0 line must be in 1 level.

11.5 PRIORITY MODES

There are different priority modes in fixing the priorities of the interrupts in 8259A. They are Fully nested mode, Automatic Rotation mode and Specific Rotation mode.

Fully Nested Mode

In general, IR0 has the highest priority and IR7 has the lowest.

IR7	IR6	IR5	IR4	IR3	IR2	IR1	IR0
7	6	5	4	3	2	1	0

Priorities can be changed as explained below.

Rotating Priority Mode

There are two variations of the rotating priority modes; the auto mode and the specific mode.

Auto Mode

In this mode, any interrupt after being serviced, receives the lowest priority. Assuming that IR4 has just been serviced, it will receive the seventh priority as shown.

IR7	IR6	IR5	IR4	IR3	IR2	IR1	IR0
2	1	0	7	6	5	4	3

In order to set this mode, in the OCW2 format, the following parameters are set

R = 1, EOI = 1, SEOI = 0

Specific Mode

In this mode, the user can change priorities by programming the bottom priority.

In order to set this mode, in the OCW2 format, the parameters are R = 1, SEOI = 1 and L2, L1 and L0 are the encoded value of the bottom priority IR.

11.6 READING THE STATUS

To read the status of the IRR and ISR, the OCW3 is used.

Format of OCW3 :

D7	D6	D5	D4	D3	D2	D1	D0
0	ESMM	SMM	0	1	P	ERIS	RIS

Reading IRR :

Just before reading the IRR, OCW3 must be written making ERIS 1 level and RIS 0 level. At the time of writing the A0 address line must be 0. Internally OCW2 and OCW3 will be recognised by sensing the D4 and D3 bits.

	D4	D3
For OCW2	0	0
For OCW3	1	0

After writing the OCW3, the Interrupt Request status can be read by using the instruction

IN 20H, since the address line A0 must be in 0 level.

Reading ISR :

Initially OCW3 is to be written with ERIS bit 1 level and RIS bit 1 level. Then in-service register content can be read using the same instruction IN 20H.

Reading IMR :

Interrupt Mask Register content can be read just by making the A0 line 1 level. The OCW3 is not written just before reading.

IN 21H

Thus the status can be read.

11.7 DIRECT MEMORY ACCESS OPERATION

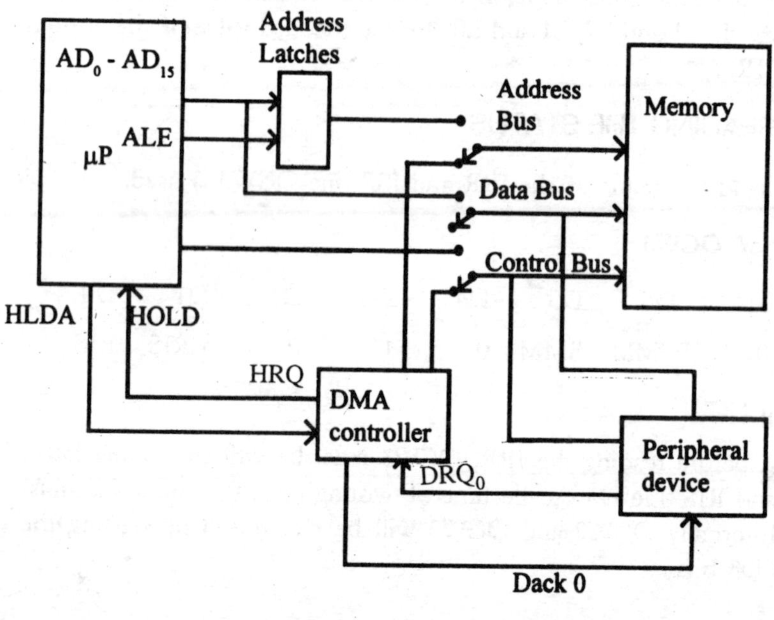

Fig.11.4 shows the DMA operation

The I/O data transfer techniques discussed so far are polled I/O and interrupt driven I/O. For bulk transfer of data between memory and a peripheral, if any one of the above techniques is followed, it takes more time since each byte of the data is transferred through the CPU. In order to transfer the data at a faster rate, the CPU is isolated and transfer of data is effected between the memory and the peripheral directly. This I/O technique is called Direct Memory Access (DMA).

Fig.11.4 shows the DMA operation. Three numbers of switches are shown in the figure. Normally, the switch positions are such that the memory and peripheral devices are connected to the CPU, i.e, the data lines, address lines and the control lines of the memory and I/O devices are connected to the CPU.

Whenever the DMA operation is to be carried out, the CPU is totally isolated and the address lines and control lines are taken over by the DMA controller circuitry.

To actuate the DMA operation, the following sequence is carried out :

1. The device which needs data transfer between the device and the memory has to send DMA request (DRQ) to the DMA controller.
2. The DMA controller raises the Hold Request (HRQ) line and it is connected to the Hold signal input of the microprocessor.
3. The microprocessor tristates all the address lines, data lines and control lines and acknowledges the Hold input signal through Hold Acknowledge (HLDA) output signal.
4. The HLDA signal is connected to the DMA controller. Once it becomes active, then DMA controller takes care of direct data transfer operation. It sends acknowledgement signal (DACK) to the device which requested for DMA operation to enable the device for data transfer.
5. DMA operation is carried out by sending suitable address to the memory and suitable control signals to transfer a byte of data. Then it increments the address and sends control signals and so on.
6. Before actually carrying out the DMA operation, the DMA controller should know

   a) the starting address of the memory location

   b) number of bytes to be transferred

   c) whether the transfer is from memory to I/O or from I/O to memory.

Block Diagram

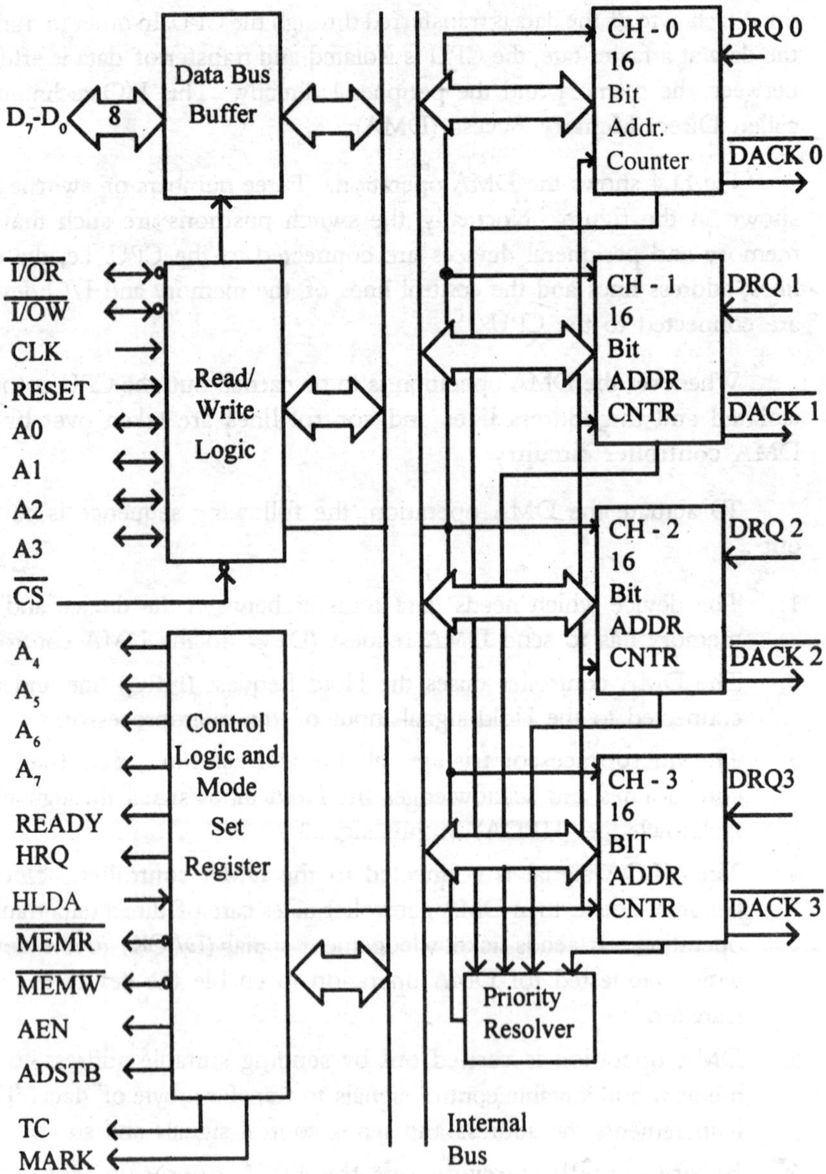

Fig.11.4 (a) Pin diagram of the 8257 DMA controller

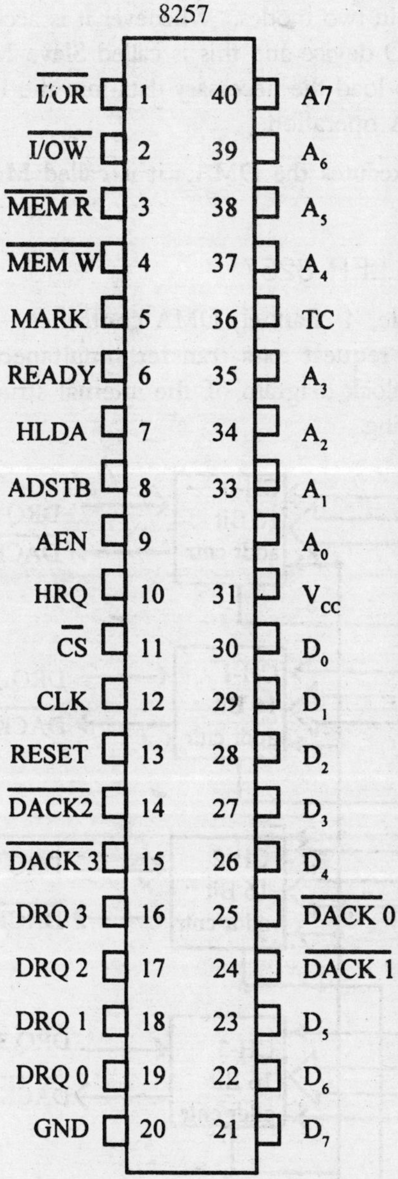

D_7-D_0	Data Bus
A_7-A_0	Address Bus
I/OR	I/O Read
I/OW	I/O Write
MEMR	Meomry Read
MEMW	Memory Write
CLK	Clock Input
RESET	Reset Input
READY	Ready
HRQ	HOLd Request (to 8085A)
HLDA	Hold Acknowledge (from 8085A)
AEN	Address Enable
ADSTB	Address Strobe
TC	Terminal Count
MARK	Modulo 128 Mark
DRQ_3-DRQ_0	DMA Request Input
$DACK_3$ - $DACK_0$	DMA Acknowledge Out put
CS	Chip Select
V_{CC}	+5 Volts
GND	Ground

Fig.11.4 (b) Block diagram of the 8257 DMA controller

The device 8257 is a Progarammable DMA controller. It is available in 40 pin dual in line package.

The device 8257 is operated in two modes. Whenever it is accessed by the CPU, it is treated as an I/O device and this is called **Slave Mode Operation**. This mode is used to load the necessary data into the DMA controller before the actual DMA operation.

When, the device actually executes the DMA, it is called **Master Mode Operation**.

11.8 THE DMA CONTROLLER 8257

The 8257 is a programmable, 4 channel, DMA controller. This means that four peripherals can request data transfer simultaneously. Fig.11.5 and Fig.11.6 shows the block diagram of the internal structure of 8257. It consists of the following.

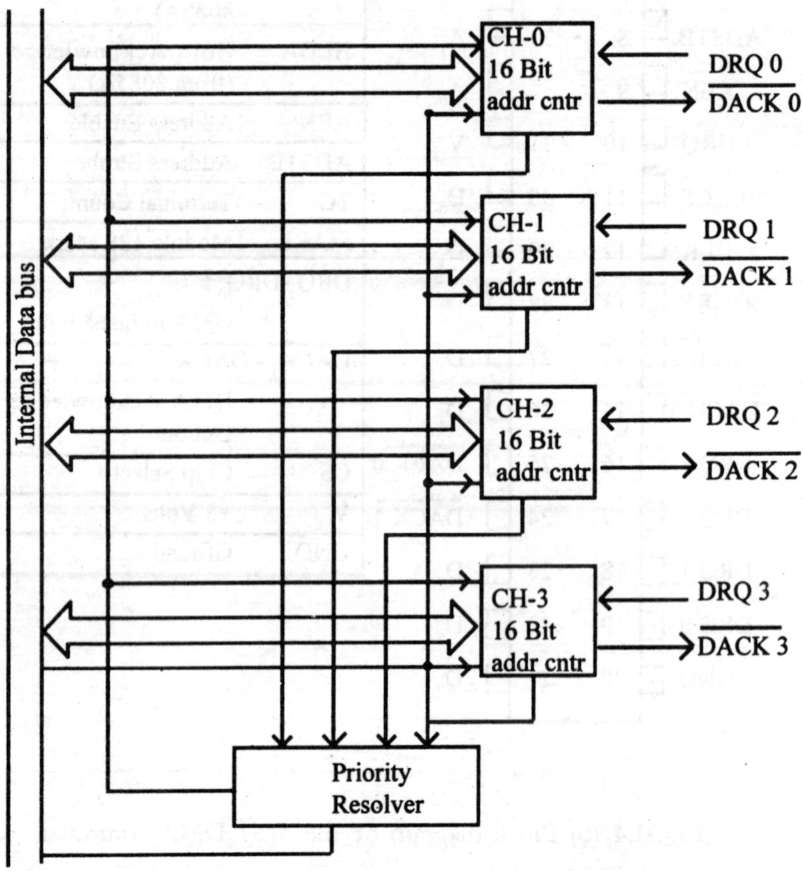

Fig.11.5 Peripheral interface side of 8257

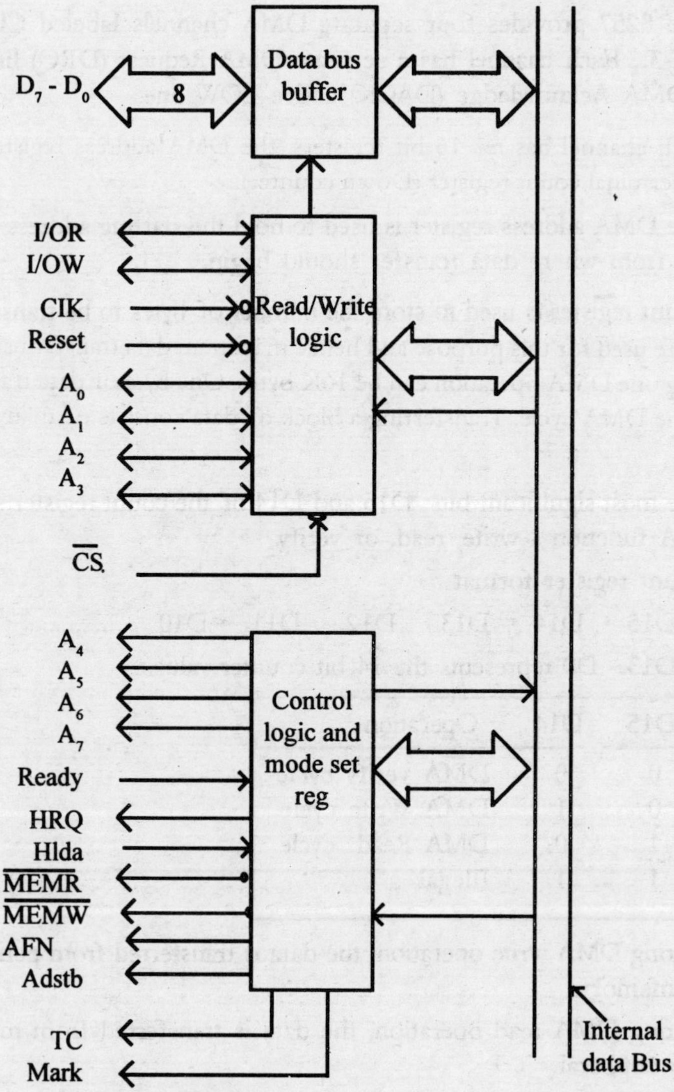

Fig.11.6 Microprocessor Interface side

- 4 DMA channels
- Control logic to manage data transfer
- Read/Write Logic
- Data bus buffer

11.9 DMA CHANNEL

- The 8257 provides four separate DMA channels labeled CH-0 to CH-3. Each channel has a separate DMA Request (DRQ) line and a DMA Acknowledge (DACK) active LOW line.
- Each channel has *two* 16 bit registers, the DMA address register and the terminal count register (Down counter).

The DMA address register is used to hold the starting address of the memory from where data transfer should begin.

Count register is used to store the number of bytes to be transferred. 14 bits are used for this purpose and hence maximum data transfer using this Ic during one DMA operation can be 16K bytes. One byte of data transfer is called one DMA cycle. Transferring a block of data consists of many DMA cycles.

The most significant bits D15 and D14 of the count register specify the DMA function - write, read, or verify.

Count register format

D15 D14 D13 D12 D11 D10 .... D0

D13 - D0 represents the 14 bit counter value.

D15	D14	Operation
0	0	DMA verify cycle
0	1	DMA Write cycle
1	0	DMA Read cycle
1	1	Illegal

1. During DMA write operation, the data is transferred from peripheral to memory.
2. During DMA read operation, the data is transferred from memory to peripheral.
3. DMA verify operation does not actually involve the transfer of data.

11.10 THE CONCEPT OF PRIORITY

Like priority interrupts facility in 8085, the DMA controller 8257 has priority facility. The Channel 0 has the highest priority in accessing the DMA controller and Channel 3 has the lowest priority. A request can be generated by *raising the request line and holding it high until DMA operation is over.*

DMA acknowledge: An active low level on the acknowledge output informs the peripheral connected to that channel that it has been selected for DMA operation.

The function of the priority resolver will be discussed later.

11.11 CONTROL LOGIC TO MANAGE DATA TRANSFER

The 8257 has two 8 bit registers internally. They are the

- mode set register and
- *status register*

The control word in the mode set register enables or disables channels and determines other functions. The mode set register can be accessed *only for write* operation.

The status register indicates which channels have reached a terminal count condition. The status register can be accessed *only for Read* operation.

Mode Word Format

The mode set format of the IC is as follows.

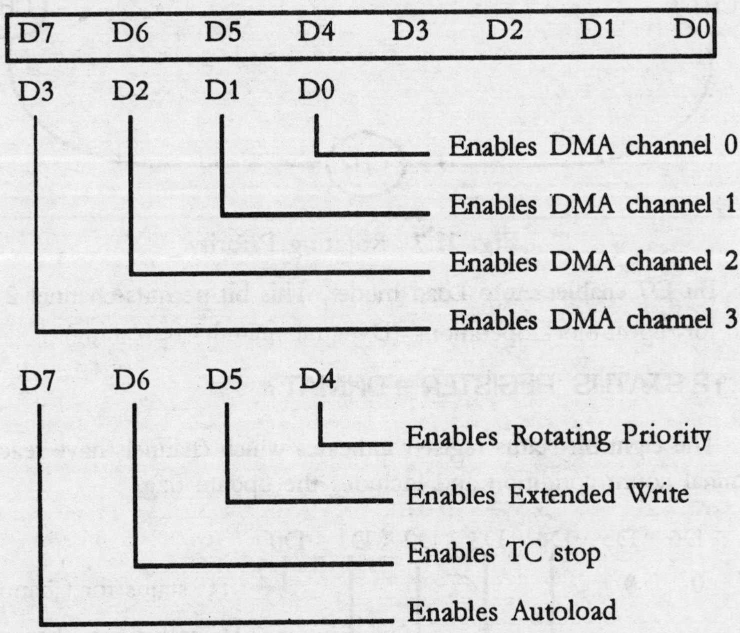

Bit D3 to D0 are used to enable/disable the DMA channel. *One level enables the channel. Bit D4 enables* ROTATING priority. In the

Rotating Priority Mode, the priority of the channels has a circular sequence. Fig.11.7 explains the Rotating Priority. After each DMA cycle, the priority of each channel changes. The channel which has just been serviced will have the lowest priority. If the bit is not set, each DMA channel has a fixed priority. In fixed priority mode, Channel 0 has the highest priority and Channel 3 has the lowest priority.

Bit D5 enables EXTENDED WRITE. If the bit is set, the duration of MEMW and I/OW signals are extended by activating them earlier in the DMA cycle and the unnecessary occurance of wait states in the 8257 are prevented.

Bit D6 enables TC STOP. If this bit is set, a channel is disabled after the Terminal Count output goes true, thus automatically preventing further DMA operation on that channel.

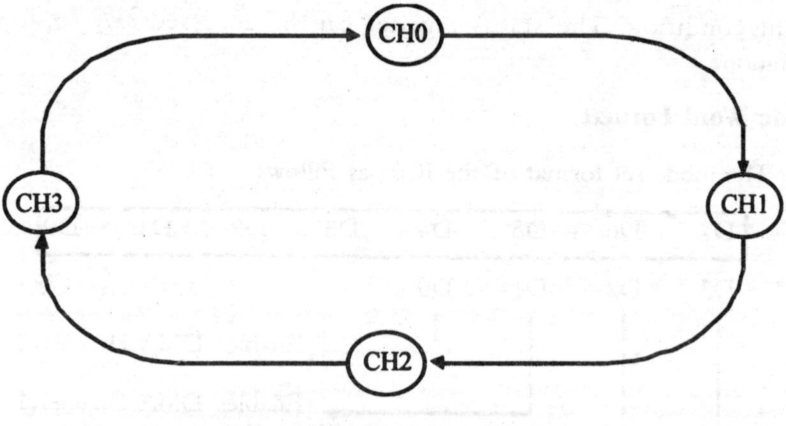

Fig. 11.7 Rotating Priority

Bit D7 enables Auto Load mode. This bit permits channel 2 to be used for repeat block operations. (Dynamic memory retreshing).

11.12 STATUS REGISTER FORMAT

The eight bit status register indicates which channels have reached a terminal count condition and includes the update flag.

D7	D6	D5	D4	D3	D2	D1	D0
0	0	0	UPDATE FLAG	TC status for Channel 3	TC status for Channel 2	TC status for Channel 1	TC status for Channel 0

The TC status bits are set when the Terminal Count (TC) output is activated for that channel. These bits remain set until the status register is read or the 8257 is reset.

UPDATE flag bit is related to repeat block operation (Auto load mode in the mode set register D7th bit)

11.13 ACCESSING THE DMA ADDRESS REGISTER, COUNT REGISTER AND MODE SET/ STATUS REGISTER

In order to access DMA address register and Count register of all the 4 DMA channels and Mode Set register/Status register, 4 address lines are needed. Table 1 shows the register selection.

Register	Byte	Address inputs A3	A2	A1	A0
CH-0 DMA Address	LSB	0	0	0	0
	MSB	0	0	0	0
CH-0 Terminal Count	LSB	0	0	0	1
	MSB	0	0	0	1
CH-1 DMA Address	LSB	0	0	1	0
	MSB	0	0	1	0
CH-1 Terminal Count	LSB	0	0	1	1
	MSB	0	0	1	1
CH-2 DMA Address	LSB	0	1	0	0
	MSB	0	1	0	0
CH-2 Terminal Count	LSB	0	1	0	1
	MSB	0	1	0	1
CH-3 DMA Address	LSB	0	1	1	0
	MSB	0	1	1	0
CH-3 Terminal Count	LSB	0	1	1	1
	MSB	0	1	1	1
Mode Set (Write only)		1	0	0	0
Status (Read only)		1	0	0	0

LSB - Least Significant Byte
MSB - Most Significant Byte

11.14 SLAVE MODE OPERATION

Fig.11.8 shows the interfacing of 8257 with the processor under Slave Mode operation. In the example, the chip is selected for the I/O addresses 70H to 7FH. In this example, the IC has been connected in I/O mapped I/O mode and the $\overline{IOW}$ and $\overline{IOR}$ pins of the IC are connected to the $\overline{IOW}$ and $\overline{IOR}$ control signals. It is to be noted that the two signals are active low. The data lines D0-D7 are connected to the data bus of the CPU.

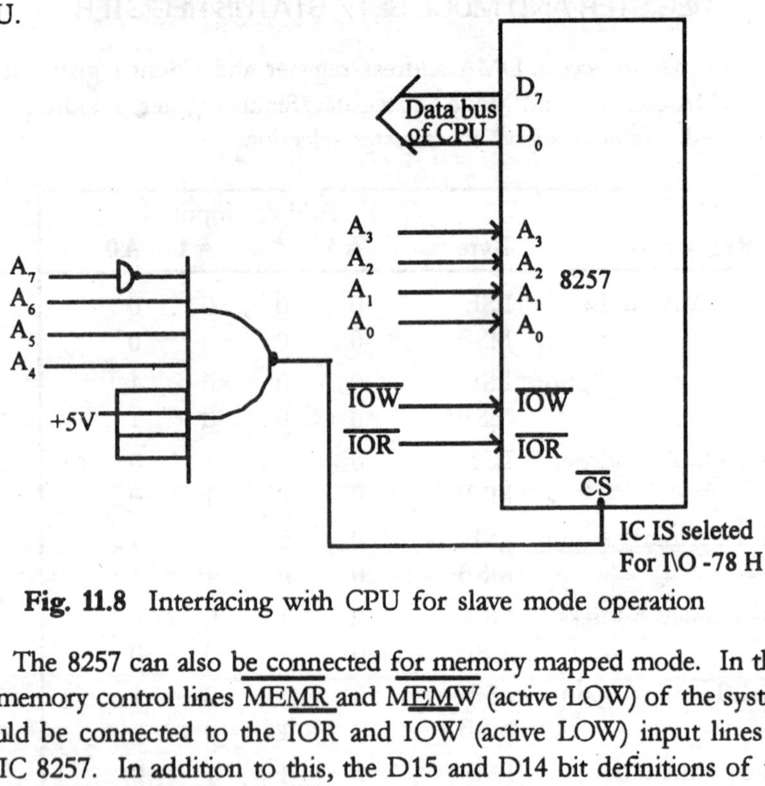

Fig. 11.8 Interfacing with CPU for slave mode operation

The 8257 can also be connected for memory mapped mode. In this, the memory control lines $\overline{MEMR}$ and $\overline{MEMW}$ (active LOW) of the system should be connected to the IOR and IOW (active LOW) input lines of the IC 8257. In addition to this, the D15 and D14 bit definitions of the Count register also varies.

In the example, explained the Mode set register address is 78H

For DMA channel 0:

The address of the DMA address register is 70H and the Terminal count register is 71H. At the time of loading the 16 bit value, the Least Significant Byte (LSB) should be loaded first and the Most Significant Byte (MSB) should be loaded next.

Assume that the data transfer is to be carried out using DMA controller as given below

i) transfer data from memory to floppy disk
ii) starting memory location 1000H
iii) number of bytes 100

The DMA controller should be INITIALISED as follows

- DMA channel 0 must be enabled and Terminal count Stop Bit is to enabled
- 1000H must be written in channel'0s DMA address register
- 100 (decimal) must be written in the channel'0 Terminal counter register and D14 and D15 bits of Terminal count register are set for memory read operation.

The following program segment will do the initialisation.

```
MVI A, 41H      ; Bit D0 should be made 1 to enable channel
OUT 78H         ; 0 and bit D6 should be made 1 to enable
                ; Terminal Count Stop bit.

                ; the Hex code 41H is written in the Mode set
                ; register (78H)

MVI A, 64H      ; demical 100 is converted into Hex and is
OUT 71H         ; written as least significant byte of the Terminal
                ; count register (71H)

MVI A, 80H      ; most significant byte of the count register
OUT 71H         ; indicates direction for read mode. The bit D7
                should be 1. It is written in the same register.

MVI A, 00       ; the 16 bit starting address is 1000H is written in
OUT 70H         ; the DMA address register, least significant byte
MVI A, 10H      ; first and most significant byte next.
OUT 70H
```

11.15 MASTER MODE OPERATION

A DMA cycle begins when one or more DMA request (DRQ) lines become active.

1. The 8257 sends a Hold Request (HRQ) to the processor and waits for the processor to return a Hold Acknowledge (HLDA).
2. When HLDA is received, the DMA Acknowledge ($\overline{DACK}$) line for the requesting channel is activated, thus selecting the channel and its peripheral for the DMA cycle. Note that the DMA request input

signal should remain high until **either** $\overline{\text{DACK}}$ (active low) is received for a "single DMA cycle service", **or** until both $\overline{\text{DACK}}$ (active low) and TC outputs are received when transferring an entire data block in a "burst" mode.

Fig.11.9 shows the Master mode operation. In this, the CPU is isolated, the DMA controller should take care of the data transfer. The address of the memory location and the control signals $\overline{\text{MEMW}}$, $\overline{\text{MEMR}}$, $\overline{\text{IOW}}$ and $\overline{\text{IOR}}$ are to be sent by the DMA controller.

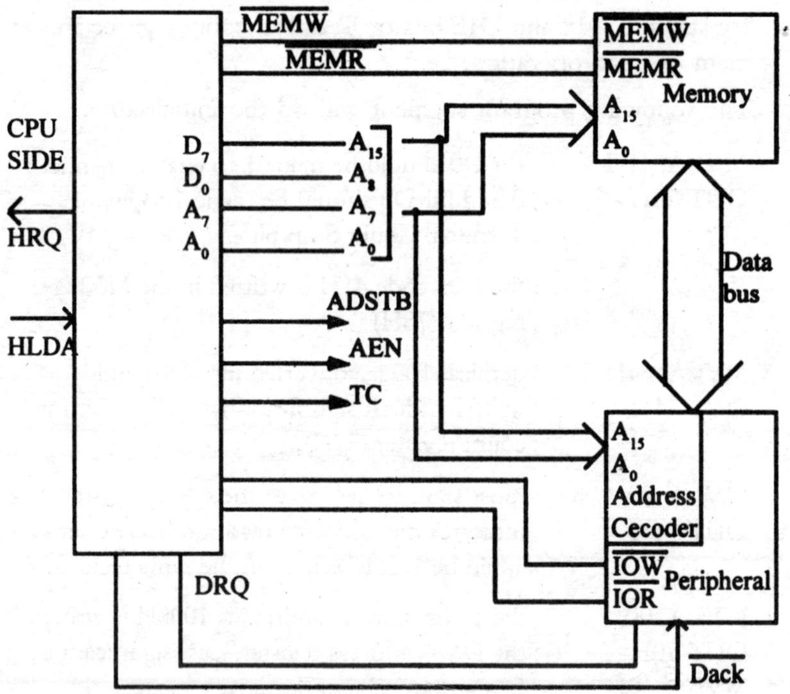

Fig. 11.9 Master mode operation

It is achieved as follows :

1. The data lines D7-D0 will act as the higher order address lines (A15-A8).
2. The A3-A0 lines which were connected to the address lines of the CPU during the Slave mode, are used as A3-A0 address lines *from* the DMA controller. It is to be noted that in the block diagram, the address lines A3-A0 lines are shown as *bidirectional* lines.

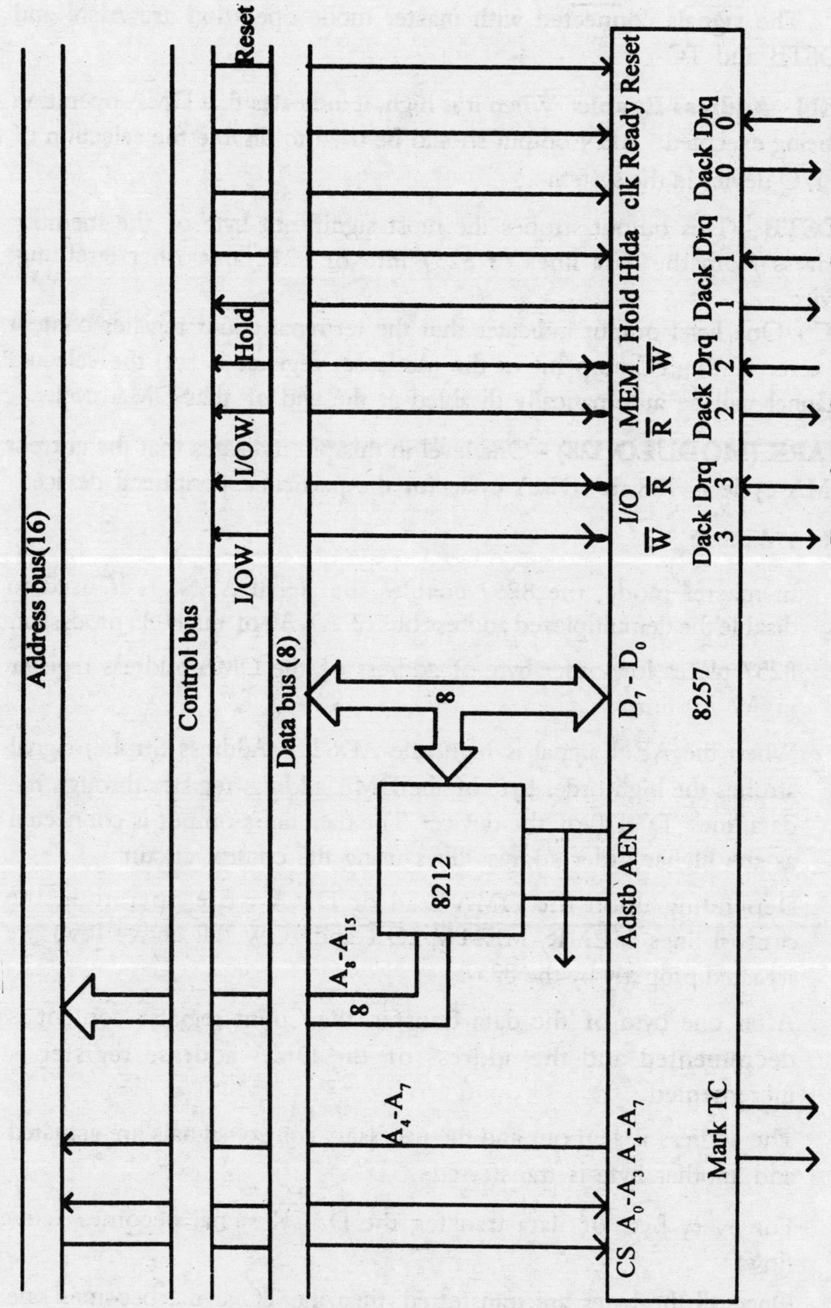

Fig. 11.10 System Interface

3. The $\overline{IOW}$ and $\overline{IOR}$ (active low lines) which were used as the input lines during the Slave mode are used as the *output lines* in this mode. They have been shown as the bidirectional lines in the block diagram.

The signals connected with master mode operation are AEN and ADSTB and TC

AEN - Address Enable: When it is high, it indicates that DMA operation is being executed. AEN output should be used to disable the selection of an I/O device in the system.

ADSTB - This output strobes the most significant byte of the memory address from the data lines of 8257 into or 8212 any other latchmig device.

TC - One level output indicates that the terminal count register content is zero. If the TC stop bit in the mode set register is set, the selected channel will be automatically disabled at the end of that DMA cycle.

MARK (MODULO 128) - One level in this pin indicates that the current DMA cycle is 128 th DMA cycle for the particular peripheral device.

DMA Action

- In master mode, the 8257 enables the signal AEN. It is used to disable the demultiplexed address bus of A7-A0 of the 8085 processor.
- 8257 places low-order byte of address of the DMA address register in A7-A0 lines.
- When the AEN signal is high, the ADSTB (Address Strobe) signal strobes the high order byte of the DMA address register through the data lines D7-D0 of the device. The data line's output is connected as the higher order address lines using the control circuit.
- Depending upon the DMA read or DMA write operation, the control lines $\overline{MEMR}$, $\overline{MEMW}$, $\overline{IOR}$ and $\overline{IOW}$ (all active low) are actuated properly by the 8257.
- After one byte of the data transfer, the Count register content is decremented and the address of the DMA address register is incremented.
- The address is sent out and the necessary control signals are actuated and another byte is transferred.
- For every byte of data transfer, the $\overline{DACK}$ signal becomes active (low).
- Once all the bytes are transferred, then the TC signal becomes one level. If the D6 bit of the Mode Set register is already set, then it automatically prevents further DMA operation on that channel and the DACK signal becomes inactive one level.
- Thus the DMA operation is carried out.
- Some times single cycle DMA is also carried out.

CHAPTER 12

MICROPROCESSOR BASED APPLICATIONS

12.1 DIGITAL CLOCK

Problem Statement

Realise a real time clock and display Hours, Minutes and Seconds on the display panel of a microprocessor trainer kit.

Background Information

Many microprocessor applications would require, doing certain tasks at specific time of the day or would involve the time of day in some other form. For example switching ON and OFF street lights at specific time in the evening and following morning, or punching entry time of every worker for a shift, at a factory gate etc. A basic requirement of this type of application is a real time digital clock with a display of current time. This program can find use in such applications.

Program Description

The program uses the address and data field to display Hours, Minutes & Seconds. It depends on a delay subroutine of 1 second duration for timing reference. Three CPU registers are used to count Hours, Minutes and Seconds. The Seconds counter is incremented for every second, and its content checked for 60. When it reaches 60, it is reset to 0 and the Minutes counter is incremented. When the Minutes counter reaches 60, it is reset and the Hour counter is incremented. When the Hours counter reaches 13 it is reset to 1. The counter incrementing is done in decimal format. Built in utilities available in the microprocessor trainer kit are used for displaying data at the address and data field. The program works in a continuous loop and displays time round the clock.

Flow Chart for Digital Clock Program

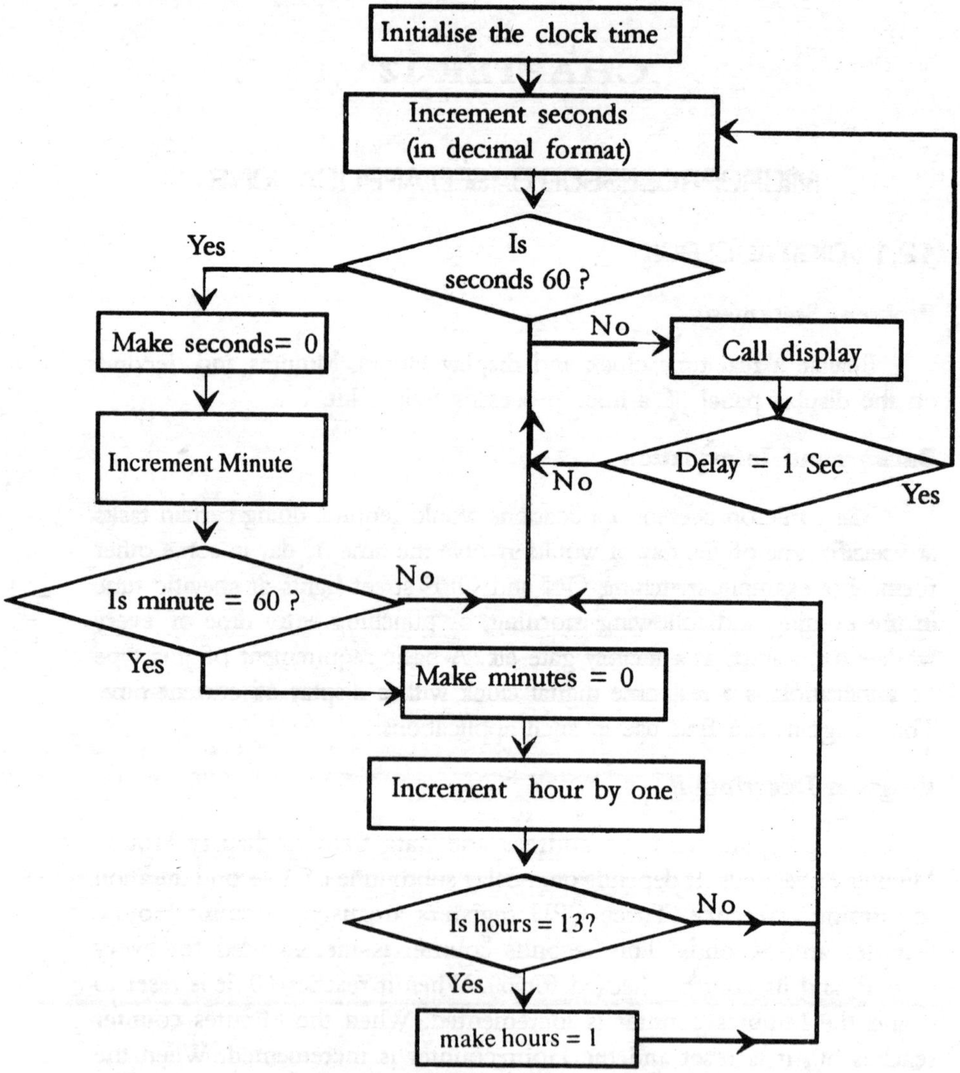

Memory Initialisation and Built-in routines used

It is assumed that the user memory area of the trainer kit starts from 3000H. The following user memory locations are used to store the initial data.

Memory location	Initialised with
3003	Hours data
3004	Minutes data
3005	Seconds data

Update data field routine

This built-in routine displays the content of the accumulator. Its starting address is 0520H.

Update address field routine

This built-in routine displays the content of the DE register pair in the address field. Its starting address is 0510H.

Program

Mem Location	Op-code	Label	Mnemonic	Comments
3006	21	BEGIN	LXI H,3003	
3007	03			
3008	30			
3009	56		MOV D,M	; Initialise Hours in D reg
300A	23		INX H	
300B	5E		MOV E,M	; Initialise Minut in E reg
300C	23		INX H	
300D	7E		MOV A,M	; Initialise Seconds in Acc
300E	C6		ADI 01	
300F	01			; Increment Accumulator
3010	27		DAA	; Convert into BCD format
3011	4F		MOV M,A	
3012	FE		CPI 60	; Compare Seconds with 60
3013	60			
3014	CA		JZ UPDATE	; If seconds = 60
3015	31			; Goto UPDATE
3016	30			
3017	21	DISP	LXI H,3005	; Initialise HL with 3005
3018	05			
3019	20			
301A	7E		MOV A,M	; Load acc. with seconds
301B	CD		CALL 0520	; Display the seconds in
301C	20			; Data field of kit
301D	05			
301E	2B		DCX H	
301F	5E		MOV E,M	; Load Minutes into E reg.
3020	2B		DCX H	
3021	56		MOV D,M	; Load Hours into D reg.

Mem Location	Op-code	Label	Mnemonic	Comments
3022	CD		CALL 0510	; Display the Hours and
3023	10			; Minutes in the Address
3024	05			; field of kit
3025	01	DELAY	LXI B,NNNN	; Initialise BC register
3026	NN			; with a value so as
3027	NN			; to get 1 Sec delay
3028	0B	TOP	DCX B	
3029	79		MOV A,C	
302A	B0		ORA B	; Check BC reg = 0000
302B	C2		JNZ TOP	; If BC is not equal to
302C	28			0000 Goto TOP
302D	30			
302E	C3		JMP BEGIN	; Goto BEGIN
302F	06			
3030	30			
3031	97	UPDATE	SUB A	; Initialise A reg with 00
3032	77		MOV M,A	
3033	7B		MOV A,E	
3034	C6		ADI 01	; Increment Minutes
3035	01			
3036	27		DAA	; Convert into BCD format
3037	32		STA 3004	; Store Minutes into 3004
3038	04			
3039	30			
303A	FE		CPI 60	; Compare Minutes = 60
303B	60			
303C	C2		JNZ DISP	; If minutes is not equal
303D	17			; to 60 Goto DISP
303E	30			
303F	97		SUB A	; Initialise acc = 00
3040	32		STA 3004	; Store 00 into Minutes
3041	04			
3042	30			
3043	7A		MOV A,D	
3044	C6		ADI 01	; Increment Hours
3045	01			
3046	27		DAA	; Convert into BCD format
3047	32		STA 3003	; Store Hours into 3003
3048	03			
3049	30			
304A	FE		CPI 13	; Check Hours = 13
304B	13			

Mem Location	Op-code	Label	Mnemonic	Comments
304C	C2		JNZ DISP	; If Hours is less than 13
304D	17			; Goto DISP
304E	30			
304F	3E		MVI A,01	; Load acc = 01
3050	01			
3051	32		STA 3003	; Store 01 into Hours
3052	03			
2053	30			
3054	C3		JMP DISP	; Goto DISP
3055	17			
3056	30			

Note

The above program has been tested in a kit having the data field display routine starting at address 0520H and address field display routine starting at address 0510H. You are requested to refer your kit manual for the relevant addresses.

Activity Sequence

1. Load the given program starting from the specified memory location or from any other suitable memory location.
2. Initialise the specified or suitable location with the starting values of Hours, Minutes and seconds.
3. Use the relevant display routines of your trainer kit for displaying data at the address and data field.
4. Run the program.

12.2 TRAFFIC LIGHT CONTROLLER

Problem Statement

Interface with the CPU, the signal lamps which control a road junction and implement a traffic control sequence.

Background Information

A typical road junction is shown in Fig.12.1 which is used as our model. Four identical sets of lights at each corner are provided. The marking on the set of lights at each corner means the following :

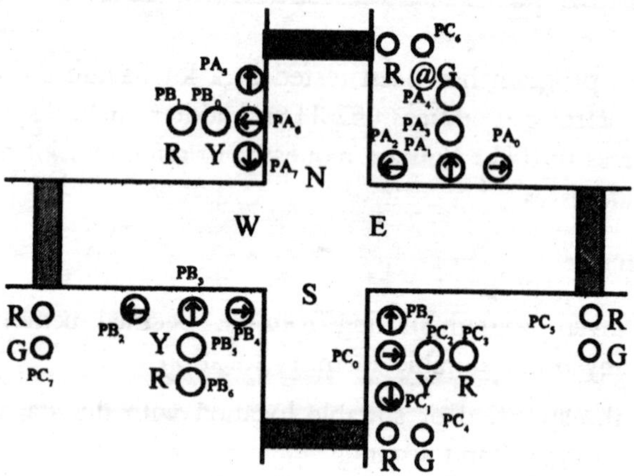

Fig. 12.1

R Red to stop the traffic

Y Yellow to caution that traffic is about to stop or about to start

P Green for pedestrians to Cross
Red for pedestrian to stop

Arrow Direction of arrow mark indicates the direction of traffic flow, which include straight, left & right.

The lights switch ON and OFF to implement the following sequence of traffic flow at the junction :

i. North and South going vehicles can go straight as well as turn left.
East and West going vehicles are stopped.
All pedestrians are Stopped.

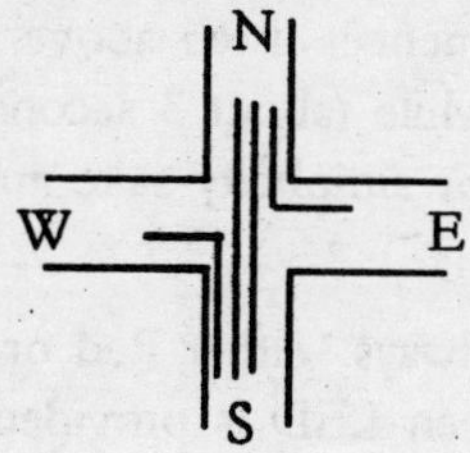

ii. North and South going vehicles can turn right.
East and West going vehicles are still stopped.
All pedestrians are stopped.

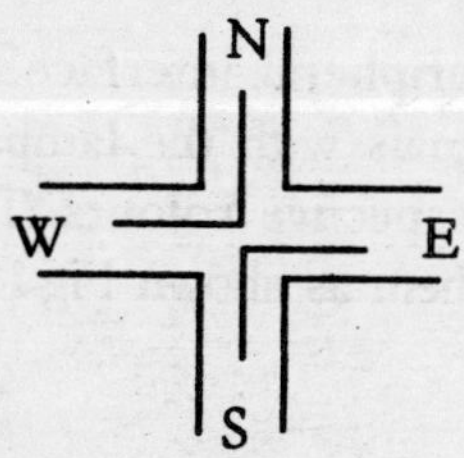

iii. North and South going vehicles are now stopped.
East and West going vehicles can go straight and also turn left.
All pedestrians are stopped.

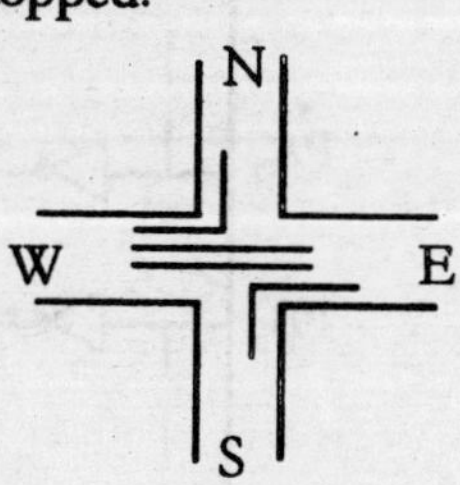

iv. North and South bound vehicles are still stopped.
East and West bound vehicles can turn right.
All pedestrians are stopped.

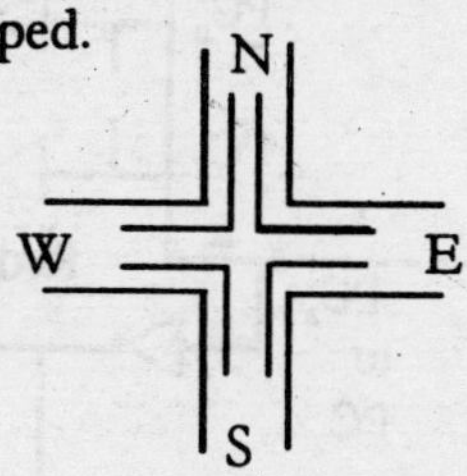

v. North and South vehicles are stopped.
East and West vehicles are stopped.
All pedestrians are allowed to cross the road.

Between every two sequences listed above, the yellow light is to be switched ON for a short while (about 3 seconds). This operation is not included in the program for simplicity sake and therefore not indicated in the flow chart.

For pedestrians it is always either Red or Green and Yellow is not used. Therefore a Red/Green LED is provided on each road to control pedestrian traffic. A Red/Green LED requires just one control signal to glow either Red or Green. Therefore the total number of logic signals to be generated works out to twenty four for the scheme given. The 0 and 1 represent the state of a lamp; OFF and ON respectively.

The programmable peripheral interface device 8255 is used to interface these 24 logic signals with the lamps. The traffic lamps are simulated with LEDs of respective colours. The 7406 open collector inverters are used to drive them as shown Fig.12.2

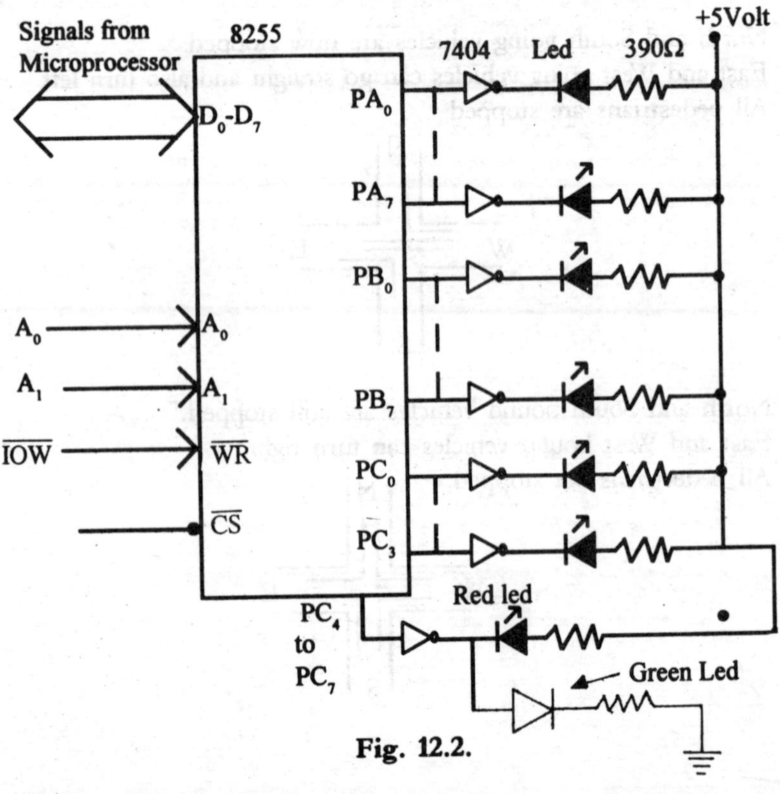

Fig. 12.2.

Flow chart for Traffic Light Control

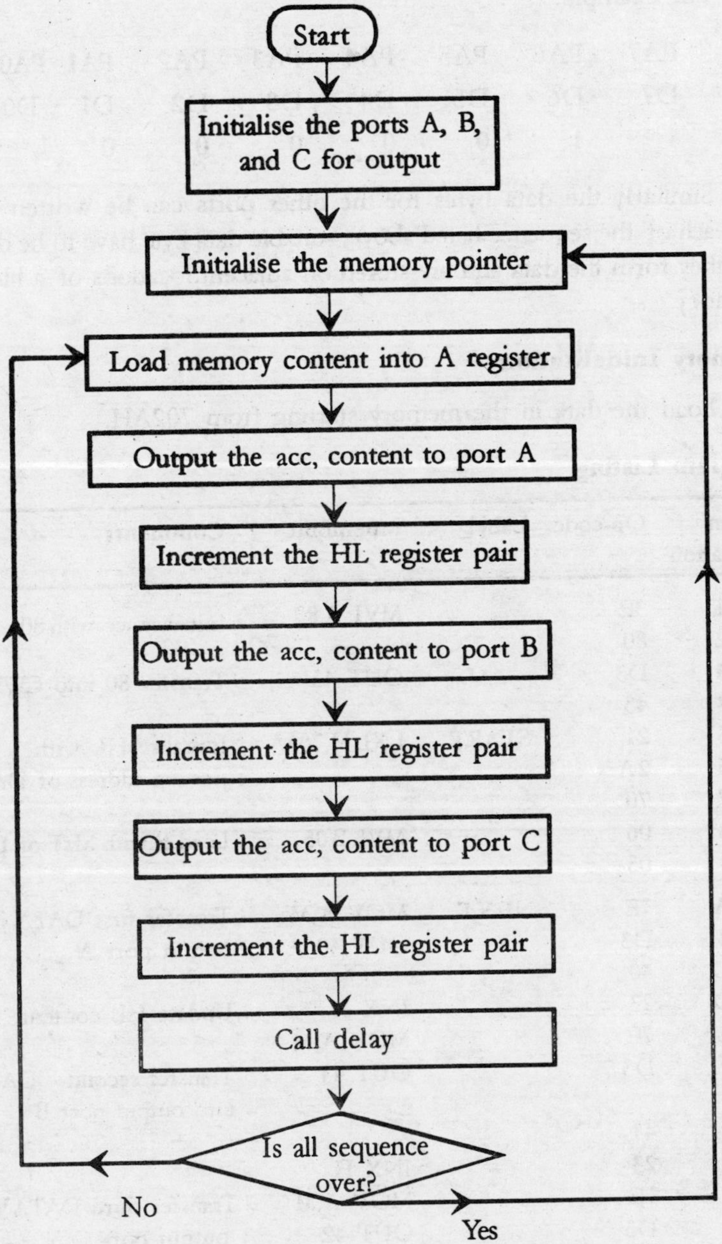

The bit assignment of ports to different LEDs is shown in the Figure. The data byte for each port can be derived by filling 0s and 1s in the appropriate position.

For example:

PA7	PA6	PA5	PA4	PA3	PA2	PA1	PA0
D7	D6	D5	D4	D3	D2	D1	D0
1	1	0	0	0	0	0	1 = CIH

Similarly the data bytes for the other ports can be written down. For each of the sequence listed above, suitable data byte have to be derived and they form the data and are stored on adjacent locations of a block of memory.

Memory Initialisation

Load the data in the memory starting from 702AH.

Program Listing

Mem Location	Op-code	Label	Mnemonic	Comments
7001	3E		MVI A,80	; Initialise acc. with 80
7002	80			
7003	D3		OUT 43	; Transfer 80 into CWReg.
7004	43			
7005	21	START	LXI H,702A	; Initialise HL with
7006	2A			; starting address of DATA
7007	70			
7008	06		MVI B,05	; Load B with SET of DATA
7009	05			
700A	7E	NEXT	MOV A,M	; Transfer first DATA into
700B	D3		OUT 40	; output port A
700C	40			
700D	23		INX H	; Update HL content
700E	7E		MOV A,M	
700F	D3		OUT 41	; Transfer second DATA
				; into output port B
7010	41			
7011	23		INX H	
7012	7E		MOV A,M	; Transfer third DATA into
7013	D3		OUT 42	; output port C
7014	42			

Mem Location	Op-code	Label	Mnemonic	Comments
7015	CD		CALL DELAY	; Execute DELAY ; program
7016	20			
7017	70			
7018	23		INX H	; Update the content of HL
7019	05		DCR B	
701A	C2		JNZ NEXT	; Check all set of DATA
701B	0A			; transfered
701C	70			
701D	C3		JMP START	; Goto START and repeat
701E	05			; the same program
701F	70			
7020	11	DELAY	LXI D,yyyy	; Load suitable number
7021	yy			; for delay
7022	yy			
7023	03	LOOP	DCX D	; decrement the DE reg.
7024	78		MOV A, E	
7025	B2		ORA D	
7026	C2		JNZ LOOP	; check for DE = 00
7027	23			
7028	70			
7029	C9		RET	
702A	C1		DATA1	; step 1
702B	C1			
702C	FA			
702D	08		DATA2	; step 2
702E	08			
702F	45			
7030	3C		DATA3	; step 3
7031	3C			
7032	F0			
7033	80		DATA4	; step 4
7034	80			
7035	5A			
7036	83		DATA5	; step 5 of the
7037	83			; traffic flow as
7038	F0			; shown in the diagram

Activity Sequence

1. Construct the circuit shown in figure.
2. Derive the data bytes for the lamp switching sequence
3. Load the data at a suitable location of the user memory.
4. Load the program at a suitable location of the user memory.
5. Execute the program.

12.3 HEX KEYBOARD INTERFACE

Problem Statement

Interface a hexadecimal keyboard (maximum of 24 keys) with the CPU using IC 8255.

Background Information

Key boards are found in almost all microprocessor based equipment/ systems. They form a very convenient means of entering information into the system. Data, commands and programs are entered into the system through such keyboards. They consist of a number of press type switches arranged in rows and columns.The switches are normally open and make contact when pressed. The microcomputer senses the closure and responds.

However mechanical keys have a problem. When pressed, the contacts vibrate for a short time (milli seconds) before settling down. The CPU gets the impression that the key is pressed many times. This is called bouncing. The bouncing is overcome by using a simple technique. The interface circuit senses a key press, then it waits for 10 to 20 milliseconds and again checks the key. If still contact is made, it takes it as a single valid key press. This is called debouncing.

Fig.12.3 shows a very common method of arranging 24 such switches to form a hexadecimal keyboard. The keys are arranged in 3 rows and 8 columns. The figure also shows how the ports of 8255 of the kit can be used to interface the keyboard to the CPU. The rows are connected to three output lines of Port C (D0-D2) and further to 8 input lines of port A (D0-D7). To get valid data from the keyboard following three steps are involved -

a) detect a key closure
b) debounce it and
c) encode it.

Each of the column lines are normally LOW as they are tied to the ground through a resistor. Pressing a key shorts a row to a column. The CPU first puts a 001 as D0-D2 on the three rows out of port C. This is followed by scanning the columns through port A for a HIGH (1) on any one of the eight lines. If a HIGH (1) is found, the CPU has to locate the exact key which is closed.

To do this one row is made HIGH at a time and the columns are scanned for a HIGH to locate the closed switch. Debouncing is done by

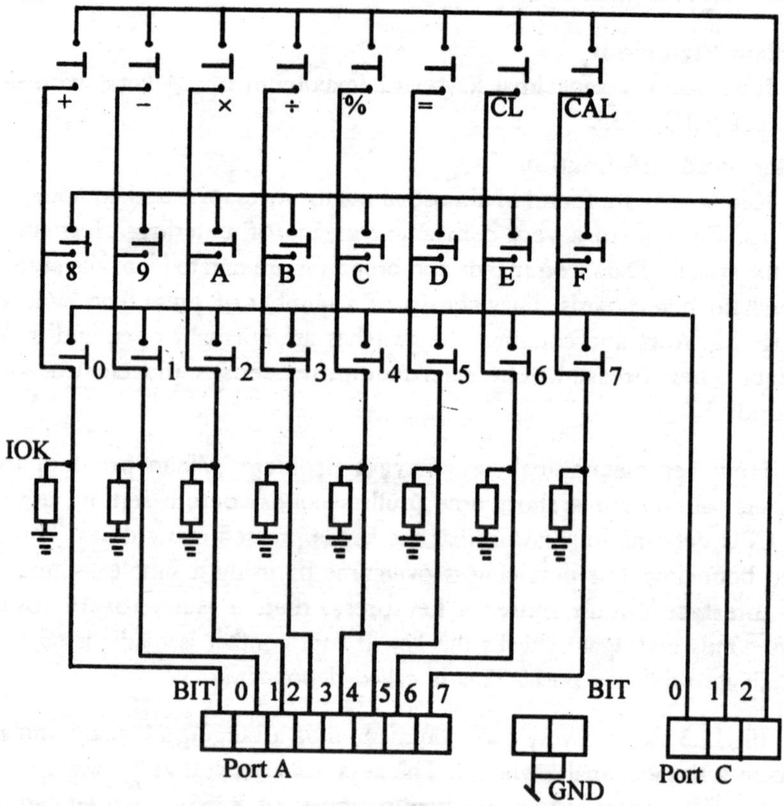

Fig. 12.3

waiting for about 20 ms and checking again to see whether the key is still pressed. Encoding each key to hex or ASCII code can be done with a ROM or through a program routine.

The flow chart shown explains the keyboard interface program. The values 001, 010 and 100 are sent one at a time on three rows. The 8 column lines on the input port are read and checked for HIGH . A HIGH indicates that a key is pressed. The program loops back until it finds all keys open before accepting the first key closure. This ensures that pressing a second key before releasing the earlier one does not have any effect.

To locate which key is pressed, the CPU outputs a 1 on the first row and 0's on all others. The columns are read and checked for 1. If it is not found the pressed key in this row, the 1 is rotated to next row and the columns are checked. If a 1 is found in a column, the 8 bit word at port

A is read in. The 8 bits of this word and three bits of port C are manipulated in the program to get the hexadecimal or ASCII code of the key pressed.

The following table indicates the port and pin assignments used for the keyboard interface with microprocessor kit.

Port	Pin lines	Connected to	Mode
A	D0 to D7	column lines	input
C	D0 to D2	row lines	output

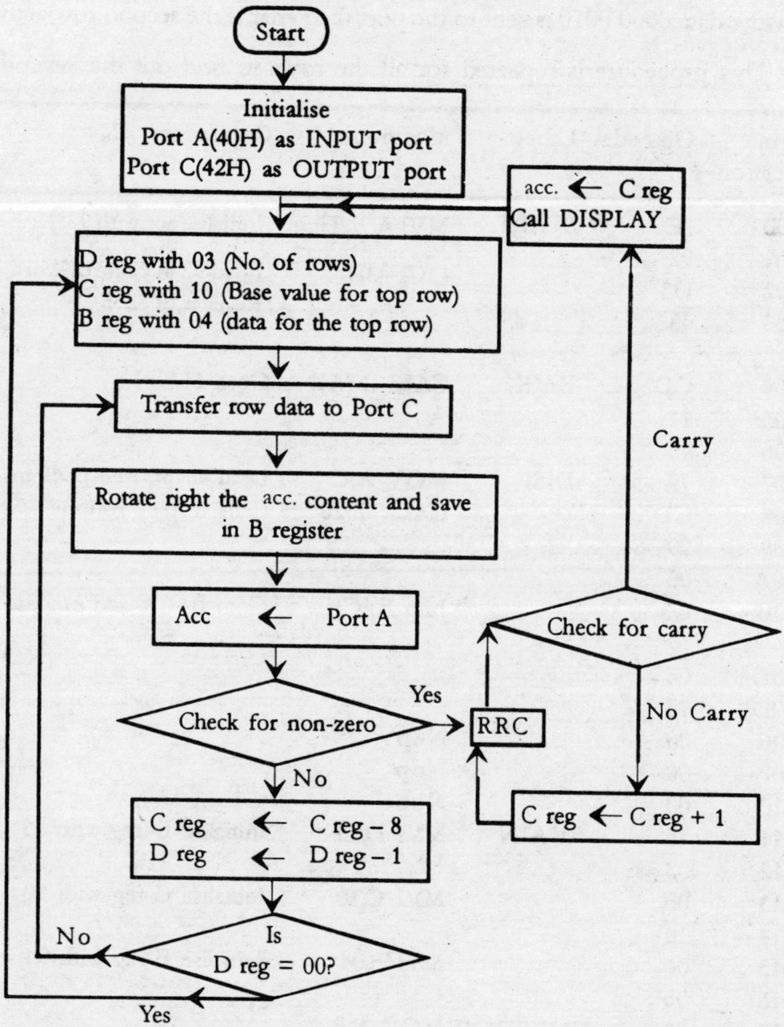

Program Description

The keyboard consists of three rows. Each row has got eight keys. The first key code of the top row is 10H. This is the base value for the top row. Initially top row is made active by sending 0000 0100 to the port C. If any key is pressed, the position of the key is found out by rotating the bit from the column information read via port A, till the bit reaches the carry. The position counter is added with the base value of the row. Thus the key code is formed.

If the data read via port A is zero, then 8 is subtracted from the base value of the top row (10H) to get (08H) as base value for the second row. Now the data 0000 0010 is sent to the port C to enable the second row active.

This procedure is repeated for all the rows to find out the keycode.

Mem Location	Op-code	Label	Mnemonic	Comments
7500	3E	START	MVI A, 92H	; Initialise acc with 92H
7501	92		OUT 43H	; Load 92 in Control Word
7502	D3			; Register of 8255
7503	43			
7504	CD	BACK	CALL MAIN	; Goto MAIN
7505	11			
7506	75			
7507	79	DISP	MOV A,C	; Load keypressed code in A
7508	CD		CALL 0520	; Calls display routine
7509	20			
750A	05			
750B	C3		Jmp BACK	; Goto BACK and execute
750C	04			
750D	75			
750E	00		Nop	
750F	00		Nop	
7510	00		Nop	
7511	16	MAIN	MVI D,03	; Initialise D reg with 03
7512	03			
7513	0E		MVI C,10	; Initialise C reg with 10
7514	10			
7515	06		MVI B,04	; Initialise B reg with 04
7516	04			
7517	78	NXTROW	MOV A,B	
7518	D3		OUT 42	; Transfer 0000 0100 in

Mem Location	Op-code	Label	Mnemonic	Comments
7519	42			output port 42
751A	0F		RRC	
751B	47		MOV B,A	Save the modified pattern
751C	DB		IN 40	Read input port 40
751D	40			
751E	FE		CPI 00	Check any key is pressed
751F	00			
7520	C2		JNZ KEYCOD	If yes, Goto KEYCOD
7521	31			
7522	75			
7523	79		MOV A,C	Load Acc with reference
7524	D6		SUI 08	
7525	08			
7526	4F		MOV C,A	Save modified reference
7527	15		DCR D	
7528	7A		MOV A,D	
7529	FE		CPI 00	Check all posibility is over
752A	00			
752B	C2		JNZ NXTROW	If no, Goto NXTROW
752C	17			
752D	75			
752E	C3		JMP MAIN	Goto MAIN
752F	11			
7530	75			
7531	0F	KEYCOD	RRC	Bring 1 bit to CY flag
7532	DA		JC DISP	Goback if CY = 1
7533	07			
7534	75			
7535	79		MOV A,C	
7536	C6		ADI 01	Add one with reference
7537	01			
7538	4F		MOV C,A	save the reference NUM
7539	C3		JMP KEYCOD	Repeat KEYCOD process
753A	31			
753B	75			

Note: Simultaneous key press checking and debouncing have not been included in the above program.

Activity Sequence

1. Construct the circuit given in Figure.12.3

   (If 24 numbers of key switches are not available, you may use the available ones at some of the locations and carry out the experiment).
2. Load the given program at the specified or convenient location of the user memory area.
3. Call display routine to display the hex code in data field.
4. Run the program.
5. Press any of one of the switch for a moment and release it.
6. See data field of the microprocessor kit to identify the pressed key.
8. Repeat this for each key position and make a table of the key pressed and the code stored. If you are managing with a few keys then relocate them after use at a given location.
9. Press any one key and before releasing it press another one. Watch the display.
10. Repeat step 9 for different pairs of keys.

12.4 SEVEN SEGMENT DISPLAY INTERFACE

Problem Statement

Interface a set of seven segment display modules with the CPU using 8255 and display a short text information.

Back ground Information

Message displays are extensively used for the purpose of displaying short alpha numeric character strings. At public places they are used to display short advertisement slogans or information such as train timings. In machines, equipment, cars etc., they may be used to display brief instructions, status information and other data.

Seven segment modules can be used to display a limited set of alphabetic characters. In Figure 12.4b, the schematic of a 4 character display is shown. The PPI chip 8255 available on the kit can be used for interfacing the display modules. The display modules used are of **common anode** type. Data is given out in serial format from the CPU. The serial to parallel shift registers (74164) convert the serial data into parallel format and their outputs drive the segments of the display modules. The CPU also outputs the necessary clock using software.

Certain English letters can not be displayed using 7 segments. Avoid such letters while writing the display message. Count the total number of characters in the message. Store it at a desired RAM location (in hex format). This forms the first entry of the data table. Convert the first character of the message into an 8 bit code and store it in the next location. The 8 bit codes of the rest of the characters are stored in successive locations. Each bit of the 8 bit code represent one segment as shown in Figure.12.4a.

A bit is made 1 if that segment is OFF;
and 0 if segment needs to be ON.

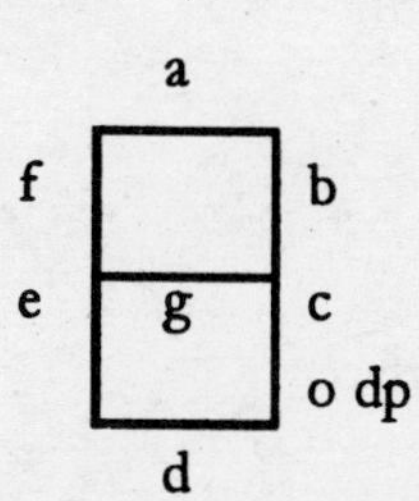

D7	D6	D5	D4	D3	D2	D1	D0
dp	g	f	e	d	c	b	a

Fig.12.4a

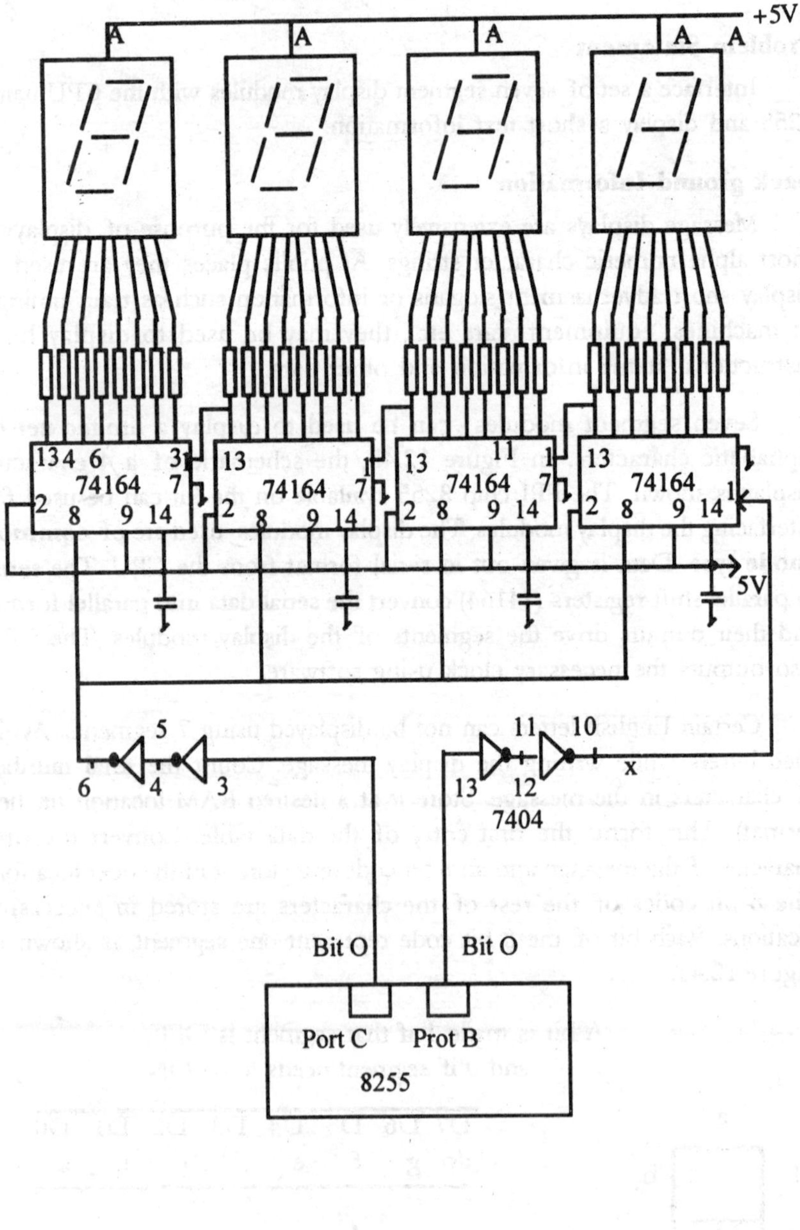

Fig. 12.4 b Seven Segment Display Interface

Example

H	=	1000 1001	= 89		G	=	1000 0010	= 82
E	=	1000 0110	= 86		O	=	1100 0000	= C0
L	=	1100 0111	= C7		O	=	1100 0000	= C0
P	=	1000 1100	= 8C		D	=	1010 0001	= A1

Program Description:

The program interfaces 4 seven segment modules with the CPU and displays a 4 letter word. The 4 byte data for the 4 letters are stored in the memory starting from the address 8030H.

The ports B & C are used for output. The first data word is brought into the accumulator. The data is shifted left by 1 bit. The MSB is sent out through port B. A single pulse is then sent out through port C. This pulse acts as the clock pulse to latch the single bit on port B into the interface circuit. The accumulator content is again shifted left by 1 bit and then sent out through port B, followed by a pulse on port C. This process is repeated 8 times, so that all the 8 bits of the first byte are latched into the interface circuit. Then the program waits for about 0.5 seconds.

This process is repeated 3 more times so that all the 4 bytes are transferred into the display interface circuit.

Memory Initialisation

The memory locations starting from the address 8030H are used to store the 4 data bytes.

Program

Mem Location	Op-code	Label	Mnemonic	Comments
8000	21		LXI H,8030	Initialise HL with DATA
8001	30			address (assumed 8030)
8002	80			
8003	3E		MVI A,80	Initialise Command Word
8004	80			Register of 8255
8005	D3		OUT 43	
8006	43			
8007	06		MVI B,04	Number of DATA = 4
8008	04			
8009	16	NXTDGT	MVI D,08	Number of BITS = 8
800A	08			
800B	7E		MOV A, M	Bring first DATA to Acc
800C	23		INX H	

Flow Chart for Seven Segment Display Interface

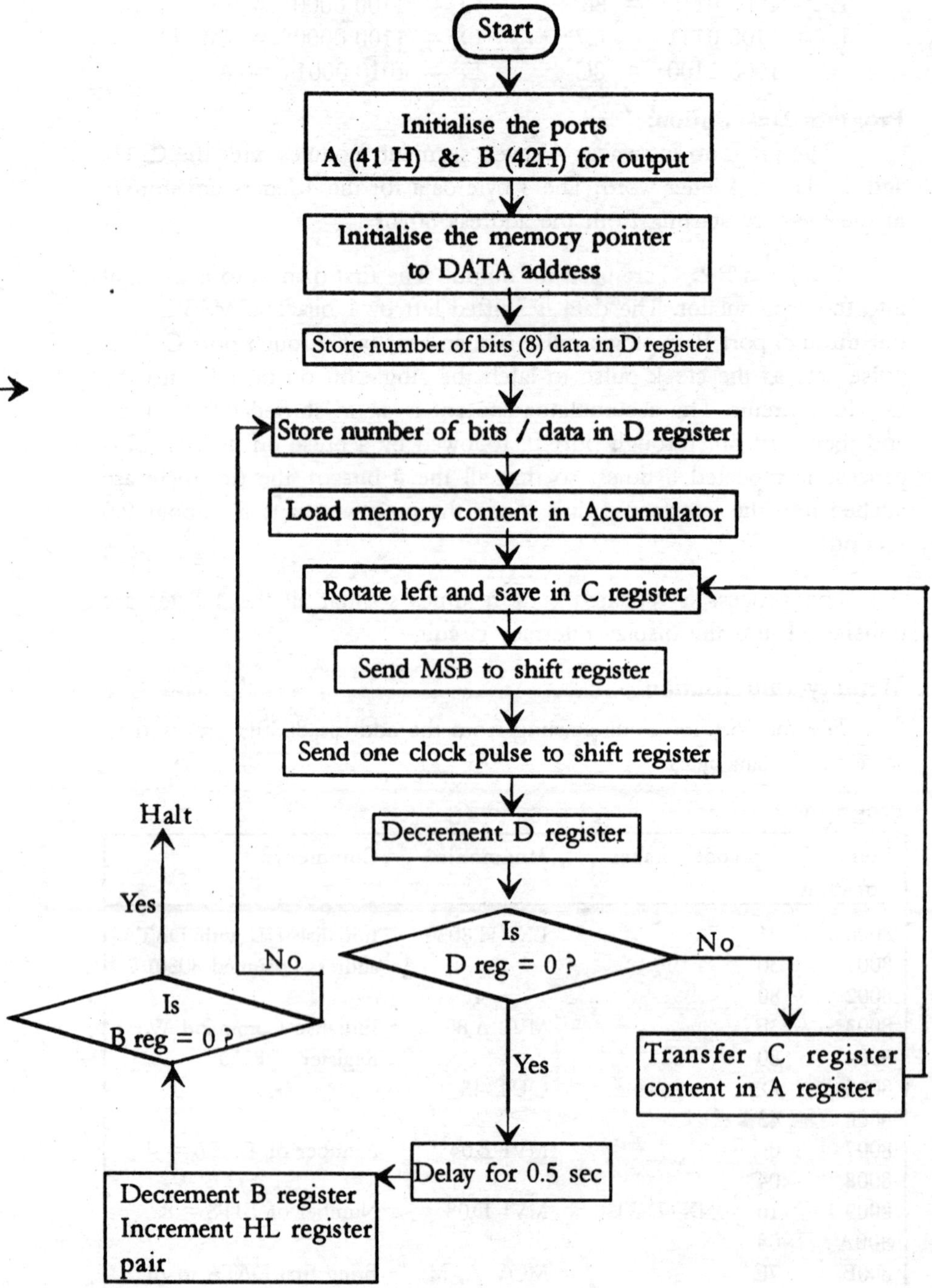

Mem Location	Op-code	Label	Mnemonic	Comments
800D	07	NXTBIT	RLC	; Rotate and save in C reg
800E	4F		MOV C,A	
800F	D3		OUT 41	; Send MSB to port 41
8010	41			
8011	3E		MVI A, 01	
8012	01			; Generate a pulse and
8013	D3		OUT 42	; send to port C
8014	42			
8015	3D		DCR A	
8016	D3		OUT 42	
8017	42			
8018	79		MOV A, C	
8019	15		DCR D	; Check all 8 bits sent
801A	C2		JNZ NXTBIT	; If no, Goto NXTBIT
801B	0D			
801C	80			
801D	CD		CALL DELAY	; It is assumed that the
801E	00			; delay sub routine is
801F	81			; available from 8100H
8020	05		DCR B	; Check all 4 DATA sent
8021	C2		JNZ NXTDGT	; If no, Goto NXTDGT
8022	09			
8023	80			
8024	76		HLT	

Activity Sequence

1. Make connections as in the diagram in Figure 12.4b.
2. Form a message with suitable characters.
3. Code each character into equivalent 8 bit with the help of fig 12.4a.
4. Choose a RAM location for the data table.
5. Load the first location of the data table with the number of characters in the message (in hex format).
6. Load the character bytes in the rest of the table, left most character first.
7. Load the program in the kit.
8. Run the program.

Q1. Suggest the changes required in hardware and data table to make the message to move from left to right.

Q2. If the display units used are common cathode type, what is the change in data word required?

Q3. Modify the program to display continuously instead of once.

12.5 STEPPER MOTOR CONTROL

Problem Statement

Interface a stepper motor with the microprocessor kit.

Background Information

A stepper motor is a specially constructed DC motor. It has 4 windings arranged such that instead of running in the usual continuous fashion the motor rotates in precise steps, from one fixed position to another. The common step sizes range from 0.9 to 30 degrees. The stepping action is acheived by proper combination of fields. Figure 12.5. shows the schematic of the stepper motor windings. Table 12.1 shows the pulsing sequence of windings when bit D0 is in 0 level the coil A1 is energised, and so on. Changing the excitation from A1 & A2 to A2 & B1 causes the shaft to rotate by one step clockwise. Each successive line of the table causes one step. Reversing the order in the sequence table causes the shaft to rotate counter clockwise. Thus the shaft can be given precise angular rotations.

Such motors can be used to provide precise movements as in robot arms, floppy drives, print head movement and paper rotation in computer printers, machine tool control etc.. In all these and many other applications stepper motors are used.

Table.12.1. Coil Pulse Sequence

clock wise	B2	B1	A2	A1	counter clockwise
	D3	D2	D1	D0	
↓	1	1	0	0	↑
	1	0	0	1	
	0	0	1	1	
	0	1	1	0	
	1	1	0	0	

Table.12.2. Port Assignments

Port	Connected to	Mode
D0 to D3 (Port A)	A1,A2,B1,B2 through drivers	output

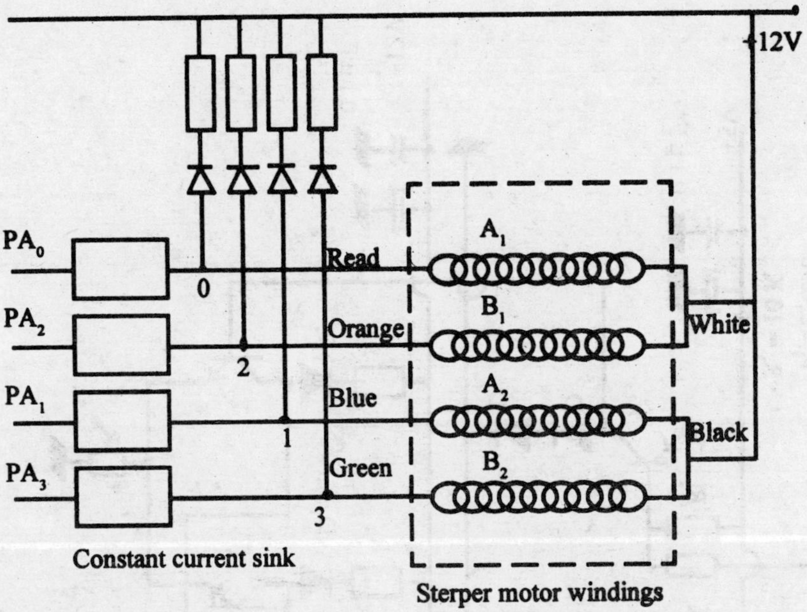

Fig. 12.5 Stepper motor windings

The coils require 1 Amp current for rotation, at 12V. The 12V power supply should be capable of suppling more current. Transistor circuits are used as driver stages as given in Figure 12.6. The PNP transistor T_1 is ON when D3 bit is 0 it is OFF when D3 bit is 1. T_2 is ON when T_1 is ON, it is OFF when T_1 is OFF. When T_2 conducts, there is a current through the coil B2. From this it is clear than when D3 bit is zero, coil B2 is energised.

Similarly there are pairs of transistor circuits to energise the coils A1, A2, and B1 as shown in the Table 12.3.

Table.12.3. Bit Assignment

Zero level in D0 bit energises coil A1
Zero level in D1 bit energises coil A2
Zero level in D2 bit energises coil B1
Zero level in D3 bit energises coil B2

Program Description

The pulsing of these stages can be done with the program given. From Table 12.1 it can be found that the starting word 1100 is essen[illegible]ally shifted left one bit in each step of the sequence. The PPI [illegible] chip 8255 on the kit can be used for the purpose of interfacin[illegible]. The port assignment

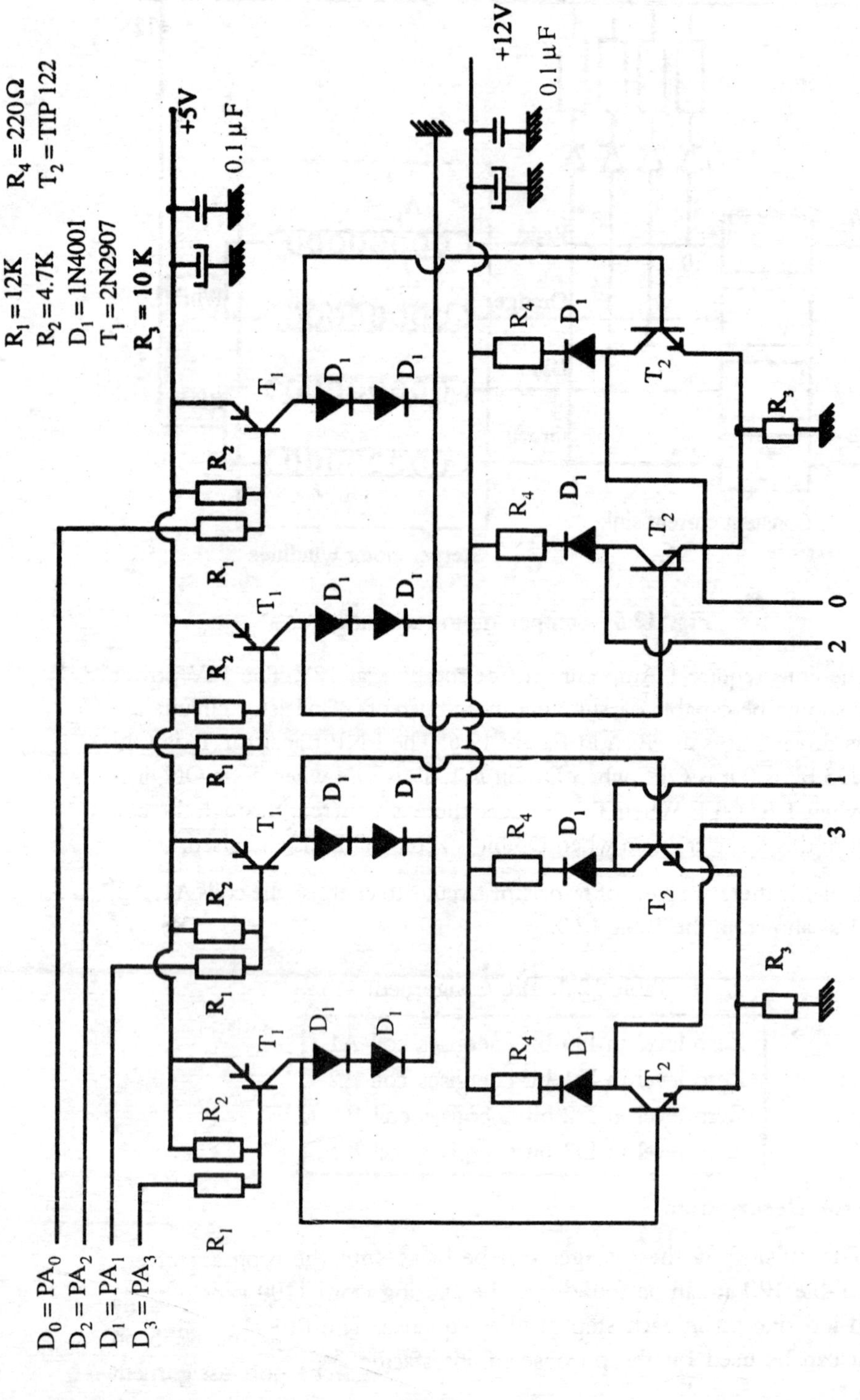

Fig. 12.6 (a) Stepper motor Interface

of the program is given in Table 12.2. The program starts with the word 1100 and outputs it through one of the ports. It shifts the word left and outputs it through the same port for each step of rotation of the shaft. For counter clockwise rotation, the word is shifted right. The number of steps required (in hex format) and the direction of rotation (D0 = 0 for clockwise, 1 for counter clockwise) are loaded in registers.

Program Listing

Mem Location	Op-code	Label	Mnemonic	; Comments
8001	3E		MVI A,80	; configure 8255 for all
8002	80			; ports as output
8003	D3		OUT 43	; 43 is the CWRegister
8004	43			
8005	0E		MVI C,XX	; counter for no of steps
8006	XX			
8007	06		MVI B,YY	; yy = 0 for clockwise
8008	YY			; 1 for anticlockwise
8009	78		MOV A,B	
800A	FE		CPI 01	
800B	01			
800C	C2		JNZ CLKWSE	;goto clockwise routine
800D	20			
800E	80			
800F	16	ANTI	MVI D,CC	; Load suitable code foe data
8010	CC			
8011	7A	LOOP1	MOV A,D	
8012	D3		OUT 40	; send data to port A
8013	40			
8014	07		RLC	
8015	57		MOV D,A	
8016	CD		CALL DELAY	
8017	30			
8018	80			
8019	0D		DCR C	; decrment the counter
801A	C2		JNZ LOOP1	; check counter = 0
801B	11			
801C	80			
801D	76		HLT	; stop
8020	16	CLKWSE	MVI D,CC	; Load suitable code for data
8021	CC			
8022	7A	LOOP2	MOV A,D	
8023	D3		OUT 40	; send data to port A

Mem Location	Op-code	Label	Mnemonic	Comments
8024	40			
8025	0F		RRC	
8026	57		MOV D,A	
8027	CD		CALL DELAY	
8028	30			
8029	80			
802A	0D		DCR C	; decrment the counter
802B	C2		JNZ LOOP2	; check counter = 0
802C	22			
802D	80			
802E	76		HLT	; stop
8030	D5	DELAY	PUSH D	; save registers
8031	11		LXI D yyyy	; Load suitable number for ; delay needed.
8032	yy			
8033	yy			
8034	1B	LOOP3	DCX D	
8035	7A		MOV A,D	; check for 0
8036	B3		ORA E	
8037	34		JNZ LOOP3	
8038	80			
8039	D1		POP D	; restore registers
803A	C9		RET	; return

Activity Sequence

1. Make the connections as shown in Figure 12.6.
2. Choose a memory location for STEP TABLE and store the direction code (00 for clockwise and 01 for counterclockwise) in the first location. Store the number of steps required (in hex format) in the next location.
3. Load the program in the kit giving the address of STEP TABLE as chosen above in line 4 of the program.
4. Calculate the angular rotation of the shaft:

   angle of rotation = no. of steps x angle per step*.
5. Run the program and observe the shaft rotation. Attach a small pointer to the shaft for measuring the angle of rotation.
6. Repeat steps 2,3 & 4 for different number of steps and directions.
7. Change the delay in the subroutine and observe the results.

Note: Refer the stepper motor data sheet for the value.

Flowchart for Stepper Motor Control

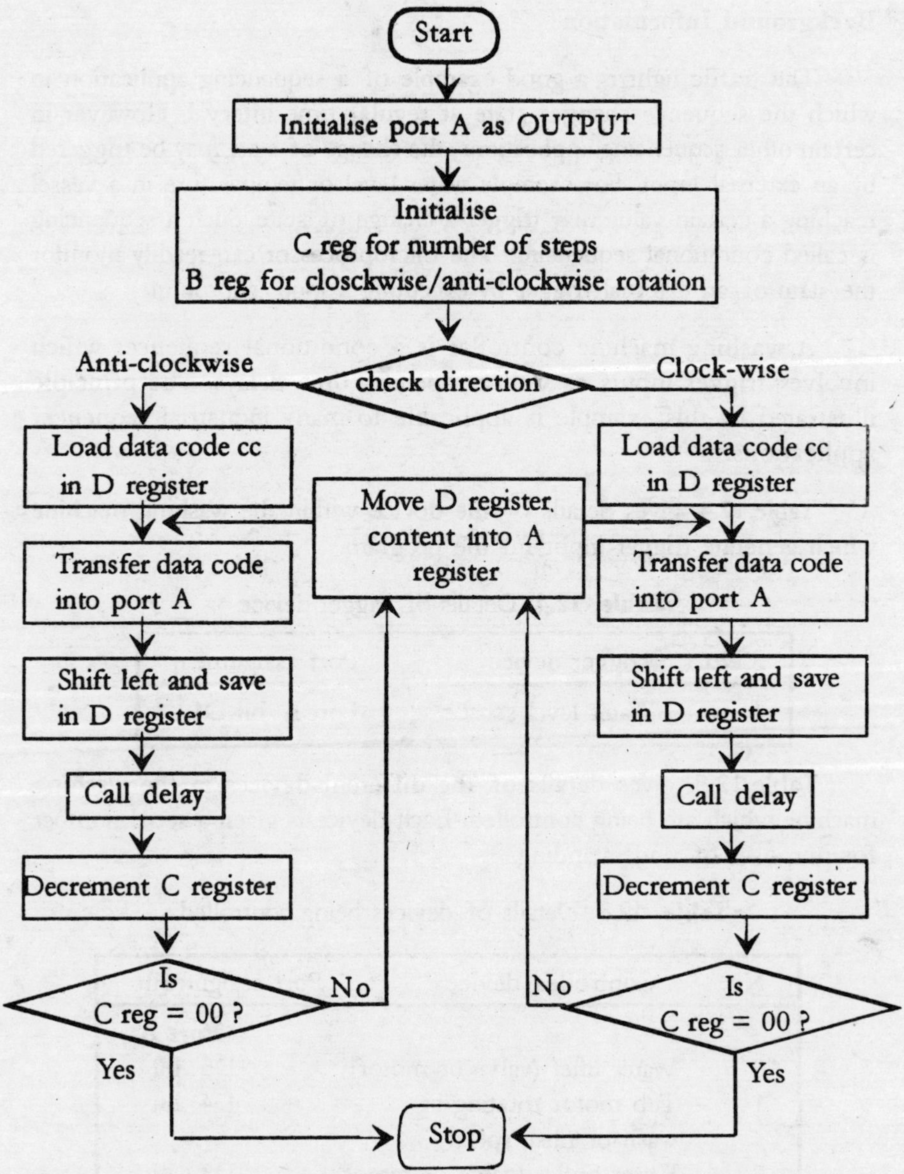

12.6 WASHING MACHINE CONTROLLER

Problem Statement

Interface different devices in a washing machine and implement a sequencing on the basis of certain conditions.

Background Information

The traffic light is a good example of a sequencing application in which the sequence changes state at regular time interval. However in certain other sequencing applications, the change of state may be triggered by an external input. For example water level or temperature in a vessel reaching a certain value may trigger a change of state. Such a sequencing is called conditional sequencing. The microprocessor can readily monitor the state of an external trigger by executing a loop (subroutine).

A washing machine controller is a conditional sequencer which involves trigger inputs as well as specific time delays. The principle illustrated by this example is applicable to many industrial sequencer applications.

Table.12.4. gives details of the device within the washing machine which generate trigger input for the program.

Table 12.4. Details of trigger device

S.No.	Trigger device	Port assignment
1	Water level sensor	Port B bit D1

Table.12.5. gives details of the different devices in the washing machine which are being controlled. Each device is given a serial number for purposes of understanding.

Table 12.5. Details of devices being controlled

No.	Controlled device	Port assignment
		Port A
0	Water inlet (valve or motor)	D5 bit
1	Tub motor rotating at wash or rinse speed	D4 bit
2	Water outlet (valve or motor)	D3 bit
3	Tub motor rotating at drying speed	D2 bit

The activites in the washing in their proper order are listed in Table.12.6. For each activity the state (ON/OFF) of each of the device is also given.

Table 12.6. Washing Machine Sequence

State Number	Controlled device 0	1	2	3	Action
0	ON	OFF	OFF	OFF	Fill the tub with water upto specified level
1	OFF	ON	OFF	OFF	Rotate tub at wash or rinse speed for a fixed time T_2.
2	OFF	OFF	ON	OFF	Empty tub for a fixed time T_1.
3	ON	OFF	OFF	OFF	Fill tub with cold water upto a specified level
4	OFF	ON	OFF	OFF	Rotate tub at wash/rinse speed for a fixed time T_2.
5	OFF	OFF	ON	OFF	Empty tub for a fixed time T_1.
6	OFF	OFF	OFF	ON	Switch ON drier for time T_1.

Table.12.7. lists along with the state of the devices the trigger which causes the change from one state to another. The bits D1 and D0 indicate change of state by the relevant time delay. The state number 7 is added as the final state when the washing machine completes the operation and is switched OFF.

Table 12.7. Washing machine controller state table

State number	Controlled device 0	1	2	3	Delay 1 T_2	Delay 0 T_1	Operation
	D5	D4	D3	D2	D1	D0	
0	1	0	0	0	0	0	Waiting for Tub full
1	0	1	0	0	1	0	signal washing for T_2
2	0	0	1	0	0	1	emptying for T_1
3	1	0	0	0	0	0	waiting for Tub full
4	0	1	0	0	1	0	signal rinsing for T_R
5	0	0	1	0	0	1	emptying for T_1
6	0	0	0	1	0	1	drying for T_1
7	0	0	0	0	System switched OFF		

The 6 bits (D5 to D0) of each state form the data byte for that state. The data byte is sent out to the devices through Port A. The tub full signal may be detected by reading the bit D1 of port B. As reference for checking the level of bit D1 of port B the data byte 000010 is added after the state 0 as well as after state 2. This results in a total of 10 bytes of data, which is stored in the memory.

Program Description

The program sends out a byte of data through port A. It then checks bits D1 & D0 of the data and implements a time delay if required. Otherwise it reads bit D1 of port B and checks for tubfull signal. It then sends out the next byte of data. This process is repeated for all the bytes of data.

Flow Chart

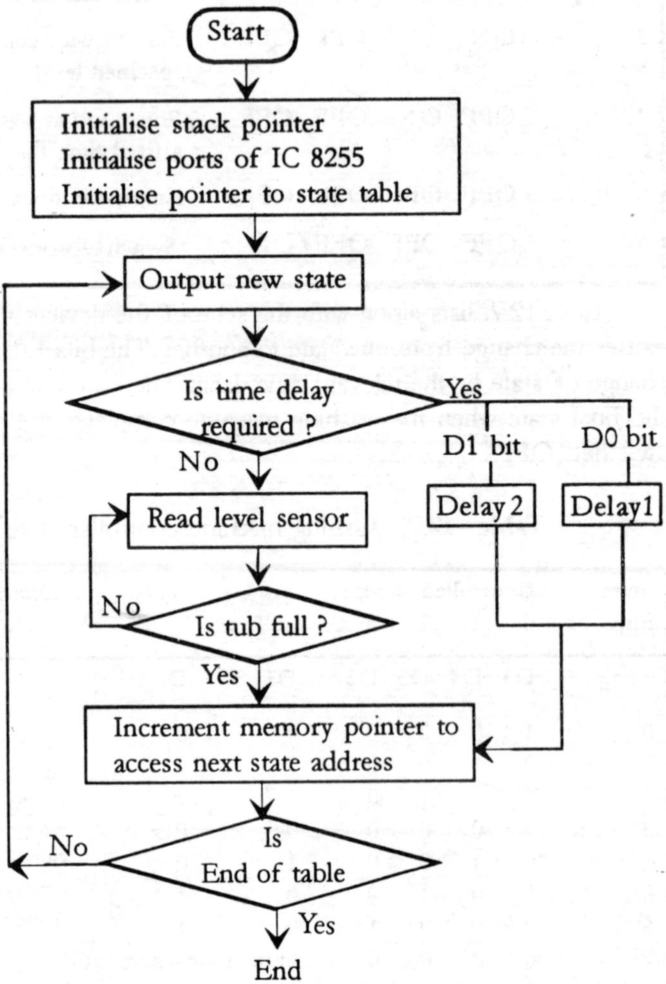

Label	Mnemonics	Comments
START	LXI SP, xxxx	; Initialise the stack pointer
	MVI A, 82	; Port A = output port
	OUT 23	; Port B = input port, 23 is CWR
	LXI H, 2300	; lookup table starting address
NEWSTATE	MOV A, M	; new state is transferred to
	OUT 20	; output port A (20 H)
	ANI 01	; check for the delay bits
	JNZ DELAY 1	; if not goto routine CONDI
	ANI 02	; check for the delay 1
	JZ Cond 1	; If not goto routine SUN
	CALL DELAY 2	; call subroutine delay 1
	JMP SKIP	; Goto SKIP
	CALL DELAY	; call subroutine delay 2
	JMP SKIP	; goto SKIP
CONDI	INX H	; update the pointer HL
LOOP	IN 21	; read the water level sensor
	SUB M	; check for the tub full condition
	JNZ LOOP	; if not go again to read the sensor
SKIP	INX H	; update the memory pointer
	MOV A, M	
	CPI 00	
	JNZ NEWSTATE	
	HLT	
DELAY1	LXI D,OEEE	; initialise delay loop.
LOOP1	DCX D	
	MOV A, E	
	ORA D	; is delay over?
	JNZ LOOP1	; no; jump to loop
	RET	; return to main program
DELAY 2	LXI D,FFFF	; initialise delay loop.
LOOP2	DCX D	
	MOV A, E	
	ORA D	; is delay over?
	JNZ LOOP2	; no; jump to loop
	RET	; return to main program

Note: It is to be noted that there are 2 motors in the washing machine, one for washing and reinsing and another for drier. The first motor is switched on by D4 bit of Port A and the drier motor is switched on by D2 bit of Port A.

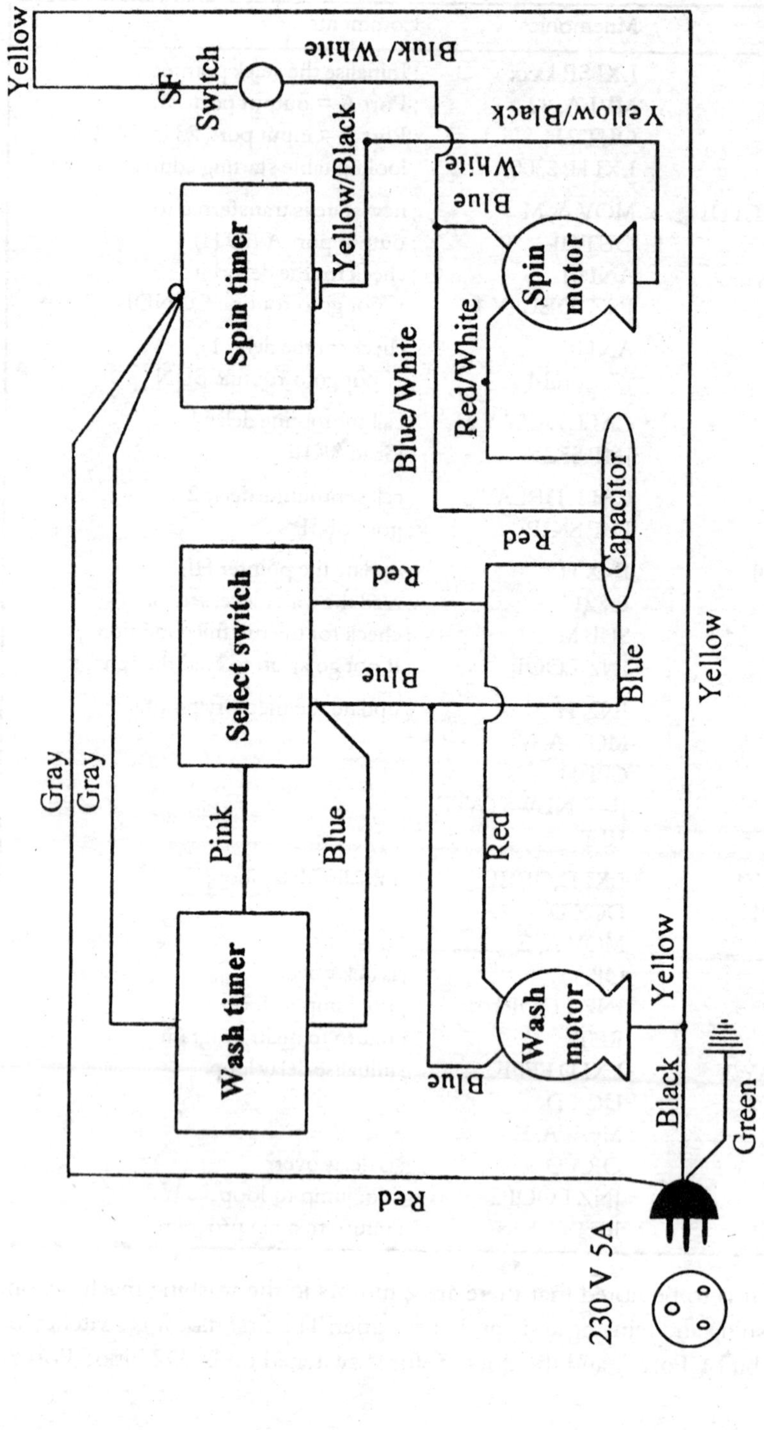

Fig. 12.6 b) Wiring Diagram

12.7 EPROM PROGRAMMER

Problem Statement

Construct and test of an EPROM programmer.

Background Information

The EPROM chip 2764 has an array of 65,536 bits of programming sites and so it can store 8192 (8K) bytes of data. The IC chip comes in a 28 pin package and has a7 mm square quartz window on the package. The chip can be erased by shining Ultra Violet (UV) light through this window. The chip operates on a single +5 volts supply. It has 13 address pins (A0 to A12) for addressing 8K bytes and 8 bi-directional data pins (D0 to D7) which are tri-state. The reading and programming modes are controlled by the 4 pins CE, OE, PGM and Vpp. The levels required at these pins for the different modes are listed in Table 12.8. The only special requirement is that the Vpp pin requires +21V while programming, otherwise this pin must be connected to +5V.

Table 12.8 Mode selection of 2764.

Mode	Pins			
	CE	PGM	OE	Vpp
Read	L	L	L	+5V
Program	L	50 ms pulse	H	+21V

The sequence of operations involved in programming a byte of data is given in the following :

1. The data byte is fed on the data pins D0 to D7.
2. The address is fed on the address pins A0 to A12.
3. Vpp pin is fed with +21V and OE is kept at logical high level.
4. The CE pin is kept at logical LOW, PGM pin is applied with a pulse of around 50 ms width. At the end of the pulse the data is stored at the selected location.

For reading the data from a location the following is the sequence of operation.

1. The address is fed on the address pins.

2. The chip is enabled by making the chip select CE low. The output OE pin must be made LOW and PGM pin is kept at HIGH level. The Vpp pin is fed with +5V.
3. The data is available on the data pins D0 to D7.

The ports available on the 8255 chip of the kit can be used for interfacing the EPROM chip with the kit. The port allotment is given in Table 12.9

To switch the voltage at the Vpp pin between +5V and +21V the circuit shown in Figure 1, may be constructed and used. It is a simple transistor switch. When the input A is 0 the transistor is ON and connects +21V to Vpp pin. When A is 1 the transistor is OFF and so Vpp gets +5V.

Fig.12.7 gives the method of interfacing the kit with the EPROM chip.

Table 12.9 Port assignment.

Port	Connected to	Purpose	Mode
A	data pins of EPROM (D0 to D7)	transferring of data between CPU &EPROM	input/ output
B	address pins of EPROM (A0 to A7)	lower byte address	output
C (lower)	address pins of EPROM (A8 to A11)	higher byte address	output
C (upper)	C4 to A12 of EPROM	MSB of address	output
	C5 to OE	output enable	
	C6 to PGM pin	Pulse must be given while programming	
	C7 to input A of transistor switch	to connect +5V or +21V	

* The levels on data bit C7 reflect the status of operation.

Blank Check

The blank check program checks a block of locations in the EPROM for blank(FF). The data to be loaded on the EPROM is stored in the user memory area starting at a convenient location. The address values of different ports used in the program is listed in Table.12.10.

Flow chart for EPROM blank check program

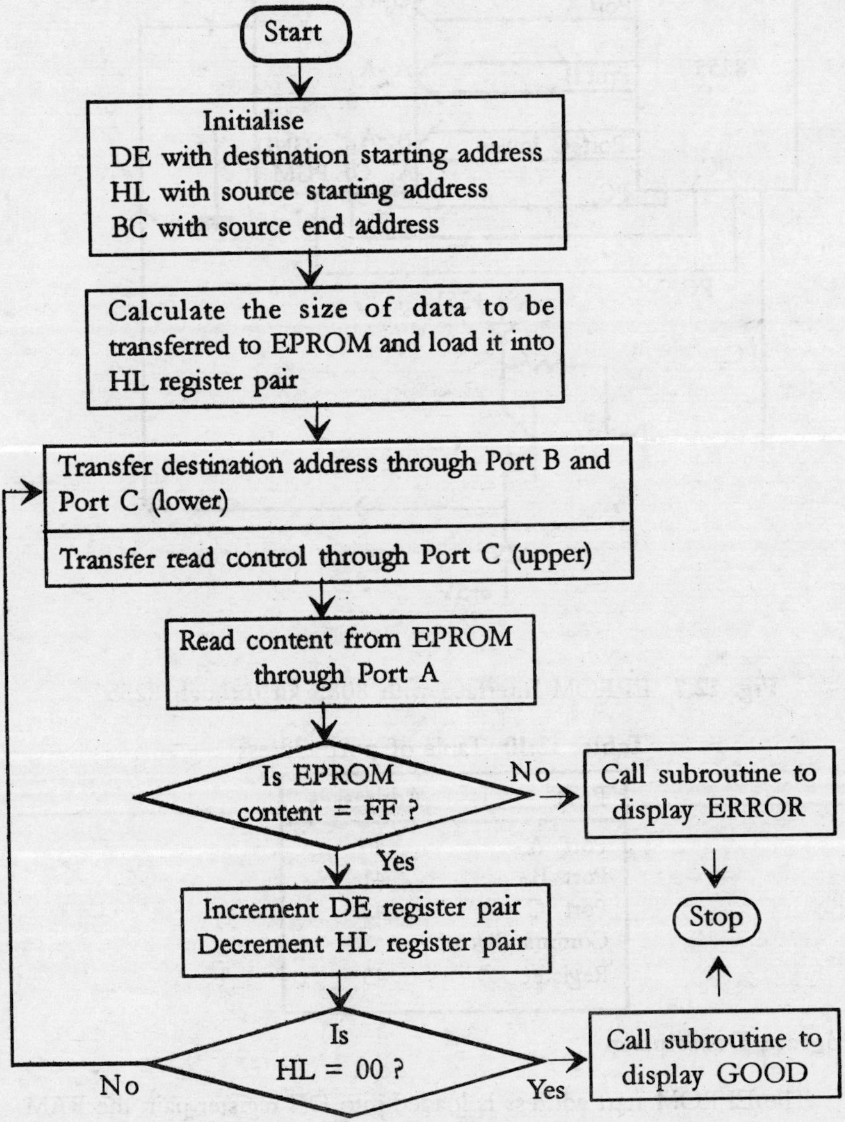

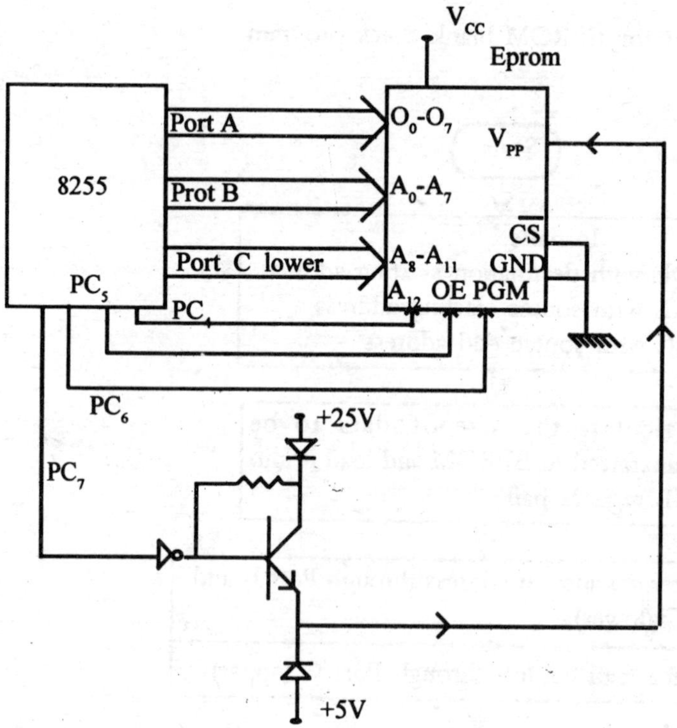

Fig. 12.7 EPROM Interface with 8085 kit through 8255

Table 12.10 Table of port address

Port	Addresses
Port A	40
Port B	41
Port C	42
Commandword Register	43

Program Description

The EPROM start address is loaded into DE register pair; the RAM start and end address in HL and BC respectively. The program subtracts the RAM end address from start address and adds 1 to get the size of the data block. The size is stored in HL pair. The lower address byte is sent out first, followed by the upper byte. In the upper byte the bit for Vpp pin is set to 1 to get +5V, the bit for PGM pin is set to 1 and the bit for OE pin is set to 0 for read operation. The data from the EPROM is read and checked for blank. If it is not blank (FF), error is displayed. Otherwise data at next location is checked. This is repeated for the whole block. If any location has data other than FF (not blank) then the subroutine meant for displaying ERROR is called to display ERROR. If all the required locations in EPROM contain FF, then the subroutine meant for displaying GOOD in the address field of the kit is called.

Blank Check Program

```
BLKCHK  LXI D,EPROM start   load starting address of EPROM
        LXI H,RAM start     load starting address of RAM
        LXI B,RAM end       load end address of RAM
        MOV A,C
        SUB L               subtract RAM end address
        MOVL ,A              from RAM start address
        MOV A,B             to get the size of the
        SBB H               block.
        MOV H,A             store the size in HL pair
        INX H               add 1 to get correct size
        MVI A,90            initialise 8255 for Port
        OUT 43              A input and B&C output.
CHECK   MOV A,E             set address low byte.
        OUT 41
        MOV A,D             set address high byte.
        ANI 1F
        ORI C0              set Vpp to +5V.
        OUT 42
        NOP                 small delay to settle address
        NOP
        IN 40               read data from EPROM
        CPI FF              is data FF?
        JNZ ERROR           no; display blank error
        INX D               yes
        DCX H
        MOV A,H
        ORA L               entire block covered?
        JNZ CHECK
        CALL BLANK
        HLT
```

```
ERROR   CALL error      display error by calling the
        HLT             user routine available in the
                        kit's monitor program.
BLANK   xxxx            user can write a routine to
        xxxx            display GOOD in the address
        xxxx            field of the kit, when the EPROM
                        is empty.
        xxxx
        xxxx
        HLT
```

Loading Data into EPROM

The data loading program loads a block of data into the EPROM starting from the indicated location. Make sure that the data block loaded into the user memory area is still intact. If required load the set of data block again at a convenient location in the user memory area (RAM).

Program Description

Since a delay subroutine is used, stack pointer is initialised to a convenient RAM location. As before, the size of the block is calculated from the RAM start and end addresses. The data byte to be loaded into EPROM is sent to the data pins of the EPROM through port A. Following this the address is sent through the ports B and C. Data bit meant for Vpp is set 0 to get +25V. Data bit meant for PGM pin is made 1, then 0 and back to 1, to generate a pulse of 50 ms duration. The delay subroutine is used for this purpose. This procedure is repeated for the entire block of data transfer. When all the data from the user memory area is transferred into the EPROM, call the subroutine to display OVER in the address field of the kit.

Flow Chart for Loading Data into EPROM

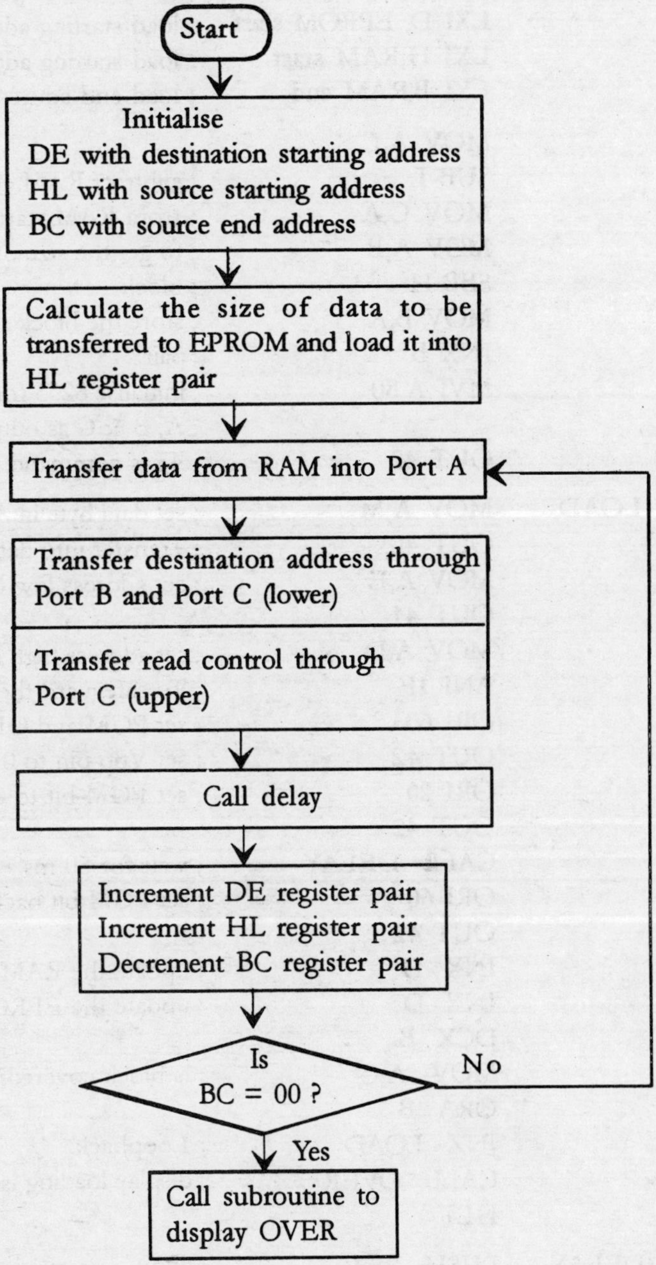

Program for Loading data into EPROM

```
DATLOD  LXI SP, stack addr   ; initialise stack pointer
        LXI D, EPROM start   ; load starting address of EPROM
        LXI H,RAM start      ; load starting address of RAM
        LXI B,RAM end        ; load end address of RAM
        MOV A,C
        SUB L                ; subtract RAM end address
        MOV C,A              ; from RAM start address
        MOV A,B              ; to get the size of the
        SBB H                ; block
        MOV B,A              ; store the block size in BC
        INX B                ; pair.
        MVI A,80             ; initialise 8255 for Port
                             ; A, B & C as output.
        OUT 43               ; 43 is command word register
LOAD    MOV A,M              ; set data byte in Accumulator
        OUT 40               ; Transfer into data bus
        MOV A,E              ; set address low byte.
        OUT 41
        MOV A,D              ; set address high byte.
        ANI 1F               ; To safeguard the higher byte addr
        ORI 60               ; set PGM and OE bit to 1 level
        OUT 42               ; set Vpp pin to 0 to get + 25 Volt
        ORI 20               ; set PGM bit to 0 for programming
        OUT 42
        CALL DELAY           ; wait for 50 ms.
        ORI 60               ; set PGM bit back to 1 level
        OUT 42
        INX H                ; update the RAM address
        INX D                ; update the EPROM address
        DCX B
        MOV A,C              ; is block covered?
        ORA B
        JNZ LOAD             ; Loopback
        CALL OVER            ; display loading is over
        HLT
DELAY   PUSH PSW             ; dump registers in stack
        PUSH H
        LXI H,0EEE           ; initialise dealy loop.
```

```
LOOP1   DCX  H
        MOV  A,H
        ORA  L               ; is delay over?
        JNZ  LOOP1           ; no; jump to loop
        POP  H               ; yes; restore registers
        POP  PSW
        RET                  ; return to main program
OVER    yyyy
        yyyy                 ; user can write a routine to
        HLT                  ; display OVER in the address
                             ; field of the kit.
```

Data Verification

The verification program, the data loaded into the EPROM is checked byte by byte with the source data at the user memory area for any errors. Make sure that the data loaded into the user memory area is still intact. If required load the data again into the user memory area.

Program Description

As before, the size of the block is calculated from the source RAM start and end addresses. An address is sent to the EPROM and the data is read from the EPROM. It is compared with the source data from the RAM. If any error is detected the program stops executing the main program and the subroutine meant for displaying ERROR will be executed. Otherwise the process is repeated for the whole block. When all the bytes loaded into the EPROM and the source bytes are equal then the subroutine meant for displaying GOOD will be executed to indicate that the EPROM is loaded properly.

Data Verification Program

```
DATCHK  LXI D,EPROM start    load starting address of EPROM
        LXI H,RAM start      load source start address of RAM
        LXI B,RAM end        load source end address of RAM

        MOV A,C
        SUB L                subtract RAM end address
        MOV C,A              from RAM start address,
        MOV A,B              to get the size of the
        SBB H                block.
        MOV B,A              store block the size in BC reg.
        INX B
```

Flow Chart for Data Verification Program

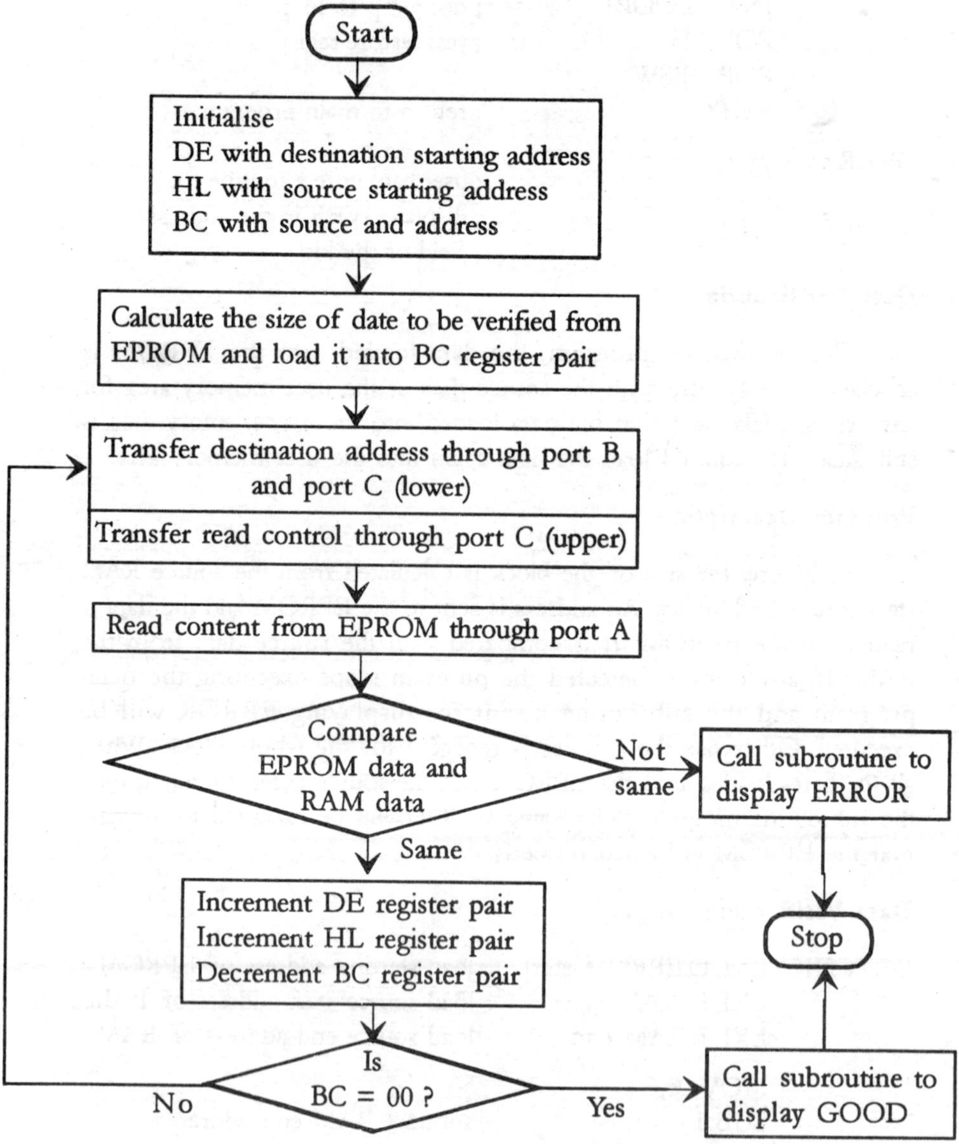

```
        MVI  A,90        initialise 8255 for Port A
                         as  input and B&C output.
        OUT 43
VERI    MOV A,E          set address low byte.
        OUT 41
        MOV A,D          set address high byte.
        ANI 1F
        ORI C0           set Vpp to +5V.
        OUT 42           set OE to 0 level
        IN 40            read data from EPROM
        CMP M            is data same as source?
        JNZ  ERROR       no; display data  error
        INX D            update EPROM address
        INX H            update source address
        DCX B
        MOV A,C
        ORA B
        JNZ  VERI        go back, check next data
        CALL GOOD        when EPROM content is correct.
        HLT
ERROR   xxxx             call the user routine to
        xxxx             display ERROR in the address
        HLT              field of the kit.

GOOD    zzzz             user can write a routine to
        zzzz             display GOOD in the address
        HLT              field of the kit.
```

Activity Sequence

1. Make the necessary connections as shown in Figure 12.7

A. Blank Checking

2. Choose a starting address in the EPROM in the vacant portion.
3. Choose a user RAM area and enter the data required to be loaded into the EPROM.
4. Enter the blank check program into the kit giving the address values as selected in steps 2 and 3 above.
5. Run the program and note the status.
6. Choose a starting address in an already loaded portion of the EPROM and repeat steps 4 & 5.

B. Data Loading into EPROM

7. Choose a starting address in the EPROM in the vacant portion.
8. Choose a user RAM area and enter the data required to be loaded into the EPROM (source data).
9. Enter the data load program into the kit giving the address values as selected in steps 7 and 8 above.
10. Run the program and note the status.

C. EPROM Data Verification

11. Make sure that the source data in the RAM as entered in step 8 is intact. Otherwise enter the data again at a convenient RAM area.
12. Enter the data verification program into the kit giving the EPROM start address and source data address values as per step 11.
13. Run the data verification program and observe the status lamps.
14. Change one or more bytes in the source data in the RAM and repeat step 13.

12.8 ANNUNCIATOR

Problem Statement

Interface and implement an annunciator system to monitor 8 faults.

Background Information

Many industries, particularly process control industries make use of a control panel to monitor and control the process from a remote control location. *The annunciator displays the status of different processes and raises alarm in case of a fault* so that the operator takes necessary action. The alarm is raised by blinking a lamp and making an audible sound.

The annunciator to be designed has to accept say 8 faults. An input port is used to sense these 8 faults. A one level on any of the bits indicate a fault. The annunciator uses an output port and 8 lamps to indicate the faults. The corresponding lamp is made blinking. In addition an audible tone is also raised. The operator acknowledges the fault by pressing the ACCEPT switch, provided. The annunciator responds by stopping the audible tone and it also stops the blinking but makes the lamp continuously ON to indicate the presense of fault. The operator tries to correct the fault and when he corrects it he presses the CLEAR switch. The corresponding lamp is switched OFF. However if he presses the CLEAR switch before the fault corrected, the blinking and audible alarm again starts. TEST push button is also provided to test whether all the lamps and alarm are in good condition or not.

Circuit Description

The programmable peripheral interface device 8255 as shown in Fig.12.8 is used to implement the ports. Port A is used for input and it accepts the 8 fault signals. Port B is used for output and drives 8 lamps. Port C (lower) is used for input, and interfaces the ACCEPT & CLEAR switches. Port C (upper) used for output and switches on the alarm. The Table.12.11. illustrates the bit assignment on Port C.

Table 1

Port C (Lower)	
PC0 -	ACCEPT push button
PC1 -	CLEAR push button
PC2 -	TEST push button
Port C (Upper)	
PC4 -	alarm

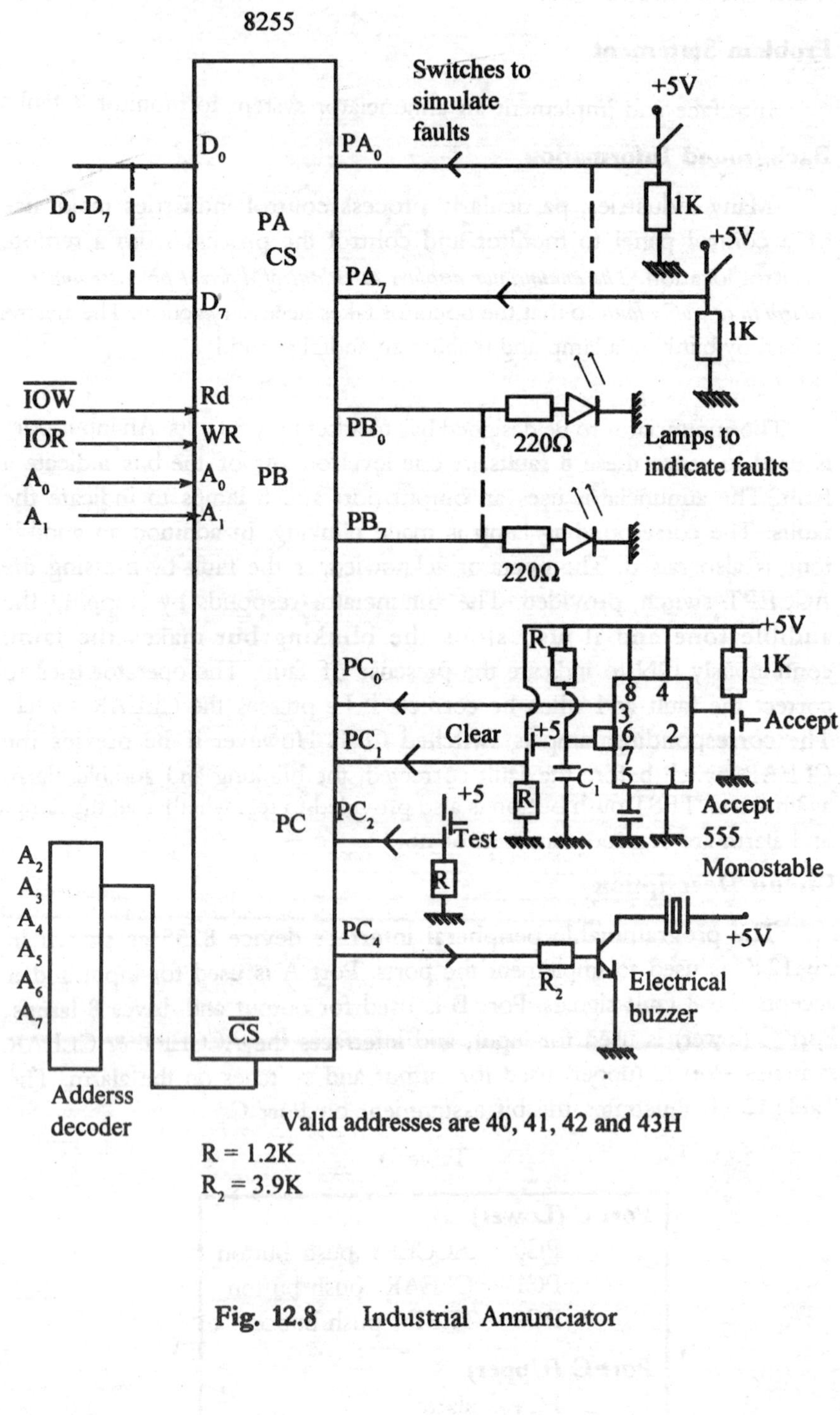

Fig. 12.8 Industrial Annunciator

Program Description

The program first reads Port A in a continuous loop. When an ONE level is sensed on any one of the bits, the corresponding lamp is made blinking and an alarm is also raised. When the ACCEPT key is sensed on Port C the alarm is stopped and the lamp is switched ON. When the CLEAR keypress is sensed the program checks for the fault on the Port A. If the fault is cleared it switches OFF the lamp. Otherwise it raises the alarm again.

Program Listing

Mem Location	Op-code	Label	Mnemonic	Comments
1800	3E	INIT	MVI A, 91	; Initialise Port A - input,
1801	91			; Port B-output, ; Port C (lower)
1802	D3		OUT 23	; -input, Port C (upper) ; -output
1803	23			
1804	3E	START	MVI A, 00	; alarm is switched OFF
1805	00			; all lamps are switched OFF
1806	D3		OUT 21	
1807	21			
1808	D3		OUT 22	
1809	22			
180A	DB	REPEAT	IN 22	; read the switches
180B	22			
180C	E6		ANI 07	; take the first 3 inputs
180D	0F			; of port C (lower)
180E	FE		CPI 04	; check whether TEST key
180F	04			; is pressed. If so, jump to
1810	CA		JZ TEST	; TEST routine
1811	51			
1812	18			
1813	DB	LOOP1	IN 20	; read the fault signals
1814	20			
1815	47		MOV B,A	; store it in reg B
1816	FE		CPI 00	; if no fault occurs, go to
1817	00			; the step REPEAT
1818	CA		JZ LOOP1	
1819	0A			
181A	18			

Mem Location	Op-code	Label	Mnemonic	Comments
181B	3E		MVI A,10	fault occured, switch ON
181C	10			the alarm
181D	D3		OUT 22	
181E	22			
181F	78		MOV A,B	switch ON the corresponding
1820	D3		OUT 21	lamps
1821	21			
1822	CD		CALL DELAY	the delay is executed
1823	5B			
1824	18			
1825	3E		MVI A, 00	all the lamps are made off
1826	00			for a delay to bring the
1827	D3		OUT 21	blinking effect
1828	21			
1829	CD		CALL DELAY	
182A	5B			
182B	18			
182C	DB		IN 22	check for ACCEPT key
182D	22			
182E	E6		ANI 07	
182F	0F			
1830	FE		CPI 01	
1831	01			
1832	C2		JNZ LOOP1	if not, goto LOOP1
1833	13			
1834	18			
1835	3E		MVI A,00	if ACCEPT key is pressed,
1836	00			alarm is switched OFF
1837	D3		OUT 22	
1838	22			
1839	78		MOV A,B	the lamps corresponding
183A	D3		OUT 21	the faults are made glow
183B	21			
183C	DB	LOOP2	IN 22	check for CLEAR key
183D	22			if not, go to LOOP2
183E	E6		ANI 07	
183F	0F			
1840	FE		CPI 02	
1841	02			
1842	C2		JNZ LOOP3	
1843	48			

Mem Location	Op-code	Label	Mnemonic	Comments
1844	18			
1845	C3		JMP START	if CLEAR switch is pressed,
1846	04			jump to the START
1847	18			
1848	DB	LOOP3	IN 20	
1849	20			
184A	B8		CMP B	
184B	C2		JNZ LOOP1	
184C	13			
184D	18			
184E	C3		JMP LOOP2	
184F	3C			
1850	18			
1851	3E	TEST	MVI A,10	test routine to blink
1852	10			the lamps and sound alarm
1853	D3		OUT 22	
1854	22			
1855	3E		MVI A,FF	
1856	FF			
1857	D3		OUT 20	
1858	20			
1859	CD		CALL DELAY	
185A	64			
185B	18			
185C	3E		MVI A,00	
185D	00			
185E	CD		CALL DELAY	
185F	64			
1860	18			
1861	C3		JMP REPEAT	it is continued till the TEST
1862	0A			key is pressed
1863	18			
1864	21	DELAY	LXI H, 0576	delay routine is written by
1865	76			taking a 16 bit number
1866	05			0576H in a reg.pair and
1867	2B	LOOPX	DCX H	decrementing to 0
1868	7C		MOV A,H	
1869	B5		ORA L	check HL = 00
186A	C2		JNZ LOOPX	if no, goto LOOPX
186B	67			
186C	18			
186D	C9		RET	

Flow Chart for Annunciator

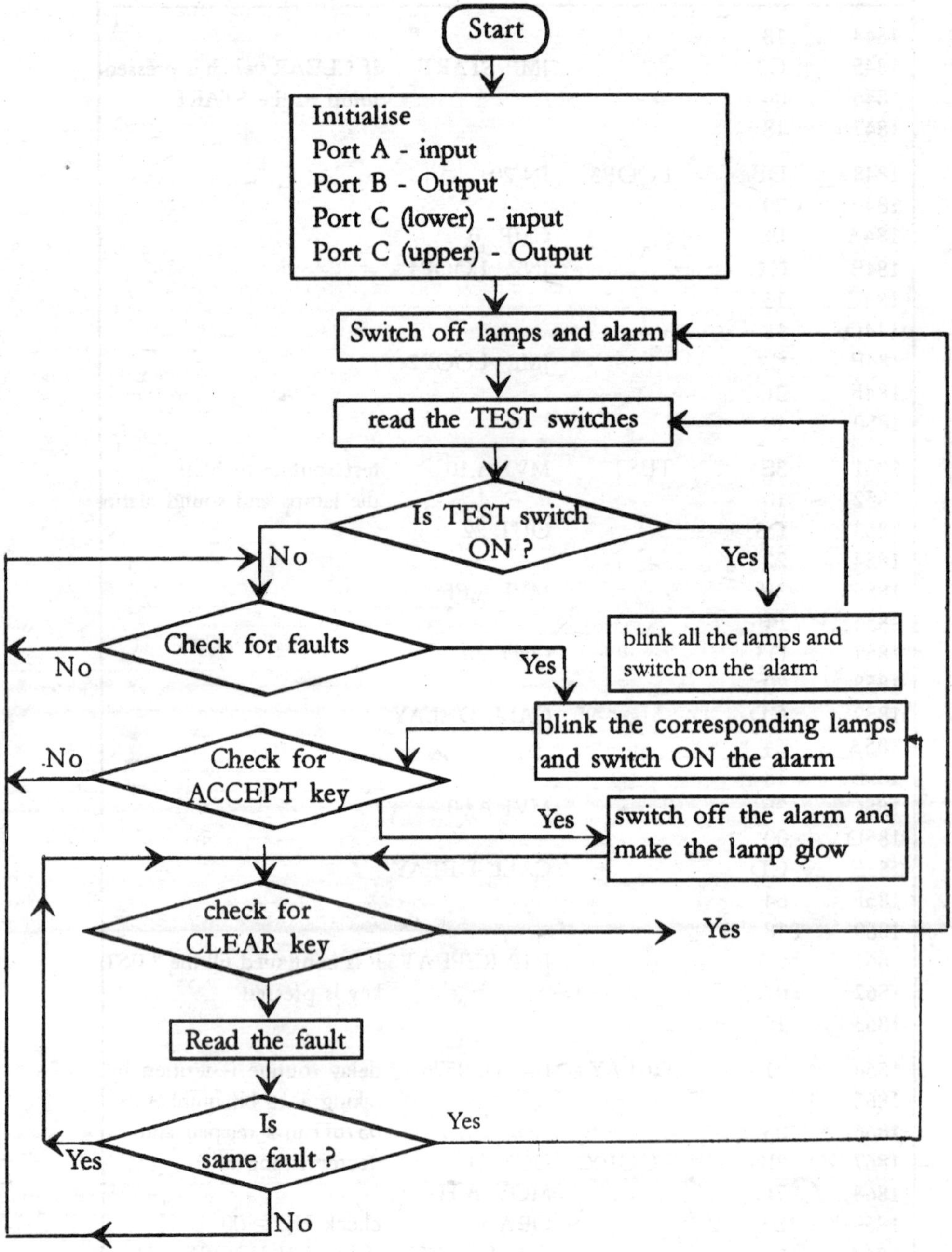

12.9 PRINTER INTERFACE

Problem Statement

Interface a printer with the microprocessor trainer kit.

Background Information

The printer is a self powered, stand alone, table top unit. It attaches to the system (computer or microprocessor kit) via a parallel signal cable of 1.5 meters length. It obtains AC power from a standard wall outlet. The printer may be of 80 column or 132 column type. The printing speed of a printer is represented in terms of characters per second (CPS).

The dotmatrix and the daisy wheel printers are the most commonly used types. The dotmatrix printer forms characters with a matrix of 5x7 or 7x7 or 7x9 or 9x9 dots, using aprint head with 9 pins. The 80 column dotmatrix printer can even print 132 characters per line in a compressed mode, with a standard font. For graphics printing and for higher resolution 24 pin head dot matrix printer are available.

The daisy wheel printer, prints fully formed characters. The characters are embossed on the tips of the spokes of a wheel. It is a slow device which can print upto 24 characters per second.

A modern printer is as complicated as a computer and has its own microprocessor, read only memory (EPROM) and read write memory (RAM). In addition each printer includes a number of electromechanical sub-systems that must work very quickly and precisely.

Most printers have a self test routine. Self test checks out most of the electronics as well as the mechanisms in the printer very qickly. During the self test mode, the printer is isolated completely from the computer. Any printer problems that are caused by the computer or that of the interface connections will not affect the self test. If the self test is satisfactory, then the fault lies either in the interface or in the computer hardware/software.

In addition, the printers have auto diagnostic alarm facility for cases like

- printer out of paper
- cover is open
- paper stuck up in the carriage
- no print ribbon etc.

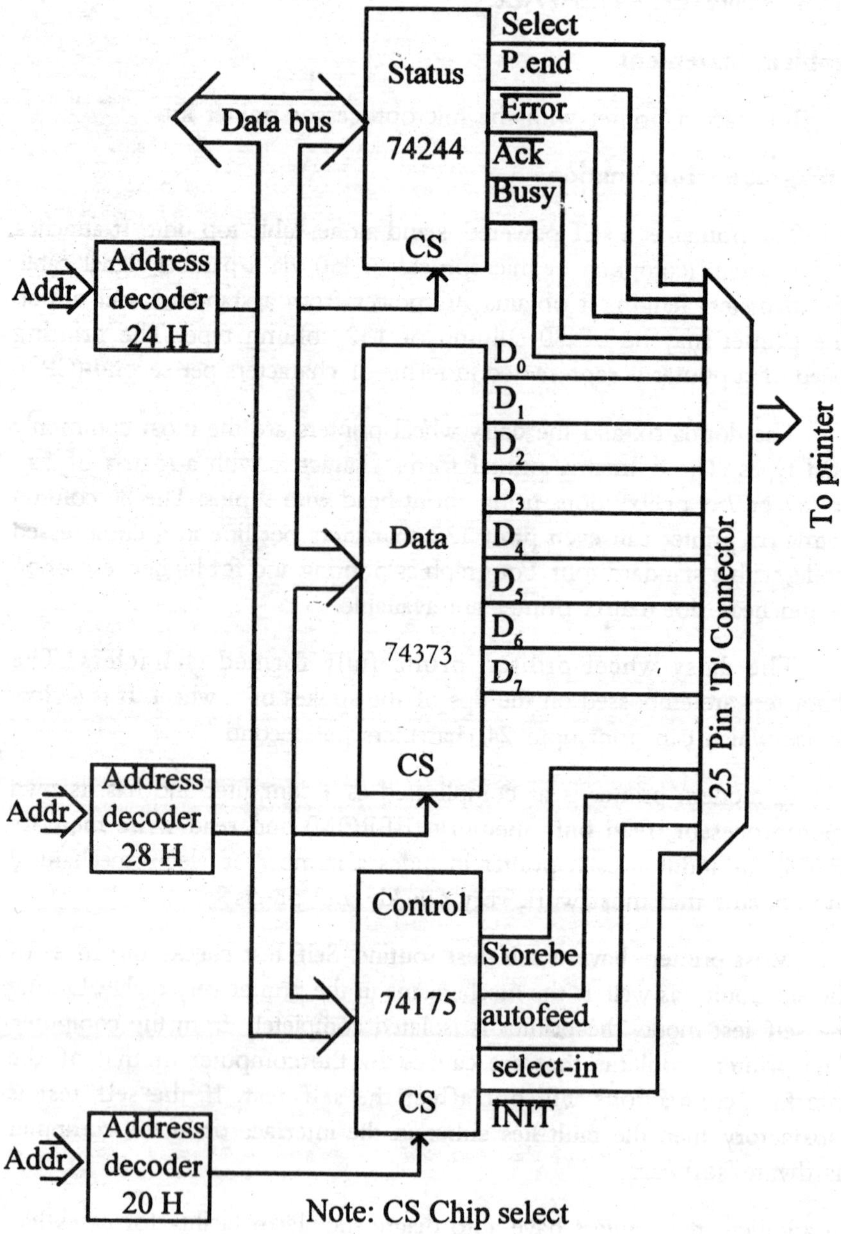

Fig. 12.9 Printer interface with microprocessor kit

The computer or a microprocessor kit can be connected by a Centronics parallel interface. This interface uses a cable with 25 leads with a 25 pin "D" type connector at the system unit end and a 36 pin connector on the printer end.

The Fig.12.9 is the interface circuit diagram to connect the microprocessor kit and the printer through this Centronics printer cable. The data bus of the microprocessor is connected to the input of IC 74273 and IC 74175. The same data bus from the microprocessor is also tied to the output of IC 74244.

The address bus of the microprocessor is connected to the address decoder circuit. The output of the address decoder circuit is connected to the chip select/enable of the IC 74273, IC 74175 and IC 74244. Let us assume that the address decoder circuit is designed in such a way that when the addresses in the following table are given, the specific IC is enabled.

Address	**Enabled IC**	**Used for**
20H	74175	To transfer printer control
24H	74244	To read printer status
28H	74373	To transfer data to printer

Note that these addresses 20H, 24H and 28H should not be the ones used in the microprocessor kit for enabling other local ICs. Otherwise these addresses may be changed suitably.

The output of ICs 74373 & 74175 and the input pins of IC 74244 is properly tied to the 25 pin "D" type female connector. For the pin connection details, refer the IBM technical reference manual or any printer manual. This interface circuit is connected to the printer using the Centronics printer cable.

The output of 74244 gives the printer status information -

- Printer selected or not
- Paper end or not
- General error
- Acknwledgement signal
- Busy or not.

Bit patern for the STATUS information

D7	D6	D5	D4	D3	D2	D1	D0
			Busy	ACK	ERR	PEND	Select

The above table gives the details of the printer status word.

The D0 bit is equal to 0 when the printer is not selected and is 1 when the printer is selected.

When the D1 bit is equal to 1, it indicates that the paper is not available in the printer. This bit is 0 when the paper is loaded in the printer.

The D2 bit of the status input from the printer is 0 only when any general error occurs in the printer, for example no printer ribbon or the cover is kept open. Otherwise this bit will be 1 level.

The D3 bit is used to get the acknowledgement signal from the printer to know that it has accepted the data, thereby we can transfer the next data from the microprocessor kit.

The D4 bit indicates that the buffer memory available in the printer is full. So the program can wait till the buffer memory is available.

The other bits D5, D6 and D7 of the status information is not used.

The output of IC 74175 transfer the following control signals as given in the following table.

- Initialisation
- Select the printer (Select-in)
- Strobe signal
- Autofeed signal.

Control word format

Bit pattern for the CONTROL information

D7	D6	D5	D4	D3	D2	D1	D0
				AF	STROB	SELEIN	INIT

The D0 bit must be 0 and this data bit must be transferred at the beginning and then this bit must be made 1 level. This bit helps the printer to adjust and position the print head in the first column.

The D1 bit must be always 0 and this bit must be transferred for each and every data transfer.

The D2 bit is a STROBE signal, used to indicate the printer that the data available in the data bus is a valid data. This helps the printer to read the data from the data bus into the printer memory. Normally this bit will be in 1 level. Only when the data is available in the data bus, this bit is made 0 and then it is made 1 level.

The D3 bit may be used in the printer for auto line feed purpose.

Program Description

The program prints all the alphabetical characters both in lower case and upper case in one line. This will be repeated for a predetermined time. If any error occurs it will display ERROR in the microprocessor kit address field. Following is the sequence of steps implemented.

- check for the paper availability
- if the paper is available proceed further otherwise display ERROR in the microprocessor kit
- check for any general error in the printer
- if any general error is found display ERROR on the kit otherwise proceed further
- transfer the first ASCII code to the printer
- make the strobe bit to 0 and then to 1 level after a predetermined time.
- check the ACK signal from the printer, if it is not available wait; otherwise proceed further
- check whether all the alphabetical characters are transferred in one line, if not transfer the next character and proceed further.
- transfer the carriage return and line feed signal to the printer for positioning the print head on the first column of the next line.
- repeat the above process to print alphabets a D7 D6 D5

Flow Chart for Data Verification Program

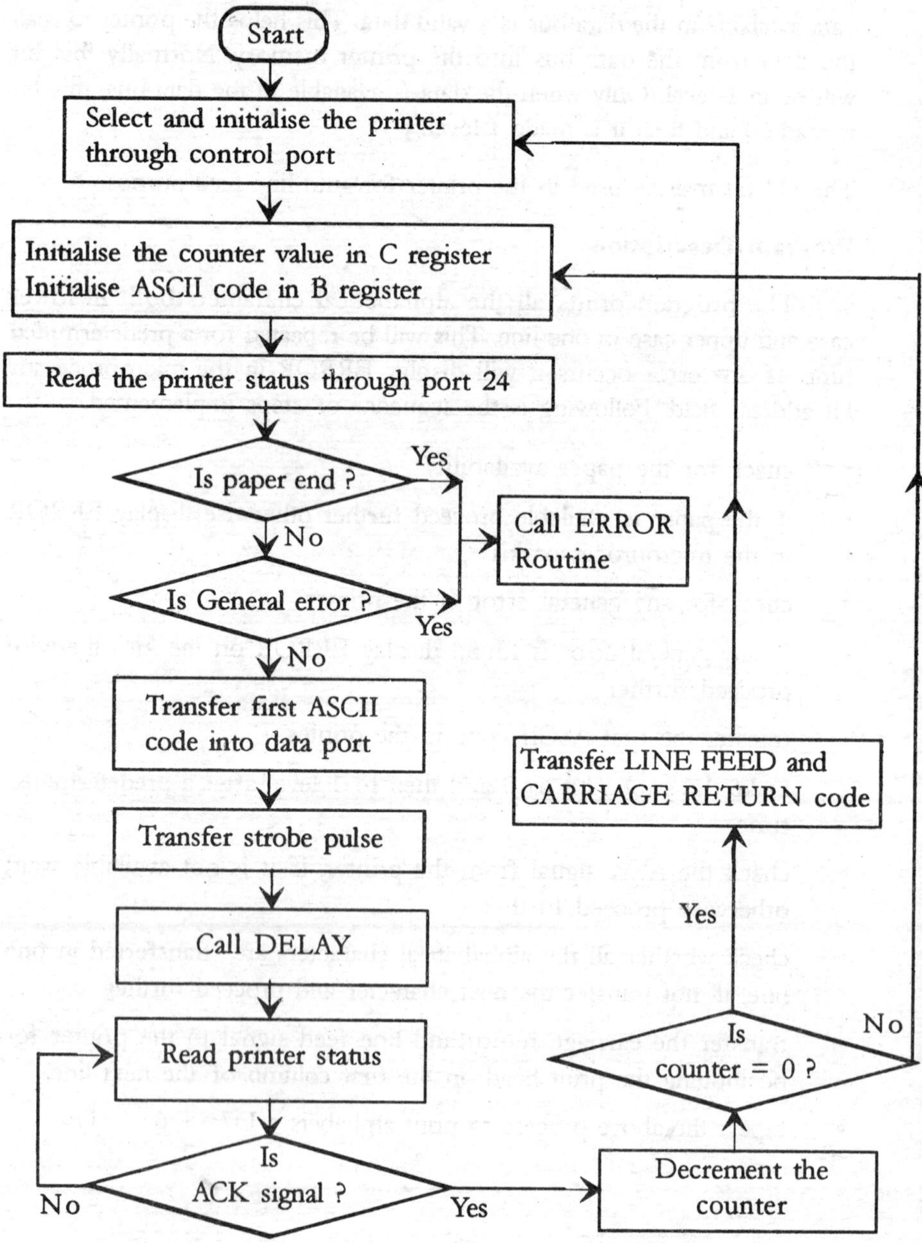

Program Listing

Mem Location	Op-code	Label	Mnemonic	Comments
5000	3E		MVI A,FC	Select and initialise
5001	FC			the printer through
5002	D3		OUT 20	control port
5003	20			
5004	A7	BEGIN	ANA A	Clear the carry flag
5005	0E		MVI C,41	Set the counter
5006	41			
5007	06		MVI B,41	Initialise the ASCII
5008	41			code for character A
5009	DB	LOOP2	IN 24	Read the printer status
500A	24			
500B	1F		RAR	
500C	1F		RAR	Check for Paper End
500D	DA		JC ERROR	If yes, call ERROR
500E	63			
500F	50			
5010	1F		RAR	Check for general error
5011	D2		JNC ERROR	If yes, call ERROR
5012	63			
5013	50			Now the printer is OK
5014	78		MOV A,B	Bring ASCII for A
5015	D3		OUT 28	Transfer into data port
5016	28			
5017	04		INR B	Update the ASCII code
5018	CD		CALL DELAY	
5019	69			
501A	50			
501B	3E		MVI A,FC	Transfer strobe +ve
501C	FC			(leading edge)
501D	D3		OUT 20	into control port.
501E	20			
501F	CD		CALL DELAY	
5020	69			
5021	50			
5022	3E		MVI A,FD	Transfer strobe -ve
5023	FD			(trailing edge)
5024	D3		OUT 20	into control port
5025	20			
5026	CD		CALL DELAY	

Mem Location	Op-code	Label	Mnemonic	Comments
5027	69			
5028	50			
5029	DB	LOOP1	IN 24	Read printer status
502A	24			
502B	E6		ANI 08	Separate the ACK signal
502C	08			
502D	FE		CPI 08	Check the ACK signal
502E	08			
502F	C2		JNZ LOOP1	
5030	29			
5031	50			
5032	0D		DCR C	Decrement the counter
5033	C2		JNZ LOOP2	If counter is not zero
5034	09			goto LOOP2
5035	50			
5036	3E		MVI A,0D	0D is the code for
5037	0D			carriage return
5038	D3		OUT 28	Transfer into printer
5039	28			control port
503A	CD		CALL DELAY	
503B	69			
503C	50			
503D	3E		MVI A,F9	Transfer strobe +ve
503E	09			(leading edge)
503F	D3		OUT 20	into control port
5040	20			
5041	CD		CALL DELAY	;
5042	69			
5043	50			
5044	3E		MVI A,FD	Transfer strobe -ve
5045	FD			(trailing edge)
5046	D3		OUT 20	into control port
5047	20			
5048	CD		CALL DELAY	
5049	69			
504A	50			
504B	3E		MVI A,0A	0A is the code for
504C	0A			line feed
504D	D3		OUT 28	
504E	28			

Mem Location	Op-code	Label	Mnemonic	Comments
504F	CD		CALL DELAY	
5050	69			
5051	50			
5052	3E		MVI A,F9	Transfer strobe +ve
5053	F9			into control port
5054	D3		OUT 20	
5055	20			
5056	CD		CALL DELAY	
5057	69			
5058	50			
5059	3E		MVI A,FD	Transfer strobe -ve
505A	FD			into control port
505B	D3		OUT 20	
505C	20			
505D	CD		CALL DELAY	
505E	69			
505F	50			
5060	C3		JMP BEGIN	Goto BEGIN, repeat
5061	04			the printing of chrs
5062	50			from A to Z and a to z
5063	3E	ERROR	MVI A,04	
5064	04			
5065	CD		CALL XXXX	Load error routine address available in the kit.
5066	XX			
5067	XX			
5068	76		HLT	
5069	11	DELAY	LXI D,05FF	
506A	FF			
506B	05			
506C	1B	LOOPX	DCX D	
506D	7B		MOV A,E	
506E	B2		ORA D	
506F	C2		JNZ LOOPX	
5070	6C			
5071	50			
5072	C9		RET	

Activity Sequence

1. Construct the circuit as shown in the figure.
2. Enter and run the program as listed above.

CHAPTER 13

OTHER 8 BIT MICROPROCESSORS

13.1 THE Z-80

The Z-80 microprocessor was introduced in 1976 and it uses N channel MOS depletion mode technology. It is available in 40 pin Dual In-line Package.

It has 16 separate address lines and 8 data lines. This eliminates the need to separate lower order address lines and data lines in a Z-80 system.

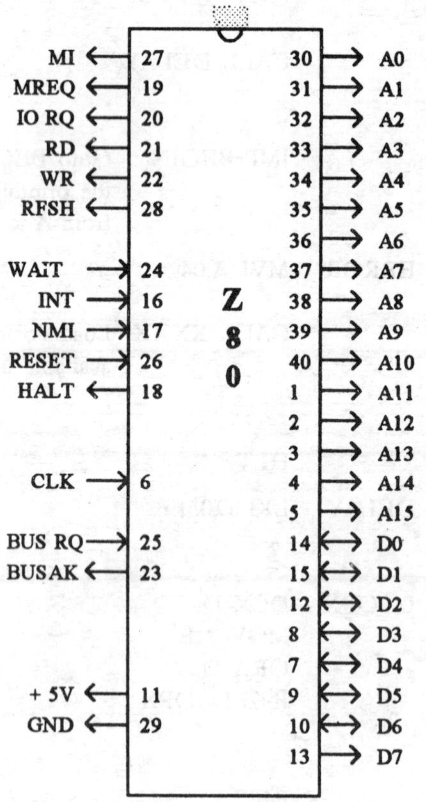

Fig. 13.1 Pin details of Z-80

The Z-80 has six control inputs:-

- Clock input (pin 6)
- Interrupt Request input (pin 16)
- Non-Maskable Interrupt request input (pin 17)
- Wait request (pin 24)
- Bus request input (pin 25)
- Reset input (pin 26)

The clock input requires a single +5V pulse train. A square wave generator that provides a fairly symmetrical square wave at 2 MHz can be used.

The Interrupt request ($\overline{\text{INT}}$) is anologous to the INT line of 8085 except that the request is initiated by an active LOW (logic zero) signal.

The Non-Maskable Interrupt input (NMI) is similar to INT except that this input cannot be disabled by software instructions.

The WAIT request is anologous to the READY line of 8085.

The $\overline{\text{RESET}}$ input is anologous to the RESET input of 8085, again this input is active LOW.

The $\overline{\text{BUSRQ}}$ (bus request) pin is used by an external device to gain access to the system address, data and control buses. If $\overline{\text{BUSRQ}}$ is placed at a logic 0 level, the processor open circuits the address, data and control bus pins. It does this so that an external device can directly address the memory and I/O. The BUSAK signal is an indicator to the external device that micro processor has indeed open circuited its buses.

The Z-80 has 8 CONTROL OUTPUT lines:-

- $\overline{\text{HALT}}$ (pin 18) pin becomes a logic 0 whenever the Halt instruction is executed. The pin is at 0 level until the processor is either interrupted or reset.
- $\overline{\text{MREQ}}$ (pin 19) Active low signal indicates that the address bus contains a valid memory address for a memory read or write operation.
- $\overline{\text{IORQ}}$ (pin 20) Active low signal indicates that the address bus contain a valid I/O port number for an IN or an OUT instruction.
- $\overline{\text{BUSAK}}$ signal (pin 23) is anologous to the HLDA signal of 8085.

- $\overline{\text{RD}}$ (pin 21) active LOW, indicates that CPU wants to READ from memory or I/O device
- $\overline{\text{WR}}$ (pin 22) goes LOW to signal a memory or I/O WRITE operation.
- MI (pin 27) is used to indicate the current machine cycle in the opcode fetch cycle of an instruction execution.
- $\overline{\text{RFSH}}$ (refresh) output (pin 28) has no counterpart in the 8085. This output is used as a control signal to simplify the refresh circuitry required with the dynamic memory.

Table 13.1 Pin Details of Z-80

Address	Data	Control Bus	
		INPUTS	OUTPUTS
16 lines	8 Bit Bidirectional	CLOCK	HALT
		INT	MREQ
		NMI	IORQ
		WAIT	RD
		BUSRQ	WR
		RESET	BUSAK
			MI
			RFSH

The internal architecture of the Z-80 is similar to that of 8085 with the most striking difference being that it has twice as many internal registers. The instruction set of the Z-80 consists of 158 instructions which included the 78 instructions of 8085. Operating with a 4 MHz clock the Z-80 has a minimum instruction execution of 1 microsecond.

The Z-80 contains a register array, a timing and control section, an arithmetic and logic unit (ALU), an instruction register and decoder, and bus connections to the outside world. Notice that there are 16 address bus connections A0-A15 and 8 bit data bus connections D0-D7. The 16 bit address bus allows the Z-80 to address 64K different memory locations and the 8 bit data bus allows the processor to access a byte of data at a time. The address bus is used to address either memory location or I/O channel. The data bus is used to transfer data between the processor and the memory location or I/O channel.

The internal Block Diagram of microprocessor Z-80 is given in Fig.13.2.

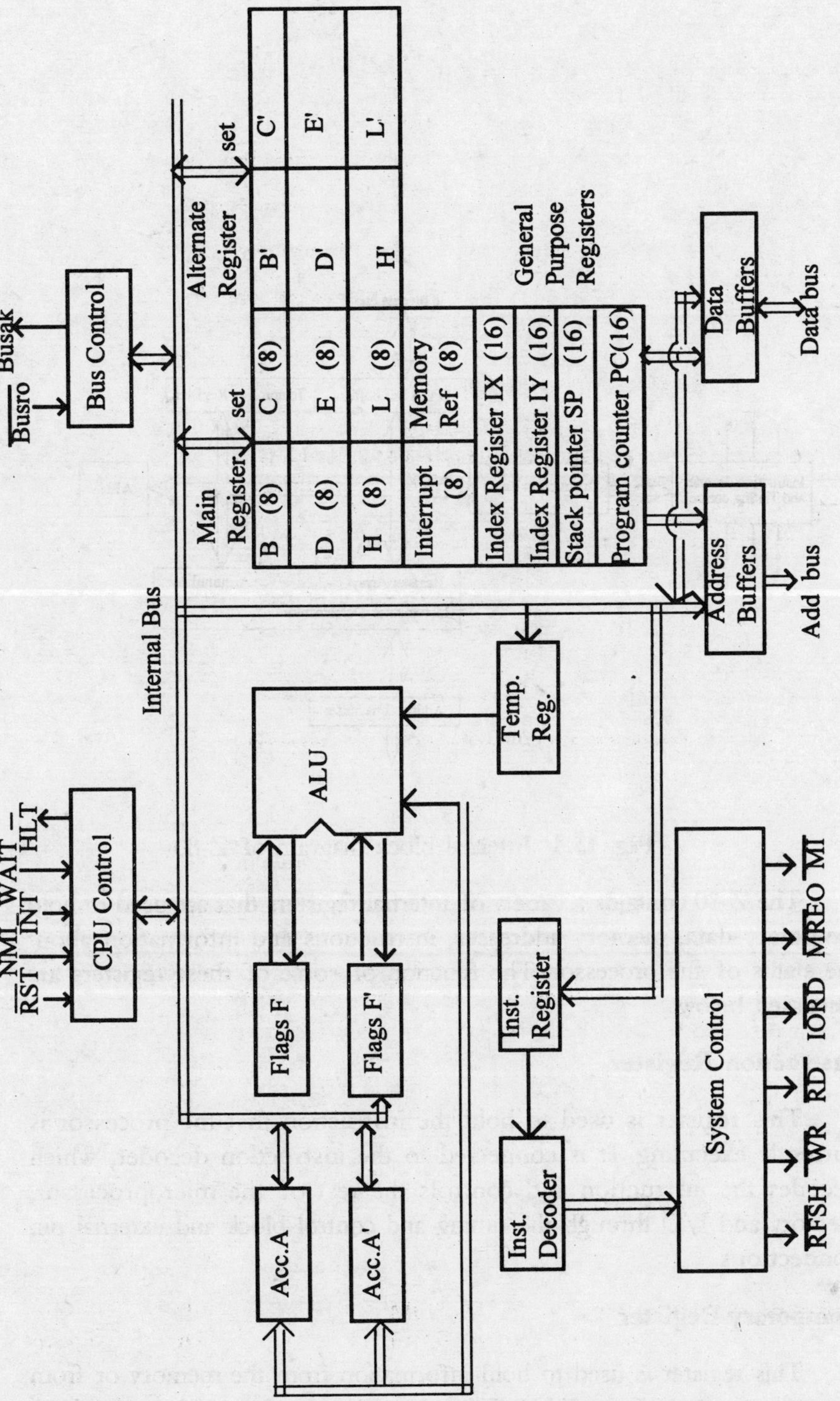

Fig. 13.2 Architecture of Microprocessor Z-80

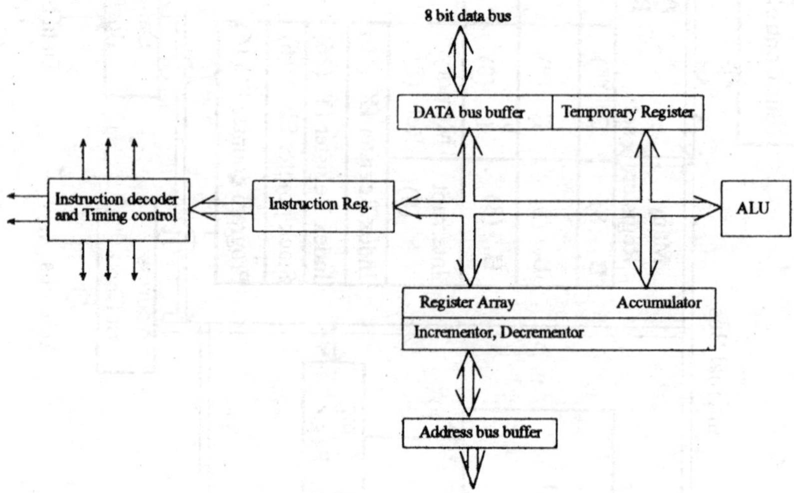

Fig. 13.3 Internal block diagram of Z-80

The Z-80 contains a variety of internal registers that are used to hold temporary data, memory addresses, instructions and information about the status of the processor. The function of some of these registers are discussed below :

Instruction Register

This register is used to hold the instruction that the processor is currently executing. It is connected to the instruction decoder, which decodes the instruction and controls the rest of the microprocessor, memory and I/O through the timing and control block and external pin connections.

Temporary Register

This register is used to hold information from the memory or from the register array of the ALU. The other input to the ALU comes from the accumulator.

The result is fed to the internal 8 bit data bus for distribution to the accumulator, register array or to the memory.

Incrementer / Decrementer address latch

This block is used to hold the address of data to be accessed in the memory or I/O. It is also used to add one or subtract one from any of the 16 bit registers in the register array.

Other Sections

The interrupt control section is used to determine the priority of the interrupt control inputs and also to supply, in some cases, an interrupt instruction to the instruction register.

The timing and control section provides the basic control bus signals $\overline{\text{RD}}$, $\overline{\text{WR}}$, $\overline{\text{MREQ}}$ and $\overline{\text{IORQ}}$. In addition to these basic system control signals, other control signals are also supplied to control the external hardware and also to control some internal functions.

General Purpose Registers

This microprocessor contains a double set of general purpose registers, which are main registers and alternative registers. These registers are selected as a group and either as the main set or as the alternative set.

The six general purpose registers are B, C, D, E, H and L. These registers are called general purpose registers because they can be used in any manner by the user. These registers can be used to hold numeric, BCD or ASCII data that may be required. They are flexible enough so that they can be used as six 8 bit registers or as three 16 bit registers.

The valid register pairs are BC, DE and HL. Register pairs can be used to hold 16 bit of data or 16 bit information. These register pairs can also be used to address memory locations.

SPECIAL PURPOSE REGISTERS

Program Counter (PC)

This counter holds the 16 bit address of the current instruction, which is being fetched from memory. After instruction fetch the PC is automatically incremented. When a program jump occurs the new value is automatically placed in PC overriding the incrementer.

B	C	B'	C'
D	E	D'	E'
H	L	H'	L'
A	F	A'	F'
IX			
IY			
SP			
PC			
I		R	

Fig. 13.4 Z-80 Register Details

Stack Pointer(SP)

It is a 16 bit register which holds the current top of stack address, located in the external RAM. The stack is organised as a last in first out file. The data can be PUSHed into the stack from CPU registers and out into the CPU from the stack. This stack allows the implementation of unlimited subroutine nesting.

Index Registers (Ix, Iy)

These two index registers hold a 16 bit base address that is used in indexed addressing modes. These registers can be used to point to a region in memory from which data is to be retrived or stored. An additional byte is included in indexed instructions to specify a displacement from this base. This displacement is a two's complement signed number.

Interrupt Page Address Register

The Z-80 CPU can be operated in a mode where an indirect call to any memory location can be achieved in response to an interrupt. This I register is used to store the higher order 8 bits of the address, and the lower order 8 bits of the address is provided by the interruption device.

Memory Refresh Register (R)

This register acts as a memory refresh counter to enable dynamic memories to be used. The data in the refresh counter is sent out on the lower portion of the address bus along with a refresh control signal while the CPU is decoding and executing the fetched instruction. This does not slow down the CPU operation.

Accumulator and Flag Registers

The CPU contains two sets of accumulator and flag registers. Any one set can be selected by the instruction EXAF. The flag register contains 6 bits that are used as flags.

In addition to the 5 flags in the 8085, it has got negative flag bit (N) which indicates whether the arithmetic operation is a subtraction or an addition. It is used with H flag bit for BCD correction. The AC flag bit is called as H flag.

D7	D6	D5	D4	D3	D2	D1	D0
S	Z	x	H	x	P/V	N	C

The 8 bit arithmetic and logical instruction of the CPU are executed in the ALU. Internally the ALU communicates with the registers and the external data bus using the internal bus. The type of functions performed by the ALU are as listed in Table 13.2.

Table: 13.2 Functions performed by the ALU

Addition Increment Compare Shift right Test bit	Subtraction Decrement Shift left Set bit	Logical AND Logical OR Logical EX-OR Reset bit

The Z-80 CPU can execute 158 different instruction types including all the 78 of the 8085 CPU. The total instructions can be classified into the following groups:

- Load and Exchange
- Block transfer and search
- Arithmetical and Logical
- Rotate and shift
- Bit manipulation
- Jump, call, return
- Input, Output
- Basic CPU control

Addressing Modes

The Z80 microprocessor uses six different addressing modes for most instructions: direct, register, register indirect, indexed, relative and immediate.

Instruction word format

There are basically four different instruction word formats used by this microprocessor. They are One byte instructions, two byte instructions, three byte instructions and four byte instructions. The one byte instructions represent a majority of the instructions for the Z-80 microprocessor. In all four formats the first byte is always the OPCODE. The opcode tells the microprocessor which operation to perform and also whether a second, third and fourth bytes are required.

The one byte instructions, which are the most numerous, are used for most of the instructions in a program. They are used for moving numbers between registers or between registers and memory, and also to do most of the arithmetic and logic operations.

In the two byte instruction the first byte is the opcode and the second byte contains 8 bit data, a 8 bit low order displacement address, an extension to the opcode or an I/O port number.

The three byte instruction contain an opcode for the first byte and then 16 bit data or a memory location address.

The last form of instruction for the Z-80 is the four byte instruction. The first byte of a four byte instruction contains the opcode, and the second byte contains the opcode extension. The remaining bytes are used for representing displacements address or 16 bit data.

Some additional features of Z-80 over 8085

1. The indexed addressing mode is available only in Z-80. This is due to the different internal architecture. When these registers IX,IY are properly loaded, they can be used to access the memory locations.

   Example: LD A,(IX)

   LD (IY+5),B

These two instructions will use the value of IX or IY and add a constant given in the instruction to get the new value. This new value will be used as the memory location address for read or write data.

2. Normally the jump instruction will contain the address. The relative addressing feature uses only the 8 bit signed number as the displacement to the next instruction. The relative jump instruction (JR dd) is a 2 byte instruction. The second byte of this instruction contains the displacement to the next instruction. It allows the program to continue upto +127 to -128 bytes from the address of the next instruction.

3. A group of registers B', C', D', E', H' and L' are called alternative registers. This alternative register set is identical to the regular register set. In order to access data in this register set, user must first exchange their contents with the regular register set.

   Example: EX AF, AF'

   This instruction will exchange the data available in A register and flag with the alternative registers A' and F'.

   Example: EXX

   This instruction will exchange the content of BCDEHL registers with alternative registers.

4. The term extended opcode refer to the Z-80 code form of the mnemonics. Let us examine the object code for the instruction

   Example: LD IX, 8A41 is DD, 21, 41, 8A

   This takes 4 bytes, all other immediate instructions required only 3 bytes. In this instruction, the first byte DD informs the processor that this is an extended op-code instruction. In this extended opcode form, the instructions may even have the same first byte.

5. The Z-80 has unique instructions designed for doing operations on blocks of data in memory. An instruction will allow the user to specify the address bound for the search, complete the search and stop when there is a match or logically inform the user there was no match.

   LDIR load increment and repeat

   LDDR load decrement and repeat

Example:

LD HL,5000	source address
LD DE,4000	destination address
LD BC,0512	byte counter
LDIR	move the entire block

The BC register pair is used to initialise the counter, which will have the number of bytes to be transferred or moved or copied. The source starting address is loaded in HL register pair and the destination starting address is loaded with DE register pair. The LDIR instruction takes care of copying block of data from the source area to destination area. The HL register pair and DE register pair are incremented and BC register pair is decremented for every data transfer till BC register pair becomes zero.

6. There are six rotate instructions that allow the contents of any register or memory location to be rotated right or left. Instructions are available for BCD operations in this group.
7. The Z-80 processor contains a complete set of BIT SET, RESET and TEST instruction that allow any bit of the memory or register to be reset to a logic 0, set to a logic 1 or tested for a 1 or 0. It is true that reset and set are also possible by the logical instructions , but this logical instructions allow multiple bits to be affected.
8. The Z-80 instruction set contains special instructions that allow a 16 bit addition and subtraction. Notice that both add, add with carry and subtract & subtract with borrow instructions are available. This 16 bit addition instruction affect only the carry flag.
9. In Z-80, it is possible to transfer any register content to the specified port address. Similarly from the specified port, data can be read into any register.

   Example: OUT 23,B
   OUT 41,D
   IN C,32

   IN register, port number
   OUT port number, register
10. The N bit flag is normally used by the Z-80 processor during BCD (binary coded decimal, 4 bit) operations. The DAA instruction will adjust the result of a decimal operation. The adjustment is different for a subtract operation as compared to an add operation. This means the DAA instruction will operate differently depending on the state of the N bit. The N bit is set to a logical 1 after subtraction and cleared to a logical 0 after an addition operation.

Z-80 Memory Map

The memory map of this microprocessor are numbered in hexadecimal from 0000 to FFFF. Each memory location holds one byte of information, which can be an instruction or any form of data or part of the address.

The memory in the Z-80 system is most often segmented into two areas. One area of the memory is devoted to the system program and is most often populated with EPROMs. The other area is used to store user programs and data in the microprocessor based systems, which is usually populated with RAMs.

The reset location is an important location in the Z-80 memory map. The reset location 0000 is where the processor will begin to execute a monitor program after the reset button is pressed or the system is activated. If the user wants to develop software for the Z-80 system, the user must start the system software at memory location 0000. This means that user programs must begin elsewhere in the RAM memory location of system. The exact memory location of the RAM varies from the system to system.

Z-80 I/O Map

The Z80 can directly address 256 different input devices and 256 different output devices. It uses 8 bit address.

A programme written on 8085 instructions can run on Z-80 without any modifications.

13.2 THE 6502

The 65xx series of microprocessor are manufactured by Raytheon Company.

Features

- Single +5 volt supply
- N channel, Silicon gate
- Eight bit parallel processing
- 56 Instructions
- Decimal and Binary arithmetic
- True indexing capability
- Programmable stack pointer
- Variable length stack
- Interrupt capability
- Use with memory of any speed.

- Addressing memory range upto 64K bytes
- Direct Memory Access capability
- Bus compatible with 6800 microprocessor
- 1 MHz, 2 MHz and 3 MHz versions
- Choice of external or onchip clock
- Commercial and Industrial temperature versions
- Pipeline architecture

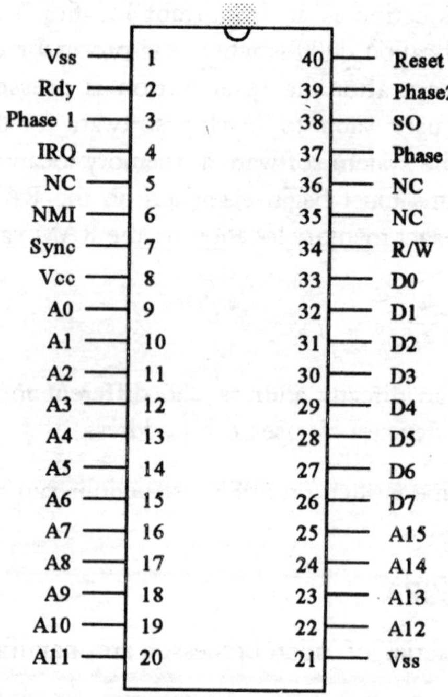

Fig: 13.4 Pin details of Microprocessor 6502

The pins marked A0-A15 (pins 9 to 20 and pins 22 to 25) are the sixteen bit address bus and D0-D7 (pins 26 to 33) are the eight bit data bus.

IRQ (pin 4) is the interrupt request input. A LOW level at this pin generates an interrupt. The interrupt service routine is executed only if the interrupt mask bit is not set. The processor automatically stores the contents of the program counter, status register on the stack memory and it sets the interrupt mask bit, so that further interrupts are ignored until the current one has been executed. The program counter is loaded with the numbers stored at address FFFEH (low byte) and FFFFH (high byte). So these two address memory locations must contain the start address of interrupt routine. After execution of the interrupt program, the processor returns to the main program.

The second interrupt is the non maskable interrupt $\overline{\text{NMI}}$ input on pin 6. This interrupt has got higher priority than the $\overline{\text{IRQ}}$ input. The routine meant for this interrupt is executed regardless of the state of the interrupt masking bit. This interrupt is also handled in much the same way as for the $\overline{\text{IRQ}}$ input, but the program counter is loaded with the address stored at FFFAH (low byte) and FFFBH (high byte).

The $\overline{\text{RESET}}$ input (pin 40) is LOW when power is switched on and this starts the microprocessor on its initialisation sequence. This input is used to take back the computer to this sequence at any time, after the computer has crashed or when it hangs. During initialisation process the program counter is loaded with the number from address FFFCH (low byte) and FFFDH (high byte). Normally these low byte and high byte address represents starting address of the operating system (monitor program).

The R/$\overline{\text{W}}$ (read / write) (pin 34) is an output pin and is used to control memory and input & output devices. This pin goes HIGH when the processor wants to read from the data bus and it switches the memory and input/output devices into the output mode, so that the particular device can be read by the processor. The read/write line goes LOW when the processor wants to place data onto the data bus and this pin sets the memory or input/output devices in the state where they are ready to receive data from the databus. The input and output devices are handled in memory mapped technique.

The pins phase 0 (pin 37), phase 1 (pin 3) and phase 2 (pin 39) are the clock terminals of the devices. This processor has a built in clock circuit which has its frequency set by an external crystal. The standard 6502 processor will operate with clock frequencies of upto 1MHz, so that it carries out instruction at the highest rate. The number of cycles taken to execute an instruction varies from one instruction to another, but for the 6502 it is about six clock cycles. 6502C is the high speed version of this group of microprocessors.

The Ready (RDY) input signal allows the user to halt or single cycle the microprocessor on all cycles except write cycles. A negative transition to the low state during or coincident with phase one will halt the microprocessor with the output address lines reflecting the current address being fetched. If ready is low during a write cycle, it is ignored until the following read operation. This feature allows interfacing the CPU with the low speed PROMs as well as for Direct Memory Access (DMA).

This SYNC output line is provided to identify those cycles in which the microprocessor is doing an OP CODE fetch. The SYNC line goes high during phase 1 of an OP CODE fetch and stays high for the remainder of that cycle. If the RDY line is pulled low during the phase 1 clock pulse in which SYNC went high, the processor will stop in its current state and will remain in the state until the RDY line goes high. In this manner, the SYNC signal can be used to control RDY to cause single instruction execution.

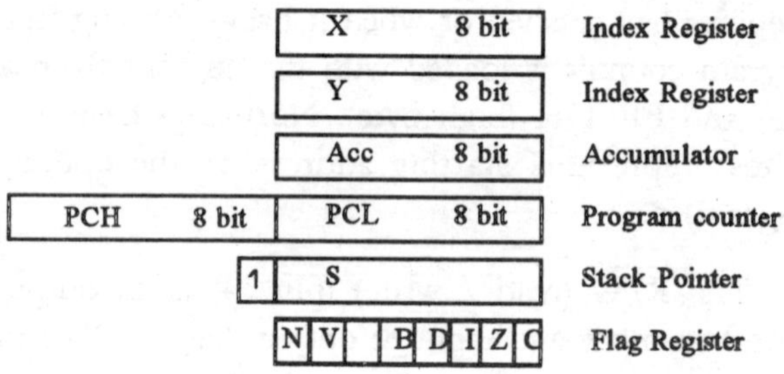

The internal register configuration of the 6502 is shown in Fig.13.5(a).

It consists of 6 registers, which are

- X Index register (8 bit)
- Y Index register (8 bit)
- Accumulator (8 bit)
- Stack pointer (9 bit)
- Program counter (16 bit)
- Status register (7 bit)

The accumulator forms the core of the processor, and any data processed by the microprocessor has to be handled by this register and the complex circuit associated with it. This circuit is called the Arithmetic Logic Unit (ALU).

The X and Y registers are Index registers. These registers act as pointers to guide the microprocessor where to find data or instruction in the memory. The 6502 can handle a maximum of 64K (65536) locations.

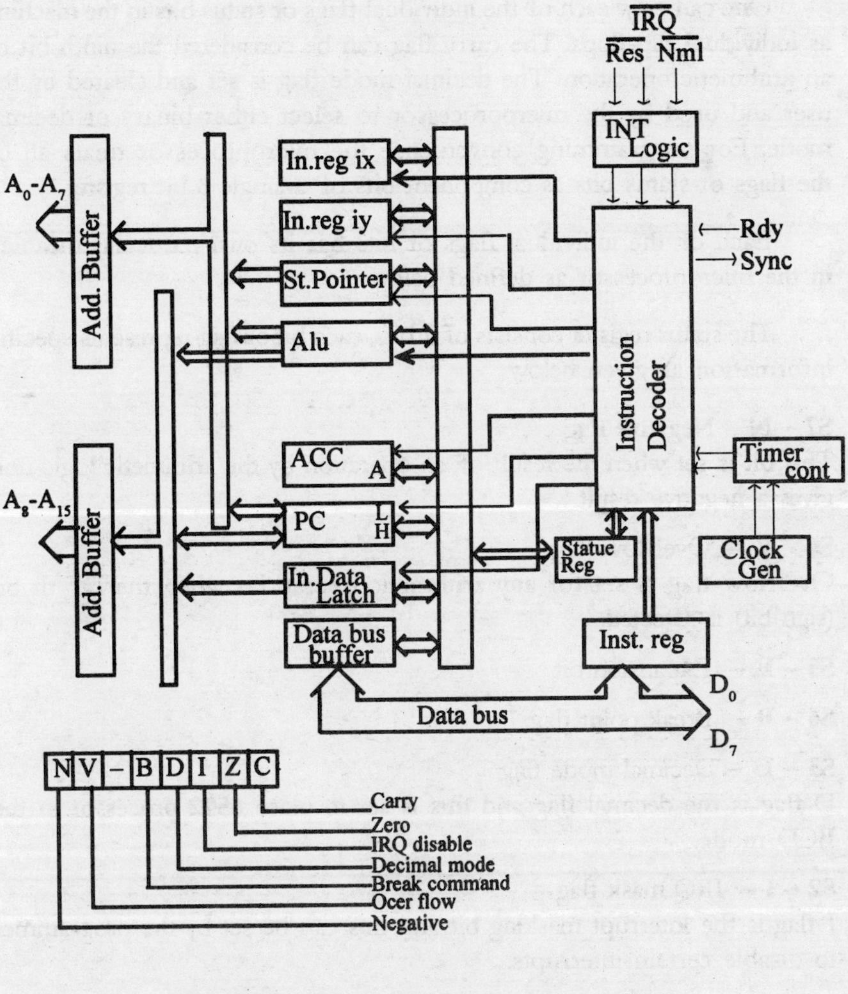

Fig. 13.5 (b) Internal Architecture of 6502

The program counter holds the address of the next instruction to be executed by the processor. This register is automatically incremented, suitably based on the instruction length (one byte, two byte or three byte), after execution of the current instruction.

The stack pointer is a 9 bit register rather than the more usual 8 bit type. However, the most significant bit is always set at 1. The stack area is from 511 th location of the RAM to 256th location. The stack grows from 511th location towards 256th location. LIFO system is used in the stack.

Concepts of Flags and Status Register

One can view each of the individual flags or status bits in the machine as individual flip-flops. The carry flag can be considered the ninth bit of an arithmetic operation. The decimal mode flag is set and cleared by the user and used by the microprocessor to select either binary or decimal mode. For programming convenience the microprocessor treats all of the flags or status bits as component bits of a single 8 bit register.

Each of the individual flags or bits has its own particular meaning in the microprocessor as defined below

The status register consists of 7 bits, each bit or flag represents specific information as given below.

S7 – N – Negative flag
This bit is set when the result of an operation by the arithmetic logic unit gives a negative result.

S6 – V – Overflow flag
Overflow flag is set for any arithmetic operations when the D7 th bit (sign bit) is affected.

S5 – E – Expansion bit

S4 – B – Break point flag

S3 – D – Decimal mode flag
D flag is the decimal flag and this is set to place 6502 processor in the BCD mode.

S2 – I – IRQ mask flag
I flag is the interrupt masking bit and this can be set by the programmer to disable certain interrupts.

S1 - Z - Zero flag

S0 - C - Carry flag

The 6502 has nine possible addressing modes.

Some instructions can use more than one addressing mode. Though the same mnemonic is used for all addressing modes, the opcode is different. Special symbols or syntax are used to indicate some modes.

The microprocessor 6502 uses the following different types of addressing modes

- Implied addressing

- Immediate addressing
- Absolute addressing
- Zero page
- Relative addressing
- Indirect addresssing (Indexed addressing)
- Absolute indexed addressing
- Indirect indexed addressing
- Indexed indirect addressing

Implied Addressing

In the implied addressing mode the address containing the operand is implicitly stated in the operation code of the instruction. All these instructions are a single byte long.

For example - INX, INY, NOP, DEX, CLC, SED

Immediate Addressing

In immediate addressing mode the operand is contained in the second byte of the instruction, with no further memory addressing required. All such instructions are two bytes long. The # symbol is used to indicate immediate mode.

For example - LDA #14, ADC #23, AND #32, CMP #41

Absolute Addressing

In this addressing mode, the second byte of the instruction specifies the eight low order bits of the effective address while the third byte specifies the eight high order bits. This addressing mode allows access to the entire 65K bytes of addressable memory. These instructions are three bytes long.

For example - CPX #0255, LDX #3241

Zero Page Addressing

The zero page instructions allow for shorter code and execution times by only fetching the second byte of the instruction and assuming a zero high address byte. Careful use of the zero page can result in significant increase in code efficiency.

For example - BIT, CMP, STA, ROR

Relative Addressing

Relative addressing is used only with branch instructions and establishes a destination for the conditional branch. The second byte of the instruction becomes the operand which is an OFFSET added to the contents of the lower eight bits of the program counter when the counter is set at the next instruction. The range of the offset is -128 to +127 bytes from the next instruction. All instructions using this mode are two bytes long.

Indirect Addressing

In indirect addressing, two bytes following the opcode contain a memory address. The contents of this address, and the byte that follows it give a further address, which is where the data is to be found.

Absolute Indexed Addressing

In this mode, the content of either the X or the Y index register is added to the address contained in the instruction. Using the X register, it is permissible to have either a 16 bit or an 8 bit address(zero page). The Y register, can only be used with 16 bit addresses.

Indirect Indexed Addressing

In this address mode, the instruction contains an address of a memory location which, as it can only be one byte long, must be in zero page.

The contents of this zero page location, plus the one following it, give an address anywhere in memory, to which the contents of the Y register are added to give the final address.

This address mode is used to access elements in a table.

Indexed Indirect Addressing

In indexed indirect adressing, the second byte of the instruction is added to the contents of the X index register,(Y register can not be used) discarding the carry. The contents of this byte plus one following it give the address where the final data are to be found.

Memory Map of 6502

As shown in the Fig.13.6, Zero page is usually reserved for important variables and pointers and this is due to the special form of addressing associated with zero page. There has to be RAM at pages 0 and 1. The stack uses page 1.

As we have seen, the six addresses at the top of memory point to the start addresses of the operating system and interrupt routines, the operating

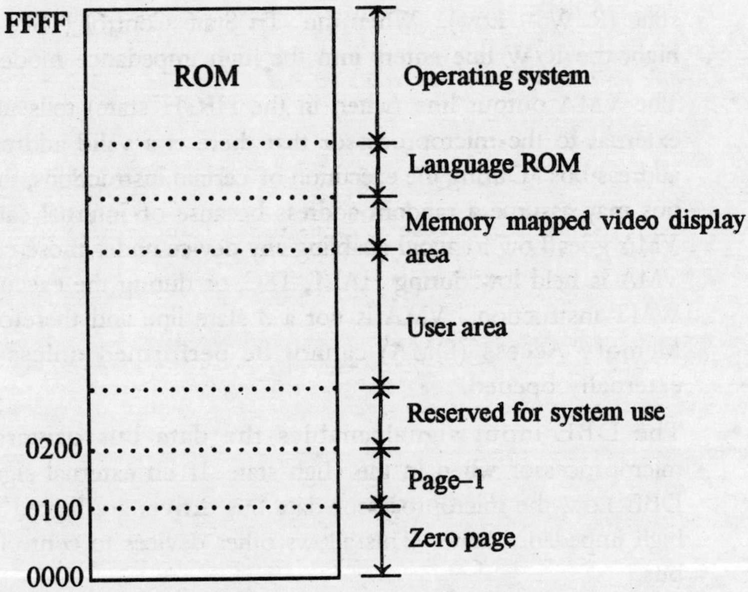

Fig. 13. 6 Memory map of the processor 6502

system ROM therefore occupies the top section of the address range. The remaining place can be used by the RAM. The space utilised for Input and Output ports, one page may be used.

13.3 THE 6800

This Motorola microprocessor is designed to suit the existing TTL IC's. It uses N-channel MOS technology. It was developed at the same time as the Intel 8080. This microprocessor has a different architecture than its competitors. It requires only +5V for its operation. Its comes in 40 pin DIP package. This processor contains 16 bit address and 8 bit data lines and other control lines. The 6800B can be driven by a clock upto 1MHz and 68B00 works upto 2MHz. The temperature range chosen for this processor is 0 to 70 degree C, which is adequate for most of the industrial and commercial applications. The 6800C has a wider range of –40 to +85 degree C. Military version of this processor can be operated from –55 degree C.

Pin details:

- This output Control line R/W is used to signal all external devices that the microprocessor is in a Read state (R/W = High), or a Write state (R/W = Low). When the Tri State Control (TSC) line goes high, the R/W line enters into the high impedance mode.

- The VMA output line (when in the HIGH state) tells all devices external to the microprocessor that there is a valid address on the address bus. During the execution of certain instructions, the address bus may assume a random address because of internal calculations. VMA goes Low to avoid enabling any device under those conditions. VMA is held low during HALT, TSC, or during the execution of a WAIT instruction. VMA is not a 3 state line and therefore Direct Memory Access (DMA) cannot be performed unless VMA is externally opened.
- The DBE input signal enables the data bus drivers of the microprocessor when in the High state. If an external signal holds DBE Low, the microprocessor data bus drivers are forced into their high impedance state. This allows other devices to control the I/O bus.
- The 6800 uses four different types of interrupts. Reset (RST), Non Maskable (NMI), Software (SWI), and Hardware Interrupt Request (IRQ). The following table gives the interrupts and the locations from which the address for the routines are taken.

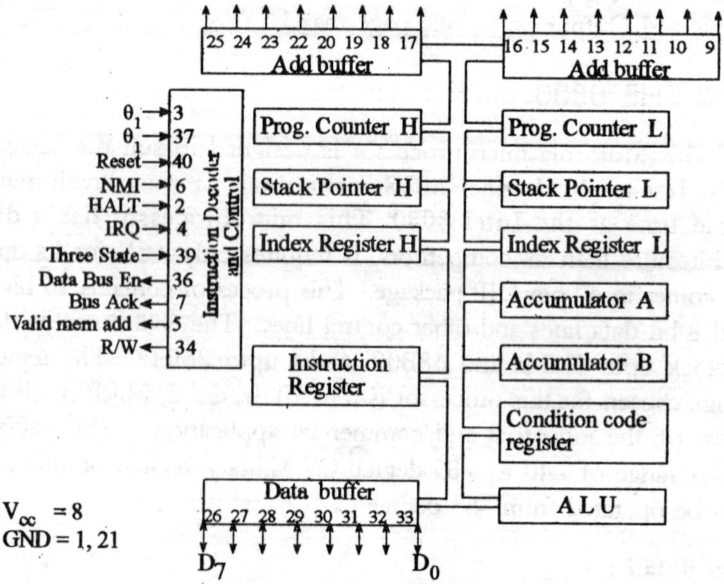

Fig: 13.7 PIN connections of M6800

1. Reset (RST)	FFFE - FFFF
2. Non Maskable Interrupt (NMI)	FFFC - FFFD
3. Software Interrupt (SWI)	FFFA - FFFB
4. Interrupt Request (IRQ)	FFF8 - FFF9

- When the system is reset, it places the content of the location FFFFH and FFFEH as the 16 bit address in the Program Counter of the microprocessor and starts executing the program from that address.
- Phase One and Phase Two of the Clock lines are non overlapping clock lines.
- The bus available (BA) signal is a normally Low signal generated by the microprocessor. High level indicates that the microprocessor has stopped and that the address bus is available. This occurs if the processor is in the Halt mode or in a Wait state when the WAI instruction is executed.
- Tri State Control (TSC) is an externally generated signal that effectively causes the microprocessor to disconnect itself from the address and control buses.

Features of 6800

___ 8 Bit parallel processing
___ Bidirectional data bus
___ 16 bit address bus (6.5 K bytes of addressing capability)
___ 72 instructions with variable length
___ Minimization of required support package
___ Simplicity of interface
___ Simplicity of power requirements (only +5 V)
___ System throughput
___ Seven addressing modes:

Direct	Relative	Immediate	
Indexed	Extended	Implied	Accumulator

___ Variable length stack
___ Vectored restart
___ Separate Non-Maskable Interrupt (internal registers saved in stack)
___ Six internal registers

Two accumulators
Index registers
Program counter
Stack pointer and
Condition Code Register

___ Direct Memory Addressing (DMA) and Multiple processor capability
___ Clock rate as high as 1 MH Z
___ Simple bus interfaces without TTL.
___ Halt and single instruction execution capability.

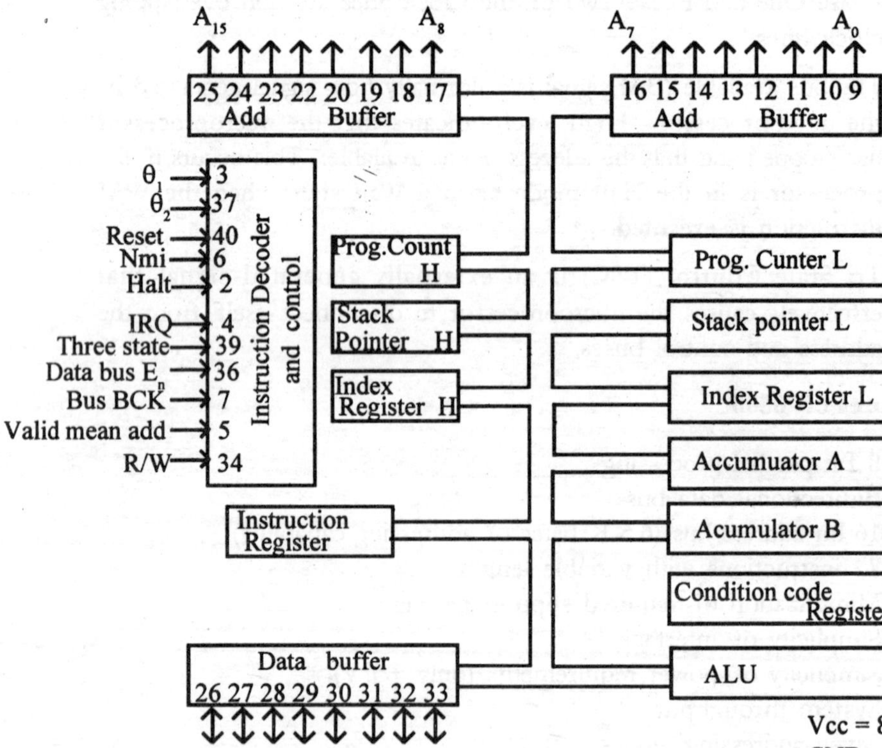

Vcc = 8
GND = 1, 21

CCR :

Carry
Over flow
Zero
Negative
Interrupt
Most carry

Fig: 13.8 6800 Internal Architecture

In the 6800 processor system, the program instructions would typically be stored in the 6830 ROM (1024 bytes of 8 bit each) or 68708 EPROM, all variable data would be written or read from the 6810 RAM (128 bytes of 8 bits each). The parallel input/output operation is carried out by using 6820 periphral interface adapter, this is equivalent/similar to Intels 8255 IC. MC6850 Asynchonous communication interface adopter is used for serial data input/output, this is similar/equivalent to Intels 8251. MC 6871A or MC6875 is used with 6800 for clock purpose. There are crystal controlled oscillator that provide the necessary two-phase non-overlapping timing pulses and are equipped with output circuits suitable for every MOS circuits. IC 6828 is used to control the Priority of interrrupting devices in the system.

The ALU included in the 6800 is an 8 bit, parallel processing, 2s complement device. It contain the condition code or processor status register. The internal bus is 8 bit wide, the index and stack pointer registers are implemented with low and high byte. The two 8 bit accumulators speed up program execution by allowing two operands to remain in the microprocessor, because they do not require additional cycles to fetch the operand.

The ALU performs the arithmetic operations of addition, subtraction, complementation, shifting and negation. The other functions like multiplication and division can be performed by software that use functions like repeated addition or shift with additions. This ALU also performs the Boolean functions like AND, OR and EX-OR.

The registers program counter (PC), index register (IX), stack pointer (SP) are all 8 bits wide. All these registers are interconnected by an 8 bit internal bus with other registers like accumulator A, accumulator B, arithmetic logic unit (ALU), data buffer (DB) and address buffers.

The 6800 uses 6 condition flags, labeled H, I, N, Z, V and C. These codes are available in Condition Code Register (CCR) or flag register as shown below:

The zero flag bit in CCR is SET (1) only when all the 8 bits of the result is zero, otherwise zero flag bit is zero. Compare instruction may be used to set or reset the zero flag.

The carry bit (CY) in the CCR is SET, when any one of the following conditions is satisfied

When the result of the addition produces a carry out (9 bit result)

During subtraction, when X is subtracted from Y, the carry bit is set if X is more than Y.

During shift and rotate operation, based on the data bits the carry bit may be 1 or 0.

When an set carry (SEC) instruction is used.

The negative (N) bit is SET whenever the results of an operation are negative. This N bit is the reflection of MSB of the result, in the 2s complement arithmatic.

The overflow (V) bit is SET when an arithmetic operation results in a 2s complement overflow or underflow. The limitation of a single 8 bit byte is restricted to numbers between +127 and -128.

The use of H bit of the CCR and the specific instruction DAA helps the user to do decimal arithmetic operation.

The interrupt (I) bit is set in one of the three ways

by the instruction (SEI set interrupt mask)

by the hardware interrupt system

by the restart procedure.

The program counter (PC) keeps track of the location in memory space the next instruction byte is to be fetched. The bytes are then loaded into the instruction register and then instructions are executed.

The 6800 processor uses four types of interrupts

- Reset (RST)
- Non Maskable interrupt (NMI)
- Software interrupt (SWI)
- Hardware interrupt (IRQ)

These four interrupts have the specific locations in EPROM, which will hold the starting address of the service routines meant for that interrupt. These service routine addresses are commonly called vector addresses.

The stack pointer is a 16 bit register and contains the address of the next location available for the stack operation.

This stack pointer decrements automatically when data or address are stored. Similarly when data or address are read from stack area, the SP is automatically incremented. So the stack pointer is initially set to the highest address in the stack memory area.

Apart from the instruction PUSH and POP available in 8085, this 6800 processor has other instructions related to stack, which are DES, INS, LDS, STS, TXS and TSX.

ADDRESSING MODES

Accumulator Addressing (ACCX)

In this either Accumulator A or Accumulator B is specified. These are ONE BYTE instruction.

Example: ASL A
DEC B

Immediate Addressing

Here the operand is contained in the second byte of the instruction set except for LDS and LDX, which have the operand in the second and third bytes of the instruction. The microprocessor unit addresses this instruction. When it fetches the immediate instruction for execution. These are TWO or THREE byte instructions.

Example: LDA A,#23
LDA B,#41

Direct Addressing

Here the address of the operand is contained in the second byte of the insturction. Direct addressing allows the user to directly address the lowest 256 bytes in the machine achieved by storing data in these locations. In most configurations it should be a RAM. These are TWO BYTE instruction.

Example: LDA A,F3
LDA B,10

Extended Addressing

Here the address contained in the second byte of instruction is used as the higher 8 bits of the address for the operand. The third byte of the instruction serves as the lower 8 bits of the address for the operand. This is an absolute address in memory. These bare THREE byte instructions.

Example: LDA A,A0F3
LDX Addr.

Indexed Addressing

Here the address contained in the second byte of the instruction is added to the index register's lower 8 bits in the microprocessor unit. The carry is then added to the higher order of 8 bits of the index register. This result is then used to address memory. The modified address is held in a temporary register so there is no change to the index register. These are TWO BYTE instructions.

Example: LDAA 3,X
CMPA 2,X

Implied Addressing

The instruction gives the address (ie. SP, index Register etc.). These are SINGLE BYTE instructions.

Example: ABA
DEX

Relative Addressing

Here the second byte of the instruction is treated as signed 8 bit number and is added to the PC. This allows the user to address data within a range of -128 to +127 bytes of the present instruction. They are 2 byte instructions.

Example: BPL * +5
BEQ FOUND

CHAPTER 14

16 BIT MICROPROCESSORS

14.1 INTEL 8086

The 8086 CPU comes in a 40 pin package and requires a single +5 Volt DC power supply. It is capable of operating at 5MHz to 10MHz of clock speed. The 8086 CPU features 16 bit wide data path and 20 bit wide address path. The enhanced clock speed, 16 bit data and 20 bit address paths makes this microprocessor suitable for applications requiring high system throughput. Performance is further enhanced by a 6 byte look ahead look ahead instruction queue. Fig 14.1 shows the pin details of microprocessors 8086. While the 8086 is internally decoding the current instruction, the processors Bus Interface Unit (BIU) fetches the contents of the next 6 address locations and loads them into the queue. Therefore when the present instruction execution is completed.

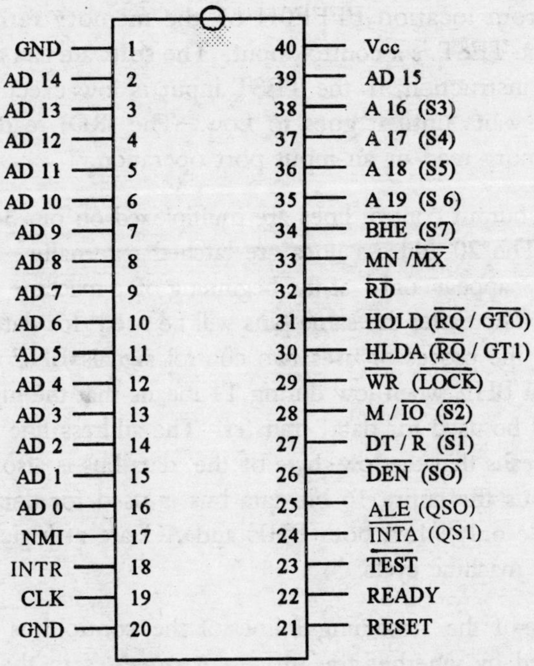

Fig. 14.1 Pin details of Microprocessor 8086

the next instruction is immediately available to the processor. The lower 16 bits of the address bits are multiplexed with the 16 bits of the data bits. This means they use the same pins. The sharing of the pins reduces the number of pins needed in the I.C, and still the data transfer rate is not slowed down because of the special timing on the bus. The 20 bit address bus permits direct access of 1 megabyte of memory.

This expanded memory capability makes multiprogramming feasible and several multiprogramming features have been added in the 8086's design. It also has a number of features which enhances multiprocessing capability, so that 8086 can be used with other processing elements; for example 8087, the numeric data processor. The device has 16 control levels for providing handshaking signals during bus transfers.

14.2 CONTROL LINES

The processor has 16 control lines for providing handshaking signals during bus transfers and also for enabling certain external control. It has a Non-Markable Interrupt (NMI) request input line and also a Maskable Interrupt request line (INTR). The RESET input is different from 8085, because after a High on the RESET pin the 8086 processor begins program execution from location FFFF0H of the memory rather than from 00000H. The TEST is a control input. The software can check its status by the Test instruction, if the TEST input is low execution continues otherwise it waits until it goes to Low. The (RD) read pin indicates either a memory read or an input port operation.

Several output control lines are multiplexed on pin 34 to 38 of the processor. The 20 address lines are latched externally therefore the address bits appear only at the beginning of a machine cycle, that is at the T1 state. Thereafter the same pins will be used for data transfer. For this purpose the processor uses two control signals BHE and AO. The control signal BHE when low during T1 means that the high byte of the data bus will be used for data transfer. The address line AO being low during T1 means that the low byte of the data bus is also used for Data transfer. Thus the entire 16 bit data bus is used for data transfer in a machine cycle only when both BHE and AO are at logic O during T1 state of that machine cycle.

The role of the remaining 8 lines of the control bus (pins 24 to 31) is determined by whether the processor operates in the minimum or maximum mode. The MN/MX line determine the mode When it is HIGH the processor operates in minimum mode and when it is LOW the processor operates in maximum mode.

The remaining 8 control lines are :

- INTA
- ALE
- BHE
- DEN
- DT/R
- M/IO
- WR
- HOLD and HLDA

In the minimum mode INTA (active LOW) signal goes low to acknowledge an interrupt. The ALE outputs a pulse to indicate that the valid address is available on the address pins. DEN (active LOW) is used to enable the outputs of the drivers. The DT/R indicates to the transeivers whether they are to transmit or receive data. The M/IO indicates a memory transfer or an I/O transfer. The WR (active LOW) indicates the write operation to memory or to an output port. The HOLD and HLDA are used just as in 8085 to start and acknowledge a DMA operation.

When the MN/MX is held LOW, the processor operates in the maximum mode. In this mode the QS0 and QS1 indicate the activity in the instruction queue during the previous clock cycle. The status bits S0, S1 and S2 are used to encode the DEN, DT/R and M/IO signals of minimum mode. These three lines are normally decoded by an 8288 bus controller. The three other signals are used for multiprocessor applications. The Lock is a software controlled output which locks the other processor from taking control of the bus. The RQ/GT pins are used by the other processors to force the active processor into a HOLD state so as to take control of the bus. The RQ/GTO has priority over RQ/GT1.

14.3 ARCHITECTURE OF 8086

Fig. 14.2 shows the internal architecture of 8086.

REGISTERS

Inside the processor information is stored in registers. The Data Register hold data for an operation. The Address Registers hold the address of a memory location. The Status Register hold the status of the processor. The 8086 has a total of 14 general purpose registers, each of which can hold 16 bits.

DATA REGISTERS

The processor has 4 register pairs which are named as AX, BX, CX and DX. The high and low bytes stored in each of the registers can be

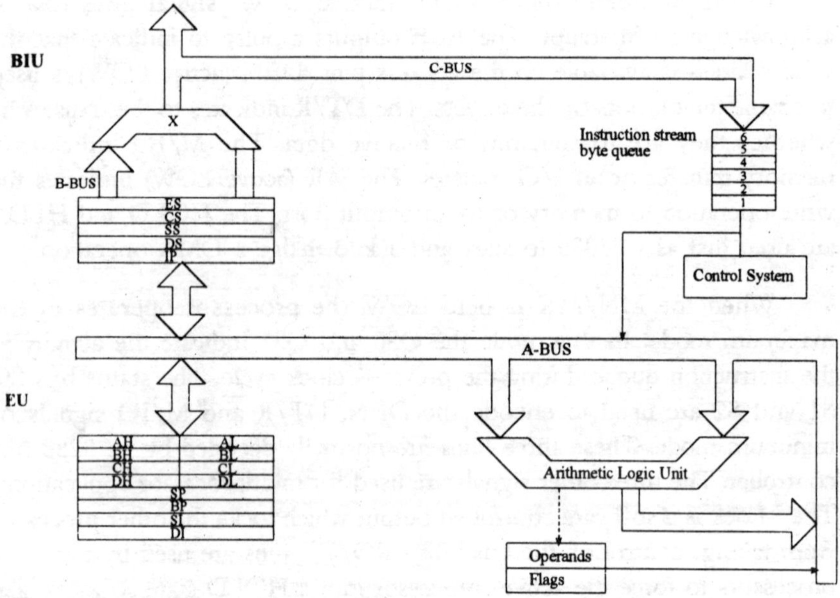

Fig. 14.2 Internal architecture of 8086

accessed seperately. The high bytes are available in AH, BH, CH and DH while the low bytes are available in AL, BL, CL, and DL. Though these four 16 bit registers are general purpose in nature they can also perform special functions. The AX register is called as the Accumulator which is used in arithmetic, logic and data transfer operations. Multiplication and division operation demand that one of the numbers must be in AX or AL register. The BX register is called the Base register. The base address is stored in this register. The CX register is called the count register. This register serves as the loop counter to construct a loop in the program. The DX register is known as the data register. This is used in multiplication, division and input and output operations.

SEGMENT REGISTERS

The 8086 is a 16 bit processor which means all its register can hold only 16 bits. However the processor has 20 address lines, which means it has to store 20 bit address information. In order to handle 20 bit address, the segmented memory concept is used. The memory is divided into segment of 64 kilobyte. Each segment is identified by a segment number which is also known as the SEGMENT ADDRESS. Within the segment, a memory location is identified by an OFFSET ADDRESS. To access the 64k memory locations in a segment only 16 bit address is required. The segment address is also of 16 bit size and therefore the entire addressing can be managed with 16 bit registers.

The proper combination of segment and offset address is called PHYSICAL ADDRESS. The physical address is obtained by multiplying the segment address by 16 (serving the segment address by 4 bits towards left and adding zero to right) and adding the offset address which results in a 20 bit number. Thus the physical address can access any location within the one MB memory space.

The 8086 has 4 segment registers to store the segment address. They are CS, DS, ES and SS. The Code segment (CS) register will hold the segment address of the memory location where the program is available. The Data segment (DS) register will hold the segment address of the data area. The Stack segment (SS) will contain the address of the system stack memory area. In some cases, if the user needs to use a second set of data, he can use the Extra Segment (ES) register to hold the address of the second data segment memory area. At any time only those memory locations addressed by the four segment registers are accessible. The contents of a segment register can be modified by the user through the program to address any segment of the memory.

POINTER AND INDEX REGISTERS

The segment registers store the segment address for different requirements. The offset address to be used with these segment registers are stored in pointers and Index registers. These registers can be used in arithmetic and other operations.

The stack pointer (SP) register is used with the stack segment (SS) register to access the stack memory area.

The Base Pointer (BP) register is also used to access data on the stack. The BP register can also be used to access data in other segment.

The Source Index (SI) register is used to hold the offset address of memory locations in the data segment, addressed by the DS register.

The Destination Index (DI) register does the same function as SI, but addressed by ES register instead of DS.

INSTRUCTION POINTER

To access the program instructions, the processor uses the Instruction Pointer (IP) register along with the code segment (CS) register. The CS registers holds the segment address and IP contains the offset address of the next instruction to be executed or to be loaded into the queue register. The IP register is incremented such that it always point to the next instruction. This IP register can not be directly munipulated by an instruction.

Suppose code segment (CS) register contains 1600H and instruction pointer (IP) contains 1300H, the CPU fetches its next instruction from the memory location 16000H + 1300H = 17300H.

FLAG REGISTER

The purpose of the FLAG register is to indicate the current status of the microprocessor. After executing the instruction the processor sets the individual bits called flags. These flags can be grouped as STATUS and CONTROL flags. The status flag reflect the result of an instruction executed by the processor. The control flag enable or disable certain operations of the processor.

The condition or status flags are

- Sign Flag (SF)
- Zero Flag (ZF)
- Parity Flag (PF)
- Carry Flag (CF)
- Auxilliary carry Flag (AF)
- Overflow Flag (OF)

The control flags are

- Direction Flag (DF)
- Interrrupt Enable Flag (IF)
- Trap Flag (TF)

ADDRESSING MODES

The way in which an operand is specified is called its addressing mode. The addressing modes for the 8086 instructions are typical. These modes are

- Immediate addressing
  The datum is either 8 or 16 bits and is part of the instruction.
- Direct addressing
  The 16 bit effective address of the datum is part of the instruction.
- Register addressing
  The datum is in the register that is specified by the instruction.
- Register indirect addressing
  The effective or offset address of the datum is in the base register or an index register specified by the instruction.
- Register Relative addressing
  The effective or offset address is the sum of an 8 or 16 bit displacement and the contents of a base register or an index register.
- Based Indexed addressing
  The effective or offset address is the sum of a base register and an index register, both are specified by the instruction.
- Relative Based Indexed addressing
  The offset or effective address is the sum of an 8 or 16 bit displacement and a based indexed address.

The addressing modes for indicating branch addresses are
- Intrasegment direct
- Intrasegment indirect
- Intersegment direct
  Intersegment indirect.

14.4 THE MOTOROLA 68000

FEATURES

- 16 bit data paths on its system bus
- Performs 32 bit arithmatic and logic operations internally.
- Can directly address 16 Megabytes of memory.
- I/O memory mapped.
- 32 bit registers (8 data reg., 7 addr.reg., 1 PC, 2 SP)
- Has two modes: Supervisory mode, User mode.
- Powerful instruction repertoire and HIGH SPEED operation
- Mostly used in Personal Computers for communication and control purposes.

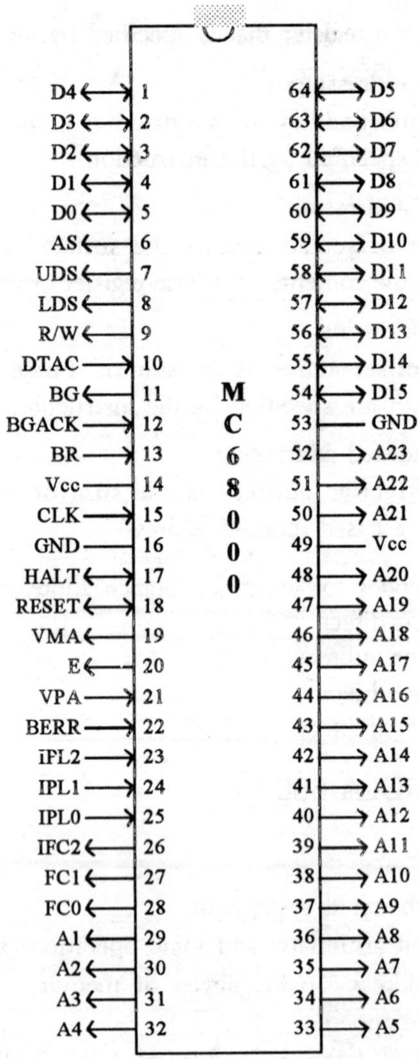

Fig. 14.3 Pin details of processor 68000

Motorola 68000 is 24 bit address bus and 16 bit data bus, which is used in Apple computers. Motorola 68008 is an 20 bit address bus and 8 bit data bus, which is used in the Sinclair computers. Motorola 68010 is an processor 68000 with virtual memory, which is used in the HP 9000 series computers.

Pin name	Description
D0 - D15	Data bus
A1 - A23	Address Bus
AS	Address strobe
R/W	Read / Write control
UDS, LDS	Upper, Lower data strobes
DTACK	Data transfer acknowledge
FC0, FC1, FC2	Function code (status) outputs
IPL0, IPL1, IPL2	Interrupt request
BERR	Bus error
HALT	Halt processor
RESET	Reset processor or external devices
CLK	clock
BR	Bus request
BG	Bus grant
BGACK	Bus grant acknowledge
E	Enable (clock) output
VMA	Valid memory address
VPA	Valid peripheral address
Vcc, GND	Power(+5 V), Ground

The pin details of the 16 bit Motorola microprocessor is shown in Fig. 14.3. The advantage of a 64 pin Dual-In-Line package enables the address and data buses to be non-multiplexed, inaddition to this a large number of control bus signals can be accommodated. So the bus controller (8288) and demultiplexing chips needed with the Intel 16 bit processor 8086 are not needed with this Motorola processor 68000. This processor does not posses maximum/minimum option pin, insead maximum configuration to be permaently selected.

The signal combination available in pins UDS and LDS indicate whether data are being transferred on the most significant byte, least significant byte or both bytes of the data bus. FC0, FC1 and FC2 represent the function code of the device. Seven interrupt levels are available in this processor. Three bus signals Br, Bg and BGACK are used when other processors or DMA controllers require to utilise the main buses. The signals E, VPA and VMA are available to interface with standard devices with synchronisation.

SUMMARY OF THE MICROPROCESSORS

Microprocessors	Manufacturers	Distinction	Introduced
4004	INTEL	First MP	1971
8008	INTEL	First 8 bit	1972
8080A	INTEL	N Channel Second Generation	1974
6800	MOTOROLA	8 bit, +5 v only	1974
PACE	NATIONAL	16 bit	1974
1802	RCA	CMOS	1974
8048	INTEL	8 bit single chip	1976
8086	INTEL	8 bit with 16 bit architecture	1976
2920	INTEL	Analog Signal Processor	1974
iAPX432	INTEL	32 bit	1982
68000	MOTOROLA	16 bit	1976
6502	ROCKWELL	8 bit	1976
80186, 80286	INTEL	16 bit	1980
80386	INTEL	32 bit	1984
Z 80	ZILOG	8 bit	1974
Z 8000	ZILOG	16 bit	1980

14.5 ARITHMETIC COPROCESSOR

The IBM compatiable personal computer family makes use of Intel CPUs 8088, 80286 and 88386. This series of CPUs are designed as general purpose CPUs. The instruction set of this series of CPU does cover arithmetic operations, yet when the software running on the systems very large number of arithmetic coprocessor is used to aid the CPU to realise high speed number crunching operations.

The arithmetic coprocessor is designed to operate in parallel with a general purpose CPU. The coprocessor gets in parallel most of the connections of the CPU. The CPU executes all normal instructions and numeric processor executes only arithmetic instructions.

The Intel family of arithmetic Coprocessor includes the 8087, 80287 and 80387. The instruction sets and programming for these devices are identical. The jonly difference is they are designed to operate with corresponding CPUs.

The arithmetic coprocessor executes 68 different instructions. Whenever a coprocessor instruction access the memory the main CPU generates the memory address required for the instruction. During normal instruction the CPU uses the data bus, and it leaves the bus to the coprocessor for coprocessor instructions.

The coprocessor is able to

- multiply
- divide
- add
- substract & calculate square root
- partial tangent
- partial arctangent
- logarithms

The coprocessor is capable of handling integers, BCD and floating point numbers. The signed integers can be 16, 32 or 64 bit long. The positive numbers are stored in true form with a 0 at MSB. Negative numbers are stored in complement form with a 1 at MSB. The binary coded decimal BCD form requires 80 bits of memory. Each number is stored as an 18 degit packed integer, which occupy 72 bits. The 10th byte contain the sign bits. Both negative and positive numbers are stored in true form. Floating print numbers are stored using scientific notation. The Intel family of coprocessor has three types of floating point numbers

- short (32 bits)
- long (64 bits) and
- temporary (80 bits)

14.6 INTERNAL STRUCTURE OF 80287

The device has a control unit and numeric execution unit. The control unit interfaces with the microprocessor system data bus. The instructions reach both the CPU and the coprocessor. If it is an ESC coprocessor instruction, the coprocessor executes it otherwise the CPU executes the instruction. The numeric execution unit executes unit has 8 sesistor stack each of 80 bits width that holds operands and results.

Instructions address, data in specific data register or can also use push and pop mechanism. Besides the coprocessor also has a status register which stores the status of operation. It has a control register, which indicates the contents of each location in the coprocessor stack.

14.7 COPROCESSOR INSTRUCTIONS

The coprocessors has arithmetic instructions for addition, substraction, multiplication, division and finding the square root. The arithmetic related instructions are scaling, rounding, absolute value and changing the sign. The comparison instruction compares the data at the top of the stack with another data and returns the result of comparison. The constant operations return constants to the top of the stack. The set of constants allowed include 0.0, 1.0, log 2 power 10 etc. Besides these instruction the coprocessor also has control instruction for initialisation, exception handling and task switching.

Appendix I

REFERENCE SHEET OF 8085

The 8080 was the first NMOS, 8 bit processor and was widely used in India. It has a good general purpose architecture and is well supported with both software and hardware. The 8085 has used the same instruction set of 8080 but needs only a 5 Volt dc supply and has many additional features like on-chip clock, serial I/O and four more interrupt lines. Extra pins needed for these functions have been manipulated by multiplexing the low order address bus with the data bus.

The 8085 has seven 8 bit general purpose registers. Six of these can be used as three 16 bit register pairs, BC, DE & HL. The HL register pair is used as memory pointer for register indirect addressing. SP is the stack pointer, which contains a 16 bit memory address of the top of a system stack and is used as address pointer. PC is the program counter which holds a 16 bit memory address which points to the next instruction to be executed. It has five, ONE bit flag registers to indicate the effect of arithmetic and logic operations, which is

- Carry flag
- Parity flag
- Auxilary carry flag
- Zero flag and
- Sign flag.

The 8085 has 80 basic instructions including RIM and SIM. One, two and three byte instructions are used. Direct, Register, Register Indirect and Immediate addressing modes are used in this processor. Fully 8 bit binary and BCD arithmetic is possible. Few 16 bit arithmetic is possible using the HL register pair as an accumulator.

Separate addresses are available for I/O using IN and OUT instructions. This INTEL chip is well supported with software like BASICS and CP/M operating system.

Features :

Memory address range	-	64 K
I/O address range	-	256 input ports and 256 output ports.
Clock frequency	-	3.125 MHz
Power Supply	-	+ 5 V
Interrupts	-	INTR, RST 5.5, RST 6.5, RST 7.5 and TRAP

High speed vertions of 8085 is also available in the market nowdays.

It has large number of support devices like

- 8251 (USART),
- 8255 (parallel I/O),
- 8253 (TIMER),
- 8259 (Interrupt controller),
- 8257 (DMA controller).

In addition to the above chips, the INTEL 8085 has two special combination I/O & Memory chips 8155 and 8355.

Execution time for

ADD register to accumulator	-	1.28 micro sec
OUTPUT accumulator to Port	-	3.20 micro sec
MOVE from memory to memory	-	5.12 micro sec

Original Source	-	INTEL
Second Sourcing	-	SIEMENS,NEC, NATIONAL SIGNETICS, AMD

Appendix I

INSTRUCTION SET OF 8085

DATA TRANSFER GROUP

MOV	A,A	7F
	A,B	78
	A,C	79
	A,D	7A
	A,E	7B
	A,H	7C
	A,L	7D
	A,M	7E
MOV	B,A	47
	B,B	40
	B,C	41
	B,D	42
	B,E	43
	B,H	44
	B,L	45
	B,M	46
MOV	C,A	4F
	C,B	48
	C,C	49
	C,D	4A
	C,E	4B
	C,H	4C
	C,L	4D
	C,M	4E
MOV	D,A	57
	D,B	50
	D,C	51
	D,D	52
	D,E	53
	D,H	54
	D,L	55
	D,M	56

MOV	E,A	5F
	E,B	58
	E,C	59
	E,D	5A
	E,E	5B
	E,H	5C
	E,L	5D
	E,M	5E
MOV	H,A	67
	H,B	60
	H,C	61
	H,D	62
	H,E	63
	H,H	64
	H,L	65
	H,M	66
MOV	L,A	6F
	L,B	68
	L,C	69
	L,D	6A
	L,E	6B
	L,H	6C
	L,L	6D
	L,M	6E
MOV	M,A	77
	M,B	70
	M,C	71
	M,D	72
	M,E	73
	M,H	74
	M,L	75

XCHG EB

Move Immediate

MVI	A,data	3E
	B,data	06
	C,data	0E
	D,data	16
	E,data	1E
	H,data	26
	L,data	2E
	M,data	36

Load Immediate

LXI	B,data	01
	D,data	11
	H,data	21
	SP,data	31

Load / Store

LDAX B 0A

LDAX D 1A

LHLD addr 2A

LDA addr 3A

STAX B 02

STAX D12

SHLD addr 22

STA addr 32

ARITHMETIC AND LOGICAL GROUP

ADD	A	87	INR	A	3C	ANA	A	A7
	B	80		B	04		B	A0
	C	81		C	0C		C	A1
	D	82		D	14		D	A2
	E	83		E	1C		E	A3
	H	84		H	24		H	A4
	L	85		L	2C		L	A5
	M	86		M	34		M	A6
ADC	A	8F	INX	B	03	XRA	A	AF
	B	88		D	13		B	A8
	C	89		H	23		C	A9
	D	8A		SP	33		D	AA
	E	8B					E	AB
	H	8C	DCX	B	0B		H	AC
	L	8D		D	1B		L	AD
	M	8E		H	2B		M	AE
				SP	3B			
SUB	A	97	DCR	A	3D	ORA	A	B7
	B	90		B	05		B	B0
	C	91		C	0D		C	B1
	D	92		D	15		D	B2
	E	93		E	1D		E	B3
	H	94		H	25		H	B4
	L	95		L	2D		L	B5
	M	96		M	35		M	B6
SBB	A	9F	ADI	data	C6	CMP	A	BF
	B	98	ACI	data	CE		B	B8
	C	99	SUI	data	D6		C	B9
	D	9A	SBI	data	DE		D	BA
	E	9B	ANI	data	E6		E	BB
	H	9C	XRI	data	EE		H	BC
	L	9D	ORI	data	F6		L	BD
	M	9E	CPI	data	FE		M	BE

DAA	27	RLC	07
CMA	2F	RRC	0F
STC	37	RAL	17
CMC	3F	RAR	1F

BRANCH CONTROL INSTRUCTIONS

JMP	addr	C3	CALL	addr	CD
JNZ	addr	C2	CNZ	addr	C4
JZ	addr	CA	CZ	addr	CC
JNC	addr	D2	CNC	addr	D4
JC	addr	DA	CC	addr	DC
JPO	addr	E2	CPO	addr	E4
JPE	addr	EA	CPE	addr	EC
JP	addr	F2	CP	addr	F4
JM	addr	FA	CM	addr	FC
PCHL		E9			

RETURN		RESTART		
RET	C9	RST	0	C7
RNZ	C0	RST	1	CF
RZ	C8	RST	2	D7
RNC	D0	RST	3	DF
RC	D8	RST	4	E7
RPO	E0	RST	5	EF
RPE	E8	RST	6	F7
RP	F0	RST	7	FF
RM	F8			

I/O and MACHINE CONTROL

STACK operation			INPUT/OUTPUT	
PUSHB	C5		OUT data	D3
PUSHD	D5		IN data	DB
PUSHH	E5			
PUSHPSW	F5			
POP	B	C1	CONTROL	
POP	D	D1		
POP	H	E1	DI	F3
POP	PSW	F1	EI	FB
			NOP	00
			HLT	76
XTRL	E3		SIM	30
SPHL	F9		RIM	20

Appendix II

REFERENCE SHEET OF Z-80

The Z-80 was developed as a "Super 8085". This processor is compatiable with 8085 at the object code level. Inspite of having many powerful new instructions and using different mnemonics, the software developed for 8085 processor can run without any modification. This Z-80 processor has new features like a set of extra registers, automatic refresh for dynamic RAMs.

The Z-80 has two banks of 8 general purpose 8 bit registers but only one bank may be accessed at a time. In addition to the usual stack pointer (SP register) and Program Counter (PC register), the Z80 has two 16 bit Index Registers and the dedicated 8 bit Interrupt Vector (I) and Refresh (R) registers. The I register points to interrupt vector page in main memory. The R register is counter for 16K DRAM refresh. This processor has six, ONE bit flag register to indicate the effect of arithmetic and logic operations, which is

- Carry flag
- Subtract flag
- Parity and Overflow flag
- Auxlary carry flag
- Zero flag and
- Sign flag

ZILOG company has taken advantage of the unused opcodes from 8085 instruction set to add new instructions to the Z-80 set. Some of these spare codes are used to get extra opcode tables, each can provide 256 extra opcode possibilities. This method makes it necessary to use two opcode bytes instead of one used in 8085. This results in the use of one byte, two byte, three byte and four byte instructions in 280.

The Z-80 has 158 different instructions compared with 80 in 8085. This processor has many new capabilities, like Relative jump, Bit set, reset & test, nibble shift, block transfer and search. Since it can execute 8085 object code, therefore it has access to the CP/$\overline{M}$ operating system.

Features

Memory address range	-	64K
I/O address range	-	256
Clock frequency	-	2.5 MHz
Power Supply	-	+ 5 V
Interrupt	-	INT & NMI

High speed versions of Z-80 is also available in the market now a days.

This Z-80 needs an external clock generator. It has large number of support devices like

- Z-80 PIO (Parallel ports)
- Z-80 CTC (Counter/Timers)
- Z-80 DMA (Direct Memeory Access controller) and
- Z-80 SI0 (dual USART)

Original Source	- ZILOG
Second Source	- NEC, SHARP, SIGNETICS, MOSTEK

Appendix II

INSTRUCTION SET OF Z-80

INSTRUCTION	OPCODE	COMMENTS
ADC A,(HL)	8E	A = A+(HL)+Cy
ADC A,(IX+dd)	DD8E dd	A = A+(IX+dd)+Cy
ADC A,(IY+dd)	FD8E dd	A = A+(IY+dd)+Cy
ADC A,B	88	A = A+B+Cy
ADC A,C	89	A = A+C+Cy
ADC A,D	8A	A = A+D+Cy
ADC A,E	8B	A = A+E+Cy
ADC A,H	8C	A = A+H+Cy
ADC A,L	8D	A = A+L+Cy
ADC A,A	8F	A = A+A+Cy
ADC A,data	CE data	A = A+data+Cy
ADC HL,BC	ED 4A	HL = HL+BC+Cy
ADC HL,DE	ED 5A	HL = HL+DE+Cy
ADC HL,HL	ED 6A	HL = HL+HL+Cy
ADC HL,SP	ED 7A	HL = HL+SP+Cy
ADD A,(HL)	86	A = A+(HL)
ADD A,(IX+dd)	DD86 dd	A = A+(IX+dd)
ADC A,(IY+dd)	FD86 dd	A = A+(IY+dd)
ADD A,B	80	A = A + B
ADD A,C	81	A = A + C
ADD A,D	82	A = A + D
ADD A,E	83	A = A + E
ADD A,H	84	A = A + H
ADD A,L	85	A = A + L
ADD A,A	87	A = A + A
ADD A,data	C6 data	A = A + data
ADD HL,BC	09	HL = HL + BC
ADD HL,DE	19	HL = HL + DE
ADD HL,HL	29	HL = HL + HL
ADD HL,SP	39	HL = HL + SP
ADD IX,BC	DD 09	IX = IX + BC

ADD IX,DE	DD 19	IX = IX + DE
ADD IX,IX	DD 29	IX = IX + IX
ADD IX,SP	DD 39	IX = IX + SP
ADD IY,BC	FD 09	IY = IY + BC
ADD IY,DE	FD 19	IY = IY + DE
ADD IY,IY	FD 29	IY = IY + IY
ADD IY,SP	FD 39	IY = IY + SP
AND (HL)	A6	A = A and (HL)
AND A,(IX+dd)	DDA6 dd	A = A and (IX+dd)
AND A,(IY+dd)	FDA6 dd	A = A and (IY+dd)
AND B	A0	A = A and B
AND C	A1	A = A and C
AND D	A2	A = A and D
AND E	A3	A = A and E
AND H	A4	A = A and H
AND L	A5	A = A and L
AND A	A7	A = A and A
AND data	E6 data	A = A and data
BIT 0,(HL)	CB 46	TEST BIT 0 of (HL)
BIT 0,(IX+dd)	DDCBdd46	TEST BIT 0 of (IX+dd)
BIT 0,(IY+dd)	FDCBdd46	TEST BIT 0 of (IY+dd)
BIT 0,B	CB 40	TEST BIT 0 of B
BIT 0,C	CB 41	TEST BIT 0 of C
BIT 0,D	CB 42	TEST BIT 0 of D
BIT 0,E	CB 43	TEST BIT 0 of E
BIT 0,H	CB 44	TEST BIT 0 of H
BIT 0,L	CB 45	TEST BIT 0 of L
BIT 0,A	CB 47	TEST BIT 0 of A
BIT 1,(HL)	CB 4E	TEST BIT 1 of (HL)
BIT 1,(IX+dd)	DDCBdd4E	TEST BIT 1 of (IX+dd)
BIT 1,(IY+dd)	FDCBdd4E	TEST BIT 1 of (IY+dd)
BIT 1,B	CB 48	TEST BIT 1 of B
BIT 1,C	CB 49	TEST BIT 1 of C
BIT 1,D	CB 4A	TEST BIT 1 of D
BIT 1,E	CB 4B	TEST BIT 1 of E
BIT 1,H	CB 4C	TEST BIT 1 of H
BIT 1,L	CB 4D	TEST BIT 1 of L
BIT 1,A	CB 4F	TEST BIT 1 of A
BIT 2,(HL) CB 56	TEST BIT	2 of (HL)
BIT 2,(IX+dd)	DDCBdd56	TEST BIT 2 of (IX+dd)
BIT 2,(IY+dd)	FDCBdd56	TEST BIT 2 of (IY+dd)
BIT 2,B	CB 50	TEST BIT 2 of B

BIT 2,C	CB 51	TEST BIT 2 of C
BIT 2,D	CB 52	TEST BIT 2 of D
BIT 2,E	CB 53	TEST BIT 2 of E
BIT 2,H	CB 54	TEST BIT 2 of H
BIT 2,L	CB 55	TEST BIT 2 of L
BIT 2,A	CB 57	TEST BIT 2 of A
BIT 3,(HL)	CB 5E	TEST BIT 3 of (HL)
BIT 3,(IX+dd)	DDCBdd5E	TEST BIT 3 of (IX+dd)
BIT 3,(IY+dd)	FDCBdd5E	TEST BIT 3 of (IY+dd)
BIT 3,B	CB 58	TEST BIT 3 of B
BIT 3,C	CB 59	TEST BIT 3 of C
BIT 3,D	CB 5A	TEST BIT 3 of D
BIT 3,E	CB 5B	TEST BIT 3 of E
BIT 3,H	CB 5C	TEST BIT 3 of H
BIT 3,L	CB 5D	TEST BIT 3 of L
BIT 3,A	CB 5F	TEST BIT 3 of A
BIT 4,(HL)	CB 66	TEST BIT 4 of (HL)
BIT 4,(IX+dd)	DDCBdd66	TEST BIT 4 of (IX+dd)
BIT 4,(IY+dd)	FDCBdd66	TEST BIT 4 of (IY+dd)
BIT 4,B	CB 60	TEST BIT 4 of B
BIT 4,C	CB 61	TEST BIT 4 of C
BIT 4,D	CB 62	TEST BIT 4 of D
BIT 4,E	CB 63	TEST BIT 4 of E
BIT 4,H	CB 64	TEST BIT 4 of H
BIT 4,L	CB 65	TEST BIT 4 of L
BIT 4,A	CB 67	TEST BIT 4 of A
BIT 5,(HL)	CB 6E	TEST BIT 5 of (HL)
BIT 5,(IX+dd)	DDCBdd6E	TEST BIT 5 of (IX+dd)
BIT 5,(IY+dd)	FDCBdd6E	TEST BIT 5 of (IY+dd)
BIT 5,B	CB 68	TEST BIT 5 of B
BIT 5,C	CB 69	TEST BIT 5 of C
BIT 5,D	CB 6A	TEST BIT 5 of D
BIT 5,E	CB 6B	TEST BIT 5 of E
BIT 5,H	CB 6C	TEST BIT 5 of H
BIT 5,L	CB 6D	TEST BIT 5 of L
BIT 5,A	CB 6F	TEST BIT 5 of A
BIT 6, (HL)	CB 76	TEST BIT 6 of (HL)
BIT 6, (IX+dd)	DDCBdd76	TEST BIT 6 of (IX+dd)
BIT 6, (IY+dd)	FDCBdd76	TEST BIT 6 of (IY+dd)
BIT 6, B	CB 70	TEST BIT 6 of B
BIT 6, C	CB 71	TEST BIT 6 of C
BIT 6, D	CB 72	TEST BIT 6 of D

BIT 6,E	CB 73	TEST BIT 6 of E
BIT 6,H	CB 74	TEST BIT 6 of H
BIT 6,L	CB 75	TEST BIT 6 of L
BIT 6,A	CB 77	TEST BIT 6 of A
BIT 7,(HL)	CB 7E	TEST BIT 7 of (HL)
BIT 7,(IX+dd)	DDCBdd7E	TEST BIT 7 of (IX+dd)
BIT 7,(IY+dd)	FDCBdd7E	TEST BIT 7 of (IY+dd)
BIT 7,B	CB 78	TEST BIT 7 of B
BIT 7,C	CB 79	TEST BIT 7 of C
BIT 7,D	CB 7A	TEST BIT 7 of D
BIT 7,E	CB 7B	TEST BIT 7 of E
BIT 7,H	CB 7C	TEST BIT 7 of H
BIT 7,L	CB 7D	TEST BIT 7 of L
BIT 7,A	CB 7F	TEST BIT 7 of A
CALL C,addr	DC addr	CALL if carry
CALL M,addr	FC addr	CALL if minus
CALL NC,addr	D4 addr	CALL if no carry
CALL addr	CD addr	CALL subroutine
CALL NZ,addr	C4 addr	CALL if not zero
CALL P,addr	F4 addr	CALL if positive
CALL PE,addr	EC addr	CALL if parity even
CALL PO,addr	E4 addr	CALL if parity odd
CALL Z,addr	CC addr	CALL if zero
CCF	3F	COMPLEMENT CARRY flag
CP (HL)	BE	COMPARE A with (HL)
CP (IX+dd)	DDBE dd	COMPARE A with (IX+dd)
CP (IY+dd)	FDBE dd	COMPARE A with (IY+dd)
CP B	B8	COMPARE A with B
CP C	B9	COMPARE A with C
CP D	BA	COMPARE A with D
CP E	BB	COMPARE A with E
CP H	BC	COMPARE A with H
CP L	BD	COMPARE A with L
CP A	BF	COMPARE A with A
CP data	FE data	COMPARE A with data
CPD	ED A9	COMPARE A with (HL) then decrement HL and BC
CPDR	ED B9	COMPARE A with (HL) then decrement HL and BC, repeat until BC=00 or A=(HL)

CPI	ED A1	COMPARE A with (HL) then increment HL and decrement BC
CPIR	ED B1	COMPARE A with (HL) then increment HL and decrement BC, repeat until BC=00 or A=(HL)
CPL	2F	COMPLEMENT A
DAA	27	DECIMAL ADJUST A reg.
DEC (HL)	35	(HL) = (HL) - 1
DEC A,(IX+dd)	DD35 dd	(IX+dd) = (IX+dd) - 1
DEC A,(IY+dd)	FD35 dd	(IY+dd) = (IY+dd) - 1
DEC B	05	B = B - 1
DEC C	0D	C = C - 1
DEC D	15	D = D - 1
DEC E	1D	E = E - 1
DEC H	25	H = H - 1
DEC L	2D	L = L - 1
DEC A	3D	A = A - 1
DEC BC	0B	BC = BC - 1
DEC DE	1B	DE = DE - 1
DEC HL	2B	HL = HL - 1
DEC SP	3B	SP = SP - 1
DEC IX	DD 2B	IX = IX - 1
DEC IY	FD 2B	IY = IY - 1
DJNZ	10 dd	DECREMENT B and JUMP if B is not zero.
DI	F3	DISABLE INTERRUPTs
EI	FB	ENABLE INTERRUPTs
EX (SP),HL	E3	EXCHANGE HL with (SP)
EX (SP),IX DD	E3	EXCHANGE IX with (SP)
EX (SP), IY FD	E3	EXCHANGE IY with (SP)
EX AF,AF' 08		EXCHANGE AF with AF'
EX DE,HL EB		EXCHANGE DE with HL
EXX	D9	EXCHANGE BC, DE and HL with BC', DE' and HL'
HALT	76	HALT for interrupt of RESET
IM 0	ED 46	Select interrupt MODE 0
IM 1	ED 56	Select interrupt MODE 1
IM 2	ED 5E	Select interrupt MODE 2

IN A,(C)	ED 78	INPUT data to A from I/O port (C)
IN A,portaddr	DB addr	INPUT data to A from specified port address
IN B,(C)	ED 40	INPUT data to B from I/O port (C)
IN C,(C)	ED 48	INPUT data to C from I/O port (C)
IN D,(C)	ED 50	INPUT data to D from I/O port (C)
IN E,(C)	ED 58	INPUT data to E from I/O port (C)
IN H,(C)	ED 60	INPUT data to H from I/O port (C)
IN L,(C)	ED 68	INPUT data to L from I/O port (C)
INC (HL)	34	(HL) = (HL) + 1
INC A,(IX+dd)	DD34 dd	(IX+dd) = (IX+dd) + 1
INC A,(IY+dd)	FD34 dd	(IY+dd) = (IY+dd) + 1
INC B	04	B = B + 1
INC C	0C	C = C + 1
INC D	14	D = D + 1
INC E	1C	E = E + 1
INC H	24	H = H + 1
INC L	2C	L = L + 1
INC A	3C	A = A + 1
INC BC	03	BC = BC + 1
INC DE	13	DE = DE + 1
INC HL	23	HL = HL + 1
INC SP	33	SP = SP + 1
INC IX	DD 23	IX = IX + 1
INC IY	FD 23	IY = IY + 1
IND	ED AA	INPUT data to (HL) from I/O port (C), decrement HL and B
INDR	ED BA	INPUT data to (HL) from I/O port (C), decrement HL and B, repeat until B = 00
INI	ED A2	INPUT data to (HL) from I/O port (C), decrement B and increment HL.

INIR	ED BA	INPUT data to (HL) from I/O port (C), decrement B and increment HL, repeat until B = 00
JP (HL)	E9	JUMP to address (HL)
JP (IX)	DDE9	JUMP to address (IX)
JP (IY)	FDE9	JUMP to address (IY)
JP C,addr	DA addr	JUMP if carry
JP M,addr	FA addr	JUMP if minus
JP NC,addr	D2 addr	JUMP if no carry
JP addr	C3 addr	JUMP to specified address
JP NZ,addr	C2 addr	JUMP if not zero
JP P,addr	F2 addr	JUMP if positive
JP PE,addr	EA addr	JUMP if parity even
JP PO,addr	E2 addr	JUMP if parity odd
JP Z,addr	CA addr	JUMP if zero
JR C,dd	38 dd	JUMP RELATIVE if carry
JR dd	18 dd	JUMP RELATIVE
JR NC,dd	30 dd	JUMP RELATIVE if no carry
JR NZ,dd	20 dd	JUMP RELATIVE if not zero
JR Z,dd	28 dd	JUMP RELATIVE if zero
LD (BC),A	02	LOAD (BC) from A
LD (DE),A	12	LOAD (DE) from A
LD (HL),B	70	LOAD (HL) from B
LD (HL),C	71	LOAD (HL) from C
LD (HL),D	72	LOAD (HL) from D
LD (HL),E	73	LOAD (HL) from E
LD (HL),H	74	LOAD (HL) from H
LD (HL),L	75	LOAD (HL) from L
LD (HL),A	77	LOAD (HL) from A
LD (HL),data	36 data	LOAD (HL) with data
LD (IX+dd),B	DD70dd	LOAD (IX+dd) from B
LD (IX+dd),C	DD71dd	LOAD (IX+dd) from C
LD (IX+dd),D	DD72dd	LOAD (IX+dd) from D
LD (IX+dd),E	DD73dd	LOAD (IX+dd) from E
LD (IX+dd),H	DD74dd	LOAD (IX+dd) from H
LD (IX+dd),L	DD75dd	LOAD (IX+dd) from L
LD (IX+dd),A	DD77dd	LOAD (IX+dd) from A
LD (IX+dd),data	DD36dddata	LOAD (IX+dd) with data
LD (IY+dd),B	FD70dd	LOAD (IY+dd) from B
LD (IY+dd),C	FD71dd	LOAD (IY+dd) from C
LD (IY+dd),D	FD72dd	LOAD (IY+dd) from D
LD (IY+dd),E	FD73dd	LOAD (IY+dd) from E

LD (IY+dd),H	FD74dd	LOAD (IY+dd) from H
LD (IY+dd),L	FD75dd	LOAD (IY+dd) from L
LD (IY+dd),A	FD77dd	LOAD (IY+dd) from A
LD (IY+dd),data	FD36dddata	LOAD (IY+dd) with data
LD (addr),A	32 addr	LOAD (addr) from A
LD (addr),BC	ED43addr	LOAD (addr) from BC
LD (addr),DE	ED53addr	LOAD (addr) from DE
LD (addr),HL	22 addr	LOAD (addr) from HL
LD (addr),IX	DD22addr	LOAD (addr) from IX
LD (addr),IY	FD22addr	LOAD (addr) from IY
LD (addr),SP	ED73addr	LOAD (addr) from SP
LD A,(BC)	0A	LOAD A from (BC)
LD A,(DE)	1A	LOAD A from (DE)
LD A,(HL)	7E	LOAD A from (HL)
LD A,(IX+dd)	DD7E dd	LOAD A from (IX+dd)
LD A,(IY+dd)	FD7E dd	LOAD A from (IY+dd)
LD A,addr	3A addr	LOAD A from address
LD A,A	7F	LOAD A from A
LD A,B	78	LOAD A from B
LD A,C	79	LOAD A from C
LD A,D	7A	LOAD A from D
LD A,E	7B	LOAD A from E
LD A,H	7C	LOAD A from H
LD A,L	7D	LOAD A from L
LD A,data	3E data	LOAD A with data
LD A,I	ED57	LOAD A from I
LD A,R	ED5F	LOAD A from R
LD B,(HL)	46	LOAD B from (HL)
LD B,(IX+dd)	DD46 dd	LOAD B from (IX+dd)
LD B,(IY+dd)	FD46 dd	LOAD B from (IY+dd)
LD B,A	47	LOAD B from A
LD B,B	40	LOAD B from B
LD B,C	41	LOAD B from C
LD B,D	42	LOAD B from D
LD B,E	43	LOAD B from E
LD B,H	44	LOAD B from H
LD B,L	45	LOAD B from L
LD B,data	06 data	LOAD B with data
LD BC,addr	ED4B addr	LOAD BC from address
LD BC,data	01 data	LOAD BC with data

LD C,(HL)	4E	LOAD C from (HL)
LD C,(IX+dd)	DD4E dd	LOAD C from (IX+dd)
LD C,(IY+dd)	FD4E dd	LOAD C from (IY+dd)
LD C,A	4F	LOAD C from A
LD C,B	48	LOAD C from B
LD C,C	49	LOAD C from C
LD C,D	4A	LOAD C from D
LD C,E	4B	LOAD C from E
LD C,H	4C	LOAD C from H
LD C,L	4D	LOAD C from L
LD C,data	0E data	LOAD C with data
LD D,(HL)	56	LOAD D from (HL)
LD D,(IX+dd)	DD56 dd	LOAD D from (IX+dd)
LD D,(IY+dd)	FD56 dd	LOAD D from (IY+dd)
LD D,A	57	LOAD D from A
LD D,B	50	LOAD D from B
LD D,C	51	LOAD D from C
LD D,D	52	LOAD D from D
LD D,E	53	LOAD D from E
LD D,H	54	LOAD D from H
LD D,L	55	LOAD D from L
LD D,data	16 data	LOAD D with data
LD DE,addr	ED5Baddr	LOAD DE from addr
LD DE,data	11 data	LOAD DE with data
LD E,(HL)	5E	LOAD E from (HL)
LD E,(IX+dd)	DD5E dd	LOAD E from (IX+dd)
LD E,(IY+dd)	FD5E dd	LOAD E from (IY+dd)
LD E,A	5F	LOAD E from A
LD E,B	58	LOAD E from B
LD E,C	59	LOAD E from C
LD E,D	5A	LOAD E from D
LD E,E	5B	LOAD E from E
LD E,H	5C	LOAD E from H
LD E,L	5D	LOAD E from L
LD E,data	1E data	LOAD E with data
LD H,(HL)66	LOAD H from (HL)	
LD H,(IX+dd)	DD66 dd	LOAD H from (IX+dd)
LD H,(IY+dd)	FD66 dd	LOAD H from (IY+dd)

LD H,A	67	LOAD H from A
LD H,B	60	LOAD H from B
LD H,C	61	LOAD H from C
LD H,D	62	LOAD H from D
LD H,E	63	LOAD H from E
LD H,H	64	LOAD H from H
LD H,L	65	LOAD H from L
LD H,data	26 data	LOAD H with data
LD HL,addr	2A addr	LOAD HL from addr
LD HL,data	21 data	LOAD HL with data
LD I,A	ED47	LOAD I from A
LD IX,addr	DD2A addr	LOAD IX from address
LD IX,data	DD21 data	LOAD IX with data
LD IY,addr	FD2A addr	LOAD IY from address
LD IY,data	FD21 data	LOAD IY with data
LD L,(HL)	6E	LOAD L from (HL)
LD L,(IX+dd)	DD6E dd	LOAD L from (IX+dd)
LD L,(IY+dd)	FD6E dd	LOAD L from (IY+dd)
LD L,A	6F	LOAD L from A
LD L,B	68	LOAD L from B
LD L,C	69	LOAD L from C
LD L,D	6A	LOAD L from D
LD L,E	6B	LOAD L from E
LD L,H	6C	LOAD L from H
LD L,L	6D	LOAD L from L
LD L,data	2E data	LOAD L with data
LD R,A	ED4F	LOAD R from A
LD SP,addr	ED7B addr	LOAD SP from address
LD SP,HL	F9	LOAD SP from HL
LD SP,IX	DDF9	LOAD SP from IX
LD SP,IY	FDF9	LOAD SP from IY
LD SP,data	31 data	LOAD SP with data
LDD	EDA8	LOAD (HL) from (DE), then decrement BC, DE and HL.
LDDR	EDB8	LOAD (HL) from (DE), then decrement BC, DE and HL, repeat until BC = 00
LDI	EDA0	LOAD (HL) from (DE), then decrement BC and increment DE and HL.

LDIR	EDB0	LOAD (HL) from (DE), then decrement BC and increment DE and HL, repeat until
	BC = 0000.	
NEG	ED44	2s COMPLEMENT A
OR (HL)	B6	A ORed with (HL)
OR (IX+dd)	DDB6 dd	A ORed with (IX+dd)
OR (IY+dd)	FDB6 dd	A ORed with (IY+dd)
OR B	B7	A ORed with B
OR C	B0	A ORed with C
OR D	B1	A ORed with D
OR E	B2	A ORed with E
OR H	B3	A ORed with H
OR L	B4	A ORed with L
OR A	B5	A ORed with A
OR data	F6 data	A ORed with data
OTDR	EDBB	OUTPUT (HL) to I/O port (C) decrement B and HL. Repeat until B = 0.
OTIR	EDB3	OUTPUT (HL) to I/O port (C) decrement B and Increment HL Repeat until B = 0.
OUT (C),A	ED79	OUTPUT A to I/O port (C)
OUT (C),B	ED41	OUTPUT B to I/O port (C)
OUT (C),C	ED49	OUTPUT C to I/O port (C)
OUT (C),D	ED51	OUTPUT D to I/O port (C)
OUT (C),E	ED59	OUTPUT E to I/O port (C)
OUT (C),H	ED61	OUTPUT H to I/O port (C)
OUT (C),L	ED69	OUTPUT L to I/O port (C)
OUT (port)	D3 port	OUTPUT A to specified port
OUTD	EDAB	OUTPUT (HL) to I/O port (C) decrement B and HL
OUTI	EDA3	OUTPUT (HL) to I/O port (C) decrement B and Increment HL
POP AF	F1	LOAD AF from stack
POP BC	C1	LOAD BC from stack
POP DE	D1	LOAD DE from stack
POP HL	E1	LOAD HL from stack
POP IX	DDE1	LOAD IX from stack
POP IY	FDE1	LOAD IY from stack

PUSH AF	F5	LOAD stack from AF
PUSH BC	C5	LOAD stack from BC
PUSH DE	D5	LOAD stack from DE
PUSH HL	E5	LOAD stack from HL
PUSH IX	DDE5	LOAD stack from IX
PUSH IY	FDE5	LOAD stack from IY
RES 0,(HL)	CB86	BIT 0 of (HL) = 0
RES 0,(IX+dd)	DDCBdd86	BIT 0 of (IX+dd) = 0
RES 0,(IY+DD)	FDCBdd86	BIT 0 of (IY+dd) = 0
RES 0,A	CB87	BIT 0 of A = 0
RES 0,B	CB80	BIT 0 of B = 0
RES 0,C	CB81	BIT 0 of C = 0
RES 0,D	CB82	BIT 0 of D = 0
RES 0,E	CB83	BIT 0 of E = 0
RES 0,H	CB84	BIT 0 of H = 0
RES 0,L	CB85	BIT 0 of L = 0
RES 1,(HL)	CB8E	BIT 1 of (HL) = 0
RES 1,(IX+dd)	DDCBdd8E	BIT 1 of (IX+dd) = 0
RES 1,(IY+DD)	FDCBdd8E	BIT 1 of (IY+dd) = 0
RES 1,A	CB8F	BIT 1 of A = 0
RES 1,B	CB88	BIT 1 of B = 0
RES 1,C	CB89	BIT 1 of C = 0
RES 1,D	CB8A	BIT 1 of D = 0
RES 1,E	CB8B	BIT 1 of E = 0
RES 1,H	CB8C	BIT 1 of H = 0
RES 1,L	CB8D	BIT 1 of L = 0
RES 2,(HL)	CB96	BIT 2 of (HL) = 0
RES 2,(IX+dd)	DDCBdd96	BIT 2 of (IX+dd) = 0
RES 2,(IY+DD)	FDCBdd96	BIT 2 of (IY+dd) = 0
RES 2,A	CB97	BIT 2 of A = 0
RES 2,B	CB90	BIT 2 of B = 0
RES 2,C	CB91	BIT 2 of C = 0
RES 2,D	CB92	BIT 2 of D = 0
RES 2,E	CB93	BIT 2 of E = 0
RES 2,H	CB94	BIT 2 of H = 0
RES 2,L	CB95	BIT 2 of L = 0
RES 3,(HL)	CB9E	BIT 3 of (HL) = 0
RES 3,(IX+dd)	DDCBdd9E	BIT 3 of (IX+dd) = 0
RES 3,(IY+DD)	FDCBdd9E	BIT 3 of (IY+dd) = 0
RES 3,A	CB9F	BIT 3 of A = 0
RES 3,B	CB98	BIT 3 of B = 0
RES 3,C	CB99	BIT 3 of C = 0

RES 3,D	CB9A	BIT 3 of D = 0
RES 3,E	CB9B	BIT 3 of E = 0
RES 3,H	CB9C	BIT 3 of H = 0
RES 3,L	CB9D	BIT 3 of L = 0
RES 4,(HL)	CBA6	BIT 4 of (HL) = 0
RES 4,(IX+dd)	DDCBddA6	BIT 4 of (IX+dd) = 0
RES 4,(IY+DD)	FDCBddA6	BIT 4 of (IY+dd) = 0
RES 4,A	CBA7	BIT 4 of A = 0
RES 4,B	CBA0	BIT 4 of B = 0
RES 4,C	CBA1	BIT 4 of C = 0
RES 4,D	CBA2	BIT 4 of D = 0
RES 4,E	CBA3	BIT 4 of E = 0
RES 4,H	CBA4	BIT 4 of H = 0
RES 4,L	CBA5	BIT 4 of L = 0
RES 5,(HL)	CBAE	BIT 5 of (HL) = 0
RES 5,(IX+dd)	DDCBddAE	BIT 5 of (IX+dd) = 0
RES 5,(IY+DD)	FDCBddAE	BIT 5 of (IY+dd) = 0
RES 5,A	CBAF	BIT 5 of A = 0
RES 5,B	CBA8	BIT 5 of B = 0
RES 5,C	CBA9	BIT 5 of C = 0
RES 5,D	CBAA	BIT 5 of D = 0
RES 5,E	CBAB	BIT 5 of E = 0
RES 5,H	CBAC	BIT 5 of H = 0
RES 5,L	CBAD	BIT 5 of L = 0
RES 6,(HL)	CBB6	BIT 6 of (HL) = 0
RES 6,(IX+dd)	DDCBddB6	BIT 6 of (IX+dd) = 0
RES 6,(IY+DD)	FDCBddB6	BIT 6 of (IY+dd) = 0
RES 6,A	CBB7	BIT 6 of A = 0
RES 6,B	CBB0	BIT 6 of B = 0
RES 6,C	CBB1	BIT 6 of C = 0
RES 6,D	CBB2	BIT 6 of D = 0
RES 6,E	CBB3	BIT 6 of E = 0
RES 6,H	CBB4	BIT 6 of H = 0
RES 6,L	CBB5	BIT 6 of L = 0
RES 7,(HL)	CBBE	BIT 7 of (HL) = 0
RES 7,(IX+dd)	DDCBddBE	BIT 7 of (IX+dd) = 0
RES 7,(IY+DD)	FDCBddBE	BIT 7 of (IY+dd) = 0
RES 7,A	CBBF	BIT 7 of A = 0
RES 7,B	CBB8	BIT 7 of B = 0
RES 7,C	CBB9	BIT 7 of C = 0
RES 7,D	CBBA	BIT 7 of D = 0
RES 7,E	CBBB	BIT 7 of E = 0
RES 7,H	CBBC	BIT 7 of H = 0
RES 7,L	CBBD	BIT 7 of L = 0

RET	C9	RETURN
RET C	D8	RETURN if CARRY
RET M	F8	RETURN if MINUS
RET NC	D0	RETURN if NO-CARRY
RET NZ	C0	RETURN if NOT-ZERO
RET P	F0	RETURN if POSITIVE
RET PE	E8	RETURN if PARITY-EVEN
RET PO	E0	RETURN if PARITY-ODD
RET Z	C8	RETURN if ZERO
RET I	ED4D	RETURN from INTERRUPT
RET N	ED45	RETURN from NON-MASKABLE INT.
RL(HL)	CB16	ROTATE(HL)LEFT THROUGH CARRY
RL(IX+dd)	DDCBdd16	ROTATE(IX+dd)LEFTTHRO CARRY
RL(IY+dd)	FDCBdd16	ROTATE(IY+dd)LEFTTHRO CARRY
RL A	CB17	ROTATE A LEFT THROUGH CARRY
RL B	CB10	ROTATE B LEFT THROUGH CARRY
RL C	CB11	ROTATE C LEFT THROUGH CARRY
RL D	CB12	ROTATE D LEFT THROUGH CARRY
RL E	CB13	ROTATE E LEFT THROUGH CARRY
RL H	CB14	ROTATE H LEFT THROUGH CARRY
RL L	CB15	ROTATE L LEFT THROUGH CARRY
RLA	17	ROTATE A LEFT THROUGH CARRY
RLC (HL)	CB06	ROTATE(HL)LEFT
RLC (IX+dd)	DDCBdd06	ROTATE(IX+dd)LEFT
RLC (IY+dd)	FDCBdd06	ROTATE(IY+dd)LEFT
RLC A	CB07	ROTATE A LEFT
RLC B	CB00	ROTATE B LEFT
RLC C	CB01	ROTATE C LEFT
RLC D	CB02	ROTATE D LEFT
RLC E	CB03	ROTATE E LEFT
RLC H	CB04	ROTATE H LEFT
RLC L	CB05	ROTATE L LEFT

RLCA	07	ROTATE A LEFT
RLD	ED6F	ROTATE LEFT DIGIT
RR(HL)	CB1E	ROTATE(HL)RIGHT THROUGH CARRY
RR(IX+dd)	DDCBdd1E	ROTATE(IX+dd)RIGHT WITH CARRY
RR(IY+dd)	FDCBdd1E	ROTATE(IY+dd)RIGHT WITH CARRY
RR A	CB1F	ROTATE A RIGHT THROUGH CARRY
RR B	CB18	ROTATE B RIGHT THROUGH CARRY
RR C	CB19	ROTATE C RIGHT THROUGH CARRY
RR D	CB1A	ROTATE D RIGHT THROUGH CARRY
RR E	CB1B	ROTATE E RIGHT THROUGH CARRY
RR H	CB1C	ROTATE H RIGHT THROUGH CARRY
RR L	CB1D	ROTATE L RIGHT THROUGH CARRY
RRA	1F	ROTATE A RIGHT THROUGH CARRY
RRC (HL)	CB0E	ROTATE(HL) RIGHT
RRC (IX+dd)	DDCBdd0E	ROTATE(IX+dd) RIGHT
RRC (IY+dd)	FDCBdd0E	ROTATE(IY+dd) RIGHT
RRC A	CB0F	ROTATE A RIGHT
RRC B	CB08	ROTATE B RIGHT
RRC C	CB09	ROTATE C RIGHT
RRC D	CB0A	ROTATE D RIGHT
RRC E	CB0B	ROTATE E RIGHT
RRC H	CB0C	ROTATE H RIGHT
RRC L	CB0D	ROTATE L RIGHT
RRCA	0F	ROTATE A RIGHT
RRD	ED67	ROTATE DIGIT RIGHT
RST 00H	C7	CALL 0000H
RST 08H	CF	CALL 0008H
RST 10H	D7	CALL 0010H
RST 18H	DF	CALL 0018H
RST 20H	E7	CALL 0020H
RST 28H	EF	CALL 0028H
RST 30H	F7	CALL 0030H
RST 38H	FF	CALL 0038H

SBC A,(HL)	9E	A = A - (HL) - CY
SBC A,(IX+dd)	DD9Edd	A = A - (IX+dd) - CY
SBC A,(IY+dd)	FD9Edd	A = A - (IY+dd) - CY
SBC A,A	9F	A = A - A - CY
SBC A,B	98	A = A - B - CY
SBC A,C	99	A = A - C - CY
SBC A,D	9A	A = A - D - CY
SBC A,E	9B	A = A - E - CY
SBC A,H	9C	A = A - H - CY
SBC A,L	9D	A = A - L - CY
SBC A,data	DEdata	A = A - data - CY
SBC HL,BC	ED42	HL = HL - BC - CY
SBC HL,DE	ED52	HL = HL - DE - CY
SBC HL,HL	ED62	HL = HL - HL - CY
SBC HL,SP	ED72	HL = HL - SP - CY
SCF	37	SET CARRY
SET 0,(HL)	CBC6	BIT 0 of (HL) = 1
SET 0,(IX+dd)	DDCBddC6	BIT 0 of (IX+dd) = 1
SET 0,(IY+dd)	FDCBddC6	BIT 0 of (IY+dd) = 1
SET 0,A	CBC7	BIT 0 of A = 1
SET 0,B	CBC0	BIT 0 of B = 1
SET 0,C	CBC1	BIT 0 of C = 1
SET 0,D	CBC2	BIT 0 of D = 1
SET 0,E	CBC3	BIT 0 of E = 1
SET 0,H	CBC4	BIT 0 of H = 1
SET 0,L	CBC5	BIT 0 of L = 1
SET 1,(HL)	CBCE	BIT 1 of (HL) = 1
SET 1,(IX+dd)	DDCBddCE	BIT 1 of (IX+dd) = 1
SET 1,(IY+dd)	FDCBddCE	BIT 1 of (IY+dd) = 1
SET 1,A	CBCF	BIT 1 of A = 1
SET 1,B	CBC8	BIT 1 of B = 1
SET 1,C	CBC9	BIT 1 of C = 1
SET 1,D	CBCA	BIT 1 of D = 1
SET 1,E	CBCB	BIT 1 of E = 1
SET 1,H	CBCC	BIT 1 of H = 1
SET 1,L	CBCD	BIT 1 of L = 1
SET 2,(HL)	CBD6	BIT 2 of (HL) = 1
SET 2,(IX+dd)	DDCBddD6	BIT 2 of (IX+dd) = 1
SET 2,(IY+dd)	FDCBddD6	BIT 2 of (IY+dd) = 1
SET 2,A	CBD7	BIT 2 of A = 1
SET 2,B	CBD0	BIT 2 of B = 1
SET 2,C	CBD1	BIT 2 of C = 1
SET 2,D	CBD2	BIT 2 of D = 1

SET 2,E	CBD3	BIT 2 of E = 1
SET 2,H	CBD4	BIT 2 of H = 1
SET 2,L	CBD5	BIT 2 of L = 1
58SET 3,(HL)	CBDE	BIT 3 of (HL) = 1
SET 3,(IX+dd)	DDCBddDE	BIT 3 of (IX+dd) = 1
SET 3,(IY+dd)	FDCBddDE	BIT 3 of (IY+dd) = 1
SET 3,A	CBDF	BIT 3 of A = 1
SET 3,B	CBD8	BIT 3 of B = 1
SET 3,C	CBD9	BIT 3 of C = 1
SET 3,D	CBDA	BIT 3 of D = 1
SET 3,E	CBDB	BIT 3 of E = 1
SET 3,H	CBDC	BIT 3 of H = 1
SET 3,L	CBDD	BIT 3 of L = 1
SET 4,(HL)	CBE6	BIT 4 of (HL) = 1
SET 4,(IX+dd)	DDCBddE6	BIT 4 of (IX+dd) = 1
SET 4,(IY+dd)	FDCBddE6	BIT 4 of (IY+dd) = 1
SET 4,A	CBE7	BIT 4 of A = 1
SET 4,B	CBE0	BIT 4 of B = 1
SET 4,C	CBE1	BIT 4 of C = 1
SET 4,D	CBE2	BIT 4 of D = 1
SET 4,E	CBE3	BIT 4 of E = 1
SET 4,H	CBE4	BIT 4 of H = 1
SET 4,L	CBE5	BIT 4 of L = 1
SET 5,(HL)	CBEE	BIT 5 of (HL) = 1
SET 5,(IX+dd)	DDCBddEE	BIT 5 of (IX+dd) = 1
SET 5,(IY+dd)	FDCBddEE	BIT 5 of (IY+dd) = 1
SET 5,A	CBEF	BIT 5 of A = 1
SET 5,B	CBE8	BIT 5 of B = 1
SET 5,C	CBE9	BIT 5 of C = 1
SET 5,D	CBEA	BIT 5 of D = 1
SET 5,E	CBEB	BIT 5 of E = 1
SET 5,H	CBEC	BIT 5 of H = 1
SET 5,L	CBED	BIT 5 of L = 1
SET 6,(HL)	CBF6	BIT 6 of (HL) = 1
SET 6,(IX+dd)	DDCBddF6	BIT 6 of (IX+dd) = 1
SET 6,(IY+dd)	FDCBddF6	BIT 6 of (IY+dd) = 1
SET 6,A	CBF7	BIT 6 of A = 1
SET 6,B	CBF0	BIT 6 of B = 1
SET 6,C	CBF1	BIT 6 of C = 1
SET 6,D	CBF2	BIT 6 of D = 1
SET 6,E	CBF3	BIT 6 of E = 1
SET 6,H	CBF4	BIT 6 of H = 1
SET 6,L	CBF5	BIT 6 of L = 1

SET 7,(HL)	CBFE	BIT 7 of (HL) = 1
SET 7,(IX+dd)	DDCBddFE	BIT 7 of (IX+dd) = 1
SET 7,(IY+dd)	FDCBddFE	BIT 7 of (IY+dd) = 1
SET 7,A	CBFF	BIT 7 of A = 1
SET 7,B	CBF8	BIT 7 of B = 1
SET 7,C	CBF9	BIT 7 of C = 1
SET 7,D	CBFA	BIT 7 of D = 1
SET 7,E	CBFB	BIT 7 of E = 1
SET 7,H	CBFC	BIT 7 of H = 1
SET 7,L	CBFD	BIT 7 of L = 1
SLA (HL)	CB26	SHIFT (HL) LEFT
SLA (IX+dd)	DDCBdd26	SHIFT (IX+dd) LEFT
SLA (IY+dd)	FDCBdd26	SHIFT (IY+dd) LEFT
SLA A	CB27	SHIFT A LEFT
SLA B	CB20	SHIFT B LEFT
SLA C	CB21	SHIFT C LEFT
SLA D	CB22	SHIFT D LEFT
SLA E	CB23	SHIFT E LEFT
SLA H	CB24	SHIFT H LEFT
SLA L	CB25	SHIFT L LEFT
SRA (HL)	CB2E	ARITH. SHIFT (HL) RIGHT
SRA (IX+dd)	DDCBdd2E	ARITH. SHIFT (IX+dd) RIGHT
SRA (IY+dd)	FDCDdd2E	ARITH. SHIFT (IY+dd) RIGHT
SRA A	CB2F	ARITH. SHEFT A RIGHT
SRA B	CB28	ARITH. SHEFT B RIGHT
SRA C	CB29	ARITH. SHEFT C RIGHT
SRA D	CB2A	ARITH. SHEFT D RIGHT
SRA E	CB2B	ARITH. SHEFT E RIGHT
SRA H	CB2C	ARITH. SHEFT H RIGHT
SRA L	CB2D	ARITH. SHEFT L RIGHT
SRL (HL)	CB3E	SHIFT (HL) RIGHT
SRL (IX+dd)	DDCBdd3E	SHIFT (IX+dd) RIGHT
SRL (IY+dd)	FDCDdd3E	SHIFT (IY+dd) RIGHT
SRL A	CB3F	SHEFT A RIGHT
SRL B	CB38	SHEFT B RIGHT
SRL C	CB39	SHEFT C RIGHT
SRL D	CB3A	SHEFT D RIGHT
SRL E	CB3B	SHEFT E RIGHT
SRL H	CB3C	SHEFT H RIGHT
SRL L	CB3D	SHEFT L RIGHT
SUB (HL)	96	A = A - (HL)
SUB (IX+dd)	DD96dd	A = A - (IX+dd)

SUB (IY+dd)	FD96dd	A = A - (IY+dd)
SUB A	97	A = A - A
SUB B	90	A = A - B
SUB C	91	A = A - C
SUB D	92	A = A - D
SUB E	93	A = A - E
SUB H	94	A = A - H
SUB L	95	A = A - L
SUB data	D6data	A = A - data
XOR (HL)	AE	A = A .XOR. (HL)
XOR (IX+dd)	DDAEdd	A = A .XOR. (IX+dd)
XOR (IY+dd)	FDAEdd	A = A .XOR. (IY+dd)
XOR A	AF	A = A .XOR. A
XOR B	A8	A = A .XOR. B
XOR C	A9	A = A .XOR. C
XOR D	AA	A = A .XOR. D
XOR E	AB	A = A .XOR. E
XOR H	AC	A = A .XOR. H
XOR L	AD	A = A .XOR. L
XOR data	EEdata	A = A .XOR. data

Appendix III

REFERENCE SHEET OF 6502

This processor was developed as a "Super 6800" by using MOS technology. Even though the same bus structure and basic design concept as the 6800, this processor is not directly compatiable at the object code level, since it has a modified register and instruction set. It has a unique pipelined architecture and the provisions of two index registers (IR). This processor performs very well when running high level languages such as BASIC. It is popular for personal computers. It is very useful for simple controller application.

It has only one general purpose data register, but has two 8 bit index registers which can access full 64K using indexed absolute addressing mode. It has short stack pointer (8 bit+1) forces stack to reside in page 2 of memory. It has seven, ONE bit flag register to indicate the effect and perform arithmetic, logical and decimal mode of operation, which is

- Carry flag
- Zero flag
- Decimal mode flag
- Break flag
- OVerflow flag
- Sign flag and
- Interrupt flag.

The 6502 has set of 56 instructions. It has a BCD mode for the ALU which removes the need for a DAA instruction but requires the new SED (SEt of Decimal modes) and CLD (CLear Decimal mode). To make maximum use of the short index registers, this processor has a full complement of addressing modes. This processor is well supported with software and literature. There is no equivalent to CP/M available.

Features

Memory address range - 64 K
I/O address range memory mapped.
Clock frequency - 1 MHz
Power suppliers - + 5 Volt dc
Interrupts - IRQ, NMI

High speed vertion of 6502 (2 MHz) is also available in the market nowadays.

Since the 6502 has the 6800 bus type, all 6800 peripherals may be used with this processor. Dedicated 6502 support chips are also available like

- 6520 (parallel I/O),
- 6522 (Parallel I/O + two 16 bit timers)
- 6541 (keyboard + Display controller)
- 6545 (CRT controller)
- 6551 (serial UART) and
- 6532 (RAM, I/O,Timer combination)

Execution time for

Add register to accumulator	- 4 micro sec
Output accumulator to post	- 4 micro sec
Move from memory to memory	- 8 micro sec
NMI Vector address	- FFFAH and FFFBH
RESET vector address	- FFFCH and FFFDH
IRQ and BRK vector address	- FFFEH and FFFFH
Original Source	- MOS technology Inc
Second Source	- ROCKWELL, SYNERTEK
NMI Vector address	- FFFA H, FFFB H
RESET Vector address	- FFFC H & FFFD H
IRQ and BAK address	- FFFE A & FFFF H

Appendix III

INSTRUCTION SET OF 6502

Hexadecimal	Instruction	Address Mode
00	BRK	
01	ORA	Indirect X
05	ORA	Zero Page
06	ASL	Zero Page
08	PHP	
09	ORA	Immediate
0A	ASL	Accumulator
0D	ORA	Absolute
0E	ASL	Absolute
10	BPL	
11	ORA	Indirect Y
15	ORA	Zero Page X
16	ASL	Zero Page X
18	CLC	
19	ORA	Absolute Y
1D	ORA	Absolute X
1E	ASL	Absolute X
20	JSR	
21	AND	Indirect X
24	BIT	Zero Page
25	AND	Zero Page
26	ROL	Zero Page
28	PLP	
29	AND	Immediate
2A	ROL	Accumulator
2C	BIT	Absolute
2D	AND	Absolute
2E	ROL	Absolute
30	BMI	
31	AND	Indirect Y
35	AND	Zero Page X
36	ROL	Zero Page X
38	SEC	
39	AND	Absolute Y
3D	AND	Absolute X
3E	ROL	Absolute X

Hexadecimal	Instruction	Address Mode
40	RTI	
41	EOR	Indirect X
45	EOR	Zero Page
46	LSR	Zero Page
48	PHA	
49	EOR	Immediate
4A	LSR	Accumulator
4C	JMP	Absolute
4D	EOR	Absolute
4E	LSR	Absolute
50	BVC	
51	EOR	Indirect Y
55	EOR	Zero Page X
56	LSR	Zero Page X
58	CLI	
59	EOR	Absolute Y
5D	EOR	Absolute X
5E	LSR	Absolute X
60	RTS	
61	ADC	Indirect X
65	ADC	Zero Page
66	ROR	Zero Page
68	PLA	
69	ADC	Immediate
6A	ROR	Accumulator
6C	JMP	Indirect
6D	ADC	Absolute
6E	ROR	Absolute
70	BVS	
71	ADC	Indirect Y
75	ADC	Zero Page X
76	ROR	Zero Page X
78	SEI	
79	ADC	Absolute Y
7D	ADC	Absolute X
7E	ROR	Absolute X
81	STA	Indirect X
84	STY	Zero Page
85	STA	Zero Page
86	STX	Zero Page
88	DEY	
8A	TXA	
8C	STY	Absolute

Hexadecimal	Instruction	Address Mode
8D	STA	Absolute
8E	STX	Absolute
90	BCC	Absolute
91	STA	Indirect Y
94	STY	Zero Page X
95	STA	Zero Page X
96	STX	Zero Page Y
98	TYA	
99	STA	Absolute Y
9A	TXS	
9D	STA	Absolute X
A0	LDY	Immediate
A1	LDA	Indirect X
A2	LDX	Immediate
A4	LDY	Zero page
A5	LDA	Zero Page
A6	LDX	Zero Page
A8	TAY	
A9	LDA	Immediate
AA	TAX	
AC	LDY	Absolute
AD	LDA	Absolute
AE	LDX	Absolute
B0	BCS	
B1	LDA	Indirect Y
B4	LDY	Zero Page X
B5	LDA	Zero Page X
B6	LDX	Zero Page Y
B8	CLV	
B9	LDA	Absolute Y
BA	TSX	
BC	LDY	Absolute X
BD	LDA	Absolute X
BE	LDX	Absolute Y
C0	CPY	Immediate
C1	CMP	Indirect X
C4	CPY	Zero Page
C5	CMP	Zero Page
C6	DEC	Zero Page
C8	INY	
C9	CMP	Immediate
CA	DEX	
CC	CPY	Absolute

Hexadecimal	Instruction	Address Mode
CD	CMP	Absolute
CE	DEC	Absolute
D0	BNE	
D1	CMP	Indirect Y
D5	GMP	Zero Page X
D6	DEC	Zero Page X
D8	CLD	
D9	CMP	Absolute Y
DD	CMP	Absolute X
DE	DEC	Absolute X
E0	CPX	Immmediate
E1	SBC	Indirect X
E4	CPX	Zero Page
E5	SBC	Zero Page
E6	INC	Zero Page
E8	INX	
E9	SBC	Immediate
EA	NOP	
EC	CPX	Absolute
ED	SBC	Absolute
EE	INC	Absolute
F0	BEQ	
F1	SBC	Indirect Y
F5	SBC	Zero Page X
F6	INC	Zero Page X
F8	SED	
F9	SBC	Absolute Y
FD	SBC	Absolute X
FE	INC	Absolute X

Appendix IV

REFERENCE SHEET OF 6800

The 6800 processor has a more elegant instruction set and hardware which makes it a good device for beginners and a better device than the 8080A when it is capable of doing the job. The 6802 processor is a simple upgrade of the 6800 processor which has an on-chip clock generator and 128 bytes of RAM. The processor 6802 is recommended for all new hardware designs. The 6802 has ROM, Timer, I/O combination chips in addition to 6800.

The 6800/6802 have two 8 bit general purpose data registers ie Accumulator A and Accumulator B and three specialised sixteen bit memory pointer, which is Index register (IR), Stack pointer (SP) and Program counter (PC). This processor has six, one bit flag register, which is

- Carry flag
- Overflow flag
- Zero flag
- Sign flag
- Auxilury flag and
- Interrupt flag

The 6800 and 6802 share a common instruction set which has been modelled after the PDP11 minicomputer. The instruction set is more elegant than the competitor 8085 processor but is hindered by a scarcity of CPU registers which is overcome to some extent by the Direct addressing mode which allows fast access to page zero of memory. Reset couses branch to address which must be stored in address locations FFFEH and FFFFH. One, two and three byte instructions are used. This processor has Direct, Extended, Immediate, Relative, Indexed and Implied addressing modes. This is well supported in software including Basic.

Features

	6800	**6802**
Memory address range	64 K	64 K
I/O address range	Memory mapped.	
Clock frequency	1 MHz	1 MHz
Power supplies	+ 5 Volt	+ 5 Volt
Interrupts	IRQ, NMI	IRQ, NMI

High speed vertion of 6800 and 6802 (1.5 MHz and 2 MHz) is also available in the market nowadays.

The processor 6800 needs an external two phase clock generator, usch as 6871 or 6875. It has a family of support devices

- 6821 (Parallel I/O)
- 6828 (Interrupt controller)
- 6840 (Timer/counter)
- 6844 (DMA controller)
- 6850 (UART)

Execution time for

Add register to accumulator	- 2 micro sec
Output accumulator to port	- 5 micro sec
Move from memory to memory	- 9 micro sec
IRQ Vector address	- FFF8H and FFF9H
SWI Vector address	- FFFAH and FFFBH
NMI Vector address	- FFFCH and FFFDH
RESET Vector address	- FFFEH and FFFFH
Original source	- MOTOROLA
Second sourcing	- AMI, HITACHI, FAIRCHILD, SESCOSEM, PLESSEY, MITEL.

Appendix IV

INSTRUCTION SET OF 6800

Operation	Mnemonics	Opcode	Addressing mode
ADD	ADDA	3B	IMMEDIATE
		9B	DIRECT
		AB	INDEX
		BB	EXTEND
	ADDB	CB	IMMEDIATE
		DB	DIRECT
		EB	INDEX
		FB	EXTEND
ADD ACC.	ABA	1B	IMPLIED
ADD+CARRY	ADCA	89	IMMEDIATE
		99	DIRECT
		A9	INDEX
		B9	EXTEND
	ADCB	C9	IMMEDIATE
		D9	DIRECT
		E9	INDEX
		F9	EXTEND
AND	ANDA	84	IMMEDIATE
		94	DIRECT
		A4	INDEX
		B4	EXTEND
	ANDB	C4	IMMEDIATE
		D4	DIRECT
		E4	INDEX
		F4	EXTEND
BIT test	BITA	85	IMMEDIATE
		95	DIRECT
		A5	INDEX
		B5	EXTEND

Operation	Mnemonics	Opcode	Addressing mode
	BITB	C5	IMMEDIATE
		D5	DIRECT
		E5	INDEX
		F5	EXTEND
CLEAR	CLR	6F	INDEX
		7F	EXTEND
	CLRA	4F	IMPLIED
	CLRB	5F	IMPLIED
COMPARE	CMPA	81	IMMEDIATE
		91	DIRECT
		A1	INDEX
		B1	EXTEND
	CMPB	C1	IMMEDIATE
		D1	DIRECT
		E1	INDEX
		F1	EXTEND
COMPARE ACC.	CBA	11	IMPLIED
COMPLEMENT	COM ONES	63	INDEX
		73	EXTEND
	COMA	43	IMPLIED
	COMB	53	IMPLIED
COMPLEMENT	NEG TWOs	60	INDEX
		70	EXTEND
	NEGA	40	IMPLIED
	NEGB	50	IMPLIED
DECIMAL ADJUST	DAA	19	IMPLIED
DECREMENT	DEC	6A	INDEX
		7A	EXTEND
	DECA	4A	IMPLIED
	DECB	5A	IMPLIED
EXCLUSIVE	EORA OR	88	IMMEDIATE
		98	DIRECT
		A8	INDEX
		B8	EXTEND

Operation	Mnemonics	Opcode	Addressing mode
	EORB	C8	IMMEDIATE
		D8	DIRECT
		E8	INDEX
		F8	EXTEND
INCREMENT	INC	6C	INDEX
		7C	EXTEND
	INCA	4C	IMPLIED
	INCB	5C	IMPLIED
LOAD ACC.	LDAA	86	IMMEDIATE
		96	DIRECT
		A6	INDEX
		B6	EXTEND
LOAD ACC.	LDAB	C6	IMMEDIATE
		D6	DIRECT
		E6	INDEX
		F6	EXTEND
OR	ORA	8A	IMMEDIATE
		9A	DIRECT
		AA	INDEX
		BA	EXTEND
	ORB	CA	IMMEDIATE
		DA	DIRECT
		EA	INDEX
		FA	EXTEND
PUSH data	PSHA	36	IMPLIED
	PSHB	37	IMPLIED
PULL data	PULA	32	IMPLIED
	PULB	33	IMPLIED
ROTATE LEFT	ROL	69	INDEX
		79	EXTEND
	ROLA	49	IMPLIED
	ROLB	59	IMPLIED
ROTATE RIGHT	ROR	66	INDEX
		76	EXTEND
	RORA	46	IMPLIED
	RORB	56	IMPLIED

Operation	Mnemonics	Opcode	Addressing mode
SHIFT LEFT	ASL	68	INDEX
		78	EXTEND
	ASLA	48	IMPLIED
	ASLB	58	IMPLIED
SHIFT RIGHT	ASR	67	INDEX
		77	EXTEND
	ASRA	47	IMPLIED
	ASRB	57	IMPLIED
SHIFT RIGHT	LSR	64	INDEX
	LOGIC	74	EXTEND
	LSRA	44	IMPLIED
	LSRB	54	IMPLIED
STORE	STAA	97	DIRECT
	ACC.	A7	INDEX
		B7	EXTEND
STORE	STAB	D7	DIRECT
	ACC.	E7	INDEX
		F7	EXTEND
SUBTRACT	SUBA	80	IMMEDIATE
		90	DIRECT
		A0	INDEX
		B0	EXTEND
	SUBB	C0	IMMEDIATE
		D0	DIRECT
		E0	INDEX
		F0	EXTEND
SUBTRACT ACC.	SBA	10	IMPLIED
SUBTRACT+	SBCA	82	IMMEDIATE
	CARRY	92	DIRECT
		A2	INDEX
		B2	EXTEND
	SBCB	C2	IMMEDIATE
		D2	DIRECT
		E2	INDEX
		F2	EXTEND

Operation	Mnemonics	Opcode	Addressing mode
TRANFER ACC.	TAB	16	IMPLIED
	TBA	17	IMPLIED
TEST ZERO	TST	6D	INDEX
	or MINUS	7D	EXTEND
	TSTA	4D	IMPLIED
	TSTB	5D	IMPLIED

1. IMMEDIATE ADDRESSING TECHNIQUE

Operations	Mnemonics	Op-code
ADD	ADDA	3B
	ADDB	CB
ADD+CARRY	ADCA	89
	ADCB	C9
AND	ANDA	84
	ANDB	C4
BIT test	BITA	85
	BITB	C5
COMPARE	CMPA	81
	CMPB	C1
EX-OR	EORA	88
	EORB	C8
LOAD ACC.	LDAA	86
	LDAB	C6
OR	ORA	8A
	ORB	CA
SUBTRACT	SUBA	80
	SUBB	C0
SUBTRACT+ CARRY	SBCA	82
	SBCB	C2

2. DIRECT ADDRESSING TECHNIQUES

Operations	Mnemonics	Op-code
ADD	ADDA	9B
	ADDB	DB
ADD+CARRY	ADCA	99
	ADCB	D9
AND	ANDA	94
	ANDB	D4
BIT test	BITA	95
	BITB	D5
Operations	**Mnemonics**	**Op-code**
COMPARE	CMPA	91
	CMPB	D1
EX-OR	EORA	98
	EORB	D8
LOAD ACC.	LDAA	96
	LDAB	D6
OR	ORA	9A
	ORB	DA
STORE ACC.	STAA	97
	STAB	D7
SUBTRACT	SUBA	90
	SUBB	D0
SUB+CARRY	SBCA	92
	SBCB	D2

3. INDEXED ADDRESSING TECHNIQUE

Operations	Mnemonics	Op-code
ADD	ADDA	AB
	ADDB	EB
ADD+CARRY	ADCA	A9
	ADCB	E9
AND	ANDA	A4
	ANDB	E4
BIT test	BITA	A5
	BITB	E5
CLEAR	CLR	6F

Operations	Mnemonics	Op-code
COMPARE	CMPA	A1
	CMPB	E1
COMPLEMENT ONEs	COM	63
COMPLEMENT TWOs	NEG	60
DECREMENT	DEC	6A
EX-OR	EORA	A8
	EORB	E8
INCREMENT	INC	6C
LOAD ACC.	LDAA	A6
	LDAB	E6
OR	ORA	AA
	ORB	EA
ROTATE LEFT	ROL	69
ROTATE RIGHT	ROR	66
SHIFT LEFT	ASL	68
SHIFT RIGHT	ASR	67
SHIFT RIGHT LOGIC	LSR	64
STORE ACC.	STAA	A7
	STAB	E7
SUBTRACT	SUBA	A0
	SUBB	E0
SUB+CARRY	SBCA	A2
	SBCB	E2
TEST ZERO	TST or MINUS	6D

4. EXTENDED ADDRESSING TECHNIQUE

Operations	Mnemonics	Op-code
ADD	ADDA	BB
	ADDB	FB
ADD+CARRY	ADCA	B9
	ADCB	F9

Operations	Mnemonics	Op-code
AND	ANDA	B4
	ANDB	F4
BIT test	BITA	B5
	BITB	F5
CLEAR	CLR	7F
COMPARE	CMPA	B1
	CMPB	F1
COMPLEMENT	COM	73
	ONES	
COMPLEMENT TWOs	NEG	70
DECREMENT	DEC	7A
EX-OR	EORA	B8
	EORB	F8
INCREMENT	INC	7C
LOAD ACC.	LDAA	B6
	LDAB	F6
OR	ORA	BA
	ORB	FA
ROTATE LEFT	ROL	79
ROTATE RIGHT	ROR	76
SHIFT LEFT	ASL	78
SHIFT RIGHT	ASR	77
SHIFT RIGHT LOGIC	LSR	74
STORE ACC.	STAA	B7
	STAB	F7
SUBTRACT	SUBA	B0
	SUBB	F0
SUB+CARRY	SBCA	B2
	SBCB	F2
TRANSFER	ACC. TST	7D

5. IMPLIED ADDRESSING TECHNIQUE

Operations	Mnemonics	Op-code
ADD ACC.	ABA	1B
CLEAR	CLRA	4F
	CLRB	5F
COMPARE ACC.	CBA	11
COMPLEMENT ONEs	COMA	43
	COMB	53
COMPLEMENT TWOs	NEGA	40
	NEGB	50
DECIMAL ADJUST	DAA	19
DECREMENT	DECA	4A
	DECB	5A
INCREMENT	INCA	4C
	INCB	5C
PUSH data	PSHA	36
	PSHB	37
PULL data	PULA	32
	PULB	33
ROTATE LEFT	ROLA	49
	ROLB	59
ROTATE RIGHT	RORA	46
	RORB	56
SHIFT LEFT	ASLA	48
	ASLB	58
SHIFT RIGHT	ASRA	47
	ASRB	57
SHIFT RIGHT LOGIC	LSRA	44
	LSRB	54
SUBTRACT ACC.	SBA	10
TRANFER ACC.	TAB	16
	TBA	17
TEST ZERO or MINUS	TSTA	4D
	TSTB	5D

Index

Symbols